Journeying to the Same Heaven

ELLEN G. WHITE, THE CIVIL WAR,
AND THE GOAL OF POST-RACIALISM

By Kevin L. Morgan

www.TEACHServices.com • (800) 367-1844

World rights reserved. This book or any portion thereof may not be copied or reproduced in any form or manner whatever, except as provided by law, without the written permission of the publisher, except by a reviewer who may quote brief passages in a review.

The author assumes full responsibility for the accuracy of all facts and quotations as cited in this book. The opinions expressed in this book are the author's personal views and interpretations, and do not necessarily reflect those of the publisher.

This book is provided with the understanding that the publisher is not engaged in giving spiritual, legal, medical, or other professional advice. If authoritative advice is needed, the reader should seek the counsel of a competent professional.

Unless otherwise indicated, all Scripture quotations are taken from the King James Version. Scripture marked NKJV is taken from the New King James Version®, copyright © 1982, by Thomas Nelson, Inc. Used by permission. All rights reserved.

Front cover design by Bill Newman, TEACH Services, Inc.
Back cover and interior design by Honor Him Publishers
Copyediting by Susan Hullquist and Carole Huddleston

Copyright © 2015 Honor Him Publishers, Millers Creek, North Carolina 28651. Second edition, April 2016.
Copyright © 2015 TEACH Services, Inc., Fort Oglethorpe, Georgia 30742.
ISBN-13: 978-1-4796-0566-8 (Paperback)

Morgan, Kevin L., 1957-

    Author
        Sabbath Rest: Is There Something Missing in Your Busy Life? (2002)
        White Lie Soap: For Removal of Lingering Stains on Ellen White's Integrity as an Inspired Writer (2013)
    Co-author with E. Marcella Anderson King
        More Than Words: A Study of Inspiration and Ellen White's Use of Sources in the Desire of Ages (2009)
    Contributing author with Daniel Knauft
        Sacred Time unRemembered: How the Original Sabbath was Lost and Why It Matters (2014)

TEACH Services, Inc.
PUBLISHING
www.TEACHServices.com • (800) 367-1844

Dedication

Abraham Lincoln,
February 9, 1864

I dedicate this book to the memory of the president I have admired ever since I first pondered his likeness on the wall of my elementary school cafeteria. He was better than most of us—in his devotion to the country, in his concern for the oppressed Negro, and in his magnanimity in dealing with the vanquished in war. Were it not for him, compromise over slavery in our country would have been prolonged. His death, one hundred fifty years ago as I write, was a tragedy on all levels—for his family, for the nation, and for the South in its efforts to heal from nearly four years of conflict and devastation. May we honor his memory and follow our better angels in dealing with people who are different from us.

Acknowledgments

I am reminded of a statement that Dr. Jeffrey Bortz, professor of Latin American History at Appalachian State University, made to me on more than one occasion: *"We do not write as individuals. We write as a community."* In presenting this book to the public, it is my duty and delight to acknowledge the *community* who helped me in preparing this book. A large part of that community is listed in the bibliographical index. However, another part, who acted more directly in the book's preparation, I wish to acknowledge here.

Dr. Judkin J. Browning gave thoughtful feedback to my term paper on Ellen White and Civil War history, which was the springboard for this book. Dr. Michael J. Turner suggested sources for England's deliberations over whether to declare war on the United States during the American Civil War, and he raised larger questions regarding Ellen White's statements on race. Lovers of Civil War history, Dennis Depew, Barry Mahorney and Henry Johnson gave encouragement in the early development of the manuscript. Geoffrey Marshall, a friend in Jamaica, gave me feedback and pointed to sources for the final chapters. R. Steven Norman, III, editor of *Southern Tidings* and lover of Adventist history who recognizes its value for the next generation, connected me with helpful people and resources for the book. Dr. Arthur V. Chadwick of Southwestern Adventist University, whose expertise is in the fields of molecular biology and geology, reviewed and validated the information in the section on horizontal gene transfer. My wife, Susan, shared her expertise in the use of genealogical tools, helping me resolve a number of issues. Kareis Wagner, recently retired from McFarland Publishers, thoughtfully reviewed the manuscript. Dr. Jud Lake at Southern Adventist University, who is soon to publish his own book on Ellen White's Civil War messages, gave me suggestions on content and resources. Dr. Benjamin Baker, whose doctorate was entitled, " 'I Do Not Mean to Live a Coward or Die a Coward': An Examination of Ellen G. White's Lifelong Relationship to Black People" (2011), pointed out several necessary corrections in the early manuscript. Dr. Brian Strayer, Professor of History at Andrews University and biographer of J. N. Loughborough and John Byington, reviewed the manuscript for the second edition of the book, making suggestions and flagging numerous corrections. My sincerest thanks to each of you!

Table of Contents

1. What "Elephant"? 7
   Adventist abolitionism in apathetic America

2. "Great Distress Coming" 19
   Ellen White's first Civil War vision in historical context, preparing Seventh-day Adventists for the severity of the coming conflict

3. "Slavery and the War" 25
   Ellen White's second Civil War vision in historical context, declaring the ending of slavery to be the legitimate moral basis for the war, with commentary about the First Battle of Manassas

4. "The North and the South" 31
   Ellen White's third Civil War vision in historical context, focusing on the South's preparedness for war and England's deliberations concerning declaring war on the United States

5. Answering a Prejudicial Charge 45
   A thorough response to the accusation that Ellen White saw Negroes as less than human

6. Early Seventh-day Adventist Ministry to the Freedmen 65
   Why Seventh-day Adventists delayed in engaging in ministry to the freed slaves

7. Appeals for Volunteers 87
   Ellen White's call for workers to educate and evangelize African Americans in the South

8. Threading the Needle 97
   Straddling reality and the ideal—Ellen White's pragmatic response to severe prejudice, allowing Seventh-day Adventists to minister in the American South

9. Education, the Road to Post-Racialism 117
   A historical summary of Seventh-day Adventist educational pursuits among African Americans

10. Calcified Pragmatism 123
    An honest look at the history of the Seventh-day Adventist Church in taking Ellen White's pragmatic accommodations as unbending rules

Endnotes 135
Bibliographical Index 184
Scriptural and Pseudepigraphal Index 203
Photo Documentation Index 204
General Index 209

Preface

An Insightful Advocate of African-American Dignity

"The pre-millennialists, or Adventists," wrote historian John R. McKivigan, "believed the second coming would precede the millennial age and were pessimistic regarding efforts to reform the world in advance of the time of Christ's direct intervention."[1] They believed that only God could eradicate slavery. Nonetheless, early Adventist and co-founder of the Seventh-day Adventist Church, Ellen G. White consistently advocated for the freedom and human dignity of African Americans. Among abolitionists of the Civil War era, she was one of the most consistent and insightful.

Ellen G. White, 1864

This book is an exploration of the history contemporaneous with Ellen White's messages on slavery and the race of people enslaved within it. It grew out of my reading and reflection in a master's level class on the American Civil War at Appalachian State University, Boone, North Carolina. In that class, Dr. Judkin J. Browning outlined readings to stimulate class discussion on various aspects of the American Civil War experience. The titles of the books that we were assigned to read outline the topics that we covered: Louis Masur's *The Civil War: A Concise History*, Michael F. Holt's *The Fate of Their Country: Politicians, Slavery Extension, and the Coming of the Civil War*, Stephanie McCurry's *Confederate Reckoning: Power and Politics in the Civil War South*, James M. McPherson's *For Cause and Comrades: Why Men Fought in the Civil War*, Michael Thomas Smith's *The Enemy Within: Fears of Corruption in the Civil War North*, Drew Gilpin Faust's *This Republic of Suffering: Death and the American Civil War*

As I read these books, I could not help but feel that I had already become acquainted with many of the major issues that they raised through my reading of the writings of Seventh-day Adventist author Ellen G. White, whose life and ministry extended through the Civil War period.

When I pitched the topic for my paper, "Until We Acknowledged the Elephant in the Room: A Prophetic Reminder of the Reason for the American Civil War," to Dr. Browning, I described White's visionary revelations about the war.[2] His response was that Mrs. White was either "well-read, well-connected, or very insightful," yet he had concerns about her description of England's deliberations over entering the war.[3]

I later conferred with Dr. Michael J. Turner, professor of British history at Appalachian State University, to see whether such deliberations had taken place. His response was unequivocal: "Of course!" I asked him how I could validate such a notion, and he suggested reading the Parliamentary debates of the period. When I later found these debates online, I was amazed how insightful Mrs. White's counsels were. I hope that you, the reader, will share my amazement.

Because of the existence of distinct black and white conferences in the Seventh-day Adventist Church, many Seventh-day Adventists have assumed that Ellen White favored some kind of segregation of the races. That is why I was surprised to read, in Ciro Sepúlveda's *Ellen White on the Color Line* (see chapter 7), Ellen White's statements about integrated gatherings of blacks and whites. As a result, I expanded my original study to include the origins of segregation in the Seventh-day Adventist Church, seeking to understand how Ellen White's counsels may have shaped ideas regarding race. I concluded—and this is the thesis for this book—that *Mrs. White wrote about slavery and the Negro race with a clear view of the shared humanity of blacks and whites. Nonetheless, she astutely avoided pushing her views politically to keep from undermining Lincoln's efforts in pursuing the war to save the Union and to avoid hampering evangelistic efforts after the war in the American South. She also recognized the role that education and the message of the gospel would play in the moral, mental and social equality of those who had been subjugated under the institution of slavery.*

The title *Journeying to the Same Heaven* comes from a key statement penned by Mrs. White: "Men may have both hereditary and cultivated prejudices, but when the love of Jesus fills the heart and they become one with Christ, they will have the same spirit that He had. They are *journeying to the same heaven*, and will be seated at the same table to eat bread in the kingdom of God. If Jesus is abiding in our hearts, we cannot despise the colored man. He is *journeying to the same heaven*, who has the same Saviour abiding in his heart."[4] The title is an apt metaphor because, from her earliest visions, Ellen White conceived of the Christian life as a journey to heaven on the narrow way.[5] The book's concerns are largely about events that took place in the United States. However, the issue of racial equality has global application.

Chapter 1 of this book provides background for Adventist views about slavery in the context of other Christian denominations, and it places Ellen White among her peers. Chapters 2 through 4 review Mrs. White's first three visionary pronouncements about the war, its cause, and its duration. Chapter 5 answers the accusation that Ellen White suggested during the war that the Negro race was not human. Chapter 6 describes the early efforts after the Civil War to minister to the former slaves in the South. Chapter 7 summarizes Ellen White's spoken and written addresses regarding the need to work in the South. Chapter 8 explains Ellen White's pragmatic stance about working in the South under racial prejudice. Chapter 9 provides a brief summary of Seventh-day Adventist educational pursuits for African Americans. Chapter 10 reviews the consequences of segregation in the Seventh-day Adventist Church following Ellen White's death, as well as the steps that were taken to remedy it.

A final note about conventions: Because the nomenclature for describing Americans of African heritage has changed over the years—from "colored people," "Negroes," and "people of color" to "blacks," "Afro-Americans," and "African Americans" (hyphenated and not hyphenated)—this book uses various terms from the more than one hundred fifty years of experience that it covers to designate this ethnic group. Since Ellen White's statements are the focus of the book, they are highlighted throughout the book in light gray. To keep the body of the book as short as possible, I have placed many interesting primary sources in the endnotes. These will be of particular interest for those who use this book in connection with classes on history.

Kevin L. Morgan, M.A.

Chapter 1

What "Elephant"?

Be it the business of the people everywhere to forget the negro and remember only the country. —The New-York Tribune[1]

The debates in the nation had run their course. Slavery had divided the nation's two largest Christian denominations—the Methodists in 1844 and the Baptists in 1845. New school Presbyterians were also divided over slavery.[2] After years of animosity, the strain between North and South was coming to a breaking point. Many believe the division of the churches was the Union's first crack.[3]

As the total separation of North and South continued to lurch forward, the major participants were unwilling to acknowledge the "elephant in the room"—the "elephant," that is, of slavery. Political elites in the South, scheming to manipulate the popular vote to gain their ends, reframed the issue as "popular liberty."[4] Southern diplomats insisted to their foreign trading partners that it was the tariff on imports that had caused them to separate, yet "the declaration adopted by the South Carolina Convention . . . said nothing of the tariff as a cause of secession."[5] In fact, Alexander Stephens, who would become the vice president of the Confederacy, wrote his brother on New Year's Day 1861 that South Carolina was seceding from a tariff "which is just what Her own Senators and members in Congress made it."[6] England seemed happy to accept the Southern explanation to maintain relations with the major supplier of cotton for her textile industry.[7] When war broke out, Northern leaders and Southern ambassadors to England would not say, "This war is about the future of slavery."[8]

Historians often explain the rift between North and South in other ways. For instance, Frank L. Owsley stated: "The North had interests which demanded positive legislation exploitative of the agrarian South; the South had interests which demanded that the federal government refrain entirely from legislation within its bounds—it demanded only to be let alone."[9] Yet being left alone with the guarantee of slavery within the Southern states would not have been enough. The real bone of contention was the extension of slavery into new western territories.[10] As John C. Calhoun asserted, the equilibrium of power was tipping towards the North in the number of states, population, and federal representation.[11] He blamed the North-South rift on "the agitation" against slavery.[12]

Polarizing of Key Politicians Over the Institution of Slavery

With Northern States made responsible to enforce Southern slavery by the Fugitive Slave Act (1850), the expansion of possible new slave states through "popular sovereignty" to the territories north of the 36° 30′ line by the Kansas-Nebraska Act (1854), and slavery made portable to all states by the Dred Scott decision (1857), Abraham Lincoln saw the nation tending toward slavery as the rule for all states.[13] He declared in his "House Divided" speech on June 16, 1858:

> "A house divided against itself cannot stand." I believe this Government cannot endure permanently half *slave* and half *free*. I do not expect the Union to be *dissolved*—I don't expect the house to *fall*—but I do expect it will cease to be divided. It will become *all* one thing or *all* the other. Either the *opponents* of Slavery will arrest the further spread of it, and place it where the public mind shall rest in the belief that it is in course of ultimate extinction; or its *advocates* will push it forward till it shall become alike lawful in *all* the States, *old* as well as *new*—*North* as well as *South*. Have we no *tendency* to the latter condition?[14]

Southern slaveholders did not miss the significance of Lincoln's speech and the aims of the Republican Party.[15] They could not risk the nation becoming completely free of slavery.[16] "During the Secession Winter of 1860–1861, radical secessionists, known as 'Fire-Eaters,' [were] . . . forthright in arguing that secession was the only means of perpetuating slavery and white supremacy and that the alternative was racial holocaust and economic ruin under 'Black Republican' rule. As they seceded, several states went on public record with declarations of the causes of secession that spelled out the Republican Party's threat to slavery and to the peace and prosperity of the South and the world."[17] One of the most forthright was Confederate Vice-President Alexander H. Stephens. Just three days before Lincoln's March 4 inauguration, in a speech at Savannah, Stephens declared that the original Union had "rested upon the assumption of the equality of races. Our new government," he said, "is founded upon exactly the opposite ideas: its foundations are laid, its cornerstone rests, upon the great truth that the Negro is not equal to the white man; that slavery is his natural and moral condition. This, our new government, is the first, in the history of the world, based upon this great . . . truth."[18] Thus, among their supporters, Southern leaders were quite candid about the "elephant in the room."

Alexander Stephens, Vice-President of the Confederacy

Jefferson Davis, President of the Confederacy

Before his election to the Confederate presidency, Jefferson Davis built his case against the Union upon their threatening of the Constitutional rights of property under the control of the various States. He saw slaves as property (though the Constitution did not use that term but, rather, used "persons held in service").[19] In an address to the Senate on February 13, 1850, he declared, "As a property recognized by the Constitution, and held in a portion of the States, the Federal Government is bound to admit it [slavery] into all the Territories, and to give it such protection as other private property receives."[20] Davis was convinced that slavery did Africans who had come to America a favor:

> In a moral and social condition they had been elevated from brutal savages into docile, intelligent, and civilized agricultural laborers, and supplied not only with bodily comforts, but with careful religious instruction under the supervision of a superior race. Their labor had been so directed as not only to allow a gradual and marked amelioration of their own condition, but to convert hundreds of thousands of square miles of the wilderness into cultivated lands

covered with a prosperous people. Towns and cities had sprung into existence, and it rapidly increased in wealth and population under the social system of the South.[21]

A product of his environment and times, Davis failed to recognize that Southern aristocracy deprived over a third of the South's human population of their *human* rights.[22] He only saw the rights of the Southern ruling class and was annoyed that the Northern States were seeking to impose controls that would affect the Southern agricultural economy.[23] He wrote: "The people of the Southern States, whose almost exclusive occupation was agriculture, early perceived a tendency in the Northern States to render a common government subservient to their own purposes by imposing burthens [*sic*] on commerce as protection to their manufacturing and shipping interests."[24] On October 16, 1860, Davis wrote privately:

> Confronted by a common foe, the South should by the instinct of self-preservation be united. ... The recent declaration of the candidate and leaders of the Black Republican party are familiar to you and need not be recited; they must suffice to convince many who have formerly doubted the purpose to attack the institution of slavery in the States. The undying opposition to slavery in the United States means woe upon it where it is, not where it is not; and the time is at hand when the great battle is to be fought between the defenders of the constitutional government and the votaries of mob rule, fanaticism, and anarchy.[25]

Slavery was such an integral part of Southern life for Davis that he took it for granted in 1881 in reflecting on the rise and fall of the Confederacy. "To whatever extent the question of slavery may have served as an *occasion*," he declared, "it was far from being a *cause* of the war."[26] Those who assert that slavery in the South would have died a natural death through the expansion of free labor, as it had already done in the North, fail to reckon with Southern aristocracy and the persistence of Southern culture built on the backs of the slaves.[27]

Northern Democrat and champion of "popular sovereignty" Stephen Douglas asserted in his July 10, 1858 debate with Abraham Lincoln in Bloomington, Illinois, that, based on Lincoln's "House Divided" speech, Lincoln was "in favor of making war by the North upon the South for the extinction of slavery" and that he was "also in favor of inviting ... the South to a war upon the North for the purpose of nationalizing slavery." Though acknowledging his hatred for slavery and his interest in limiting the institution within Constitutional provisions, Lincoln countered the pro-war charge:

Lincoln defending his "House Divided" speech during the Lincoln-Douglas debate

I did not say that I was in favor of anything in it. I only said what I expected would take place. I made prediction only .... I am tolerably well acquainted with the history of the country, and I know that it has endured eighty-two years half slave and half free. I *believe*—and that is what I meant to allude to there—I *believe* it has endured, because during all that time, until the introduction of the Nebraska bill, the public mind did rest all the time in the belief that slavery was in course of ultimate extinction.[28] That was what gave us the rest that we had through that period of eighty-two years,—at least, so I believe. I have always hated slavery, I think, as much as any

Abolitionist,—I have been an Old Line Whig,—I have always hated it, but I have always been quiet about it until this new era of the introduction of the Nebraska bill began.[29] I always believed that everybody was against it, and that it was in course of ultimate extinction.... I have said a hundred times, and have now no inclination to take it back that I believe there is no right, and ought to be no inclination, in the people of the Free States to enter into the Slave States and interfere with the question of slavery at all. I have said that always.... I believe each individual is naturally entitled to do as he pleases with himself and the fruit of his labor, so far as it in no wise interferes with any other man's rights; that each community, as a State, has a right to do exactly as it pleases with all the concerns within that State that interferes with the right of no other State; and that the General Government, upon principle, has no right to interfere with anything other than that general class of things that does concern the whole.[30]

Notice that twice Lincoln declared his belief that slavery was endured so long because it was "in course of ultimate extinction." After the election, Lincoln wrote Alexander Stephens, reassuring him that he would not "directly, or indirectly, interfere with the slaves or with the southern people about their slaves," but ended his letter saying, "I suppose, however, this does not meet the case [i.e., is not enough]. You think slavery is right and ought to be extended, while we think it is wrong and ought to be restricted...." Writing back, Stephens reminded Lincoln that the restriction of slavery was the central plank in the Republican platform.[31]

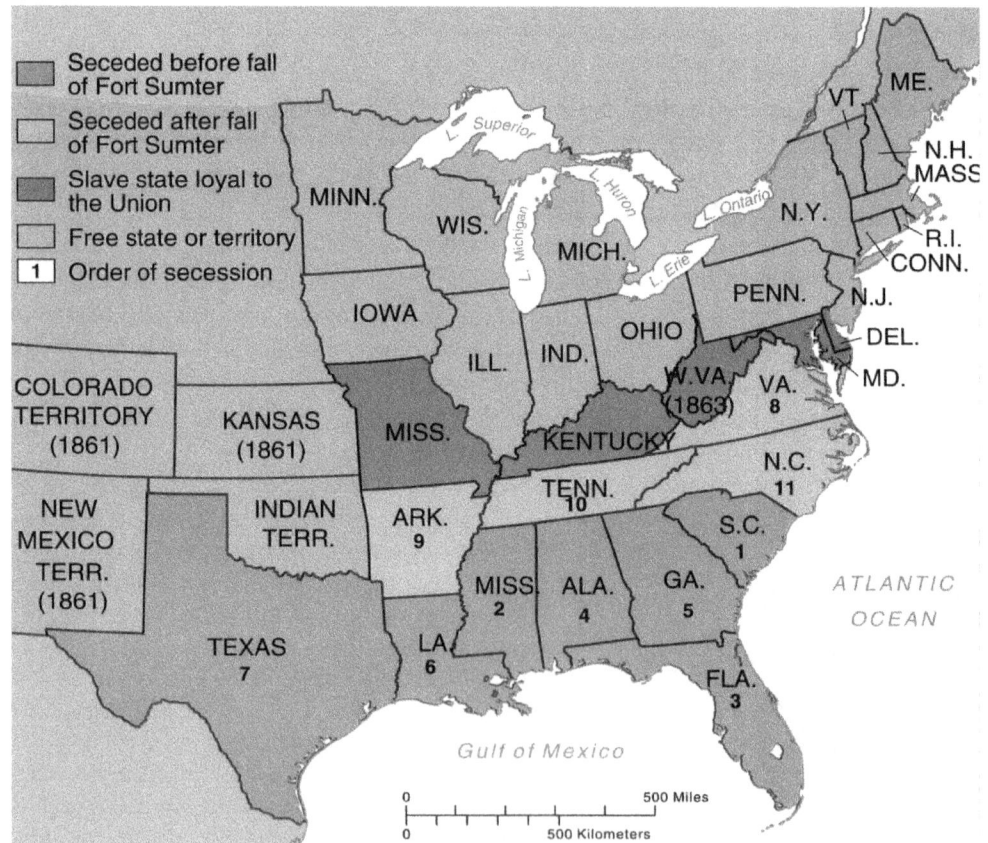

Map of Southern Secession, 1860–1861

Southern Secession, a Last-Ditch Effort to Save a Way of Life

Despite Lincoln's reassurances after his election, South Carolina seceded from the Union on December 20, 1860, believing the Republican agenda would soon eclipse their Southern way of life. During the next few weeks, six other Southern states followed suit—Mississippi on January 9, 1861, Florida on January 10, Alabama on January 11, Georgia on January 19, and Louisiana and Texas on January 26. On February 4, they formed the Confederacy. Still hoping to hold the nation together, Lincoln confirmed in his first inaugural address his promise not to interfere with slavery in the Southern states. "I have no purpose, directly or indirectly, to interfere with the institution of slavery in the States where it exists. I believe I have no lawful right to do so, and I have no inclination to do so."[32] Even after war broke out, denial of the "elephant" continued. Pastor A. L. Stone, of the Boston Park Street Church, declared on April 21, 1861: "It is not an anti-slavery war we wage, not a sectional war, not a war of conquest and subjugation; it is simply and solely a war for the maintenance of the Government and the Constitution."[33] Ex-governor of New York Horatio Seymour declared in December 1861: "I deny that slavery is the cause of this war."[34] August 22, 1862, Lincoln wrote New York editor Horace Greeley:

> If there be those who would not save the Union, unless they could at the same time *save* slavery, I do not agree with them. If there be those who would not save the Union unless they could at the same time *destroy* slavery, I do not agree with them. My paramount object in this struggle *is* to save the Union, and it is *not* either to save or to destroy slavery. If I could save the Union without freeing *any* slave, I would do it; and if I could save it by freeing *all* the slaves, I would do it; and if I could save it by freeing some and leaving others alone, I would also do that. What I do about slavery and the colored race, I do because I believe it helps to save this Union, and what I forbear, I forbear because I do *not* believe it would help to save the Union.[35]

Moral Apathy Regarding Slavery

How was it that the elephant of slavery could be so easily ignored and even denied? Prominent Presbyterian clergyman Albert Barnes held the churches of America responsible for not employing their moral voice to curtail slavery.[36] So did Harriet Beecher Stowe, whom the *Advent Review and Sabbath Herald* quoted as saying, "Not to condemn is to approve."[37] "It is probable," Barnes declared, "that slavery could not be sustained in this land if it were not for the countenance, direct and indirect, of the churches."[38] Northern teacher Charles Stearns asserted in 1849: "There is scarcely a church throughout New England, all the members of which, who voted at all, voted against the extension of Slavery."[39] Many Christians had abdicated their duty to vote against slavery's spread into the new western territories.

Harriet Beecher Stowe, author of *Uncle Tom's Cabin*

Albert Barnes, Presbyterian clergyman

At its greatest strength in the latter 1830s, about 160,000 church people belonged to the American Anti-Slavery Society and its affiliates. This was only a fraction of the approximately four million Americans who attended church.[40] In the summer of 1836, evangelist Charles Finney, who was affiliated with the abolitionist Oberlin College, feared

Evangelist Charles G. Finney

that the abolition movement was pushing the country into civil war and wrote his fellow abolitionist Theodore Weld that the solution was for abolition to become "an appendage of a general revival of religion."[41] In other words, Finney thought that abolition should become a standard plank in the platform of general religious reform. Neither Weld nor anyone else accepted Finney's suggestion. Overall, Northern Christians took no official stance either for or against slavery. As McKivigan wrote in *The War against Proslavery Religion*, "all but a few denominations refused to condemn slaveholding."[42] The churches' strongest leverage against slavery would have been to disfellowship slave-holding members. However, as McKivigan noted, "Liturgical denominations refused to deny fellowship to slaveholders because the idea that individuals could be held responsible for the sins of other church members was contrary to their established doctrines. In many denominations, sweeping guidelines on acceptable moral behavior were opposed as infringements upon the local autonomy of lower judicatories.[43] Even moderate antislavery churchmen argued that slaveholders' consciences could be enlightened better inside the religious bodies than outside them. . . ." In addition "many church leaders hesitated to endorse any position on slavery that might drive away southern members."[44] Even the American Tract Society and the American Bible Society refused to condemn slavery.[45]

Abolitionists "harshly criticized the churches for their lack of conviction and decisive action."[46] Nonetheless, not all preachers and churches abdicated their moral role regarding slavery.[47] The American Board of Commissioners for Foreign Missions in Boston for the Episcopal Church declared the slave trade "an enormous evil—that pollutes whatever it touches and desolates wherever it goes."[48] The 1818 General Assembly of the Presbyterians voiced what many individual Christians believed—"that it considered the voluntary enslaving of one part of the human race by another, as a gross violation of the most precious and sacred rights of human nature, as utterly inconsistent with the law of God."[49]

Adventist Concern for a People Held in Slavery

It is significant that Seventh-day Adventists, who were outspokenly against slavery before the Civil War, formalized as a denomination during the years of the war. Their roots were in the millennial movement of William Miller, which culminated in 1844 under the fervor of the Second Great Awakening. Miller, a military veteran, farmer, and justice of the peace turned Baptist preacher, proclaimed the imminent advent of Christ based upon his interpretation of Bible prophecy. Those who believed like Miller were called Adventists. The cross-cultural and cross-denominational nature of the Advent movement lent itself to considering African Americans as brethren. Among the early Adventists, there were several prominent African-American preachers, including William Still, Charles Bowles, William Ellis Foy, and John L. Lewis. These made "the case that a new day was coming for Blacks, which, due to the return of Christ, would see a new social order established."[50]

William Miller

Though Adventists looked to God's intervention at the second coming of Christ as that which would end slavery, many Adventists were active abolitionists. William Lloyd Garrison considered William Miller himself to be an "outspoken friend" of "the cause of temperance, of anti-slavery, of moral reform, of non-resistance."[51] "Miller . . . believed that benevolent reform groups were forerunners to his movement."[52] A friend of William Miller, Truman Hendryx, wrote Miller, critical of the American Anti-Slavery Society's call for immediate abolition, preferring the less radical approach of the American Colonization Society, which assisted free African Americans in immigrating to Africa. In his February 25, 1834 response, Miller employed sarcasm in scorning Hendryx's reserve on the issue and in critiquing the American Colonization Society for treating blacks as less than human: "These Abolitionists, Emancipators, Liberators must be put down," he taunted. "What[,] emancipate 2,000,000 of brutes, unless we call molatoes [sic] half brutes only, then say 1,000,000 brutes & 1,000,000 half brutes. No, no this would flood our country with beasts surely. . . . God knew what a dilemma we should be placed in, and therefore made [them] black, and so we may beat them, bruise them, sell them, buy them, not teach them, not give them Bibles, not preach to them, hang them, burn them, shoot them, and cut their throats if they should try to get free. . . . I think, Br. Hendryx," he wrote facetiously, "that the Abolitionists who say that the Negroes are to be free aught in justice to have their throats [cut] from e[a]r to ear for saying these things. What think you Br. Hendryx? . . . the great, the good benevolent Colonisation Society transports and banishes them to Liber[i]a where one half die from starvation and the 'seasoning' as they call it. Now we know they would not do it if they were men because it would be murder. That Society are Christians, & they murder [?], no. For 'as much as ye have done it unto the least of these ye have done it unto me' says Christ."[53] Disappointed by the division he witnessed at an Abolitionist meeting in New York City in 1840, Miller lamented, "The poor slave, has but little chance to be liberated by these two parties. . . . The slaveholder may call in his piquets, he may need no additional guards, his citadel is safe.[54] While the pretended friends of the slave, are expending all their ammunition on each other, the release of the captive will be little thought of."

Abolitionist William Lloyd Garrison

William Lloyd Garrison also described Charles Fitch, another prominent Adventist preacher, as being "well known to the abolitionists of the United States." In Fitch's tract, "Slaveholding Weighed in the Balance of Truth, and its Comparative Guilt Illustrated," he wrote: "Up my friends, and do your duty, to deliver the spoils out of the hands of the oppressor, lest the fire of God's fury kindle ere long upon you."[55] Joshua V. Himes, a key Millerite organizer and preacher, was a close friend of William Lloyd Garrison and also an abolitionist.[56] Ultimately, Miller taught that God would be the slaves' liberator: "God can and will release the captive. And to him alone we must look for redress."[57] Many disillusioned abolitionists agreed with Miller and joined his movement, which "presented the ultimate cure for slavery in the form of the apocalyptic return of Jesus Christ."[58]

Adventist preachers Charles Fitch and Joshua V. Himes

An Anti-Slavery Faith Formed Under the Fire of War

Following their disappointment that Jesus did not return in 1844 as expected, the Adventists who accepted the seventh-day Sabbath held study conferences during the late 1840s and 1850s to work out their doctrinal framework.[59] Having been shunned by their former churches for believing in Christ's imminent return, they were resistant to formal church organization. Notwithstanding, they were eager to publish their Scriptural views, and legal standing for their publishing association required the choice of a name. The name "Seventh-day Adventists" was selected on October 1, 1860. The "Seventh-day Adventist Publishing Association" was incorporated on May 3, 1861, and the association's bylaws were adopted on May 23, 1861. These latter two events, just after war had been declared in the United States, were the first steps toward formal denominational status. The next would not come for another two years, in the midst of the war, following the Emancipation Proclamation.[60] On May 21, 1863, the Seventh-day Adventists formally organized with 125 churches and about thirty-five hundred members.[61] Theirs was a religious faith birthed under the fire of war.

Established denominations were divided over slavery. So too were the Christadelphians, who, like the Seventh-day Adventists, emerged as a denomination during the Civil War. Though Seventh-day Adventists had spread west as far as Wisconsin, they had made no inroads into the South before the Southern states seceded.[62] This by itself would not have ensured their united anti-slavery stance were it not for the leadership of Mrs. Ellen G. White, whose statements framed the American Civil War for Seventh-day Adventists and kept them united.[63] For those who do not know Ellen White, past secretary of the trustees of Ellen White's writings and Ellen White's grandson, Arthur L. White, has prepared a synopsis of her accomplishments:

> In brief, she was a woman of remarkable spiritual gifts who lived most of her life during the nineteenth century (1827-1915), yet through her writings she is still making a revolutionary impact on millions of people around the world. During her lifetime she wrote more than 5,000 periodical articles and 40 books; but today, including compilations from her 50,000 pages of manuscript, more than 100 titles are available in English. She is the most translated woman writer in the entire history of literature, and the most translated American author of either gender. Her writings cover a broad range of subjects, including religion, education, social relationships, evangelism, prophecy, publishing, nutrition, and management. Her life-changing masterpiece on successful Christian living, *Steps to Christ*, has been published in more than 140 languages. Seventh-day Adventists believe that Mrs. White was more than a gifted writer; they believe she was appointed by God as a special messenger to draw the world's attention to the Holy Scriptures and help prepare people for Christ's second advent. From the time she was 17 years old until she died 70 years later, God gave her approximately 2,000 visions and dreams.[64] The visions varied in length from less than a minute to nearly four hours. The knowledge and counsel received through these revelations she wrote out to be shared with others. Thus her special writings are accepted by Seventh-day Adventists as inspired, and their exceptional quality is recognized even by casual readers. As stated in *Seventh-day Adventists Believe* . . . "The writings of Ellen White are not a substitute for Scripture. They cannot be placed on the same level. The Holy Scriptures stand alone, the

Ellen G. White, 1859

unique standard by which her and all other writings must be judged and to which they must be subject."[65] Yet, as Ellen White herself noted, "The fact that God has revealed His will to men through His Word, has not rendered needless the continued presence and guiding of the Holy Spirit. On the contrary, the Spirit was promised by our Saviour to open the Word to His servants, to illuminate and apply its teachings."[66]

That Seventh-day Adventists consider Ellen White's writings to be inspired does not mean that they believe she received every word by heavenly dictation—any more than they believe that the inspired writers of Scripture wrote without the use of sources.[67] Ellen White's son, William C. White, described his mother's use of sources in bringing "vividly to her mind scenes presented clearly in vision" and in helping her "perfect her descriptions of details."[68] Ellen White herself described her use of history that was "well known and universally acknowledged by the Protestant world" in writing *The Great Controversy*, her first published volume in the Conflict of the Ages series.[69]

Like many other Adventists, Ellen White was against slavery. Though the Fugitive Slave Act of 1850 was decried by many, it was generally enforced, and Mrs. White encouraged Adventists to disobey it—whatever the consequences might be.[70] In 1859, she pronounced:

> The law of our land requiring us to deliver a slave to his master, we are not to obey; and we must abide the consequences of violating this law. *The slave is not the property of any man.* God is his rightful master, and man has no right to take God's workmanship into his hands, and claim him as his own.[71]

Mrs. White would later write: "The system of slavery has reduced and degraded human beings to the level of the brutes, and the majority of slave masters regard them as such." She believed: "The whole system of slavery was originated by Satan, who delights in tyrannizing over human beings."[72]

A Review of Adventist Anti-Slavery Views

Among sabbatarian Adventists, Ellen White was not an isolated voice in opposition to slavery. Their official organ, the *Advent Review and Sabbath Herald*, contained many submissions that demonstrate disdain for the institution. For example, in 1853, the periodical's editor, Uriah Smith, included the following lines in an exposition on America in prophecy:

> O land of boasted freedom! thou hast given
> The lie to all thy loud professions, fair,
> Of justice, liberty and equal rights;
> And thou hast set a foul and heinous blot
> Upon the sacred page of liberty;
> And whilst thou traffickest in souls of men,
> Thou hurl'st defiance, proud, in face of Heaven
> Soon to be answered with avenging doom.[73]

The next year, Edwin R. Seaman of Rochester, New York, wrote in the same periodical: "A man made in God's own image is torn from friends and society and all that is dear in life, and dragged back into slavery by the power of that atrocious bargain, the fugitive slave law, the foulest stain that ever blotted the history of any nation, especially one whose professions are entirely of an opposite character."[74] Early Adventist scholar John Nevins Andrews asked: " 'If all men are born free and equal,' why then does this power hold three millions of human beings in the bondage of slavery? Why is it that the Negro race is reduced to the rank of chattels personal, and bought and sold like brute beasts?" Andrews called the Fugitive Slave Act the "most infamous law of the nineteenth century" and lamented that, "not satisfied with this act of infamy," Congress had enacted the Kansas-Nebraska Act of May 30, 1854.[75] Joseph Clarke of Ohio was another vocal opponent of slavery before and during the Civil War among sabbatarian Adventists. His writings on the subject will be considered in Chapter 6. In opposition to slavery, Uriah Smith quoted the honorable Joshua R. Giddings, U.S. Congressman from Ohio from 1838 to 1859 and opponent of slavery:

J. N. Andrews

> *Three distinct and separate wars* have been waged to uphold and maintain the system of American Slavery. More than *three hundred millions of dollars* have been drawn from the pockets of our laboring people, and paid out by government for that purpose; and more than *five hundred thousand human victims* have been sent to premature graves, to uphold and maintain the interests of an institution which the present administration and its supporters are seeking to extend and eternize. . . . [A]nd the groans of men and women, murdered in Kansas by employees of the government, have not yet ceased to ring in our ears.[76]

Joshua R. Giddings

As Seventh-day Adventist historian Douglas Morgan has asserted, most sabbatarian Adventists believed that "only Christ's Second Coming . . . would free the slaves."[77] Because of belief in the nearness of Christ's return, they focused on preparing themselves and others for that grand event rather than on engaging in political activism. They believed that the spreading of the Advent message was the resolution to slavery. This can be seen in an entry in the autobiography of Joseph Bates, a co-founder of the Seventh-day Adventist Church who had helped organize a local anti-slavery society in Fairhaven, Massachusetts.[78] Bates wrote:

> Some of my good friends that were engaged in the temperance and abolition cause, came to know why I could not attend their stated meetings as formerly, and argued that my belief in the coming of the Saviour should make me more ardent in endeavoring to suppress these growing evils. My reply was, that in embracing the doctrine of the second coming of the Saviour, I found enough to engage my whole time in getting ready for such an event, and aiding others to do the same, and that all who embraced this doctrine would and must necessarily be advocates of temperance and the abolition of slavery . . . .[79]

Joseph Bates

Uriah Smith voiced a similar view in 1856:

Uriah Smith

With the belief that the people generally entertain, that there is yet a long future before the world, we cannot blame them for using every effort to prevent soil which is now free from being blasted by the mildew of Slavery [referring to Kansas]. . . . To the question, why we do not with our votes and influence labor against the evil tendency of the times, we reply, that our views of prophecy lead us to the conclusion that things will not be bettered. . . . We do not therefore feel it incumbent upon us to labor, in this respect, either to hasten or retard the fulfillment of prophecy. God's purposes will surely be accomplished.[80]

Because of Uriah Smith's apparent "passivity on the issue of slavery," Anson Byington, elder brother of John Byington (who would become the first president of the General Conference of Seventh-day Adventists), announced that he would be discontinuing his subscription to the *Advent Review and Sabbath Herald*.[81] Byington added:

> I dare not tell the slave that he can afford to be contented in his bondage until the Saviour comes however near we may believe his coming. Surely the editor of the *Review* could not afford to go without his breakfast till then. If it was our duty to remember those in bonds [Heb. 13:3] as bound with them eighteen hundred years ago, it must be our duty still. When saw we thee hungry or athirst, sick or in prison, and did not minister unto thee [Matt. 25:38, 39].[82]

Smith responded to Byington in the same issue of the *Review:*

> Our feelings in regard to slavery could hardly be mistaken by any who are acquainted with our position on the law of God, the foundation of all reform, the radical stand point against every evil. Slavery as a sin we have never ceased to abhor; its ravages we have never ceased to deprecate; with the victims locked in its foul embrace, we have not ceased to sympathize. But what is to be done? The tyranny of oppression secludes them from our reach. In saying this, we do not tell the slave that he can afford to be content in slavery, nor that he should not escape from it whenever he can, nor that all good men should not aid him to the extent of their power, nor that this great evil should not be resisted by any and all means which afford any hope of success. All this should be done.[83]

Lack of political activism did not mean that Smith questioned the immorality of slavery. In August 1861, Smith introduced an article from the *American Missionary*, which showed that Seventh-day Adventists were not alone in censuring Americans for condoning slavery:

> Well does the writer remark that the "Almighty has a controversy with this nation;" and not only with this nation, we may add, but he has a controversy with all nations [Jer. 25:31], upon which he is evidently now about entering [Luke 21:25, 26]; and of the cup of God's fury from which all nations will be required to drink [Jer. 25:15] we believe the dregs will be administered to our own [Jer. 25:26; Psalm 75:8]; for the guilt of any people is in proportion to the strength and brightness of the light which they reject; and how much light has been rejected by this government may be learned from the fact that a black and revolting iniquity which all other nations pretending to any degree of civilization have repudiated, and from

which they are hastening to cleanse their hands, is still hugged by our own with a sottish tenacity, the people in one portion of the country blasphemously endeavoring to defend it by the Bible, and too many of the rest conniving at both its existence and its arrogant claims. . . .

Then Smith quoted the article. Tipping their hat to those who recognized the Negro as "their countryman and brother," the *American Missionary* lamented the nearly universal indifference "to the welfare, improvement and advancement of the colored Americans" and held "the Church and those who minister at God's altar" responsible for the suffering of free and enslaved blacks in America. Despite the assertion of the Declaration of Independence that "all men are created equal," the article continued, "yet, from the foundation of the government to the present time the free people of color have been maltreated and scorned, at the North as well as at the South, and their enslaved brethren inhumanly peeled and goaded at the South, aided in the inhumanity by the North." Noting that other nations of the world saw the hypocrisy and indifference and ridiculed America for it, the *American Missionary* concluded:

> Professing to be a Christian nation, the people—we allude to the masses—have set at naught the precepts of Christianity, in their treatment of their colored brethren, forgotten the exhortations of God, and unheeded his warnings, until the patience of the Father of all appears to have been exhausted, and he has come out against us in judgment. . . .[84]

Three months later, Smith unhesitatingly declared:

> Slavery is the cause of the present war, and consequently *no efforts can be effective* which do not embrace within their purposes the removal of this diabolical iniquity; and yet slavery is persistently ignored on the part of the government as having any bearing on the settlement of this controversy. . . . [U]ntil the North shall cleanse its hands from all the stains of this sin, and take a bold stand of uncompromising opposition to its very existence, and seize upon every opportunity to abolish and crush it out, God cannot make bare his arm nor manifest his power to aid them in the struggle.[85]

Though their denomination was yet in its infancy, Seventh-day Adventists were united in believing that the abolition of slavery needed to become a primary object of the Civil War, and they were not afraid to declare their convictions in the *Advent Review and Sabbath Herald*.[86] Because of this, the periodical was banned in many slave states.[87] Though they would not pray for the saving of the Union without the liberation of the slaves, Seventh-day Adventists, as "conscientious co-operators," were "rigidly anti-slavery, loyal to the government, and in sympathy with it against the rebellion."[88] This was due, in part, to Ellen White's "testimonies" on slavery and the Civil War, which we will consider in the next three chapters.

Chapter 2

"Great Distress Coming"

A day of heart-rending anguish is before us. —Ellen G. White

In the critical months leading up to and following the outbreak of the Civil War, Mrs. Ellen G. White had several visions relating to the war. Written out as "testimonies," they dealt largely with the spiritual preparedness of Seventh-day Adventists for the coming crisis.[1] The first of these visions came on January 12, 1861, at Parkville, Michigan, after the initial string of Southern secessions.[2] The second came on August 3, 1861, at Roosevelt, New York, after the defeat of the Union forces at the First Battle of Manassas (Bull Run).[3] Mrs. White first published the content of the vision in the *Advent Review and Sabbath Herald* of August 27, 1861.[4] The third vision came on January 4, 1862, at Battle Creek, Michigan.[5] Shortly after receiving the third vision, Mrs. White published the content of all three visions in a pamphlet entitled, "Testimony for the Church, No. 7," leading off with the third vision followed by the first and the second.[6] The pamphlet was later reprinted in *Testimonies for the Church*, vol. 1. Besides these three visions, Mrs. White had at least one other vision on the war, published in January of 1863 in "Testimony for the Church, No. 9" under the title "The Rebellion." Only aspects of the first three visions that deal with the Civil War will be covered here.[7] (All of her Civil War visions will be covered in Jud Lake's forthcoming book, *A Nation in God's Hands: The Civil War Visions of Ellen G. White*).[8]

> **COMMUNICATION FROM SISTER WHITE.**
>
> SLAVERY AND THE WAR.
>
> GOD is punishing this nation for the high crime of slavery. He has the destiny of the nation in his hands. He will punish the South for the sin of slavery, and the North for so long suffering its overreaching and overbearing influences.
>
> All heaven beholds with indignation, human beings, the workmanship of God, reduced to the lowest depths of degradation, and placed on a level with the brute creation by their fellow-men. And professed followers of that dear Saviour whose compassion was ever moved as he witnessed human woe, heartily engage in this enormous and grievous sin, and deal in slaves and souls of men. Angels have recorded it all. It is written in the book. The tears of the pious bond-men and bond-women, of fathers, mothers and children, brothers and sisters, are all bottled up in heaven. Agony, human agony, is carried from place to place, and bought and sold. God will restrain his anger but a little longer. His anger burns against this nation, and especially against the religious bodies who have sanctioned, and have themselves engaged in this terrible merchandise. Such injustice, such oppression,

The first portion of Ellen White's counsel about the Civil War, published in the *Review and Herald* following the Battle of Bull Run

Mistaken Projections of a Short Conflict

Familiar with threats of secession, the *New-York Daily Tribune* editor Horace Greeley stated in 1851 that a state that was let go without exercise of military force "would be glad to walk in again before she had been out two years."[9] Many Northerners were hopeful that there would be a peaceful resolution to any rising conflict between the States or that armed conflict would be limited and short. A pro-Lincoln paper in Boston announced shortly after Lincoln's election: "The only results to the rebellious States would be a bloody strife confined entirely to their own territory, [and] the immediate and violent abolition of slavery."[10] The *New York Times* projected the possibility of "scattered collisions" but that whatever war there was could be managed from sea.[11] On May 17, 1861, after war had begun, anti-slavery Kentuckian Cassius Clay wrote to the London *Times*, overestimating support for the Union:

Horace Greeley, editor

Cassius Marcellus Clay

> But can you conquer the South? Of course we can. We can blockade them by sea and invade them by land, and close up the rebellion in a single year, if let alone, for the population of the Slave States is divided, perhaps equally, for and against the Union, the loyal citizens being for the time overawed by the organized conspiracy of the traitors; while the North is united to a man.[12]

Most Northerners had no idea that the nation was heading for a war that would continue until the spring of 1865 or that it would cost as many as 750,000 Northern and Southern lives.[13] The January 11, 1861 *New-York Tribune* suggested: "The Secession of the Southern States appears to be inevitable; the excitement and feeling of the people run in that direction; the exasperation is increasing; it must eventually culminate in a separation, even if contrary to their interests. Under such circumstances, the true policy of the North is to effect a just, peaceful and dignified separation."[14] Reflecting the view that the secession could take place with little or no armed conflict, Alexander Stephens boasted on March 21, 1861, to a Savannah, Georgia audience that the Southern revolution had thus far been accomplished "without shedding a drop of blood."[15]

Abraham Lincoln, February 9, 1861

There is no doubt that influential men viewed the rising conflict as being one of short duration. The editor of *Harper's Weekly* of May 4, 1861, questioned publicly whether Northern men would respond to the provocation of the Southern rebellion and the insulting of the flag. If they had the gumption to fight, the editor asserted, and "Abraham Lincoln is equal to the position he fills, this war will be over by January, 1862."[16] Lincoln likewise cherished the "hope that powerful advances in Virginia and down the Mississippi would end the fighting in 1862 . . . and expected to see slavery shaken and eroded."[17] On July 4, Lincoln called on Congress to authorize him with the "legal means for making this contest a short and decisive one, that you place at the control of the government for this work at least 400,000 men and $400,000,000. . . ."[18]

"Great Distress Coming, and God's People Not Prepared For It"[19]

Three months before the attack on Fort Sumter, James and Ellen White, J. H. Waggoner, Uriah Smith, and J. N. Loughborough officiated at the dedication of the meeting-house of the Sabbath-keeping Adventists at Parkville, Michigan.[20] It was January 12, 1861. The day was clear and cold, and it had snowed the day before.[21] Loughborough recorded that Waggoner had the sermon, James White had the dedicatory prayer, and Ellen delivered a moving presentation and sat down.[22] Then she went into a visionary state without noticeable respiration for about twenty minutes.[23] As on other occasions, her eyes were "open, not with a glassy appearance,

Ellen G. White

or a vacant stare, but with a look more like that of one looking intently at a distant object."[24] The people in the crowded house waited with deep interest. When the vision was over and Mrs. White had resumed normal respiration, she stood up and described what she had seen:

There is not a person in this house who has even dreamed of the trouble that is coming upon this land. People are making sport of the secession ordinance of South Carolina, but I have just been shown that a large number of States are going to join that State, and there will be a most terrible war.[25] In this vision, I have seen large armies on both sides gathered on the field of *battle. I heard the booming of the cannon,* and saw *the dead and dying on every hand.* Then I saw them rushing up engaged in *hand-to-hand fight*ing. Then *I saw* the field after the battle, all *covered with the dead and dying.* Then I was carried to prisons, and saw the *suffering* of those in *want,* who were wasting away. Then I was taken to the homes of those who had lost husbands, sons, or brothers in the war. I saw there *distress* and anguish. . . . There are those in this house who will lose sons in that war.[26]

Parkville officiants James and Ellen White, J. H. Waggoner, Uriah Smith, and J. N. Loughborough

Some present in the audience did not take the potential of war very seriously. Discussion in the local papers was not of war but of the dissolution of the Union.[27] Loughborough noted the reaction of two prominent guests in the audience—Judge Nathan Osborn and wool manufacturer Leonard E. Schellhous. Both listened and shook their heads in disbelief.[28] They, like many others, did not believe that the brewing conflict would be as serious as Ellen White portrayed it.[29]

A Harvest of Death, Gettysburg, July 4, 1863

A related event that occurred the day of the dedication was etched in the memory of those present. Loughborough described it the year after the war: "I saw a noted Spiritualist and mesmerizer present . . . when she had a vision at Parkville, Michigan. He had given out before she came that if she should have a vision there, as it was nothing but mesmerism, he could bring her out of it. When he saw her in vision he came forward where she was, but instead of trying to bring her out, he went staggering toward the door, saying to the congregation, 'She don't breathe,' and declaring that he did not know what it was, turned deadly pale and left the room."[30] No one present could disregard the supernatural nature of Mrs. White's vision. What she revealed left a deep impression on the people.[31] That a woman who had never witnessed battle was able to capture the horrors of battle and the ravages of its aftermath caught everyone's attention. Yet, her account assured the people that God was not caught off guard by human affairs.

Living conditions at Andersonville prison

J. N. Loughborough, accompanied by John Byington, returned to Parkville on November 1 and 2, 1862, to organize the church. In teaching on spiritual gifts, he reminded the audience of the vision.[32] The same two men who had been skeptical in hearing Ellen White's pronouncement were present on this occasion as well. However, this time they were fighting back tears. Judge Nathan Osborn's adopted sons, Frank and George, ages 18 and 16, had volunteered for the 17th Michigan Infantry, Company C, on July 24, 1862.[33] The older brother was one of 114 in the 17th Infantry wounded in action at the Battle of South Mountain, Maryland, on September 14, 1862.[34] He died from his wounds

J. N. Loughborough and John Byington

on October 4 at nearby Middleton, Maryland.[35] The loss was doubly painful for Judge Osborn because Frank's mother, who was Osborn's second wife Rebecca, had died on February 3 that same year.[36] Schellhous had his own reason for fighting back tears. He had lost a nearly two-month-old baby just two months prior. In the fall of 1883, Harvey Keeney, who was the head elder of the Parkville Adventist Church in 1861, told Loughborough that he remembered Mrs. White's statements about the war and could name several people in attendance the day of the vision that had lost sons in the war.[37]

The *New York Herald* of January 11, 1861, pessimistically projected that Virginia and the border slave states would secede from the Union and form an army to remove the symbols of the Union "from every fortress or public building within the Confederate States, including the White House, the Capitol and other buildings of Washington" and that "civil war of five, ten or twenty years' duration" would follow.[38] Either President Lincoln did not anticipate the severity of the war, or at least he did not let on that he did. Relying "upon a provision of a 1795 militia law" to call for troops on April 15 to put down the insurrection in South Carolina, he called for only 75,000 volunteers from the State militias, with an enlistment of just three months.[39] Virginia interpreted Lincoln's call for volunteers to take back the federal forts as an act of aggression toward the South and, two days later, seceded from the Union. Jefferson Davis accused Lincoln of acting outside his authority and took Lincoln's actions as a declaration of war on the Confederacy.[40] Davis believed that the Southern states had acted constitutionally in seceding from the nation and in claiming federal forts as their property. "Far from being revolutionaries seeking to overthrow the existing government, secessionists insisted they were merely withdrawing from the existing 'compact' of states and creating a government of their own among the other like-minded Southern states."[41] On May 3, Lincoln "issued a proclamation calling for an additional 42,034 three-year volunteers and 18,000 sailors, as well as expanding the regular army by 22,714 men."[42] Arkansas, North Carolina, and Tennessee joined the Confederacy on May 6, 20, and June 8, respectively.

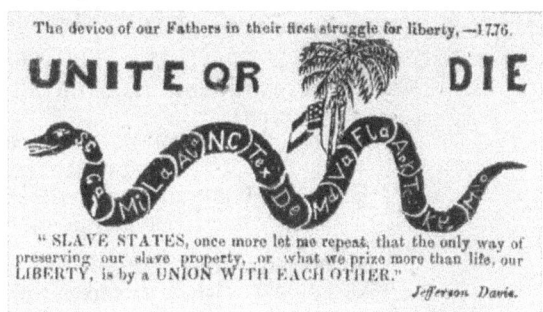

Confederate pictorial envelope, Charleston, S.C., ca. 1861.

Despite early hopes of a peaceful separation, Ellen White predicted a "terrible war" with the "booming of the cannon" and "hand-to-hand fighting." In November 1861, after touring a Union army camp near Washington, DC, Julia Ward Howe wrote new words to "John Brown's Body," which she had heard Union soldiers sing.[43] The new lyrics, published as "The Battle Hymn of the Republic," anticipated a quick and decisive conclusion to the war—"He hath loosed the fateful lightnings of His terrible *swift* sword."[44] In August 1861, Ellen White saw, in her second Civil War vision, that God would not allow the war to end so long as Americans neglected the great moral stain of slavery.

Julia Ward Howe

BATTLE HYMN OF THE REPUBLIC.

BY MRS. JULIA WARD HOWE.

Mine eyes have seen the glory of the coming of the Lord:
He is trampling out the vintage where the grapes of wrath are stored;
He hath loosed the fateful lightnings of His terrible swift sword:
    His truth is marching on.
  Chorus—Glory, glory, hallelujah!
      Glory, glory, hallelujah!
      Glory, glory, hallelujah!
      His truth is marching on.

I have seen Him in the watch-fires of a hundred circling camps;
They have builded Him an altar in the evening dews and damps:
I can read His righteous sentence by the dim and flaring lamps:
    His day is marching on.
  Chorus—Glory, glory, hallelujah, &c.
      His day is marching on.

I have read a fiery gospel writ in burnished rows of steel:
"As ye deal with my contemners, so with you my grace shall deal;
Let the Hero, born of woman, crush the serpent with his heel,
    Since God is marching on."
  Chorus—Glory, glory, hallelujah &c.
      Since God is marching on.

He has sounded forth the trumpet that shall never call retreat:
He is sifting out the hearts of men before His judgment seat:
Oh, be swift, my soul, to answer Him! be jubilant my feet!
    Our God is marching on!
  Chorus—Glory, glory, hallelujah, &c.
      Our God is marching on!

In the beauty of the lilies Christ was born across the sea,
With a glory in His bosom that transfigures you and me;
As he died to make men holy, let us die to make men free,
    While God is marching on.
  Chorus—Glory, glory, hallelujah, &c.
      While God is marching on.

"Battle Hymn of the Republic," first published in *The Atlantic Monthly*, February 1862

Chapter 3

"Slavery and the War"

The North have had no just idea of the strength of the accursed system of slavery. It is this, and this alone, which lies at the foundation of the war. —Ellen G. White

Ellen White's second Civil War vision came August 3, 1861, at Roosevelt, New York, after the defeat of the Union forces at the First Battle of Manassas (Bull Run). One might mistakenly think that the vision delivered a prediction of a battle not yet fought. However, the vision was a post-battle explanation, from a spiritual standpoint and not a tactical one, of why the North lost the first major battle in the war. It was that God was holding both the South and the North accountable for the perpetuation of slavery, and the Northern armies would not succeed in preserving the Union until the abolition of slavery was a stated objective of the war.

The Roosevelt Seventh-day Adventist Church

The accounts of the events of July 21, 1861 vary, leaving readers searching for a consistent thread among them. Confederate Lieutenant Henry Kyd Douglas, who rode with "Stonewall" Jackson in the war, could not explain how the reversal took place.[1]

Lieut. Henry Kyd Douglas, CSA

> My part of the line was driven back at first; then we went in again and fought it through, and found, when the smoke cleared and the roar of artillery died away and the rattle of musketry decreased into scattering shots, that we had won the field and were pursuing the enemy. This is not very historical but it's true.[2]

Confederate Lieutenant Colonel William Willis Blackford filled in more details of the reversal that took place that day after 4 p.m.:

Lieut. Col. William Willis Blackford, CSA

> Now the most extraordinary spectacle I have ever witnessed took place. I had been gazing at the numerous well-formed lines as they moved forward to the attack, some fifteen or twenty thousand strong in full view, and for some reason had turned my head in another direction for a moment, when some one exclaimed, pointing to the battlefield, "Look! Look!" I looked, and *what a change had taken place in an instant*. Where those "well dressed," well-defined lines, with clear spaces between, had been steadily pressing forward, the whole field was a confused swarm of men, like bees, running away as fast as their legs could carry them, with all order and organization abandoned. In a moment more

the whole valley was filled with them as far as the eye could reach. They plunged through Bull Run wherever they came to it regardless of fords or bridges, and there many were drowned.[3]

Journalist Henry J. Raymond was one of several reporters to witness the battle, but only one of two reporters at the battle who had previously seen combat. (British journalist William Howard Russell was the other.) At half past 3:00 p.m., as Union forces were holding their own, Raymond traveled to Centerville to find a courier to send a report to the *New York Times*. At that point in the battle, the results were yet uncertain. While still in Centerville, he had heard about the retreat of Union forces and rode to Washington, running into a "fresh stampede" from "an enormous Pennsylvania army wagon."[4] In a letter he described his surprise that the battle had gone against the North:

Henry J. Raymond

> I had gone but a quarter of a mile when we met a great number of fugitives, and our carriage soon became entangled in a mass of baggage-wagons, the officer in charge of which told me it was useless to go in that direction, as our troops were retreating. Not crediting the story, which was utterly inconsistent with what I had seen but a little while before, I continued to push on. I soon met Quarter-master Stetson, of the Fire Zouaves, who told me, bursting into tears, that his Regiment had been utterly cut to pieces, that the Colonel and Lieutenant-Colonel were both killed, and that our troops had actually been repulsed. I still tried to proceed, but the advancing columns rendered it impossible, and I turned about.[5]

In an address delivered at the Concord, Massachusetts, town hall on July 21, 1886, Edwin S. Barrett, a civilian observer, described his experience at the Battle of Bull Run. Observing the earlier fighting from a treetop perch, he descended from the tree at about two o'clock to go to a nearby house to quench his thirst. The house had become a makeshift hospital, and he assisted the wounded for a time. Then he left the house, going south, and arrived at a wooded area previously held by Confederate General Barnard Elliott Bee. There he spoke with several Confederate soldiers. Barrett returned to the battlefield to see what was taking place:

> It was now between four and five o'clock, and I had noticed for some time a lull in the battle, and felt sure we were the victors. I passed through the woods and came out in front of the valley previously held by our infantry, while within rifle shot were the rebel lines. As I came out of the woods and looked back across the valley and up the hill, to my utter astonishment I saw our whole army retreating in confusion and disorder. No lines, no companies, no regiments could be distinguished. . . . I went slowly up the hill, occasionally halting and looking back. I stopped on the summit while our panic stricken army drifted by, and I can compare it to nothing better than a drove of cattle, so entirely broken and disorganized were our lines. The enemy had ceased firing, except from their extreme left, where the cannonading was kept up with vigor. I did not leave the hill until the enemy's fresh reinforcements of infantry moved slowly forward, their guns glistening in the declining sun, but they showed no disposition to charge and only advanced a short distance. Had they precipitated their columns upon our panic stricken army, the slaughter would have been dreadful, for so thorough was the panic that no power on earth could have stopped the retreat and made our men turn and fight. They were exhausted with fifteen hours of marching and fighting, having had little to eat, their mouths parched with thirst, and no water in their canteens.[6]

Ellen White read the conflicting war reports in Detroit at the dentist on July 26: "Abraham [Dodge] brought in the paper containing the war news, and while Dr. White was filling my husband's teeth I was reading the news."[7] Then, about two weeks after the battle—and two decades before Barrett published his account—she saw in vision why the inexperienced Union forces, who had double-timed it to the battle, suddenly became confused and retreated in panic:

> August 3, 1861. I had a view of the disastrous battle at Manassas, Virginia. It was a most exciting, distressing scene. The Southern army had everything in their favor and were prepared for a dreadful contest. The Northern army was moving on with triumph, not doubting but that they would be victorious. Many were reckless and marched forward boastingly, as though victory were already theirs. As they neared the battlefield, many were almost fainting through weariness and want of refreshment.[8] They did not expect so fierce an encounter. They rushed into battle and fought bravely, desperately. The dead and dying were on every side. Both the North and the South suffered severely. The Southern men felt the battle, and in a little while would have been driven back still further. The Northern men were rushing on, although their destruction was very great. Just then an angel descended and waved his hand backward. Instantly there was confusion in the ranks. It appeared to the Northern men that their troops were retreating, when it was not so in reality, and a precipitate retreat commenced. This seemed wonderful [i.e., "astonishing"] to me.[9]
>
> Then it was explained that God had this nation in His own hand, and would not suffer victories to be gained faster than He ordained, and would permit no more losses to the Northern men than in His wisdom He saw fit, *to punish them for their sins*. And had the Northern army at this time pushed the battle still further in their fainting, exhausted condition, *the far greater struggle and destruction which awaited them would have caused great triumph in the South*. God would not permit this, and sent an angel to interfere. The sudden falling back of the Northern troops is a mystery to all. They know not that God's hand was in the matter.

First Battle of Bull Run, by Kurz and Allison, with Angel, by Joe Maniscalco

> God is punishing this nation for the high crime of slavery. He has the destiny of the nation in His hands. He will punish the South for the sin of slavery, and the North for so long suffering its overreaching and overbearing influence.[10]

According to Ellen White, the confused retreat of the Union forces, following the backwards wave of the angel's hand, stopped much greater destruction.[11] Various explanations have been offered for the retreat. Author, biographer, historian, and editor Orville James Victor attributed the panic to the civilians who had come from Washington to watch the Union troops beat the Confederates, revealing their ignorance of the brutality of war. Victor wrote: "With regard to this flight, much was, at the time, written as to the bad effects of the civilians present. It was stated and believed that their scampering away from danger first alarmed the teamsters, and thus produced the panic." Yet the civilians were reacting to a retreat already in progress, as escaping Union soldiers "ran past" the startled spectators.[12] Writer Jim Murphy attributed the Union's panicked retreat to smoke, emotions, and the non-standard uniforms of the Confederate reinforcements from Virginia whom the Union officers did not fire upon because they mistook them for "friendly infantry." The "blue-clad arrivals (who were really Confederate troops from Virginia) marched up and routed the Union forces without much opposition."[13] General James Longstreet, who participated in the battle, attributed the confusion, in his 1896 recounting of events, to the flag. He wrote: "The mistake of supposing Kirby Smith's and Elzey's approaching troops to be Union reinforcements for Irvin McDowell's right was caused by the resemblance, at a distance, of the original Confederate flag to the colors of Federal regiments. . . ."[14] Until then, Union forces had possessed the advantage. Union General Irvin McDowell described the reinforcements' arrival and the ensuing retreat:

General Edmund Kirby Smith, CSA

> Johnston's army . . . threw themselves in the woods on our right, and toward the rear of our right, and opened a fire of musketry on our men, which caused them to break and retire down the hillside. This soon degenerated into disorder, for which there was no remedy. Every effort was made to rally them, even beyond the reach of the enemy's fire, but in vain. . . . The plain was covered with the retreating troops, and they seemed to infect those with whom they came in contact. The retreat soon became a rout, and this soon degenerated still further into a panic.[15]

General Irvin McDowell, USA

Union Colonel Andrew Porter of Hunter's division added: "Soon the slopes ... were swarming with our retreating and disorganized forces, while riderless horses and artillery teams ran furiously through the flying crowd. All further efforts were futile. The words, gestures, and threats of our officers were thrown away upon men who had lost all presence of mind, and only longed for absence of body."[16]

Pennsylvania Union infantryman John W. Urban described their sense of panic when Confederate forces surrounded them:

> The regiment on the extreme left of the Union lines, which was still fighting desperately to hold in check the advancing host of the enemy, discovering that a part of the line had given way, and that the rebel column was winding itself around their left, thus threatening to cut off their retreat, and not being able to see or hear of a single regiment being sent to their relief, now commenced to fall back, at first contesting fiercely with the enemy; but at last becoming panic-stricken, they broke and fled in dismay from the field. The panic now spread with fearful rapidity from one part of the line to the other, and then ensued that stampede that will always be a blot on the history of the Union army; regiment after regiment now broke and fled in the utmost confusion.[17]

John Wesley Urban, Infantry, USA

Attempting to explain why the Confederates did not pursue the Union forces back to Washington, Urban surmised: "They evidently considered their victory as being won merely by a lucky accident . . ."[18] Former slave Louis Hughes recalled his master exclaiming, "Why, that was a great battle at Bull Run! . . . If our men had only known, at first, what they afterwards found out, they would have wiped all the Yankees out, and succeeded in taking Washington!"[19] Many Southerners attributed the Confederate victory to divine intervention, thereby honoring Southern claims of moral superiority.[20] ". . . [S]ome devout Christians explained the Union defeat as God's punishment for the North's initiating combat on Sunday."[21] Congregationalist clergyman Horace Bushnell believed the reversal of the battle was simply a test of the nation's resolve and devotion.[22] It was Mrs. White alone who described the turnaround as God's intervention to keep the North from further slaughter while punishing them for abdicating the cause of freedom for the slaves. She insisted that God was holding both the South and the North accountable. Calling attention to the central issue behind the war with its spiritual implications, Mrs. White gave examples of Northern complicity in maintaining the institution of slavery:

Horace Bushnell, Congregationalist clergyman

> The fugitive slave law was calculated to crush out of man every noble, generous feeling of sympathy that should arise in his heart for the oppressed and suffering slave. It was in direct opposition to the teaching of Christ. . . . The sin of Northern proslavery men is great. They have strengthened the South in their sin by sanctioning the extension of slavery; they have acted a prominent part in bringing the nation into its present distressed condition.[23]

Mrs. White also described the naiveté of believing that the war could be settled by a quick blow. This did not merely have to do with Northerners. Southerners also entertained the mistaken notion that the war would soon be over. Southerner Edward Pollard declared: "The victory of Manassas proved the greatest misfortune that could have befallen the Confederacy. It was taken by the Southern public as the end of the war, or at least as its decisive event. . . . President Davis, after the battle, assured his intimate friends that the recognition of the Confederate States by the European powers was now certain."[24] Ellen White wrote:

> The North and the South were presented before me. The North have been deceived in regard to the South. They are better prepared for war than has been represented. Most of their men are well skilled in the use of arms, some of them from experience in battle, others from habitual sporting. They have the advantage of the North in this respect, but have not, as a general thing, the valor and the power of endurance that Northern men have.[25]

Three months earlier, *Harper's Weekly* also called attention to Southern preparedness, though it put the bravery of the North and the South on equal footing:

> Lastly, we desire to caution northern people against the fatal error of underrating Southerners. The Southern States combined constitute a powerful nation. Southern men are accustomed to the use of arms. The South is able to raise a great army; the men will all be found brave, and at least as highly skilled in military tactics as our northern men; they have as much money as they need for the present.[26]

The editors of *Harper's Weekly* believed that Lincoln could bring the war "to a speedy close." Mrs. White entertained no such notion.[27] We return to her testimony and its recurring theme:

> The system of slavery has reduced and degraded human beings to the level of the brutes, and the majority of slave masters regard them as such. The consciences of these masters have become seared and hardened, as was Pharaoh's . . . God alone can wrench the slave from the hand of his desperate, relentless oppressor. All the abuse and cruelty exercised toward the slave is justly chargeable to the upholders of the slave system, whether they be Southern or Northern men.[28]

Like Nathan the prophet, who identified David's sin of adultery and its cover up, and Micaiah and the later prophets, who identified the ongoing sins of Judah and Israel, Ellen White's prophetic voice held the nation accountable for upholding slavery.[29] Many people saw the abolitionists as speaking to the nation with a prophetic voice. Senators Henry Wilson and Charles Sumner, William Lloyd Garrison, Joshua R. Giddings, Congregationalist ministers Henry Ward Beecher and George B. Cheever, Gerrit Smith, and Orestes A. Brownson advocated that "no peace should be made that did not remove the cause of the difficulty altogether."[30] In the spring of 1862, Uriah Smith pondered, "What then will be the end of these things? One of the two things must follow: either a continuation of our national difficulties, or a peace upon dishonorable and disgraceful terms."[31] Ellen White simply asserted that the North could not win the war without ending slavery, and she knew that the freeing of the slaves would be an act of God.

Chapter 4

"The North and the South"

In the North there was not, perhaps, one person out of ten who desired to see it [that is, slavery] abolished. —William Schaw Lindsay

Ellen White's third Civil War vision came on January 4, 1862, at Battle Creek, Michigan, just two months after the Trent Affair nearly sparked a British declaration of war on the United States and just over a week after the release of Confederate ambassadors James Mason and John Slidell from Union detention (on Dec. 26, 1861). Mrs. White published the content of all three visions in "Testimony for the Church, No. 7" in mid–February. In describing what she learned in vision, she depicted the degree of Southern preparedness for war:

> January 4, 1862, I was shown some things in regard to our nation. My attention was called to the Southern rebellion. The South had prepared themselves for a fierce conflict, while the North were asleep as to their true feelings. Before President Lincoln's administration commenced, great advantage was taken by the South. The former administration planned and managed for the South to rob the North of their implements of war.[1] They had two objects for so doing: 1. They were contemplating a determined rebellion, and must prepare for it; 2. When they should rebel, the North would be wholly unprepared. They would thus gain time, and by their violent threats and ruthless course they thought they could so intimidate the North that they would be obliged to yield to them and let them have everything their own way.[2]

Southern efforts to amass weaponry for war are observable in contemporary sources. In December 1860, Jefferson Davis, then United States senator from Mississippi, scoured Washington, DC, to locate "every Maynard Rifle (about five hundred) to be found in the city."[3] On January 3, 1861, Louisiana governor T. O. Moore "ordered the seizure of federal forts on the lower Mississippi River, the barracks and arsenals at Baton Rouge and Fort Pike on the Rigolets—all of this weeks before the state's secession convention assembled, before even the election of delegates."[4] The January 11, 1861 *Kalamazoo* [Michigan] *Gazette* reported: "The United States arsenal was taken [January 4] ... by the Mobile troops, without resistance.—The arsenal contains six stands of arms, fifteen hundred barrels of powder, 300,000 rounds of musket cartridges, and other munitions of war."[5]

Mrs. White went on to describe the North's patronizing view of the South:

> The North did not understand the bitter, dreadful hatred of the South toward them, and were unprepared for their deep-laid plots. The North had boasted of their strength and ridiculed the idea of the South leaving the Union. They considered it like the threats of a willful, stubborn child, and thought that the South would soon come to their senses, and, becoming sick of leaving the Union, would with humble apologies return to their allegiance.

John C. Calhoun, South Carolina Senator

At the beginning of the year, many Northerners viewed Southern secession as a ploy for concessions. The Senate had seen the brinkmanship, characteristic of South Carolina Senator John C. Calhoun, many times before.[6] The editor of the Boston *Daily Advertiser* was of the opinion that South Carolina would not secede, but if she did, she would come back. He jadedly added: "The other States only want to make terms and to come back into the Union after having extorted new concessions as the price of reconciliation."[7] On January 29, after more Southern states had seceded, the editor of the Philadelphia *Inquirer* projected the establishment of a Southern Confederacy, but believed they would "certainly come back into the Union, if Virginia, Kentucky, Maryland, North Carolina and Tennessee continue in it."[8] Of course, Virginia, North Carolina, and Tennessee did not remain in the Union, and the cotton states did not return to the Union.

Ellen White next discussed Southern tenacity in extending slavery, which she called "human traffic," into new territories.

> The North have had no just idea of the strength of the accursed system of slavery. It is this, and this alone, which lies at the foundation of the war. The South have been more and more exacting. They consider it perfectly right to engage in human traffic, to deal in slaves and the souls of men. They are annoyed and become perfectly exasperated if they cannot claim all the territory they desire. They would tear down the boundaries and bring their slaves to any spot they please, and curse the soil with slave labor. The language of the South has been imperious, and the North have not taken suitable measures to silence it.[9]

The losses were already considerable at this early point in the war, and Mrs. White believed that many soldiers were disappointed to learn that the war was not to end slavery. She wrote:

> Thousands have lost their lives, and many have returned to their homes, maimed and crippled for life, their health gone, their earthly prospects forever blighted; and yet how little has been gained! Thousands have been induced to enlist with the understanding that this war was to exterminate slavery; but now that they are fixed, they find that they have been deceived, that the object of this war is not to abolish slavery, but to preserve it as it is.[10]

Much anecdotal evidence can be presented to show the expectations of those who volunteered for service in the Union army to end slavery. John Beatty, who volunteered with the 3rd Ohio Infantry in late April 1861, wrote: "I believe the war will run into a war of emancipation, and when it ends African slavery will have ended also. It would not, perhaps, be polite to say so, but if I had the army in my own hands, I would take a short cut to what I am sure will be the end—commence the work of emancipation at once, and leave every foot of soil behind me free."[11] A Massachusetts infantry captain, who graduated from Harvard, wrote his mother in November 1861: "Slavery has brought death into our households already in its wicked rebellion. . . . There is but one way [to win the war] and that is emancipation. . . . I want to sing 'John Brown' in the streets of Charleston, and ram red-hot abolitionism down their unwilling throats at the point of the bayonet."[12] In his book *The Life of Billy Yank*, Bell Wiley estimated that perhaps only one in ten Union soldiers "had any real interest in emancipation per se." Nonetheless, Wiley quoted one soldier as writing, "I have no heart in this war if the slaves cannot go free" and another as asserting that the cause of the Union was "nobler even than the Revolution for they fought for their own freedom, while we fight for that of another race.... If the doom of slavery is not sealed by the war I shall curse the day I entered the Army or lifted a finger in the preservation of the Union."[13] A private in the 5th Iowa infantry wrote in January 1862: "I believe that Slavery (the worst of all curses) was the sole cause of this Rebellion, and until this cause is removed and slavery abolished, the rebellion will continue to exist." A corporal in the 65th Ohio infantry wrote: "We are now fighting to destroy the cause of these dangerous diseases, which is slavery and the slave power." A private in the 1st Minnesota infantry said: "The War will never end until we end slavery."[14] James M. McPherson estimated that three out of ten Union soldiers saw slavery as the reason for the war. Yet he cited many other enlistees who did *not* want to free the slaves.[15]

On the Southern side, Mary Beckley Bristow of Kentucky certainly saw the war as a battle over slavery: "I can call them nothing else [but "Abolition forces"], though some of them indignantly reject the name, but as they are fighting with and for abolitionism I can't see what else they are at...."[16] Ellen White pondered whether it was worth the great sacrifice of life and limb if slavery remained intact:

> Those who have ventured to leave their homes and sacrifice their lives to exterminate slavery are dissatisfied. They see no good results from the war, only the preservation of the Union, and for this thousands of lives must be sacrificed and homes made desolate. Great numbers have wasted away and expired in hospitals; others have been taken prisoners by the rebels, a fate more to be dreaded than death. In view of all this, they inquire: If we succeed in quelling this rebellion, what has been gained? They can only answer discouragingly: Nothing. That which caused the rebellion is not removed. The system of slavery, which has ruined our nation, is left to live and stir up another rebellion. The feelings of thousands of our soldiers are bitter. They suffer the greatest privations; these they would willingly endure, but they find they have been deceived, and they are dispirited. Our leading men are perplexed, their hearts are failing them for fear. They fear to proclaim freedom to the slaves of the rebels, for by so doing they will exasperate that portion of the South who have not joined the rebellion but are strong slavery men.[17] And again they have feared the influence of those strong antislavery men who were in command, holding responsible stations. They have feared the effects of a bold, decided tone, for it fanned to a flame the strong desire of thousands to wipe out the cause of this terrible rebellion, by letting the oppressed go free and breaking every yoke.[18]

Abolitionist Wendell Phillips believed that the preservation of the union was not reason enough to continue fighting. "The present war, conducted without a reasonable object, is a total loss of blood and treasure. Better the South should go to-day than lose another life to prolong the war upon the present detestable policy.... We shall never have peace until slavery is destroyed."[19] Yet he also erroneously predicted: "Jefferson Davis's successes are far greater than he anticipated; and if he can possibly float upon them and a few more, thus holding his own to the 4th of March 1863, England will, as she ought to, recognise the Southern Confederacy.... Let this Union be dissolved, in God's name, and the

Wendell Phillips, abolitionist crusader and orator

corner-stone of a new one be laid, on which shall be engraved for ever, 'Equality in a political sense for every man who is born in the world.' "[20]

National Calls for Fasts to End the War Without Addressing Slavery

Mrs. White also asserted that men in "high command," who were against the abolition of slavery, were using their influence to silence men with anti-slavery views.[21] It was in this context that she addressed the national calls for all Christians to fast and plead with God to end the war. She referred readers to the fast described in Isaiah 58:5–7, which speaks of undoing heavy burdens, letting the oppressed go free, and breaking every yoke. She then juxtaposed the proposed national fast beside the betrayal of slaves who were returned when they had fled to the North for protection.[22] She also described the propaganda that Southern masters had fed their slaves to frighten them from seeking freedom—that Abolitionists would treat them more cruelly than had their Southern masters.[23] (One popular story in Southern papers was that Abolitionists proposed to murder the slaves to exterminate slavery!)[24] The betrayal they received in fleeing to the North and being returned left many slaves believing that Northerners would not welcome them. Ellen White affirmed that God would only recognize fasts and hear prayers when Americans decided to break every yoke.[25] It is for this reason that Seventh-day Adventists waited in joining the nation in prayer and fasting until after the Emancipation Proclamation.

A slave family near Savanna, Georgia. Insuring a steady supply of cotton for their factories helped English businessmen and politicians overlook Southern slavery.

England's Deliberations over Declaring War on the United States

The January 4, 1862 vision also addressed England's key reason for not supporting the North: "I was shown that if the object of this war had been to exterminate slavery, then, if desired, England would have helped the North."[26] This same thought was expressed in debate in the House of Commons by the honorable William Schaw Lindsay, a member of Parliament who supported the Confederacy's bid for recognition, when he declared: "Though there had been an outcry on the part of a small section of the people of the North against slavery in the South, the suppression of slavery had very little, if anything, to do with the civil war. If it had, the North would have received more sympathy from the people of England." The speaker went on to cite an article in a New York paper in which the writer "disowned entirely that slavery had anything to do with this war, and combated the argument that slavery was a sin."[27]

Though Queen Victoria declared neutrality, many of England's leaders sympathized with the South, the main supplier of cotton for England's mills and whose aristocracy reflected British social order.[28] Duncan Andrew Campbell, a lecturer in the Department of American

Studies at the University of Maryland in Baltimore County, argued in *English Public Opinion and the American Civil War* that "most in England were suspicious of both sides in the conflict, and even those who did take sides did not consist largely of any one particular social or political group."[29] Richard I. Lester argued that, if it were not for England's material aid to the South in exchange for the South's continued cotton supply, it is possible that the war "would have ended within a year to eighteen months."[30] Being divided over the issue of slavery, the North sabotaged its hopes of support from England. John D. Bennett wrote: "At the time of secession, leading newspapers had been fairly sympathetic to the North, but when it became clear that Lincoln's principal war aim was preserving the Union rather than freeing the slaves, press opinion shifted."[31] (Factory workers had also favored the North.) Some ten years after the war, a letter to the *New York Times* described this period as a time "when the public feeling in London was almost universally in favor of the South."[32] Though England took no direct action against the North, her commerce raiders inflicted damages of $15.5 million on the United States merchant fleet during the war. Then, when the North violated British neutral rights by halting one of England's ships to remove Confederate diplomats, she nearly declared war, sending eleven thousand regular troops to Canada and putting the British fleet "on a war footing."[33] "War was days away in 1861. . . . They were going to bomb . . . major port cities."[34] Ellen White explained why England did not support the Union: "England fully understands the existing feelings in the Government, and that the war is not to do away [with] slavery, but merely to preserve the Union; and *it is not for her interest to have it preserved.*"[35]

Mr. William Schaw Lindsay cited another Member of Parliament who "believed it was for the interest of [England], both politically and commercially, that that separation should take place. We knew that the South would be prepared to adopt a free trade policy; that they would be prepared to enter into relations with this country, and to exchange directly their cotton and the other products of the South for our manufactures. Therefore, commercially, it was for our interest. Politically it would be well for us that a vast power like the United States should be divided."[36] On May 1, 1862, Lord Earl Russell, the British foreign minister, told Lord Richard Lyons, the British Ambassador to the United States from 1858 to early 1865: "[S]eparation would be best for the North as well as for the South . . . for the future welfare of the free, and the future emancipation of the slave."[37] The Southern Independence Association in England proclaimed in December 1863: "Our commercial classes are also beginning to perceive, that our best interests will be promoted by creating a direct trade with a people so enterprising as the Confederates, inhabiting a land so wide and so abundant in the richest gifts of Providence, and anxious to place themselves in immediate connection with the manufacturers and consumers of Europe. In short, the struggle is now felt to be, according to Earl Russell's pregnant expression, one for independence on the part of the South, and for empire on the part of the North . . ."[38]

England vigorously debated recognition of the Confederacy. After General George B. McClellan's failure to capture Richmond during the Seven Days' Battle, the pro–Southern Edmund Hammond, who was Permanent Under-Secretary at the Foreign Office, "was of the opinion that the Confederacy had almost completely established its claim to recognition, but that the British should not interfere until 'the Northern cause [was] more thoroughly degraded.'" The cabinet was discussing "the matter of funds for a mission to the Confederacy," yet "by the end of October [1863, it] had to admit that the idea of recognizing the South had been abandoned because of 'its inexpediency.'"[39] James Spence, a British businessman who served as the Confederacy's financial agent in Europe from October 1862 to December 1863 but who held anti-slavery views, explained in a letter to the *Times* of London how England could favor the South in spite of the Confederacy's support of the institution of slavery: "It will surely depart as a result of Southern independence and the world's action upon it, as a taper will die out in the sunlight."[40] Nonetheless, as long as the war was not framed as being about slavery, British popular opinion could side with the South.

Mrs. White described England's deliberations in terms of conditional "ifs":

> Said the angel: "Hear, O heavens, the cry of the oppressed, and reward the oppressors double according to their deeds." This nation will yet be humbled into the dust. England *is studying whether* it is best to take advantage of the present weak condition of our nation, and venture to make war upon her. *She is weighing the matter*, and trying to sound other nations. She fears, *if* she should commence war abroad, that she would be weak at home, and that other nations would take advantage of her weakness. Other nations are making quiet yet active preparations for war, and are hoping that England will make war with our nation, for then they would improve the opportunity to be revenged on her for the advantage she has taken of them in the past and the injustice done them.[41] A portion of the queen's subjects are waiting a favorable opportunity to break their yoke; but *if England thinks it will pay*, she will not hesitate a moment to improve her opportunities to exercise her power and humble our nation. When England does declare war, all nations will have an interest of their own to serve, and there will be general war, general confusion. England is acquainted with the diversity of feeling among those who are seeking to quell the rebellion. She well knows the perplexed condition of our Government; she has looked with astonishment at the prosecution of this war—the slow, inefficient moves, the inactivity of our armies, and the ruinous expenses of our nation. The weakness of our Government is fully open before other nations, and they now conclude that it is because it was not a monarchial government, and they admire their own government, and look down, some with pity, others with contempt, upon our nation, which they have regarded as the most powerful upon the globe. Had our nation remained united it would have had strength, but divided it must fall.[42]

Readers of the British newspapers and street pamphlets certainly knew about their country's sympathies with the South.[43] England's willingness to consider war with America at the provocation of the Trent Affair, when Union ship captain Charles Wilkes captured the Confederate ambassadors James Mason and John Slidell, is an indication of one aspect of England's war deliberations.[44]

James Mason and John Slidell, Confederate diplomats

In 1862, Parliament also debated whether England's recognition of the Confederacy would require military intervention.[45] The *Spectator* of London, on March 15, 1862, reported: "An American war . . . is now the possibility which forms the touchstone of every argument . . . we are thinking, as we have been within the last few months, of an American war. . . ."⁴⁶ Peter Alfred Taylor of Leicester, British politician and member of the radical Emancipation Society, which promoted the cause of the Northern States, described it this way: "Intervention was only a longer word for war. Never was so tremendous an issue so easily, so lightly, and with so slight a recognition of its importance, raised, as had been this issue by the hon. [Member]. . . . It would be a fratricidal war, almost as truly as that which was being fought between the South and North—a war which would strike terror into all the friends of progress and liberty, and be rejoiced at by all who were their foes."⁴⁷

Taylor's thought is reflected in the conditionality of Mrs. White's statement. She wrote: England "fears, *if* she should commence war abroad, that she would be weak at home"; "but *if* England thinks it will pay, she will not hesitate a moment to improve her opportunities to exercise her power and humble our nation." The conclusion, "When England does declare war, all nations will have an interest of their own to serve, and there will be general war, general confusion," is conditional. It is built on *if* and not on *because*.⁴⁸ It means: *At such a time that England should declare war, other nations will have an interest*. War would not happen *unless* England so chose.⁴⁹ Ultimately, she did not so choose, deciding that it was not in her best interest to intervene.⁵⁰ The "general war" that Ellen White envisioned was staved off for another half century and the liberation of England's colonies even longer.⁵¹ However, the major point remained: as long as the North ignored slavery, England would side with the South.

The Southern Rebellion

Mrs. White and President Lincoln both framed Southern secession as "rebellion." From the start, Mrs. White saw the rebellion in moral terms. As the losses from the war piled up, Lincoln saw it increasingly in those terms. In his second inaugural address, he declared regarding the war: "If God wills that it continue until every drop of blood drawn with the lash, shall be paid by another drawn with the sword, as was said three thousand years ago, so still it must be said, 'the judgments of the Lord are true and righteous altogether.' "⁵²

Many described the war in terms of punishment, though most meant the punishment *of the South*. Advent Christian historian Isaac C. Wellcome laid all blame on the South, referring to the "wickedness of the rebels."⁵³ Others believed the South was being punished for the Southern people's "misplaced ambition . . . greed, rapacity, drinking, gambling, [and] dissipation."⁵⁴ Some Southern ministers interpreted "Stonewall" Jackson's death in 1863 by Confederate pickets at the Battle of Chancellorsville "as God's punishment for Southern sins, including the idolization of Jackson himself."⁵⁵ As the cost in lives and suffering mounted, some wondered aloud "if God was not punishing Southerners for failing to live up to the ideal of Christianity that slavery could exemplify." Southern Methodist Bishop George Foster Pierce appealed to the Georgia legislature for laws to curb slavery's harsher practices, saying: "If the institution of slavery cannot be maintained except at the expense of the black man's immortal interests, in the name of Heaven I say *let it perish*."⁵⁶ Phillip Shaw Paludan viewed Pierce's appeal as mere "rhetoric" since Pierce was only condemning the worst abuses of slavery and not slavery itself. Northern

Methodist Bishop George Foster Pierce

preachers told the people that, if they "did not meet their holy obligation to destroy slavery once and for all, God would punish the United States by permitting the infidel secessionists to succeed." The boldest of abolitionist preachers "courageously campaigned against racial discrimination as well."[57]

Though some claim otherwise, Mrs. White never promoted the view that the North would lose the war.[58] Six months before the Battle of Gettysburg, in "Testimony for the Church, No. 9," Ellen White predicted ultimate victory for the North.[59] Of the South, she said: "Their foot shall slide in due time." "God is punishing the North, that they have so long suffered the accursed sin of slavery to exist; for in the sight of heaven it is a sin of the darkest dye. God is not with the South, and He will punish them dreadfully in the end."[60] The point of her statement in "Testimony for the Church, No. 7" was that America would be humbled, and America was indeed humbled by the Civil War. Nonetheless, she found assurance that, though both North and South were being chastised for permitting slavery to continue, the Union would prevail. She wrote:

> I saw that God would not give the Northern army wholly into the hands of a rebellious people, to be utterly destroyed by their enemies. I was referred to Deuteronomy 32:26–30: "... How should one chase a thousand, and two put ten thousand to flight, except their Rock had sold them, and the Lord had shut them up?"[61]

As the war raged on, vain hope in an early termination gave way to depressing resignation that the struggle for the Union would go on. Adventist J. H. Waggoner wrote pessimistically: "In my opinion, education and gradual emancipation would be the best for all parties. But who has any hope for such a thing?"[62] In mid–1862, an article in the *Republican Standard* of New Bedford, Massachusetts, remarked:

> A few weeks ago it was proclaimed with a great flourish of trumpets that the armies of the nation were full, and orders were given to stop recruiting and the enlistment of volunteers. Now it is announced that a call is made for a hundred thousand additional men, to be used "as a reserve." A sudden change seems to have come over the administration, and they appear to be convinced that the struggle in which we are engaged is not to be terminated in any thirty or sixty days, as some of the leading men at the capital have been fond of asserting.

The *Republican Standard* went on to appeal: "[I]t is time to put into vigorous exercise that severity which is the truest mercy; it is time to proclaim freedom to the slave, and thus strike treason to the heart."[63] At long last, there was more general agreement that the Union could not triumph in the war as long as the nation allowed slavery to exist.

When, on January 1, 1863, President Lincoln proclaimed the emancipation of slaves in the States that had seceded, he made the war about slavery, and the tide of war began to turn.[64] Now England could no longer ignore the slavery of the South. Speaking about England's attitude toward the North, U.S. agent John Forbes remarked in March 1863: "All the mercantile and upper classes are entirely against the North." Yet he added, "The emancipation movement is coming to our rescue, and the people are with us and ... the vicious London *Times* shakes to hear them."[65]

Nonetheless, steely-headed Southern and British businessmen held onto the hope that the South would yet triumph. As late as January 1865, Alexander Collie wrote to Lord Wharncliffe, a prominent Confederate supporter: "Bad news have [sic] reached us as regards military matters from the South . . . but my faith in its ultimate triumph is as strong as it ever was. . . . The South will wear the North out and gain its independence."[66] Yet the North hung on until victory was theirs, as Ellen White had predicted.[67]

Lincoln's preliminary reading of the Emancipation Proclamation before his cabinet in July 1862. Francis Bicknell Carpenter, artist.

Leadership, strategies, manpower, and weaponry certainly had their place in winning the Civil War. (One thinks particularly of Grant's leadership in the latter part of the war and Sherman's demoralizing march across the South.) Yet even though England may have at first taken it as a political ploy, the Emancipation Proclamation, which freed the slaves in the rebel states, played a defining role in the war's direction. That is how former governor of Kansas John P. St. John depicted it in his speech in Ottawa, Illinois, on June 29, 1891: "I was never so disappointed as I was when the [Confederates] whipped us at Bull Run. But it was all a part of God's plan. Had we whipped the [Confederates], the politicians would have patched up a peace, and the Union would have been continued with slavery, and we would have had it to-day. For two years the [Confederates] had the advantage; but after Lincoln issued the famous emancipation proclamation we had swung round to God's side, and could not lose."[68] Israel E. Dwinell, of the South Side Church of Salem, Massachusetts, had the same conviction when he declared on October 19, 1862: "The cause of the war is clearly slavery, and we tried for a long time . . . to fight the war, and save sin; and God would not suffer it. . . . Now we are openly and directly on the side of God; and now we may hope to have His favor."[69] As illustrated in the following chart, the tides of war did begin to change from early July on, and Seventh-day Adventists were then able to join enthusiastically with other citizens of the Union in fasting and praying to Almighty God for a speedy end to the war.[70]

Emancipation Proclamation (excerpt)

"That on the first day of January, in the year of our Lord one thousand eight hundred and sixty-three, all persons held as slaves within any State or designated part of a State, the people whereof shall then be in rebellion against the United States, shall be then, thenceforward, and forever free; and the Executive Government of the United States, including the military and naval authority thereof, will recognize and maintain the freedom of such persons, and will do no act or acts to repress such persons, or any of them, in any efforts they may make for their actual freedom. . . ." —Abraham Lincoln

Ellen G. White's VISIONS in relation to CIVIL WAR events
① **January 12, 1861, Parkville, Michigan, vision "Great Distress Coming"**
▶ April 12, 1861 – Fort Sumter attacked, South Carolina
May 13, 1861 – *Seventh-day Adventist Publishing Association organized*
▶ July 21, 1861 – First Battle of Manassas (Bull Run), northern Virginia
② **August 3, 1861 – Roosevelt, New York, vision "Slavery and the War"**
▶ August 10, 1861 – Battle of Wilson's Creek, Missouri
▶ October 21, 1861 – Battle of Ball's Bluff, Virginia
November 8, 1861 – *Trent Affair nearly sparked British declaration of war*
③ **January 4, 1862 – Battle Creek, Michigan, vision "The North and the South"**
▶ February 1862 – Capture of Ft. Henry and Ft. Donelson (Tennessee rivers)
▶ March 1862 – *Monitor* vs. *Merrimac* (off Hampton Roads, Virginia), the Confederate *Merrimac* withdrew, believing it had won the battle
▶ April 1862 – Shiloh (Pittsburgh Landing, Tennessee)
▶ April 25, 1862 – New Orleans, Louisiana
▶ March-July 1862 – Peninsular Campaign in Yorktown, Seven Days Battle, Fair Oaks, southern Virginia
▶ August 1962 – Second Battle of Manassas/Bull Run, northern Virginia
▶ September 14, 1862 – Battle of South Mountain stopped Lee's entry in the North, though not so costly in terms of loss of life as the Battle of Antietam
▶ September 17, 1862 – Battle of Antietam, Maryland
September 23, 1862 – *preliminary Emancipation Proclamation*
▶ December 1862 – Battle of Fredericksburg, central Virginia
▶ December 1862 / January 1863 – Battle of Stones River, Tennessee
January 1, 1863 – *Emancipation Proclamation*
④ **January 1862 – Testimony for the Church, No. 9, "The Rebellion"**
April 30, 1863 – *National fast appointed*
▶ May 1863 – Battle of Chancellorsville, northern Virginia – "Stonewall" Jackson killed
May 21, 1863 – *General Conference of Seventh-day Adventists organized*
▶ July 1863 – Battle of Gettysburg, Pennsylvania
▶ July 1863 – Battle of Vicksburg, Mississippi
▶ September 1863 – Battle of Chickamauga, Georgia
▶ November 1863 – Battle of Chattanooga, Tennessee
March 1864 – *Grant given command of all Union troops*
▶ May 1864 – Battle of the Wilderness – great losses on both sides
▶ May 1864 – Battle of Spotsylvania, central Virginia – J. E. B. Stewart killed
▶ June 1864–April 1865 – Battle of Petersburg (south of Richmond, Virginia)
▶ September-December 1864 – Sherman's march from Atlanta to Savannah
February 11, March 1–4, 1866 – *Seventh-day Adventists fasted and prayed for the war's end*
▶ April 9, 1865 – Lee surrenders at Appomattox Court House, Virginia[71]
Key: visions	*additional events*	Union victory	Confederate victory	draw

A Broad View of the War from Start to Finish

Many commentators had denied that secession would lead to war (or at least hoped that it would not). As we noted, one newspaper had projected five to twenty years of armed conflict. Yet before war broke out and without having seen any battle, Mrs. White not only declared that war was certain to come, but she also portrayed the war's hand-to-hand combat and anticipated the loss of life and the misery of the prison camps. Some people certainly assumed that the war would be short. When the war dragged on, they vainly hoped that it would quickly end. Mrs. White predicted that there would be no rapid victory but that the war would continue until the abolition of slavery was an objective of the war.

The uniqueness of Mrs. White's views was not in her opposition to slavery, for many besides her opposed slavery and viewed it as the cause of the war. The uniqueness of her view is that she insisted that God was punishing *both* the North and the South for allowing slavery to continue and that only the termination of slavery could bring an end to the war. She also uniquely asserted that the inexplicable reversal of the First Battle of Manassas was the result of divine intervention, delaying the outcome of the war until the North dealt with the moral rights of the slave. Had there not been great losses from a prolonged war, the North likely would have continued to tolerate slavery in the South to maintain the Union. No other anti-slavery advocate made the same claim as Mrs. White, though national leaders did eventually recognize that the abolition of slavery was the only way to end the war. Until the abolition of slavery was declared an object of the war, Mrs. White insisted, national fasts to implore God to bring an end to fighting were useless. Also unique is Mrs. White's description of England's deliberations over whether to enter the American Civil War. They exceeded what she could know from American newspapers.

Unlike many Abolitionist preachers of the day, Mrs. White's insightful statements about the war were not sent to Abraham Lincoln to lobby for a change in national policy, which would have precipitated a crisis within a nation that was unready to make the abolition of slavery the major object of the war.[72] She wrote "Testimony for the Church, No. 7" to Seventh-day Adventists to keep them united and focused during the precarious years of their church's infancy. "Slavery and the War," published in the *Advent Review and Sabbath Herald*, was written to all subscribers of the periodical, including interested non-Seventh-day Adventist readers. When the North embraced the dual objectives of ending Negro slavery and saving the Union, Seventh-day Adventists were able to anticipate the war's end. We take a moment, as we close this discussion of Ellen White's Civil War visions, to share a celebratory moment with the liberated slaves of Charleston, South Carolina, as published in the *Advent Review and Sabbath Herald*.

The Jubilee at Charleston

Following the capture of Charleston, South Carolina, by Union forces in February 1865, a celebration march took place among the emancipated slaves on March 21. The celebration was reported in the *Charleston Daily Courier* and republished in the *New-York Daily Tribune*.[73] The *Advent Review and Sabbath Herald* republished the article with the introductory statement: "There is no place where it is more gratifying to a loyal man to see or hear of public manifestations of joy over the downfall of the great barbarism that has cursed our nation, than in that slave mart and hot-bed of secession, the city of Charleston, South Carolina. But whether there or elsewhere, the joy of the long down-trodden bondman over his newly acquired freedom is a pleasing feature of the great drama passing before us...."[74] The *Tribune*'s account followed:

Major General John Porter Hatch assumed military command of Charleston from February to August 1865, following the city's surrender

There was the greatest procession of loyalists in Charleston last Tuesday that the city has witnessed for many a long year. The present generation has never seen its like. For these loyalists were true to the Nation without any qualifications of State rights, reserved sovereignties, or other allegiances; they gloried in the flag, they adored the Nation, they believed with the fullest faith in the ideas which our banner symbols [sic] and the country avows as its own. It was a procession of colored men, women and children—a celebration of their deliverance from bondage and ostracism; a jubilee of freedom, a hosannah to their deliverers.

The celebration was projected and conducted by colored men. It met on the Citadel green at noon. Upward of ten thousand persons were present—colored men, women and children—and every window and balustrade overlooking the square was crowded with spectators.

This immense gathering had been convened in 24 hours, for permission to form the procession was given only on Sunday night, and none of the preliminary arrangements were completed till Monday at noon.

Gen. Hatch, Admiral Dahlgren and Col. Woodruff gave their aid to the movement; and thereby the 21st Regiment of U.S.C.T. [United States Colored Troops], a hundred colored marines and a number of national flags gave dignity and added attractions to the procession.

The procession began to move at one o'clock, under the charge of a committee and marshals on horseback, who were decorated with red, white and blue sashes and rosettes.

First came the marshals and their aids, followed by a band of music; then the 21st Regiment in full force; then the clergymen of the different churches, carrying open Bibles; then an open car, drawn by four white horses, and tastefully adorned with National flags. In this car there were 15 colored ladies dressed in white—to represent the 15 recent Slave States. Each of them had a beautiful bouquet to present to Gen. Saxton after the speech which he was expected to deliver. A long procession of women followed the car. Then followed the children of the Public Schools—or part of them; and there were 1,800 in line, at least. They sang during the entire length of the march:

John Brown's body lies a mouldering in the grave, ...
    His soul is marching on!
Glory! Glory! Glory! Hallelujah! ...
    We go marching on!

This verse, however, was not nearly so popular as one which it was intended should be omitted, but rapidly supplanted all the others, until at last all along the mile or more of children, marching two abreast, no other sound could be heard than

We'll hang Jeff. Davis on a sour apple tree! ...

Many of the children already knew the song, and took the advice not to sing that verse contrariwise—as perhaps, they were expected to do by their volunteer teacher....

Very few of these children had ever been at school before; not one of them had ever walked in a public procession; they had only one hour's drill on their playground; and yet they kept in line, closed up, and were under perfect control and orderly up to the last. They only ceased to sing in order that they might cheer Gen. Saxton, Col. Woodford, various groups of Union officers or sailors, or one or two Northern men whom they recognized as their friends. Gen. Saxton and lady were in a carriage at one street where the procession passed, and Col. Woodford and lady at another; and one continuous cheer greeted them, mingled with cheers for an officer whom they supposed to be Gen. Hatch. The colored people know all these officers as their friends. Gen. Saxton is their favorite every where in the Department, and they have all learned that Gen. Hatch and Col. Woodford gave them equal rights in the public schools—an advantage which they prize next to freedom. . . .

Brigadier General Rufus Saxton organized the first regiment of liberated slaves—the First South Carolina Colored Volunteers

The most original feature of the procession was a large cart, drawn by two dilapidated horses with the worst harness that could be got to hold out, which followed the trades. On this cart there was an auctioneer's block, and a black man, with a bell, represented a negro trader, a red flag waving over his head; recalling the days so near and yet so far off, when human beings were made merchandise of in South Carolina. This man had himself been bought and sold several times; and two women and a child who sat on the block had also been knocked down at public auction in Charleston. As the cart moved along, the mock-auctioneer rang his bell and cried out: *"How much am I offered for this good cook?" "She is an 'xlent cook, ge'men." "She can make four kinds of mock-turtle soup—from beef, fish or fowls." "Who bids?" "200's bid." "Two hundred?" "200's bid," "250," "300," "350," "400," "450." "Who bids? "who bids? 500."* And so he went on imitating in sport the infernal traffic of which many of the spectators had been the living victims. Old women burst into tears as they saw this tableau, and forgetting that it was a mimic scene, shouted wildly: *"Give me back my children! Give me back my children!"* The wringing of hands seen on the sidewalks caused more than one looker-on to curse the policy that would even suggest the possibility that the wretches who had bought and sold loyal men might be or ought to be readmitted to the rights of citizenship. But there are people here who would even recommend that these persons alone should be regarded as citizens! There is no officer in all the United States who could stand up before the storm of righteous indignation which a fearless record of the lives of the oath-takers here would arouse. And that chronicle of crime is being made here. If ever they attempt to put down the true loyalists here, this record will be sent to THE TRIBUNE.

Freed slaves watching parade

Behind the auction-car 60 men marched, tied to a rope—in imitation of the gangs who used often to be led through these streets on their way from Virginia to the sugar-fields of Louisiana. All of these men had been sold in the old times.

Then came the hearse—a comic feature, which attracted great attention, and was received with shouts of laughter. There was written on it with chalk,

"Slavery is Dead."
"Who Owns Him?"
"No One."
"Sumter Dug His Grave on the 13th April, 1861." . . .

Various societies were represented. The procession was more than two miles and a-half in length, and officers said that it marched in better military style than the great procession on the 6th of March in New-York. There was no drunkenness, no riotous disposition, no insolent airs, no rudeness. . . .

The great procession took one hour and twenty minutes to pass any point. On its return to the citadel where a stand was prepared for Gen. Saxton and the other speakers, there were at least 10,000 persons assembled. There were 4,200 men in the procession by count, exclusive of the military, the women and the children.

A shower of rain, which began to fall as the procession arrived at the citadel, rendered it expedient to postpone a speech. Rev. Mr. French led in singing a doxology, and the great assembly dispersed in an orderly manner . . . .[75]

With the war at a close, Seventh-day Adventists began to consider what would be required to extend their mission into the South in reaching the white population and helping educate the former slaves.[76] Along with all other educators entering the South, they would face Southern resentment. We will discuss their mission after we have responded to a lingering charge against Mrs. White from this period.

A hand-scrawled message on a hearse declared: "Slavery is Dead."

Chapter 5

Answering a Prejudicial Charge

Then what about all this ado over the charge . . . that the visions teach that the negro is not a human being? . . . It is simply an effort to create prejudice in the minds of the people.
—Uriah Smith

Because some have alleged that Ellen White's early statements on the amalgamation of man and beast denigrate the Negro race, it is important that we carefully evaluate her statements.[1] These are presented below, with key words italicized.

Ellen White's Amalgamation Statements

But if there was one sin above another which called for the destruction of the race by the flood, it was the base crime of *amalgamation* of man and beast which defaced the image of God, and caused *confusion* everywhere. God purposed to destroy by a flood that powerful, long-lived race that had corrupted their ways before him. He would not suffer them to live out the days of their natural life, which would be hundreds of years. It was only a few generations back when Adam had access to that tree which was to prolong life. After his disobedience he was not suffered to eat of the tree of life and perpetuate a life of sin. In order for man to possess an endless life he must continue to eat of the fruit of the tree of life. Deprived of that tree, his life would gradually wear out.[2]

Every species of animal which God had created were preserved in the ark. The *confused species* which GOD did not create, which were the result of *amalgamation*, were destroyed by the flood. Since the flood there has been *amalgamation* of man and beast, as may be seen in the almost endless varieties of species of animals, and in certain races of men.[3]

The same points are repeated in 1870 in *Spirit of Prophecy*, volume 1, *after* the Civil War and *after* the 1866 publication of Snook and Brinkerhoff's accusations (more on this later). The identical phrasing between 1864 and 1870 indicates that she consistently had two effects in view—she wrote: "*in* the almost endless varieties of species of animals and *in* certain races of man."[4] She did not repeat the amalgamation statement in the 1890 *Patriarchs and Prophets*. The first of the two amalgamation statements, while related to the second, does not have any direct bearing on modern races. Only the second statement, which describes conditions after the Flood, has such implications. Yet, understanding the second statement requires understanding "amalgamation" in the first. The *Ellen G. White Encyclopedia* gives four possible interpretations for the "amalgamation" that took place before the Flood:

(1) the practice of bestiality, (2) genetic combination of human and animal genomes to create chimeras, (3) corruption of both humans and animals by sin, thus marring God's original creation, and (4) intermarriage and/or other kinds of union between righteous and unrighteous people, so that the distinction between righteous and wicked is lost.[5]

How shall we determine which of these interpretations is what she intended? There are difficulties whichever interpretation we take. For the view that the "base crime" was bestiality, the difficulty is whether sexual relations between man and beast were ever able to produce an inheritable physiological effect. For the view that the amalgamation was the genetic production of chimeras, the difficulty is whether humans before the Flood had the capability of manipulating genes, and, if they did, whether that was the amalgamation that Ellen White described as taking place after the Flood. For the view that she was speaking of the general corruption of man and beast, the difficulty is whether Ellen White would have called attention to a particular sin as being worse than others if she were only making a general statement. The difficulty for the view that the human side of amalgamation before the Flood was intermarriage (the amalgamation of animals could still be by genetic manipulation) is in how the amalgamation *after* the Flood could be seen "in certain races of men" if the amalgamation of humans *before* the Flood was the union of the righteous line with the unrighteous.

Several approaches have been suggested for discerning what she meant. These include:

1. Reading contemporary prejudice into Ellen White's statements
2. Letting those who knew Ellen White interpret her statements
3. Reading Ellen White's statements in light of the Bible, and
4. Letting Ellen White interpret her own statements.

Defining "Amalgamation"

Before we consider each approach, it would be helpful to understand how the term "amalgamation" was used in the nineteenth century. According to Noah Webster's dictionary of 1828, "amalgamation" meant "the mixing or blending of two different things."[6] Besides the forging of different metals in metallurgy, Victorians generally used "amalgamation" to refer to the co-mingling of different races, classes, or groups of people. Sometimes the distinction of people groups was not racial, but ideological or spiritual. It should be noted that no dictionary definition or source consulted used amalgamation to refer to the mixing of animals and humans. Following are several examples of Victorian uses of "amalgamation," often revealing the era's prejudices.[7] The first of these are given in chronological order:

- "By *amalgamation*, I mean the union of natives with settlers in the same community, as master and servant, as fellow-labourers, as fellow-citizens, and, if possible, as connected by intermarriage." (Herman Merivale, 1842).[8]
- "The sudden *amalgamation* of all denominations would be productive of great evils." (Benjamin Parham Aydelott, 1846).[9]
- "It should be borne in mind, that what we term Caucasian races are not of one origin: they are, on the contrary, an *amalgamation* of an infinite number of primitive stocks, of different instincts, temperaments, and mental and physical characters. Egyptians, Jews, Arabs, Teutons, Celts, Sclavonians, Pelasgians, Romans, Iberians, etc., etc., are all mingled in blood; and it is impossible now to go back and unravel this heterogeneous mixture, and say precisely what each type originally was." (Samuel George Morton, 1854)[10]
- "I believe that the effect of general emancipation will be to discourage *amalgamation*. ... John Kinney, an intelligent colored man, said, 'The majority of the colored people don't like the intermarriage of colored and white people.'" (Robert Dale Owen, 1864)[11]

- "Let any one who doubts the evils of this mixture of races, and is inclined, from a mistaken philanthropy, to break down the barriers between them, come to Brazil. He cannot deny the deterioration consequent upon an *amalgamation* of races, more widespread here than in any other country in the world, and which is rapidly effacing the best qualities of the white man, the negro, and the Indian, leaving the mongrel nondescript type, deficient in physical or mental energy." (Louis Agassiz, 1869)[12]

Louis Agassiz, biologist and geologist

- "But the leading idea, as well as the hardest task, which Alexander had set before him was the *amalgamation* of his diverse subjects into one people." (Arthur Mapletoft Curteis, 1890).[13]
- "While the Southerners frequently charged that *amalgamation* of the two races was the aim of the Northern abolitionists, to an impartial judge it was apparent that where the negro was free, no danger existed of a mixture of blood." (James Ford Rhodes, 1892).[14]

Significant uses of "amalgamation" appear in the *Advent Review and Sabbath Herald*:

While visiting the hermitage or tomb of President Gen. Jackson, I had some conversation with quite an intelligent negro, who freely admitted that his condition was worse since his freedom than before, while at the same time, he said that with many it was bettered. Parting families by selling, and the whipping they received, he said was the worst of slavery; and I thought he might have added also, the *amalgamation* of their race, which looks to me the greatest of all sins found in slavery or elsewhere. When human beings are propagated as the beasts, for wealth or gain, to the destruction of all moral principles that should be held sacred, and when men even traffic in their own blood, I wonder that God has been so longsuffering as he has. (E. B. Lane, 1871)[15]

Elbert B. Lane

Lane's concern was the effect of amalgamation on the Negro race. He laments the disregard for moral standards in breeding slaves like livestock and the effect of illicit sexual unions that produced offspring with mixed African and European features.

Another significant example quotes from a sermon by Charles Hadden Spurgeon:

The former destruction of the world by water was in consequence of sin and was a declaration of God's wrath against it. It did not happen as an accident, or occur without design. Man sinned, was warned and sinned again, until God saw that the wickedness of man was great in the earth. The *amalgamation* of the people of God with the world was *the crowning offense of all*, for, "the sons of God saw the daughters of men, that they were fair, and they took them wives of all which they chose." Thus were Church and State set up and the Church and the world were blended till the Lord's Spirit was grieved and would no longer strive with man. Floods of sin called for floods of destruction. So will it be with the last fire. It will not happen as an inevitable result of physical causes, but because God intends to purge this material world from all traces of sin. (Charles Hadden Spurgeon, 1873)[16]

Charles Haddon Spurgeon

Notice Spurgeon's language parallels that of Ellen White's. *"The crowning offense of all"* is the equivalent of *"if there was one sin above another."* For Spurgeon, the "crowning offense" of the antediluvian world was the union of "the sons of God" with "the daughters of men," a union that he described as the *"amalgamation* of the people of God with the world." Protestant reformer Martin Luther also described the "sons of God" as having become "amalgamated" with the "daughters of men" before the Flood. In commenting on Genesis 6:4, he declared:

> But, I ask you, why does it not also complain about the males? Or why does it not also complain about the daughters of God? It merely states: 'They saw the daughters of men.' The reason obviously is that after the Cainites had been shut out of the true church, the holy family of Seth had the special directive to beware even of marrying into that family, of becoming *amalgamated* with them either in respect to the state through marriage or in respect to the church through worship. The godly must beware of all opportunities for stumbling. When the godly fathers forbade marriages with the Cainites, it was their chief concern to preserve their family uncontaminated. For into the homes of their husbands daughters bring the thoughts and even the ways of their own parents. Thus one reads in the history of the kings that Solomon was led astray by a foreign woman (1 Kings 11:1–8). Similarly, Jezebel introduced the wickedness of the Syrians into the kingdom of Israel (1 Kings 16:31–33).[17]

Martin Luther

If Spurgeon and Luther used "amalgamation" to refer to the rebellious marital unions that precipitated the judgment of the Flood, could it not also be possible that Ellen White was doing the same? We will see how Ellen White emphasized the corruption of the line of Seth through marriage with the line of Cain as the fundamental cause of the conditions that precipitated God's judgment of the Flood, as we evaluate the usefulness of the various approaches in understanding Ellen White's amalgamation statements.

1. Reading Contemporary Prejudices into Ellen White's Statements

Dr. T. Joe Willey asserted in 2007 at the San Diego Chapter of the Association of Adventist Forums in a presentation on the amalgamation statements that Ellen White's insight about amalgamation was a reflection of the prejudices of her contemporaries.[18] (He is not alone in this charge, though all that we have seen thus far in our study reveals that, unlike her contemporaries, she consistently upheld the human dignity of Negroes.) Assuming Ellen White's amalgamation statement to have been an unscientific reflection of the thinking of the nineteenth century, Willey looked for a statement from that era to support his assumption. Finding one, he drew the stunning conclusion that Ellen White considered the black man to be "the beast" in her statement.[19] At the San Diego presentation, he did not sound completely convinced of his find, saying, "And, in my search of these 200+ books, *I came very close* to finding parallel words from a pamphlet entitled, 'The Negro: What is His Ethnological State?' "[20] Here is the contemporary statement he offered in support of his conclusion. Notice the key words in *italics*:

T. Joe Willey, PhD

> He [God] determined to destroy them [antediluvian humans], and with them the world, by a flood, and for the *crime of amalgamation* or miscegenation of the white race with that of the *black—mere beasts of the earth*. We can now form an opinion of the *awful nature of the crime*, in the eyes of God, when we know that he *destroyed the world by a flood*, on account of its perpetration. But it is probable that we should not, in this our day, have been so long in the dark in regard to the sin, the particular sin, that brought the flood upon the earth . . . our translators believing it *impossible* that *brute beasts could corrupt themselves with mankind*, and then, not thinking, or regarding, that the negro was the very *beast* referred to.[21]

Willey noted that Buckner H. Payne, who authored the above statement under a pseudonym, was a pro-slavery Southerner who published his book in Cincinnati to make it appear as though it was written by a Northerner. To bolster his conclusion about the identity of the "beasts" in her statement, Willey marshaled Ellen White's second published statement on slavery, ignoring the fact that Ellen White was most definitely *not* pro-slavery:

> God cannot take the slave to heaven, who has been kept in ignorance and degradation, knowing nothing of God, or the Bible, fearing nothing but his master's lash, and not holding so elevated a position as his master's *brute beasts*. But he does the best thing for him that a compassionate God can do. He lets him be as though he had not been . . . .[22]

The quotation proves the very opposite of what Willey has alleged. If we include the portions of the statement that Willey omitted, we see that Ellen White's point was that the slave-master would be held accountable for keeping the slave in ignorance.[23] The opening sentence reads: "I saw that the slave-master would have to answer for the soul of his slave whom he has kept in ignorance; and all the sins of the slave will be visited upon the master." The second half of the closing sentence, also omitted by Willey, describes the slave-master's punishment: ". . . while the master has to suffer the seven last plagues, and then come up in the second resurrection, and suffer the second, most awful death."[24] In another early statement, Ellen White emphasized the slave's humanity, holding the slave master responsible for the Negro's ignorance:

> This scene was presented before me to illustrate the selfish love of slavery, the desperate measures the South would adopt to cherish the institution, and the dreadful lengths to which they would go before they would yield. The dreadful system of slavery has reduced and degraded *human beings* to the level of the brutes, and the majority of slave-masters regard them as such. Their consciences have become seared and hardened as was Pharaoh's; and if compelled to release their slaves, their principles are unchanged, and they would make the slave feel their oppressive power if possible. It looked to me like an impossibility now for slavery to be done away. God alone can wrench the slave from the hand of his desperate, relentless oppressor. All the abuse and cruelty exercised toward the slave is justly chargeable to the upholders of the slave system, whether they be Southern men or Northern men (Ellen G. White, 1861).[25]

Certainly the treatment of African Americans after the ratification of the Thirteenth Amendment confirmed Ellen White's assertion about the principles of former slave owners remaining unchanged. Yet, before emancipation, Ellen White consistently upheld the humanity of the Negro slaves. In other early statements, she wrote:

> All heaven beholds with indignation, *human beings*, the workmanship of God, reduced to the lowest depths of degradation, and placed on a level with the brute creation by their fellow men. And professed followers of that dear Saviour whose compassion was ever moved as he witnessed *human* woe, heartily engage in this enormous and grievous sin, and deal in slaves and souls of men. Angels have recorded it all. It is written in the book. The tears of the pious bond-men and bond-women, of fathers, mothers and children, brothers and sisters, are all bottled up in heaven.[26] Agony, *human* agony, is carried from place to place, and bought and sold. God will restrain his anger but a little longer. His anger burns against this nation, and especially against the religious bodies who have sanctioned, and have themselves engaged in this terrible merchandise. Such injustice, such oppression, such sufferings, many professed followers of the meek and lowly Jesus can witness with heartless indifference. And many of them can inflict with hateful satisfaction, all this indescribable agony themselves, and yet dare to worship God. It is solemn mockery, and Satan exults over it, and reproaches Jesus and his angels with such inconsistency, saying, with hellish triumph, *Such are* Christ's *followers*!
>
> These professed christians read of the sufferings of the martyrs, and tears course down their cheeks. They wonder that men could ever possess hearts so hardened as to practice such inhuman cruelties towards their *fellow-men*, while at the same time they hold their *fellow-men* in slavery. And this is not all. They sever the ties of nature, and cruelly oppress from day to day their *fellow-men*. (Ellen G. White, 1858)[27]
>
> Christ died for the whole *human* family, whether white or black. God has made man a free moral agent, whether white or black. The institution of slavery does away with this and permits man to exercise over his *fellow man* a power which God has never granted him, and which belongs alone to God. The slave master has dared assume the responsibility of God over his slave, and accordingly he will be accountable for the sins, ignorance, and vice of the slave. He will be called to an account for the power which he exercises over the slave. The colored race are God's property. Their Maker alone is their master, and those who have dared chain down the body and the soul of the slave, to keep him in degradation like the brutes, will have their retribution. The wrath of God has slumbered, but it will awake and be poured out without mixture of mercy. (Ellen G. White, 1863)[28]

Thus we see that Ellen White's use of the word "beast" related to the slave's treatment and not to his nature. Unlike Payne, who saw blacks as creatures made before Adam and Eve, Ellen White always considered blacks to be humans, declaring: "[W]hether a man is white or black, he still bears the image of God . . ."[29] Unlike Payne, Ellen White did not see the results of the "crime" of amalgamation as surviving the Flood.[30] So, even if certain of her words correspond to Payne's statement, there is no evidence of her possessing, reading, or using his book.[31] The approach of superimposing contemporary prejudices on her statements makes no sense.

2. Letting Those Who Knew Ellen White Interpret Her Statements

The survey of Ellen White's amalgamation statements in *The Ellen G. White Encyclopedia* gives special weight to the interpretation of those who knew her.[32] So does Dr. Ronald Osborn, who asked in *Spectrum*:

> How was White understood by her readers at the time? And how did White respond, or not respond, to these interpretations? For Adventist scholars committed to rigorous methods of historical research as well as principles of reasonable inference from all of the available

evidence, the answers to these questions will provide the most likely answer to the question of what White herself believed at the time.[33]

Prominent among her interpreters is Uriah Smith, who ran a series in the *Advent Review and Sabbath Herald* in 1866 in response to the "objections" of former Seventh-day Adventist ministers B. F. Snook and W. H. Brinkerhoff, which they published in a 27-page pamphlet entitled, "The visions of E. G. White, Not of God" (1866). Snook was at one time the president of the Iowa Conference of Seventh-day Adventists, and Brinkerhoff was the conference secretary.

Benjamin F. Snook and William H. Brinkerhoff

They had rejected counsels that Ellen White had given them.[34] Smith's response was printed in a book entitled *The Visions of Mrs. E. G. White: A Manifestation of Spiritual Gifts According to the Scriptures* (1868).[35] One of the objections of Snook and Brinkerhoff relates to the amalgamation statements:

> These visions teach that the Negro race is not human. This charge they deny ... but we will let the reader decide for himself. Here is what she says; "Since the flood there has been amalgamation of man and beast, as may be seen in the almost endless varieties of species, and in certain races of men."—Sp. Gifts. Vol. 3, p. 75. But what are we to understand by certain races of men? She has not informed us in her writings, but left us to fix the stigma of amalgamation where we may see fit. But the interpretation has come to light. She told it to her husband, and he made it known to Eld. [W. S.] Ingraham, and he divulged the secret to the writer, that Sister White had seen that God never made the Darkey. Paul says, "And hath made of one blood all nations of men, for to dwell on all the face of the earth." —Acts 17:26. Which shall we believe, Paul or E. G. White? I beg leave to believe the Apostle. I must believe that the colored man is a creature of God. If he is not, why preach to him and try to save him. Oh shame on such visions! Is not the poor Negro debased low enough with chains and shackles, without depriving him of the honor of being a creature of God, a human being?[36]

In light of Ellen White's many statements emphasizing the humanity of the Negro race, it is remarkable that Snook and Brinkerhoff could accept a third-hand innuendo that contradicts every published statement of Ellen White on the matter, and then, on the basis of that innuendo, condemn "the visions." Notice Uriah Smith's response:

Uriah Smith

> The visions teach, says the objector, that the negro race is not human. We deny it. They do not so teach. Mark the language: "Since the flood there has been amalgamation of man and beast, as may be seen in the almost endless varieties of species of animals, and in certain races of men." This view was given for the purpose of illustrating the deep corruption and crime into which the race fell, even within a few years after the flood, that signal manifestation of God's wrath against human wickedness. There was amalgamation; and the effect is still visible "in certain races of men." Mark, those excepting the animals upon whom the effects of this work are visible,

are called by the vision, "men." Now we have ever supposed that anybody that was called a man, was considered a human being. The vision speaks of all these classes as races of men; yet in the face of this plain declaration, they foolishly assert that the visions teach that some men are not human beings! But does any one deny the general statement contained in the extract given above? They do not. If they did, they could easily be silenced by a reference to such cases as the wild Bushmen of Africa, some tribes of Hottentots, and perhaps the Digger Indians of our own country, &c. Moreover, naturalists affirm that the line of demarcation between the human and animal races is lost in confusion.[37] It is impossible, as they affirm, to tell just where the human ends and the animal begins. Can we suppose that this was ordained of God in the beginning? Rather has not sin marred the boundaries of these two kingdoms? But, says the objector, Paul says that "God hath made of one blood all nations of men for to dwell on all the face of the earth," [Acts 17:26] and then they add, "Which shall we believe, Paul or E. G. White?" You need not disbelieve E. G. White, in order to believe Paul; for there is no contradiction between them. Paul's language will apply to all classes of men who have any of the original Adamic blood in their veins; and that there are any who have not this, is not taught by the visions, nor claimed by any one. But for this text to weigh anything in favor of the objector, he must take the ground that God made every particle of blood that exists in any human being. Is this so? Then God made all the scrofulous, leprous, or syphilitic blood that courses in the worst transgressor's veins! From any view which leads to such a blasphemous conclusion, we prefer to be excused.

But what has the ancient sin of amalgamation to do with any race or people at the present time? Are they in any way responsible, or to be held accountable for it? Not at all. Has any one a right to try to use it to their prejudice? By no means. The fact is mentioned simply to show how soon men relapsed into wickedness, and to what degree. But we are to take all races and peoples as we find them. And those who manifest sufficient powers of mind to show that they are moral and accountable beings, are of course to be esteemed as objects of regard and philanthropic effort. We are bound to labor, so far as in our power, for the improvement of their mental, moral, and physical condition. Whatever race of men we may take, Bushmen, Hottentots, Patagonians, or any class of people, however low they may apparently be in the scale of humanity, or their mental capabilities are in every instance the basis on which we are to work, and by which we determine whether they are subjects of moral government or not. Then what about all this ado over the charge, which is itself false, that the visions teach that the negro is not a human being? What does it amount to? It is simply an effort to create prejudice in the minds of the people, unworthy any one who makes any pretensions to being a Christian, or even a gentleman.[38]

People groups mentioned by Uriah Smith in his rebuttal: the Bushmen, the Hottentots, and the Digger Indians

In this explanation, Smith appears to be eliminating possibilities rather than directly identifying what she meant. In a later response, he acknowledged the difficulty of producing a viable species through the union of dissimilar species.[39] It should be remembered that he was responding to the charge that Ellen White implied that "the Negro race is not human" in her statement about "certain races of men." To do so would be a direct contradiction of terms since "races of *men*" cannot be anything but human. Smith argued from what he understood to be the common beliefs of naturalists. Frank Lewis Marsh commented on Smith's limitations in responding. He mistakenly assumed that all scientists of that era accepted Darwinism.[40]

Frank Lewis Marsh

> Where Uriah Smith got his biological information is a question, but evidently the naturalists he referred to were pseudo-naturalists. His other informants must have been travelers who had listened to fanciful stories told by superstitious natives. There is something about a man-beast cross which is intriguing and which captures the imagination of many. It makes good material for novels. Stories of this sort may be had in abundance but they do not circulate among biological scientists, except as an illustration of the gullibility of humans. The evolutionary biologist believes that man descended from ape-like ancestors. But notwithstanding the advantage it would be to this theory of common descent, he is honest enough to admit that man cannot and apparently never could, as a man, cross with any sort of animal to produce offspring. Smith was misinformed concerning the explanation of similarity of body structure between man and higher apes. He flatly implies that this similarity of body structure between man and higher apes was due to a crossing of man and beast. Such was never the teaching of accepted biologists. Evolutionary biologists teach, rather, that similarity of man and some higher animals is due to a common origin, *not* to *crossbreeding*![41]

Whatever questions Smith's defense may raise, he makes it quite clear that Ellen White never called those of the Negro race anything but human. In light of Mrs. White's statements about the humanity of the suffering slaves at the outset of the Civil War, anyone's accusation that Ellen White taught that "the negro race is not human" is a pure contrivance.

W. C. White

W. G. Kneeland

Some have argued that "Smith's line of reasoning" was Ellen White's reasoning and that it was "endorsed by James White," and "accepted and expanded over the course of time by Ellen White's secretary Dores E. Robinson, her son William C. White, and scientist Harold Clark, among others."[42] However, in publishing the 1866 rebuttal series, Smith issued the specific disclaimer, "[I]n preparing these answers we have had no consultation whatever with Sister White, nor received any suggestion or explanation from her on any point. We take the visions as they are published, and base our explanation of any apparent discrepancy, on the language as it stands."[43] Later, W. C. White responded to Warren G. Kneeland, superintendent of the Bahamas Mission, that his mother did *not* endorse the explanation in Uriah Smith's booklet.[44] Marsh explained her silence: "Some hold tenaciously to Smith's view because the servant of the Lord did not brand it as incorrect. The Lord gave her no message for or against his opinion. Therefore, as was her custom in such a situation, she remained silent. Her silence on the point no more proves that he was correct in his opinion than her similar silence concerning historical inaccuracies in one of his later books proved that *they* were correct."[45] Thus, what her supporters thought is not the final word on what Ellen White meant.

3. Reading Ellen White's Statements in Light of the Bible

"*Sola scriptura* is the Christian doctrine that the Bible is the supreme authority in all matters of doctrine and practice."[46] Mrs. White was an adherent to the doctrine of *sola scriptura*. In her first published book she declared: "I recommend to you, dear reader, the Word of God as the rule of your faith and practice. By that Word we are to be judged. God has, in that Word, promised to give visions in the 'last days'; not for a new rule of faith, but for the comfort of His people, and to correct those who err from Bible truth." On this basis, it is appropriate to infer that Ellen White's statements link to biblical concepts and vocabulary. Several terms in Ellen White's first amalgamation statements have linguistic roots in Scripture. Notice the italicized expressions and how they relate to scriptural concepts:

> They loved to destroy the lives of animals. They used them for food, and this increased their ferocity and *violence*, and caused them to look upon the blood of human beings with astonishing indifference. But if there was one sin above another which called for the destruction of the race by the flood, it was the *base crime* of *amalgamation* of man and beast which *defaced the image of God*, and caused *confusion* everywhere. God purposed to *destroy* by a flood that powerful, long-lived race that had *corrupted* their *ways* before him.[47]

The first linked term is "*violence*." Before the paragraph about amalgamation, Mrs. White had called attention to the destructive nature of the antediluvians and how killing animals led them to shed human blood "with astonishing indifference." Genesis 6:11, 13 describes the extreme degree of *violence* in the antediluvian world.

The second linked term is "confusion." Leviticus 18:23 describes *bestiality* as causing *confusion*: "Neither shalt thou lie with any beast to defile thyself therewith: neither shall any woman stand before a beast to lie down thereto: it is *confusion*." In Exodus 22:19, God is said to assign a penalty for this "confusion": "Whosoever lieth with a beast shall surely be put to death." Another instance of *confusion* is in Leviticus 20:12: "And if a man lie with his daughter in law, both of them shall surely be put to death: they have wrought *confusion*; their blood shall be upon them." The Hebrew word translated "confusion" means "perversion." When a human has sexual relations with animals or with a relative, it is a perversion and is deserving of death, regardless of whether it produces offspring. If applied to Ellen White's use of "confusion," it would indicate that her concern was the practice of bestiality before the flood, whether or not it produced offspring.

The third linked term is "*corruption*." A later statement of Mrs. White's impugns "corruption," in the sense of perversion, as causing the Flood. It says:

> Filled with the keenest remorse for his own sin, and doubly bereaved in the death of Abel and the rejection of Cain, Adam was bowed down with anguish. He witnessed the wide-spreading *corruption* that was finally to cause the destruction of the world by a flood; and though the sentence of death pronounced upon him by His Maker had at first appeared terrible, yet after beholding for nearly a thousand years the results of sin, he felt that it was merciful in God to bring to an end a life of suffering and sorrow. (Ellen G. White, 1890)[48]

Genesis 6 indicates how the antediluvians had "*corrupted* their *ways*":

> The earth also was *corrupt* before God, and the earth was filled with *violence*. And God looked upon the earth, and, behold, it was *corrupt*; for all flesh had *corrupted* his *way* upon the earth. And God said unto Noah, The end of all flesh is come before me; for the earth is filled with *violence* through them; and, behold, I will destroy them with the earth. (Gen. 6:11–13, emphasis added)

Notice that the judgment of the Flood was not merely against the actions of human beings. Genesis says that *the earth* was filled with *violence*; *all flesh* upon the earth had been *corrupted*. The great sins of the antediluvian world were *corruption* and *violence*.

Parenthetically, the pseudepigraphal Book of Jubilees points to the same causes for the Flood as does Genesis—the *corruption* of man and beast and the *violence* in the earth. The commentary of Jubilees illustrate how Genesis has been understood for centuries: "And lawlessness increased on the earth and all flesh *corrupted* its way, alike men and cattle and beasts and birds and everything that walks on the earth—all of them *corrupted* their ways and their orders, and they began to devour each other, and *lawlessness* increased on the earth and every imagination of the thoughts of all men [was] thus evil continually."[49] Jubilees also declares: "And everyone sold himself to work iniquity and to shed much blood, and the earth was filled with iniquity. And after this they sinned against the beasts and birds, and all that moves and walks on the earth: and much blood was shed on the earth, and every imagination and desire of men imagined vanity and evil continually. And the Lord destroyed everything from off the face of the earth; because of the wickedness of their deeds, and because of the blood which they had shed in the midst of the earth He destroyed everything."[50]

In describing the *corruption* of the antediluvians, Ellen White used the phrase, "defaced *the image of God*," which links to Genesis 1:27. Human beings were made in God's image. As His children, they were to reflect His character. Sin mars that image. That the statement about *confusion* is immediately followed by "God purposed to destroy by a flood that powerful, long-lived *race*" implies that the perversion did not create new races.

Ellen White began the chapter in *Spiritual Gifts*, volume 3, describing how God's plan was *corrupted* and how it affected the "*sons of God*." They were *corrupted* through *intermarriage* with those who did not worship the true God. Mrs. White wrote:

> Those who honored and feared to offend God, at first felt the curse but lightly; while those who turned from God and trampled upon his authority, felt the effects of the curse more heavily, especially in stature and nobleness of form. The descendants of Seth were called the *sons of God*—the descendants of Cain, the sons of men. As the *sons of God* mingled with the sons of men, they became *corrupt*, and *by intermarriage* with them, lost, through the

influence of their wives, their peculiar, holy character, and united with the sons of Cain in their idolatry. Many cast aside the fear of God, and trampled upon his commandments. But there were a few who did righteousness, who feared and honored their Creator. Noah and his family were among the righteous few."[51]

Her statement corresponds to the description in Genesis 6:

Now it came to pass, when men began to multiply on the face of the earth, and daughters were born to them, that the *sons of God* saw the *daughters of men*, that they were beautiful; and they took wives for themselves of all whom they chose" (Gen. 6:1, 2)

Though Genesis does not use the term "amalgamation" to describe these unions, the contrast between "sons of God" and "daughters of men" is so striking that some have erroneously interpreted this statement as representing the union of angels and human beings! However, the "sons of God" who "took wives for themselves" cannot have been angels, for Jesus plainly declared: "[I]n the resurrection they neither marry, nor are given in marriage, but are as the angels of God in heaven" (Matt. 22:30; see also Mark 12:25). The term "sons of God" is more in keeping with the human beings who are spiritually described as "sons of God" in John, chapter 1: "But as many as received him, to them gave he power to become the *sons of God*, even to them that believe on his name" (John 1:12).

Genesis itself points to a demarcation of the faithful line: "And as for Seth, to him also a son was born; and he named him Enosh. *Then* men began to call on the name of the LORD" (Gen. 4:26, emphasis added). The birth of Seth's son is a point of demarcation. Therefore, the "sons of God" in Genesis 6:2 are men from the line of Seth who called on the name of the LORD. Since the "daughters" spoken of are not daughters of God but "daughters of *men*," it is logical to assume that they were part of the group that did *not* call on the name of the LORD, which would have been the unfaithful line of Cain.

There is no violation of principle in people of different ethnic backgrounds marrying, for, contrary to the view of Ellen White's contemporaries, there is no such thing as a person of "mixed blood." The Bible declares that God "hath made of *one blood* all nations of men for to dwell on all the face of the earth" (Acts 17:26, emphasis added).[52] Ellen White concurred. She wrote:

The Lord looks upon the creatures He has made with compassion, no matter to what race they may belong. God "hath made of one blood all nations of men for to dwell on all the face of the earth. . . ." Speaking to His disciples the Saviour said, "All ye are brethren." God is our common Father, and each one of us is our brother's keeper.[53]

Nonetheless, there is indeed a violation of principle for followers of God to yoke themselves with unbelievers (2 Cor. 6:14). One might think that such a union would not be so harmful because the possibility exists that the unbelieving spouse may become a believer. Though this does sometimes happen, such a marriage is a great risk. Very often the believer ends up sacrificing his or her principles to please the spouse. Such was the sinful compromise in the time of Solomon that Nehemiah decried. Nehemiah wrote:

In those days I also saw Jews who had married women of Ashdod, Ammon, and Moab. And half of their children spoke the language of Ashdod, and could not speak the language of Judah, but spoke according to the language of one or the other people. So I contended with them and cursed them, struck some of them and pulled out their hair, and made them swear by God, saying, "You shall not give your daughters as wives to their sons, nor take their daughters for your sons or yourselves. Did not Solomon king of Israel sin by these things? Yet among many nations there was no king like him, who was beloved of his God; and God made him king over all Israel. Nevertheless pagan women *caused* even *him to sin*. Should we then hear of your doing all this great evil, transgressing against our God by marrying pagan women?" (Neh. 13:23–27, NKJV, emphasis supplied)[54]

"Do not be deceived," Paul said, quoting Menander's comedy *Thais*, " 'Evil company corrupts good habits' " (1 Cor. 15:33). Such was the case in Noah's day when the faithful merged with the unfaithful by intermarriage. Genesis points to an amalgamation—"intermarriage" (*Spiritual Gifts*, vol. 3, p. 60)—of people groups that should have remained distinct, not because of their color but because of their spiritual commitment to God.[55]

Jesus pointed to the apparent ease with which the antediluvians entered marriage as a characteristic of those destroyed by the Flood: "For as in the days that were before the flood they were eating and drinking, marrying and giving in marriage, until the day that Noe entered into the ark, and knew not until the flood came, and took them all away; so shall also the coming of the Son of man be" (Matt. 24:38, 39). The flippancy implied in their "eating and drinking" would seem to be mirrored by a lack of seriousness in entering marriage as well.

Many overlook one remaining interpretive approach, assuming that Ellen White made no further comment about what she had meant by "amalgamation" between the publication of *The Spirit of Prophecy*, vol. 1 (1870), and *Patriarchs and Prophets* (1890). The fourth interpretive approach demonstrates that Ellen White did leave comments that help readers understand what "base crime" brought on the Flood.

4. Letting Ellen White Interpret Her Own Statements

> If there was one sin above another which called for the destruction of the race by the flood, it was the *base crime* of amalgamation of *man and beast* which *defaced the image of God*, and caused *confusion* everywhere. (*Spiritual Gifts*, vol. 3, p. 64)

In reviewing Ellen White's amalgamation statement, we notice that what she described as "the base crime" is in a chapter entitled, "Crime Before the Flood," indicating that she was looking at "crime" as a single moral matter, and she used "base" to qualify the degree of its *depravity*. Later in the book she used "base crime" to describe a false accusation against Joseph:

> After speaking of the great confidence of his master in him, by intrusting all that he had to him, he exclaims, "How then can I do this great wickedness, and sin against God." He would not be persuaded to deviate from the path of righteousness, and trample upon God's law, by any inducements, or threats. And when he was accused, and a *base crime* was falsely laid to his charge, he did not sink in despair.[56]

In this statement "base crime" is equivalent to what Joseph called "this great wickedness." Mrs. White also used the adjective "*base*" in several other early statements:

> The news of man's fall spread through Heaven. Every harp was hushed. The angels cast their crowns from their heads in sorrow. All Heaven was in agitation. The angels were grieved at the *base* ingratitude of man, in return for the rich bounties God had provided. A council was held to decide what must be done with the guilty pair. The angels feared that they would put forth the hand, and eat of the tree of life, and be immortal sinners. (*Spiritual Gifts*, vol. 1, p. 21, emphasis added; with minor variations in *Spiritual Gifts*, vol. 3, p. 44; *The Spirit of Prophecy*, vol. 1, p. 42)
>
> Infidelity has seized upon the sad history of apostasy, which occupies so large space in the Old Testament, and has deceived many with the *base* insinuation that the men of the Bible, without distinction, were bad men, and has even blasphemously asserted that the Sacred Scriptures sanction crime. (*Spiritual Gifts*, vol. 3, p. v, emphasis added)
>
> Intemperance in eating and in drinking, and the indulgence of *base* passions have benumbed the fine sensibilities, so that sacred things have been placed upon a level with common things. (*Spiritual Gifts*, vol. 4a, p. 124, emphasis added)

In each instance, "base" means "great wickedness." None has specifically to do with sexual relations between humans and animals.

Whichever way one is inclined to interpret Ellen White's statement, one must recognize that, for Ellen White's statement to be wholly unambiguous, she would have needed to have written either "amalgamation of man *with* beast" or "amalgamation of man and *of* beast." That the phrase "of man and beast" can mean "of man and *of* beast" is confirmed by Ellen White's use of the phrase "of man and beast" in two other early statements: "When the destroying angel was to pass through Egypt, to destroy the first-born *of man and beast*, Israel was commanded to gather their children and families into their houses with them, and then mark their door-posts with blood, that the destroying angel might pass by their dwellings, and if they failed to go through with this process, there was no difference made between them and the Egyptians."[57] Here the phrase means "the firstborn of man and the firstborn *of* beast"—not the hybridized firstborn of man and beast. The other statement using the phrase "*of man and beast*," which is found in the same volume where the "amalgamation *of man and beast*" first occurs, also relates to the Flood.[58] The statement says:

> The violence of the storm increased, and there were mingled with the warring of the elements, the wailings of the people who had despised the authority of God. Trees, buildings, rocks, and earth, were hurled in every direction. The terror *of man and beast* was beyond description.[59]

Here the phrase "of man and beast" means that the breakup of the natural world caused all who could experience it to fear for their existence. It is the terror *of* man and *of* beast.

We should note that Ellen White used the term "confused species" to refer to the results of amalgamation before the Flood. She does not use it in connection with the amalgamation after the Flood, and the context indicates that "*confused* species" means confused species *of animals* and that those species were destroyed by the Flood:

> *Every species of animal* which God had created were preserved in the ark. The *confused species* which God did not create, which were the result of *amalgamation*, were destroyed by the flood. Since the flood there has been amalgamation of man and beast, as may be seen in the almost endless varieties of species of animals, and in certain races of men.
>
> After Noah had come forth from the ark, he looked around upon the powerful and ferocious beasts which he brought out of the ark, and then upon his family numbering eight, and was greatly afraid that they would be destroyed by the beasts. But the Lord sent his angel to say to Noah, "The fear of you, and the dread of you, shall be upon every beast of the earth, and upon every fowl of the air, upon all that moveth upon the earth, and upon all the fishes of the sea; into your hands are they delivered. Every moving thing that liveth shall be [meat] for you; even as the green herb have I given you all things." [Gen. 9:2, 3][60]

In 1880, Ellen White linked the defacing of *the image of God* with *sin* itself.

> Everything has been done that God could do to save man from *the power of sin*, which *defaces the divine image*, frustrates God's purpose in man's existence, degrades his God-given powers, narrows his capacity, leads to unholy imaginations, and gives loose rein to unsanctified passions. Sin! How hateful in the sight of God! Holy angels look upon it with abhorrence.[61]

In light of the breadth of Ellen White's statement about the power of sin, how could the single sin of bestiality have been responsible for defacing the divine image and bringing on the flood? No single sin is responsible for defacing the image of God. Yet, an *underlying* sin can be. When Mrs. White wrote, "if there was one sin above another," this could mean that she was either declaring a particular sin to be the most depraved of all sins or that she was doubling back to reiterate the two-pronged *fundamental cause* of the "corruption" and "violence" before the flood—the mingling of animals to create violent species and the mingling of the "daughters of men" with the "sons of God," which defaced God's image in human beings. In 1890, Ellen White specifically linked the *defacing of the image of God* to the weakening of the marriage institution. She wrote: "It was Satan's studied effort to pervert the marriage institution, to weaken its obligations and lessen its sacredness; for in *no surer way could he deface the image of God* in man and open the door to misery and vice."[62] Even before publishing this statement, Ellen White made several comments between 1868 and 1888 that point to the unions of Genesis 6:2, 4 as the key to understanding the "base crime" that initiated the Flood. Notice the italicized words:

> The marriage relation is holy, but in this degenerate age it covers vileness of every description. It is abused, and has become a *crime* which now constitutes one of the signs of the last days, even as marriages, managed as they were previous to the flood, were then a *crime*. (Ellen White, 1868)[63]

> The descendants of Seth had separated themselves from the wicked descendants of Cain. They cherished the knowledge of God's will, while the ungodly race of Cain had no respect for God and his sacred commandments. But when men multiplied upon the earth, the children of Seth saw that the *daughters* of the descendants of Cain were very beautiful, and they departed from God and displeased him by taking wives as they chose of the idolatrous race of Cain. (Ellen White, 1879)[64]

> Unhallowed marriages of the *sons of God* with the *daughters of men*, resulted in apostasy which ended in the destruction of the world by a flood. (Ellen White, 1881)[65]

> The Scriptures briefly state the reason for the prevailing iniquity in Noah's day. The *sons of God* married the *daughters of men*. Those who still cherished the knowledge of God united themselves with the ungodly and *corrupt*, and as a result became assimilated to them in character. The message of warning would have been received by a larger number, had it not been for their connection and association with those who despised and derided the word of God. (Ellen White, 1882)[66]

> The *great crime* in the marriages of the days of Noah, was that the *sons of God* formed alliances with the *daughters of men*. Those who professed to acknowledge and revere God, associated with those who were *corrupt* of heart; and without discrimination, they married whom they would. (Ellen White, 1888)[67]

Notice that Ellen White considered these marriages to be "*the* great crime" of Noah's day (echoing "if there was one sin above another"). These statements provide a bridge to her final statement in *Patriarchs and Prophets*, which deals with the intermarriage of two spiritual groups:

> For some time the two classes remained separate. The race of Cain, spreading from the place of their first settlement, dispersed over the plains and valleys where the children of Seth had dwelt; and the latter, in order to escape from their contaminating influence, withdrew to the mountains, and there made their home. So long as this separation continued, they maintained the worship of God in its purity. But in the lapse of time they ventured, little by little, to mingle with the inhabitants of the valleys. *This association was productive of the worst results.* "The *sons of God* saw the *daughters of men* that they were fair." The children of Seth, attracted by the beauty of the daughters of Cain's descendants, displeased the Lord by intermarrying with them. Many of the worshipers of God were beguiled into sin by the allurements that were now constantly before them, and they lost their peculiar, holy character. Mingling with the depraved, they became like them in spirit and in deeds; the restrictions of the seventh commandment were disregarded, "and they took them wives of all which they chose." The children of Seth went "in the way of Cain"; they fixed their minds upon worldly prosperity and enjoyment, and neglected the commandments of the Lord.[68]

Under Solomon, intermarriage with unbelievers caused *confusion* and effaced the divine *image*, as we see in a statement of Ellen White's published in 1906:

> It came to be a common practise to intermarry with the heathen. The Israelites rapidly lost their abhorrence of idolatry. Heathen customs were introduced. Idolatrous mothers brought their children up to observe heathen rites. The Hebrew faith was fast becoming a mixture of *confused* ideas. Commerce with other nations brought the Israelites into intimate contact with those who had no love for God, and their own love for Him was greatly lessened. Their keen sense of the high and holy character of God was deadened. Refusing to follow in the path of obedience, they transferred their allegiance to Satan. The enemy rejoiced in his success in effacing *the divine image* from the minds of the people that God had chosen as His representatives. *Through intermarriage with idolaters* and constant association with them, Satan brought about that for which he had long been working,—a national apostasy.[69]

Osborn argued, "wicked human beings are clearly assumed by White to be the cause and not the result of 'the base crime of amalgamation,' " having "already mentioned intermarriage between the righteous and wicked in *Spiritual Gifts* as a separate and lesser sin."[70] It is curious that Osborn would conclude that Ellen White considered the union of the faithful with the unfaithful a "lesser sin" when she identified it as the fundamental cause of the depravity leading up to the Flood. In 1888, Ellen White insisted in unambiguous terms: "Unhallowed marriages of the *sons of God* with the *daughters of men*, resulted in apostasy which ended in the destruction of the world by a flood."[71] There is no doubt that she considered the unholy union of the line of Seth with the line of Cain to be the primary reason for the Flood.

After *The Spirit of Prophecy*, vol. 1 (1870), why would Mrs. White omit the term "amalgamation" in all of her explanations of the cause of the Flood? There is a good reason. Ellen White's son W. C. White wrote: "The answer is easily found. It was the fear that wicked men, with hatred in their hearts, for certain races of men, better than themselves, would misapply and misuse it to the injury of those they hate."[72] To have used the word "amalgamation" for a book intended for the general public would carry unintended implications. As we have seen, "amalgamation" became the term of choice for intermarriage between whites and blacks. Some would have erroneously read into Mrs. White's statement the intermarriage of blacks and whites.[73]

Mrs. White made another early statement about animals that "were destroyed by the flood." She described "a class of very large animals which perished at the flood" because "God knew that the strength of man would decrease, and these mammoth animals could not be controlled by feeble man."[74] It is natural to think of dinosaurs as "mammoth animals," for many were very large. Amateur paleontologist Robert Correia asserted that the dinosaurs were also anatomically "confused" in some way and that it was their aberrant anatomy that merited their exclusion from Noah's floating zoological refuge.[75] Molecular biologist and geologist Arthur Chadwick contends that size and not aberrant anatomy was reason enough for their exclusion.[76] Since the animals arrived after Noah and his family had already entered the ark, we would assume that God was responsible for selecting which animals survived the Flood (Gen. 7:1, 2).

Amateur paleontologist Robert Correia

Presuming that Ellen White meant the interbreeding of humans with animals, Dirk Anderson, a critic of Ellen White, has asserted that Ellen White got her amalgamation statements from the pseudepigraphical book of Jasher.[77] However, if that was indeed her source, then it only corroborates the view that there are two amalgamations: one of the sons of God with the daughters of men and the other of the mixing of animals. Notice how Jasher distinguishes the two amalgamations. Notice also that, in speaking of "*their* judges and rulers," it is speaking of judges and rulers of the "sons of men."

> And all the sons of men departed from the ways of YAHWEH in those days as they multiplied upon the face of the earth with sons and daughters, and they taught one another their evil practices and they continued sinning against YAHWEH.
>
> And every man made unto himself a god, and they robbed and plundered every man his neighbor as well as his relative, and they *corrupted* the earth, and the earth was filled with violence.

And their judges and rulers went to the *daughters of men* and took their wives by force from their husbands according to their choice, and the sons of men in those days took from the cattle of the earth, the beasts of the field and the fowls of the air, and taught *the mixture of animals of one species with the other*, in order therewith to provoke YAHWEH; and YAHWEH saw the whole earth and it was *corrupt*, for all flesh had *corrupted* its ways upon earth, all men and all animals.

And YAHWEH said, I will blot out man that I created from the face of the earth, yea from man to the birds of the air, together with cattle and beasts that are in the field for I repent that I made them. (Jasher 4:16–19)

Most critics of Mrs. White focus on her mention of the amalgamation that can be seen "in certain races of men."[78] Yet she pointed first to amalgamation that can be seen "in the almost endless varieties of species of animals." To assume that the amalgamation after the Flood was the genetic blending of man *with* beast creates a problem: it would mean that "the almost endless varieties of species of animals" were the result of the crossbreeding of humans and animals. Such a conclusion stretches credulity. It makes more sense to take the statement as meaning that different animals combined to produce "the almost endless varieties of species of animals" and that certain "races" of humans have overlapping features from the blending of the "three great races."[79] It should be noted that Mrs. White did not describe the "amalgamation" after the Flood as being sinful or as resulting in "confused species."

How could the amalgamation of different kinds of animals take place biologically? Species with related genetics can certainly "amalgamate" through sexual union. Though it is commonly assumed that hybrid offspring are infertile, the truth is that this is generally not the case. What has puzzled scientists, as they have decoded the genetics of various animals, is that there are common strands of genetic code that would not be expected in unrelated species. Evolutionary biologists have long assumed that the relationships of all living things can be represented genetically in a simple tree-like structure based on similarity of DNA—with more closely related species having more similar DNA.[80] Unexpected entanglement of the genetics of bacteria, archaea, and eukarya led the periodical *New Scientist* to publish an article in 2009 entitled, "Why Darwin was wrong about the tree of life."[81] Scientists have attempted to explain this mixing of genetics by invoking the concept of horizontal gene transfer (HGT).[82] However, this explanation is puzzling, for, though it is reasonable to invoke HGT for microorganisms, which may be able to transfer segments of DNA between species directly through their cell walls, the entanglement of DNA for larger organisms, such as monkeys, dogs, and pigs, is not so easily explained.[83] Scientists have hypothesized from endogenous retro-virus (ERV) sequences in the chromosomes that the transfer of genetics in larger organisms took place through viral infections and that mosquitoes may have been the vector, or vehicle, of transfer. Such a suggestion would have required the virus to have strategically infected the animal's sex cells with the foreign DNA. Since the

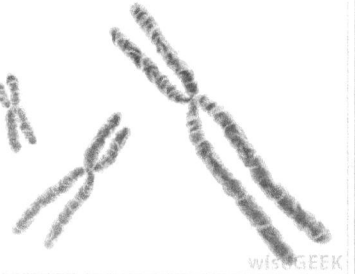

Chromosomes within the nucleus of a cell

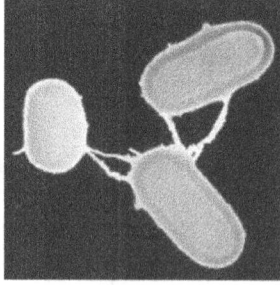

Bacterial horizontal gene transfer

matching strands of DNA are longer than those normally carried by viruses, this mechanism is suspect.[84] Suffice it to say that the entanglement of DNA is consistent with the view that the original design of the programming code was modular and that animals were indeed amalgamated after the Flood. (Molecular palaeobiologist Kevin Peterson has recently compared microRNA to build an evolutionary tree of "relatedness," and he ended up with something that almost completely contradicts the traditional tree.)[85]

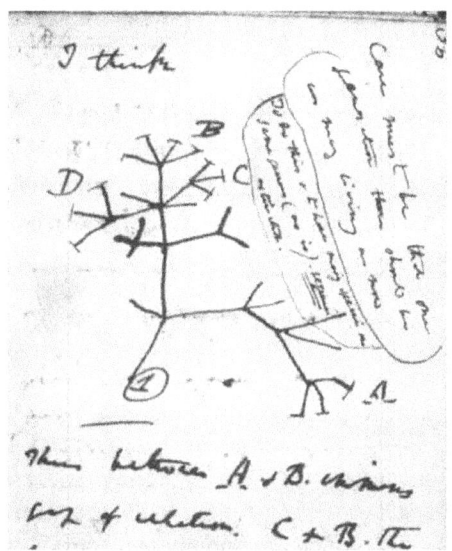

Darwin's 1837 simplistic sketch of his conception of the relation between life forms

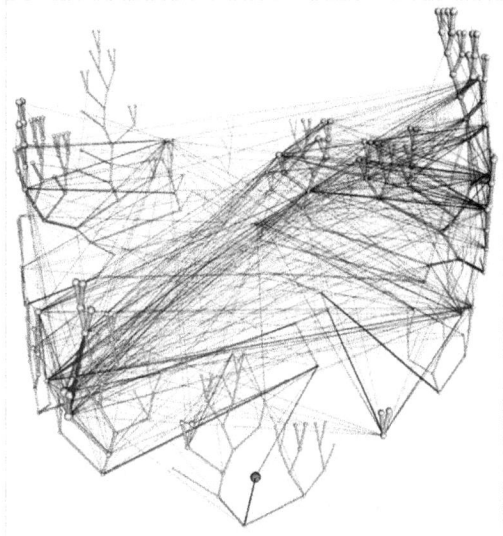

A representation of the actual relations of organisms after DNA comparisons

In recent years, scientists have developed techniques to infuse the genetics of one species into another. Yet, were ancient humans capable of gene manipulation, and is that what Ellen White meant by amalgamation? Mrs. White described early humans as ingenious: "The world today takes much satisfaction in talking of the progress of the age. But in this God does not delight. It may be said of the men of this time, as of those before the flood, They have sought out many inventions [Eccl. 7:29]. In the antediluvian world there were many wonderful works of art and science. These descendants of Adam, fresh from the hand of God, possessed capabilities and powers that we do not now look upon."[86] That early humans had greater capabilities than we might assume is witnessed by many intriguing man-made structures recovered from beneath the earth's surface. In Ellen White's thinking, humans were culpable for the pre–Flood amalgamation, yet they may have had help, particularly for the amalgamation after the Flood. In 1899, she implicated another amalgamating agent: "All tares are sown by *the evil one*. Every noxious herb is of his sowing, and by his *ingenious methods of amalgamation* he has *corrupted* the earth with tares."[87] Her statement is in keeping with Jesus' statement in the parable of the sower, in which He represented the master as asking his servant, "Didst not thou sow good seed in thy field? from whence then hath it tares?" To which the master responded, "An enemy hath done this" (Matt. 13:27, 28).

So what did Ellen White mean by "*confusion*" in her amalgamation statement? Was it the mixing of human and animal genetics, or was it the union of humans that should have remained distinct because of one group's spiritual commitment?[88] Sincere people are convinced by both sets of arguments.[89] For the purpose of this book, it is not necessary to make a final determination of the matter for us to know that Ellen White was not describing the Negro race. We do not need to determine whether she meant that, before the Flood, genetic meddling produced chimeras and denigrated the genetics of human beings, or whether she meant that the majority of humankind was denigrated by the union of the righteous with the rebellious. We do not need to determine whether she was suggesting a mechanism for the proliferation of animal life forms after the Flood by the blending of various of the biblical "kinds" that survived the flood with some blending of animal traits in certain races of humans or whether she simply meant that some races today reveal a blending of Negro, Caucasian, or Mongoloid traits.[90] Nonetheless, there is ample evidence from 1864 to 1890 to show that Ellen White considered the evil that resulted from the demise of the righteous line to be the reason that God chose to destroy the earth with a flood. Nonetheless, that she did not directly dispossess her readership of the conclusion that a particular perversity of mankind was instrumental in *corrupting* the DNA of the original kinds—including mankind—lends weight to that conclusion as well. Whichever she intended, the evidence consistently shows that she accepted those of the Negro race as possessing the full dignity of beings created in the image of God.

Was Ellen White Black?

As a side note, Charles Edward Dudley, Sr. suggested in his book *The Genealogy of Ellen Gould Harmon White* (1999) that Ellen White was herself of African-American descent, thereby explaining, in part, her "deep interest in the welfare of *Colored* people during her lifetime."[91] He does this on the basis of the apparent similarity of facial features between Ellen White and the mulatto Goulds of Gouldtown, New Jersey and the *lack* of evidence to contradict his assertion that Ellen White's mother, Eunice Gould Harmon, was related to the New Jersey Goulds. However, in 2000, the Ellen G. White Estate hired a certified and independent genealogist, Roger D. Joslyn, currently President of the American Society of Genealogists, to investigate Ellen White's maternal roots. In 2002, Joslyn delivered his careful report, which determined that there is no connection between the Goulds of New Jersey and the Goulds of Maine from which Ellen White arose but that there is, rather, solid evidence of the connection of Eunice Harmon's Gould lineage to England through her parents Joseph Goold/Gould and Lydia Lowell (both born in Maine), her grandparents Joseph Gould and Ruth Remick (both also born in Maine), her great grandparents Joseph Gould and Bethia[h] Furbush/Furbish (born in Plymouth Colony and Dover, New Hampshire), and her great-great grandparents John Gould and Mary Crossman (born in Massachusetts Bay Colony and Plymouth Colony).[92] If Ellen White were of African-American heritage, it would certainly be well received by black Seventh-day Adventists as well as by most white Seventh-day Adventists. However, the evidence indicates that she was not. Her interest in the welfare of African Americans came from her commitment to all people through her love of Christ and desire to fulfill the Gospel Commission.

In the next chapter, we will consider the Seventh-day Adventist mission to the virtually unentered Southern states, explaining why such work took so long to begin.

Chapter 6

Early Seventh-day Adventist Ministry to the Freedmen

Resolved, That a field is now opened in the South for labor among the colored people and should be entered upon according to our ability.
—Seventh-day Adventist annual meeting, Battle Creek, May 17, 1865

The resolution of Seventh-day Adventists regarding work among the freedmen of the South came during the third annual meeting of the newly organized Seventh-day Adventist Church—just one month after Lee's surrender.[1] Past editor of the *North American Regional Voice*, Stephanie D. Johnson, suggested why the church did not follow through immediately with the resolution: "Several reasons could be offered: The church was still in its infant stages and its main concern was the stabilizing of the denomination. The denomination had no formal educational society to establish a school among white students. Therefore, no systematic ministry to the Negro was present in the South."[2] Truthfully, all work in the South was limited during this period. The first Seventh-day Adventist church in the South, the Edgefield Junction, Tennessee, Church, with its thirteen members, would not be organized until June 1873.[3] (For another reference point, the first church in North Carolina would not be organized until May 15, 1881.[4]) In reporting to the 1883 General Conference on missions in the South, J. O. Corliss listed membership at "267 white Sabbathkeepers and 20 colored."[5]

The Continuation of "Slavery" by the Denial of Voting Rights

Just two months after Lee's surrender, Wendell Phillips commented at the New England Convention on what would happen to the freedmen if they were not granted the right to vote: "The first admission of a seceded State without black suffrage would settle the whole question, and then Slavery would exist in reality, though not in name."[6]

Immediately after the ratification of the Thirteenth Amendment (Jan. 31, 1865) and the end of the Civil War (June 22, 1865) major and rapid changes took place. Radical Republicans, who came into power with the 1866 elections, used the military to dissolve Southern state governments and ensure that Confederate nationalism was dead. Freedmen were given the right to vote in the new elections.[7] "The result was a Republican coalition that took power in ten states for varying lengths of time, staying in power with the help of U.S. Army units and black voters. Grant was elected president in 1868 and continued the Radical policies. Meanwhile the Freedmen's Bureau, started by Congress in 1865, helped freedmen by providing food, housing, medical care, educational opportunities and legal assistance."[8]

Yet the North itself was just beginning to grant blacks the right to vote. The *Advent Review and Sabbath Herald* reported the African American's right to vote in the nation's capitol: "The bill granting the right of suffrage to the colored citizens of the District of Columbia, has been passed over the President's veto."[9] Then it reported when the same right was gained in Ohio: "The Legislature of Ohio has finally voted in favor of admitting colored men to the right of suffrage."[10] Ultimately, 19 of the 24 Northern States did not give blacks the right to vote.[11] In the South, having the right to vote and actually exercising that right were two different things. Regarding the forthcoming election in Tennessee, the *Advent Review and Sabbath Herald* reported: "If a Union man informs a freedman of his rights, he is in constant peril of his life. Men of the late slaveholding class openly threaten to shoot any colored man who votes the Radical ticket . . . ."[12]

Attacks on Freedmen and Those Who Assisted Them

Kessia Reyne Bennett asserted: "[Seventh-day] Adventists were basically unacquainted with the South, and considered it 'a closed field, where violent men defended their prejudices with guns and whips.' "[13] Newspaper articles of the day, chronicling developments in the South under Reconstruction and reprinted in the *Advent Review and Sabbath Herald*, corroborate this appraisal. These undoubtedly affected the willingness of individual members to launch into the South. An article published just after the war called attention to attacks on the freedmen. It said:

> If one tenth part of the reports are true in regard to the ill-treatment of the blacks, which are coming from all parts of the South, thicker and faster, a most shocking state of things exists. From localities where there are no National troops, come reports that these unfortunate creatures, are being hunted down like dogs, and despatched [sic] without ceremony. The newspapers in the South are filled with accounts of these brutal murders, which foot up [sic] to an aggregate of several hundred deaths per day, which is doubtless only a small portion of the number noticed.[14]

Another article revealed challenges facing would-be educators from the North attempting to set up schools for African Americans in the South:

> Emile Bertrand, a teacher employed by the Freedmen's Bureau, was taken by the chivalry in the parish of Point Coupee, where he was teaching, and severely cowhided and his life threatened if he continued to teach a nigger school. This occurred in January last.
>
> Lieut. P. F. Burnham, formerly of the 8th Vermont Volunteers, having been mustered out of service, proceeded to Monroe, La., in February last, for the purpose of opening a school. He called a meeting of the colored population. This was set upon by ruffians armed with pistols and knives, and several of the negroes were murdered, and the Lieutenant barely escaped with his life, having received a cut with a knife, five inches in length, across the small of his back.[15]

Commenting on an assault on Rev. J. P. Bradwell and the murder of Lieutenant Blanding, the *American Missionary* commented:

> The purpose evidently is to drive away every friend of the colored man, from the South, not only the missionaries and teachers, but every one who would lift up a voice for the poor and lowly. Whether this effort succeeds or not, depends, under God, upon the action of our General Government. If such scenes are, permitted to pass unrebuked, the whole South will be overrun by violence worse than ever before, and, no faithful friend of God or man will be able to abide there. At last dates, it seemed probable that our teachers would leave.[16]

The *Advent Review and Sabbath Herald* of February 27, 1866, lamented the expiring of the Freedmen's Bureau bill, saying, "The rebels are jubilant, and drink toasts to Jeff. Davis, Gen. Lee, and President Johnson."[17] The *Advent Review and Sabbath Herald* of March 27, 1866, printed an article from the *New York Independent* entitled, "The President and Congress," written by Congregationalist pastor John Putnam Gulliver of Norwich, Connecticut. In it, Gulliver declared:

> The freedmen are not protected in any one of their rights, nor are they permitted to protect themselves. The history of the Freedman's Bureau bill has demonstrated the impossibility of securing for them anything more than a nominal protection, with the consent of the present President. We are to stand before high Heaven guilty of inviting the negroes to our banner, of using them to win a triumph which we could have gained without them only after long years of desolating war, and then abandoning them to their merciless foes. Is there a God of justice? and will he not visit us in vengeance for such treachery as this? Is the history of oppression and cruelty written in vain upon the world's annals? Is the lesson of this war so soon forgotten?[18]

Commenting on this article, Uriah Smith reminded readers of Ellen White's statement in "Testimony for the Church, No. 7": "It looked to me like an impossibility now for slavery to be done away. God alone can wrench the slave from the hand of his desperate, relentless oppressor."[19] Then he declared:

> Here was a view into the depth of the hellish spirit that reigns supreme in the slave holder's heart, which the most enlightened abolitionist would have then been scarcely willing to acknowledge, but the truth of which people are now beginning to see. While the Testimony does not say that slavery never will be abolished, it signifies that there are more difficulties in the way of accomplishing that event, than were then anticipated, or than have yet been overcome. We would that the bondman (it seems we cannot yet say freedman) might be released from the hand of the oppressor, even if the whole Egyptian host of slaveholders had to be led forth into the midst of some Red Sea, and disposed of as summarily as was Pharaoh and his minions of old. But these are events which we can leave with Heaven. God has the nation in his hand. And they who are true to his service through these eventful and perilous times, need not fear.[20]

Paramilitary groups, such as the Ku Klux Klan (which was organized in 1865 in Pulaski, Tennessee), used violence to overturn the new freedoms of the former slaves.[21] Their objective was to return to social order based on white supremacy and the segregation of the races. The Freedmen were returned to virtual slavery—a type of slavery that, for many, would persist for another century.[22] The *Advent Review and Sabbath Herald* quoted another report from the *Religious Telescope*:

Ku Klux Klan robe

> It is a very difficult thing for a freedman to get justice in the courts. Almost every day some poor fellow makes his way to Nashville, wounded and distressed. His employer or some other villain, in a moment of excitement, has fired on him with the intention of killing him. The truth is, there is a class in the South,

who would rather shoot at a negro than at a fox or a squirrel. They think it sport. They have no regard for his life or limbs. Half a dozen freedmen have been shot dead or dangerously wounded in this county within a few months past, and yet no man has been punished, and I doubt whether any one of the cold-blooded murderers of freedmen I see on the streets every day, will ever be punished.[23]

The *Advent Review and Sabbath Herald* brought a similar report from a Georgia man writing to the *Independent* (New York): "Freedmen are murdered almost every day in some part of the State, and *in no instance have the murderers been punished by the civil authorities*. . . . Two attempts have been made to take my life since my return. This makes four attempts that I *know* have been made to assassinate me. I cannot say how many more have been made that I did not discover."[24] In news from Texas, the *Advent Review and Sabbath Herald* reported: "The trial of a white man for the murder of a freedman in Texas would be a farce. It is strange that over the killing of a white man by the Indians on the remote frontier the greatest excitement will take place, but over the killing of many freedmen in the settlements, nothing is done."[25] On February 2, 1867, a teacher in Wilmington, North Carolina, wrote the *American Missionary*:

Reports are constantly brought from the country, showing the horrible abuses that are practiced there. The whites seem to wax more and more lawless. After the laborer's "contract time," for work has expired, they are driven off or "run off" the lands, as they call it, in which case they flee for their lives, for if they refuse to go they are shot. Robbing is carried on constantly, and has become in some places, quite an organized thing. Formed into companies, robbers come disguised, and sweep off the hard earned stores, and the few effects of many a colored family. To-day I saw a woman who fled to this place to save her children from being torn from her by her former master, and "bound out," as it is called, which is nothing more or less than slavery.[26]

Despite the violence, some progress could be reported. The August 13, 1867 *Advent Review and Sabbath Herald* reported on the state of education for the freedmen—1,207 schools, 1,406 teachers, and 75,456 pupils. "In addition to those in schools, thousands of scholars who have made some progress, are now teaching parents, brothers and sisters at home, so that nearly every freedman's house in the land has become a school house, and families in every section have become pupils." The *Advent Review and Sabbath Herald* also printed the summary of the sixth annual report of the Freedman's Savings and Trust Co., showing that "in 32 branches of the association, the balance due depositors was $2,454,836.11. The total in 1866 was only $199,283.42."[27]

New Forms of Bondage

As Samuel Eliot Morison contended in his history of the United States: "The North may have won the war, but the white South won the peace. It preserved the essence of slavery:—a pool of cheap, subservient labor—but escaped the capital outlays and social obligations that slavery imposed on the master."[28] Historian David Burner wrote: "The Civil War officially ended slavery in the United States, but in the postwar decades of Reconstruction and the rebuilding of the 'New South' slavery was replaced by other forms of economic and social bondage. Sharecropping and peonage plus the persistence of racial segregation in the form of 'Jim Crow' laws, assured white Southerners of continued control over the black population."[29]

> Cheap labor was another economic asset, as abundant and as available in the South in 1865 as it had been in 1850. The four million former slaves had not fled the South or even the plantation; and after a holiday of a few weeks they were back at work under conditions not unlike those that prevailed before the war. Even after the repeal of the short-lived black codes by Radical legislatures the relationship of freedman to planter gave evidence of no social or economic revolution.[30]

Hearing reports of such conditions, it is not strange that Seventh-day Adventists were hesitant to work in the South in the 1860s. Yet the "silent preachers" of literature and periodicals were doing their work.

Robert K. McCune Moves South

Ohio-born Robert Kirkwood McCune was farming in Princeton, Minnesota, when he began reading the *Advent Review and Sabbath Herald* in 1866 as a result of a gift subscription that he received from Mrs. Louisa M. Gates of Beaver Dam, Wisconsin.[31] (Mrs. Gates had herself received a gift subscription to the periodical from Lucia Morris of Wisconsin in 1857 and had subsequently joined the church.)[32] McCune appreciated what he was reading, and, in May 1868, he ordered a book through the periodical.[33] By July, he was subscribing to the paper on his own and ordering more books.[34] Relocating with his wife and four children to Edgefield Junction, Tennessee, ten miles north of Nashville, McCune, now working as a carpenter, requested the assistance of a Seventh-day Adventist minister.[35]

Elbert B. Lane Preaches in Tennessee

Elbert B. Lane, first Seventh-day Adventist minister in the South

A slave cabin

In March 1871, Elder Elbert B. Lane responded to McCune's request and began his first brief visit to the South. Lane described his impressions: "I had not long left the Ohio river [*sic*] before I saw what I had often read of and seen pictured, that is, the large plantation with its mansion and many negro huts or cabins, sometimes built of brick, but usually of boards or logs. They are small, one story buildings, often without windows or ventilation, except by means of the door. These buildings are now rented to the negroes who are in the employ of the planter. They receive low wages, ranging from five to ten dollars per month. The condition of this unfortunate race is truly lamentable. It is often remarked here in the North that the slave is worse off now than before he was liberated." Lane found white Southerners amenable to the freedman so long as he "kept his place," but "deeply resentful and hostile toward the meddling Northerner" who used the freedman for political or financial advantage.[36]

Since the schoolroom was too small, Lane's first venue for preaching was a railway station house, "the white people occupying one room and the colored the other."[37] He was only able to stay about a month before having to return to Indiana. Yet before he left, he baptized McCune and four others and left others preparing for baptism.[38] It would be two more years until he could return. In August, McCune wrote the *Advent Review and Sabbath Herald*:

Elbert B. Lane preaching in a train station

> DEAR BRETHREN: We would acknowledge our gratitude to God, to the church, and to Bro. E. B. Lane, that we have been permitted to receive the ordinance of baptism and to hear the truth spoken from a living witness. Truly, it was a feast of good things. Eld. Lane's discourses here made a deep impression on the people, and quite a number seem willing to accept the doctrine taught, but are not ready to obey. Two have commenced to keep the Sabbath since he left, and very many are anxious to hear him again and wish him to come and spend next winter here. We would not be selfish, but hope Conference will see it proper to send him again. Brethren, let your prayers go up daily for the lonely ones who have to stand up and breast the great current of popularity, and meet the sneers and scorn of the (would-be-called) respectable Christians. Yet it is comforting to look to the reward; and while we keep our eyes fixed on Christ, the troubles are so much in the dark as to be hardly visible. We have a deep sorrow that all our friends and neighbors will not receive the message and be companions with us in keeping the commandments of God and the faith of Jesus.[39]

Then, in November, McCune wrote, "The *Review* is the only preacher we have. It is, however, a good one, and comes about the beginning of the Sabbath filled with precious truth and valuable instruction. We should be very lonesome without our weekly visitor. And that is not all: it passes round from hand to hand, and neighbor to neighbor, with a happy greeting for all, until it is about worn out." McCune reported that four families of ten adults and eight or ten children were keeping the Sabbath and said: "There are also some others convinced, who talk as if they would take hold if there was a church organized here. One colored preacher has, by reading, discovered the true Sabbath. He was a missionary Baptist."[40] The next year McCune wrote: "It is cheering to read the reports from the various portions of this great nation, yet sad to think there are so few from the southern States. I think among all the people of those States, perhaps not one in ten thousand ever heard of the Advent faith; yet many of those who have heard, have received it gladly. But most of them think they must see a church organization, before they can throw off their old habits, and follow the new. Could not some of our preachers come this way this summer?"[41] Lane came back in May 1873 for just two weeks, lecturing in the railway station again. This time he left an organized church with thirteen members.[42]

The little church soon faced a major test. In September 1873, a lady wrote Lane from Edgefield Junction, describing the situation. Though the letter was not intended for publication, Lane gave his permission for McCune to publish it, "believing it will interest, and touch the sympathies of all who read it. In the prayers of God's people may the interest of the cause in the South be remembered." Here is the letter:

> DEAR BRO. LANE: I have postponed writing to you from time to time, hoping to have something of interest to write, and I can now only write a gloomy letter. About a week after you left us, we were visited by a plague; the doctors, at first could not agree upon a name for it; but finally, concluded to call it cholera, which had a run of about four weeks, and made the most distressing time I ever saw. It was the most fatal among the negroes, but spared neither high nor low. Some buried the whole family but perhaps the father, or one other member. One man buried seven, and put up a monument, "All dead but me." One family was found all dead and dying but an infant, which was sucking its dead mother's breast. And another black family of five were all found lying around over the floor in their filth, dead, with the doors and windows all open. It is said that the mortality was greater than Calcutta ever produced, ranging from ten to twenty per cent of the inhabitants left who remained in the country. . . .
>
> All the Sabbath-keepers are still holding on to the truth, and all cheerfully take part in our little meetings which have not failed a single Sabbath through all our troubles, while all other meetings were more or less postponed. One of our members has moved to Murray Co., where

The Jonathan Allison family, charter members of the Edgefield Junction Church in Tennessee. Two Allison sons became ministers—Thomas H. Allison, known for his musicianship and preaching in the South and Midwest, and Jonathan W. Allison, Sr., who worked in the South and West. Allison's son, Jonathan W. Allison, Jr., pastored in the Midwest and at the University Boulevard church in Los Angeles.

I think is an excellent opening for a course of lectures. It has been quite healthy there all summer. We hope you will remember us in your prayers, that we may all live to the honor and glory of God. May you soon return to labor here, bringing a tent. We look for much good to be done. All join in sending love.

R. K. McCune, Edgefield Junction, Tennessee, September 15, 1873.[43]

McCune's last entry from Tennessee was in May 1874. It included an appeal to send a minister.[44] McCune moved his family to Mackford, Wisconsin, where he worked as a wagon maker.[45] The little church in Edgefield Junction continued faithfully and contributed to the establishment of other churches.[46]

Squire Osborne in Kentucky

Squire Osborne (1825–1903) was a Kentuckian who migrated to Iowa in 1851 where he accepted the Seventh-day Adventist message by May 1859 and sent literature to his family in Kentucky.[47] His father, with whom he had visited in 1870, was his first convert.[48] Though Osborne was not an ordained minister, at his brother's urging he held meetings on Bible prophecy in Kentucky and Tennessee for the first time in 1871. "[B]ecause he had written freely of the new truths he had embraced," his brother, "with the Kentuckian's readiness to bestow honor and titles, before his arrival made an appointment for the Rev. S. Osborne to speak upon the prophecies of the Bible at the neighboring schoolhouse. When ... Osborne arrived, he was dismayed to find himself in such a dilemma, and protested that, never having spoken in public, he could not now begin." His brother would not give in, and Squire abruptly began his long labors in Kentucky.[49] A year later he received a license to preach.[50]

He returned to Kentucky several times more in the ensuing years, his visits punctuated by labors back in Iowa. In January 1872, Jacob Hare of Mt. Pleasant, Iowa, traveled back from Battle Creek to Springville, Kentucky, and reported on Osborne's preaching there and the six people who had begun keeping the Sabbath.[51] In April, Osborne himself reported on eleven Sabbath-keepers in Greenup County, Kentucky, and on his stay there of twenty-four weeks.[52] He returned to Iowa to minister through November 1872 and back to Greenup, Kentucky from March 1873 through at least October 1889.[53] On December 23, 1874, Osborne rejoiced in the "four colored people who have decided to keep the Sabbath" in Green County, Kentucky.[54] In March 1875, he held meetings at Hammondsville, Hart County, Kentucky. July 31 and August 1, he met with the Sabbath-keepers in Locust Grove. August 4–8, he raised up a church of seventeen members near Powder Mills.[55] August 12–18, 1875, he visited Edgefield Junction, Tennessee, the believers there having been without a minister for two years. "Worn in body and mind," he wrote, "I rested one day, and then started for Edgefield Junction, Tenn. The Sabbath-keepers there had had no preaching for about two years. Found the young very much discouraged.

Powder Mills, Kentucky, Seventh-day Adventist Church, built 1878

After speaking the first evening, I felt that my work there was for the Sabbath-keepers especially. I stayed until the 18th, laboring in prayer and social meetings, and giving close, practical discourses, until it was apparent to all that the Lord was moving upon hearts. Those that were discouraged made hearty confessions. It was truly affecting to see them plead with their unconverted friends. One brother and his wife came twenty-eight miles through the mud, traveling nearly all of one night to reach the place before the Sabbath. It was the first time they had ever heard a Seventh-day Adventist preach, and they drank in the precious truths of the third [angel's] message with joy and eagerness. On first-day they were buried in baptism, giving every evidence of genuine conversion." On the same trip, Osborne described a baptism in Powder Mills, Greenup County, Kentucky, of nine people, two of whom were black, concluding: "This was the most joyous baptismal scene I ever witnessed." Yet the work was lonely, and Osborne ended the report, writing: "I do not know how long I can endure laboring alone so constantly. May the Lord direct the mind of some consecrated minister to come South."[56] In February, he reported that members at the November 28 business meeting in Springville, Kentucky, had voted to buy a tent for evangelism.[57] On March 31, the General Conference voted to purchase it for him.[58] By April, there were five organized Seventh-day Adventist churches in Kentucky and two in Tennessee.[59] D. M. Canright described the meetings in Elizabethtown, Kentucky, where he and the other visitors were received warmly: "There are three colored people here who keep the Sabbath, and they are members of the church with the others. These feel anxious to have a mission started among the colored people. All agree that the way is now fully open for that work, if persons can be found to do it."[60]

Osborne labored many years in eastern Kentucky for the cause that he loved, dying suddenly in 1903 at camp meeting "with his armor on."[61] Notice of his death was reported in Kentucky newspapers.[62]

Charles O. Taylor in the Deep South

Charles O. Taylor was first to preach in the Deep South, following up on requests from the people who had received literature sent to them in Georgia, North and South Carolina, Alabama, Mississippi, Louisiana, and Florida.[63] Moving with his wife to Quitman, Georgia in 1876, Taylor held meetings early the next year. He observed: "I do not know of one in all this State that is keeping the Bible Sabbath. If there are any, I would like to have them write to me. … The colored people have places of worship by themselves, occupying the same house with the whites, only sitting by themselves. Last Sunday one-third of the congregation were colored persons. They gave good attention, as did all present."[64] On August 22, he wrote: "If

Charles O. Taylor

any of our T. and M. workers wish to send the *Signs* to such, on trial, they will please inform me, and the number of names they wish. Reading matter is doing much in the South in calling the attention of the people to the message. Sixty or seventy families are reading the *Signs*. Hundreds have read the *Review*, and are learning for the first time, that there is such a people as Seventh-day Adventists."[65] In Griffin, Georgia, Taylor described his work: "I spoke three times to the colored people while here. They seemed much interested, and wanted to hear more. One minister spoke at the close of one of the meetings, expressing very clear views on the nature of man, the state of the dead, and not receiving rewards at death. Many in this Southern field are waiting for the truth."[66]

Regarding meetings in Reynolds, Georgia, in 1878, he wrote: "There was a large congregation, composed of all classes. They wanted to hear on the end of the wicked. There was the very best of attention while I read the Bible. Some were more than commonly anxious to catch every word and get every idea. One gentleman expressed himself much interested, and pleased with the manner of the preaching in appealing to the Scriptures. The freedmen improved the opportunity of attending, as the meeting was in the court-house. They were much interested, and urged me to send the truth to them. I know of no one. Should any go there, they will have a good hearing."[67] The next year he wrote: "I was in Houston county a week ago, and spoke three times at the courthouse in Perry. The congregation was not large, but the most were very attentive. Forty received the ordinance of baptism. There are now thirteen in that county keeping the Sabbath. Nine are freedmen. Two of the number have been ministers in other denominations."[68]

Literature Societies

The April 5, 1877 *Advent Review and Sabbath Herald* included examples of correspondence from African-American readers in North Carolina, Alabama, and West Virginia.[69] One of these was a minister from North Carolina who had received copies of the *Signs of the Times*. He wrote:

> I am very highly pleased with such reading matter as I find in the *Signs of the Times*; and I see many books advertised in the *Signs* on such subjects that I want, not only the *Signs*, but also those books and pamphlets advertised in it, but have not the money to pay for them. I am all the time traveling and preaching among thousands of my people, and they always look for some book, paper, or tract. If you send them I can distribute thousands to great advantage. I feel that God has heard, and is now about to answer, my long continued and incessant prayers for help of this kind. I was born and brought up in slavery, and emancipated in 1865; got my learning, or much of it, in the dark days of slavery and oppression, by the fireside, when all on the plantation were asleep. I have worked hard all day, and then studied all night many a time. For seven years past I have been traveling, and trying to preach the gospel of Christ. I am going on preaching and pursuing my studies, and do earnestly desire to grow up into the full measure and stature of a man in Christ and in the pulpit.[70]

The second reader, who was also from North Carolina, wrote:

> I have been reading your paper with great care, and my dear wife, who is unconverted, seems to take great delight in them. I do think if she had more of them they would cause her to think more about her soul. I wish I was able to take the paper. Many of my friends hope to take it after a while.[71]

Another African American reader wrote from Alabama:

> I am thankful, yea, more than thankful, to feel that we have friends North who are willing to take an interest in the welfare of the colored race. The *Signs* and *Herald* come to me regularly. I am just as proud of them as any one could be. I feel as though they were *God-sent blessings*.[72]

Still another expressed his appreciation and offered to send the names of other subscribers, and yet another in West Virginia wrote:

I have been praying that the Lord would open the way through which I might get some good reading matter, and I feel that my prayers are being heard and answered. They are good religious papers, but I am so situated I am not able to pay for them. My church is hardly able to rent my house. I would have left here long since, but when I think of the condition of my people I forget my own condition, and am willing to spend and be spent for them. I am glad of any reading material you will send, if it is old books, tracts, or papers.[73]

Such literature also found a receptive audience in 1876 in at Shull's Mill, six miles from Valle Crucis in Watauga County in the mountains of western North Carolina. Charles Taylor reinforced the work of the literature by holding meetings.[74] Though there were few freedmen in this region, Taylor played a key role in evangelizing it.

Other Preachers in the South

There were other Seventh-day Adventist ministers who held evangelistic meetings in Southern cities in the early years. D. T. Bourdeau held public meetings from January to May 1872 in Kentucky, G. K. Owen assisted in middle Tennessee, and R. F. Cottrell preached in Maryland.[75] E. B. Lane and J. O. Corliss reported in March 1876 that "quite a number of colored people," as well as white folk, in New Market, Virginia, kept the Sabbath for the first time.[76] Corliss followed up on their work in Virginia and in other Southern states.[77] Orlando Soule preached east of Nashville on the Cumberland plateau and in middle Tennessee and Kentucky.[78] D. M. Canright, and E. B. Lane's brother Sands H. Lane (who was also the half brother of Otho Godsmark, who will be quoted later) also held meetings in the South.[79]

Mrs. H. M. Van Slyke in Missouri

Mrs. Hanna Maria Van Slyke was a white Seventh-day Adventist, originally from New York state, who had moved with her husband and children to Hamilton, Caldwell County, Missouri. She served as secretary of the Missouri Tract and Missionary Society for several years.[80] In late 1876 she started a school for black children in Taitsville, Ray County, Missouri—just south of Caldwell County.[81] Her students ranged from six to 24 years of age and were mostly orphans. Mrs. Slyke reported that the prejudice against the education of former slaves limited her volunteer help, yet she glowingly reported that ten of her pupils had progressed enough that they were able to read the Bible.[82] The school closed after only a few months of service. Perhaps it was because of the prejudice that Mrs. Van Slyke mentioned, or perhaps it was because of her poor health. Either way, she continued her role as secretary of the Tract and Missionary Society.[83]

Joseph Clarke in Texas

D. M. Canright, who was visiting Texas in May 1876, described the pioneering work of Eddie Capman, a young layman who was running a night school for freedmen in Texas:

> It was held in a little log cabin about 12 x 14. In this were rude seats with a rough table in the center. On this was an ordinary lantern for light. Around this table were seated about a dozen colored people, ranging from parson Green Medlin, with white locks, down to the little

children of eight or ten years. All the older ones had been slaves. Now they were learning to read, spell, write, etc. The younger ones seem to get along well; but the older ones have hard work of it. To me it was really touching to see a man of forty trying to learn his letters. But the effort is commendable, and many of them do better than could be expected.

Canright ended his report with an appeal:

D. M. Canright

It seems to me that the time has come for labor among the freedmen. But it will have to be a distinct mission. A man can not labor for them and for the whites too as the white would not associate with him if he did.[84] There is objection to laboring for them and teaching them, but it must be separately. The colored people can not attend schools nor churches with the whites, and little or nothing is done for them by the whites. They are left to shift for themselves a sheep without a shepherd. At least that is the way it is here. They are anxious to be taught, and would welcome laborers among them. They are locating in small settlements where they can get land. Could a man and his wife come among them with a tent in which to hold school for the younger ones and meetings for the others, I am sure many would embrace the truth readily.[85]

In 1877, Joseph Clarke, a key supporter of church organization and a frequent contributor to the *Advent Review and Sabbath Herald,* together with his wife Sarah, responded to Canright's appeal and moved to Texas. Clarke wrote on March 1:

Last evening, Parsons G. M. and F. Jordan, both freedmen, spent the evening here arranging for building a school-house for the freedmen, toward which, the citizens will assist. Until this is done, Mrs. Clarke will teach freedmen's school in a tent. I am hoping to teach school in this vicinity.

Joseph Clarke

Then, two weeks later, Clarke described their future plans and the support of the white townsfolk, which may explain why work with freedmen could begin at this location in Texas:

The white citizens are helping to raise means for the house, and quite a number have subscribed towards it. There is a favorable sentiment in this direction. Bro. and Sr. Rust have been here some over a year, and have done much to enlighten the public mind upon the views of S. D. Adventists; and the people know that we are not politicians nor fortune hunters.[86]

It was not long before Clarke was calling for the help of "a licensed preacher to come and organize churches."[87] He had become a Seventh-day Adventist in 1855.[88] From early on, he had concerns about human rights. In 1857, he described his views in the *Advent Review and Sabbath Herald.* His third and fourth points are:

Third, This government does sanction, and has from the first sanctioned, Slavery. Let him who doubts this examine the constitution giving to the slaveowner three-fifths of a vote for every one of his human chattels. Witness the Fugitive Slave Law, a damning feature of this our vaunted free government; and the foul stain extending to the very doors of the capitol.[89]

Fourth, The policy of this government has from the first been destructive of the true interests of the unfortunate Red Man. By violence and deceit, by plausible pretext and corrupt design, by artifice and fraud, and strength of hand, the poor child of the forest has been wasted and driven from station to station, from fort to fort, till despair has entered his poor heart, and he now drowns his sorrows in debauchery and drunkenness.[90]

This was the same Clarke who wrote a year into the war:

I HAVE been very anxious to know duty respecting the war, not so much for fear of the draft, as because I want to see treason receive its just deserts.

Consequently, I have written to Bro. White, to know if it would be allowable for us to go into the ranks.

... Often as I have thought of the baseness of slave treason, and how it hinders the message from moving forward, how it instigates Kansas raids, how it prompts to fugitive slave laws, and Dread [sic] Scott decisions, how it separates families, how it does violence to innocence, how it tars and feathers, and hangs, innocent travelers, peddlers, school-masters, etc., how it makes the soil barren, and the government corrupt, how it tantalizes, how it tyrannizes, how it traduces, in fact how it sums up in itself every horrid crime, how it brands every good patriot as a fanatic, I have wished sometimes that I had it where Joab had Absalom, and almost fancied that the time might come when a regiment of Sabbath-keepers would strike this rebellion a staggering blow, in the strength of Him who always helped his valiant people when they kept his statutes.[91]

Dred Scott

Last winter I had the war fever so high, that it injured me somewhat. I am well aware, that I felt too deeply on the matter, and when I mentioned my feelings to a judicious friend, he warned me of my danger. But I find as I look to God for light, he does not seem to frown upon me for my hatred to treason.

Well I know, that the North has sinned, and this is the greatest of our sins. We have not abhorred the deeds of the bloody deceitful southern tyrants, but have bowed, and scraped, and truckled meanly to the monstrous system of slavery.

While I have been going probably somewhat to an extreme in my hatred to treason and oppression, I see that on the other hand, many are whining lest they might be drafted.

Now brethren, let us all stop pestering Bro. White on this subject, and go to God for guidance. I have no doubt that when the time for drafting arrives, God will shed light on the path of the S. D. Adventists.[92] We have the gift of prophecy, and if we look to God, he will guide our leaders, and they will walk in the light. Praise the Lord. ...

I do not expect the full destruction of slavery; but the south must be humbled, else the slave cannot get the present truth. Still we must be patient, for we at the North have sinned by our cowardly submission to the monster in years past, and must meet our punishment. After that, let southern traitors tremble.[93]

Clarke also wrote in the middle of the war:

The youth is [*sic*] taught from infancy to despise the colored race, and even now, while the hand of Jehovah is put forth in wrath for the scourging of this proud oppressive nation, while almost every train of cars brings home more or less of coffined corpses, from the scene of conflict, even now, as thousands of our men are falling in battle, and by disease, we may daily witness on all our great thoroughfares, the proudest bearing toward, and contempt for, the colored race; scorn, and indignity, are heaped upon them; often, too, is this manifested toward men of worth and character, merely because of their color. Oh, pride, to what lengths hast thou attained! And how few can plead innocent of complicity with the gigantic sin of slavery. Who has felt for the slave as for a brother in bonds, as bound with him? Who has persistently protested against these evils?[94]

Clarke also commented on the Thirteenth Amendment:

But the act of congress [*sic*] abolishing the "peculiar institution" of slavery, which should take effect December 18, 1865, was the final stunning blow to slavery. Alas who can tell the agony of the statesmen of the chivalric and proud Southern dynasty, as on Christmas the freedmen celebrated the jubilee of freedom. To say that the freedman can, in all cases, avail himself of the blessings of liberty; to say that he is in all cases fit to govern himself, is, more than we can affirm. It is still in the power of the citizen to make the freedman's life a life of misery. But one thing is certain; the proud oppressor has been terribly rebuked.[95]

In an article entitled "Is the Rebellion Quelled?" he raised concerns about safety in the South, quoting a letter dated April 26, 1871 from Hamilton Jay, Esq., "who went to Florida, strong in the belief that there was nothing to be apprehended from the Ku Klux":

"MY DEAR GENERAL: Another one of our band has just been killed. Hon. John P. Mahoney was assassinated at Lake City this morning.[96] He was a young, ardent Republican, a member of the Legislature from Columbia County. He was my personal friend, possessing many noble qualities. Congress must pass a strong Ku Klux bill, or we have no safety, for Republicanism in this State means death. This makes the fifth murder since I came here, all Republicans. . . ."

In the same article, Clarke also quoted a letter from Senator William G. Brownlow of Tennessee, regarding conditions in the South:

The rebel party that we are dealing with are as bitter and insulting as they were in 1861, and are as haughty and overbearing as when in the field with arms in their hands. . . . The truth is, this rebel party hate the old flag, and hate the Government of the United States. They have hopes of destroying it, and now seek to accomplish through legislation that which they failed to accomplish on the field of battle. They are sailing under the colors of Democracy and under false pretense of upholding the Constitution. The same Democracy furnished a Governor to each of the eleven seceded States just preceding the rebellion, hence their unanimity of voting themselves out of the Union. Their present plans and purposes are to elect a President, both branches of Congress, and to repeal all the reconstruction acts and grant pensions to the rebel soldiery. Also, to either have pay for their negroes or restore slavery, and by all means to do away with negro suffrage.[97] Many of them openly avow that their toleration of negro suffrage and emancipation, is only an experiment, and if it don't [*sic*] work to their notion, they will put it down. . . . It will be seen that I characterize the opposition to the Republicans as rebels. There are but two parties in this country. The one is the Union Republican party, that has saved the country thus far, and proposes to take care of it from this time forward. The other is the rebel party, which fought for four years to destroy the Government. The one is an army of patriots, the other an army of traitors. And the great mistake of the party in power was that they did not hang the leaders.[98]

The Second Enforcement Act of 1871, also known as the Ku Klux Klan Act, did curtail some of the violence for a period of time, allowing Seventh-day Adventist forays into the South to intensify for a time.[99] In 1875, Clarke wrote about continued rebellion in the South:

> We deprecate the sword with all its warlike accompaniments, but as lookers on, we ask, Is not the South daily gaining back her lost victories? Is not the conflict still going on quietly and surely? Is not the oppressor as active as ever, and is he not winning back his laurels? . . .
> We pity the slave. We pity his once rich master, now his foe. We hope each will do all he can for a prolongation of peace; but we see no signs of permanent prosperity while rebellion holds the reins of power.[100]

A year before he and his wife began teaching the freedmen, Clarke wrote:

> Why is it that our nation has not set up schools for Freedmen in every town and village in the South? Why is it that good people at the North have not taken this matter in hand? Why is it that our excellent President, General Grant, has not defended their cause? Why is it that every kind of lawlessness is still tolerated at the South? These questions are easily answered; but one question is not so easily replied to: Why is it that Christians can rest so quietly while their colored brother pines in ignorance and neglect? The day for labor is fast passing away, and shall not the light yet reach the Freedman?[101]

Obviously Joseph Clarke was already motivated when he heard D. M. Canright's appeal for teachers to come to Texas.[102] He and his wife held school for freedmen in Dallas County, Texas, from February 17, 1877, to June 12, 1878.[103] Though Elder Robert M. Kilgore commended the Clarkes for their self-sacrificing work when he arrived in May 1877, he differed with them over the work's efficacy.[104] Clarke wrote to Uriah Smith: "Bro. Kilgore and S. H. King are of the opinion it is not important as an agency for the propagation of present truth and that we cannot effect much here under the circumstances."[105] Their appraisal was not from racial bigotry, for Kilgore had been raised by a father (John Lindsay Kilgore) who provided his home as a station on the Underground Railroad. The appraisal was based on the real "circumstances" of the minimal response on the part of the freedmen and Kilgore's being "threatened with death or being driven out of the county if he allowed the Clarkes to continue teaching."[106] Only one of the Clarkes' twenty-four or so students had embraced the Sabbath—a 25-year-old man from Alabama. Yet fearing public opinion, the young man had "not come to meeting with" the Seventh-day Adventist believers, and the Clarkes would visit him Sabbath afternoons.[107] The school for the freedmen closed, Kilgore made great strides among white Texans, and the Clarkes moved to Missouri, where they engaged in a productive ministry until the 1890s.[108]

William F. Killen in Georgia

William Francis Killen, a lawyer, tax assessor and collector, and county school superintendent of Houston County, Georgia, accepted the Sabbath as the biblical day of worship in 1877 after hearing Charles Taylor "talk privately on the Lord's Sabbath" and reading literature on the subject.[109] Uniting with the Seventh-day Adventists in 1878, Killen "brought with him many of his colored laborers, some of whom had been his slaves and bore his name."[110] Among these was a preacher who worked his land on shares named Edmund Killen.[111] Results of Edmund Killen's preaching have not been recorded.[112] However, W. F. Killen himself baptized into the faith a number of freedmen and labored as a self-supporting minister for many years, being ordained a gospel minister in 1880.[113]

William Francis and Martha Killen

Why was there so little progress among freedmen in these early years? Killen's description of one of Taylor's return trips and the response of Georgians may give some clues about the Southern reactions to them:

> I have just returned from Brooks Co., Ga. I found there four Sabbath-keepers, who are very firm indeed in the truth. Three of them, one man and two women, were baptized by Eld. C. O. Taylor before he left Georgia for Battle Creek. The other, the husband of one of these ladies, told me that he was ready for baptism, but was in feeble health, and thought it best to wait until the weather became warmer. A colored woman says she thinks I will have her to baptize when I go back there. I preached eight discourses in the county, four of them in the immediate neighborhood where I was stopping, the others in different parts of the county. I had attentive audiences. *There was considerable opposition to Eld. Taylor, because he was a Northern man.* They treated me very kindly indeed, and the way for the truth to be spoken in that county is fully open. Several freely acknowledged that we have the Bible Sabbath. The preaching was of a practical nature, and everywhere apparently well received.[114]

Otho C. Godsmark described an evangelistic series in the South that gives indications of how Southerners read the efforts of Northern Seventh-day Adventists:

Otho C. Godsmark

> In response to a call of the General Conference in 1888, my brother [half brother, Sands H. Lane], my wife and myself came to the South in March.[115] After some preliminary work, visiting the brethren in Georgia and Florida, we began tent meetings in a town not far from Atlanta.[116] Our first town was an educational center, a female seminary being located there. I started out at the first to find a musical instrument; and in one of the stores of the town was inquiring where there might be found an organ for rent, stating that if it should be out of repair, I could put it in order. The principal of the school happened to be there; and hearing me say this, he asked if I could tune pianos. I told him I could, so he asked me to examine their two pianos, which I did, and put them in perfect unison. They were so highly pleased

with the work that notice was made of it in the paper, and that public notice gave me entrance into the homes, including the home of the mayor. While I was tuning pianos, my brother was talking the truth to them. Our stay at this place seemed finally to accomplish no great results, except to make a friendly impression, which extended through the country, and caused a cordial invitation to come to us from another town named Social Center.

Here the people received us in a very friendly manner, and showed us many kindnesses. We had no stove, and were cooking over a gas torch light. One day when we returned from making a visit, we found sitting out in front of our tent a full equipment, a brand new cook stove, with pots and skillets and kettles and pipe, everything complete. The citizens had made up a purse and bought a complete outfit.

As soon as we began our meetings, there arose a splendid interest, the best people, and all classes crowding the tent. The colored people would come out behind the white people, and lie round in hundreds in the grass about us. We were in a large open meadow, having some shade, right at the edge of the village.

Sands H. Lane

We, of course, were anxious to do something for both colored and white. So my brother went to the mayor of the city, and said to him, 'Now, we are strangers here in the South, and while we are from the North, we are here to preach, of course, to the white people, and we have no desire to do anything at all contrary to the customs of the Southern people. Yet if there is anything we can do to reach these colored people, we should be glad to do so.'

The Mayor replied that probably the way we were then doing would accomplish as much for the colored people as anything we could do; they were listening and taking it in; though, he said, if we could at any time go out in the country and hold meetings in their houses, that would be all right. But he was afraid if we held meetings in the tent for them, it would hurt our influence with the white people, and also with the colored.

But we rather pressed the matter with him, and asked if it would not be proper for us to give one night in the week to the colored people in the tent. He stated that if we announced it fully, so the white people would understand it would not necessarily raise any special prejudice, but it was a question in his mind whether it would be best; it would hurt our influence with the colored as much as with the white.

We didn't see how it could hurt us with the Negroes, for they had been coming to the tent during the daytime to talk with us, and to buy our literature, and we thought if we should show them special favor, they would come much more freely. So we publicly announced that each Thursday night we should hold a meeting especially for the colored people. We announced this about a week ahead.

Immediately our attendance decreased, both of white and colored people, and the colored people quit coming to the tent to visit us in the daytime. And when Thursday night came, instead of hundreds of colored people flocking out to hear us, as we had expected, and as they had come before our announcement, not a soul showed himself, either colored or white. We thought maybe they did not understand about the meeting, so we raised the walls of the tent all around, and we played the organ and sang as loud as we could, to make every one think the meeting had begun. But only one little old colored woman put in an appearance, leading two little children.

She sat down on the back seat, looked at us dubiously for about five minutes, and then went out of the tent as though shot out of a gun. Never a colored person came near us after that. The Negroes immediately started the story that we were low-down white trash that had been run out by the respectable people of the North, and had come South to live off the colored folks. They retorted that we did not believe colored men had any souls, and so forth.

At that time a colored woman was doing our laundry. She had our washing out this week, and she refused to bring it home. I had to walk four miles in the hot sun down to her cabin and actually demand of her to finish the washing. I sat in the front yard under my umbrella while she ironed the clothes, and then through the broiling sun I toted them home myself on my back. Beautiful corroboration it was to the colored people of the report that we were low-down white trash![117] After that we could get our washing done only by the courtesy of a white woman, who took it in with hers for a colored woman to do.

That closed our interest out. We stayed there about two weeks, but our interest was dead. The whites treated us kindly, but did not come to hear us, after having given us the stove, and all that!

My brother now felt that he had a call to survey the country, from North Carolina to Alabama, to find opportunities for good tent efforts; while I, with an English brother, essayed another one of the good tent efforts at another town in Georgia. This time it was our English brother, a little more unused than ourselves to Southern Americanism, who, under stress of a rainstorm and Christian philanthropy, again put us in bad odor with both races. This time we were not only left with our empty tent, but received a scathing denouncement in the county paper. We heard that yellow fever had broken out somewhere in the South, and we felt that it was time to leave for the General Conference at Minneapolis, which fortunately just then offered a plausible reason for closing up our work.

Ours was a flat failure, and it affected us sadly. We felt the field was impossible, and we did not come back. It was thirteen years before I gained the courage and the sense to return, and start to learning before I tried to teach.[118]

What Godsmark did not understand was that, in separating the blacks from the whites, the blacks felt vulnerable. They had been taken advantage of by Northern whites during Reconstruction.[119] It was not reasonable to expect a people, who had been so dependent on a ruling class for so long, to think and reason for themselves. Yet this was not the only effect of slavery. Arthur W. Spalding described the typical freedman:

> Slavery had been a poor school to teach him morality. Often pinched by hunger, he would steal; always fearful of punishment, he would lie; wronged by the auction-block, by concubinage, and by a system that had more regard to scientific breeding than to conjugal happiness, he had little or no conception of family life or marital faithfulness. With his equipment he was ill fitted to face as a freeman the requirements of Christian civilization. ... His education had not taught him independence of opinion; he had only known it safe to agree. Ask him, "This river runs up hill, Sandy, doesn't it?"—"Yes sah, reckon hit mus', sah!"[120]

Seventh-day Adventist historian A. W. Spalding

The extreme prejudice of the time made work among both races difficult. "Elder Osborne and Elder Killen, being Southern men, had no difficulty in dealing with their converts, to the satisfaction of both races."[121] In Georgia, indeed, the color-line [or segregation] question hardly appeared, the colored members being few and scattered. In Kentucky Elder Osborne formed the two races into separate companies and churches. Upon Elder Osborne's visit to Battle Creek in 1877, he laid the question before Elder James White, then president of the General Conference of Seventh-day Adventists who listened to his presentation of conditions and resulting necessities, and agreed with him in his plans.[122] But a few years later, Northern laborers being sent to aid in the work in Kentucky and one of them being elected president of the little conference to succeed Elder Osborne, insistence was made that the two races be joined in the churches. Neither of these laborers stayed long, but the results of their work remained in enfeebled churches, injured public feeling, and conditions which were a source of weakness till long after the superintendence of the Southern field was assumed by Elder R. M. Kilgore in 1890. When Elder Osborne, saddened and oppressed by this state of things, wrote an appeal to headquarters, the response of the General Conference, under a new regime, was anything but favorable."[123] Yet Seventh-day Adventist minister of Wisconsin David Downer could report in 1874: "The colored people are becoming educated with a rapidity that is beyond all our former hopes. Is it not the work of God, preparing their minds for this last message?"[124]

Robert M. Kilgore in Texas

Robert M. Kilgore of Iowa mustered out of the Union army in 1864 and returned to his Iowa home to discover that his parents were observing the seventh-day Sabbath. He soon united with them. In 1868, he volunteered as tent master for George I. Butler and Merritt E. Cornell in a meeting in the South. After that meeting, James White ordained him to the ministry.

In 1877, Kilgore responded, on the behest of the General Conference, to Joseph Clarke's request for licensed ministerial help in Texas. During the eight years that he worked in Texas, he faced threats of lynching and once had his tent burned down.[125] Kilgore wrote: "The opposition against us is strong, and every effort is made to scare the people away from the tent. The best arguments they have are brought to bear against us, such as, 'He is a Yankee;' 'he has come here to preach nigger equality;' etc. While some of the ministers are preaching such tidings, we are preaching an entirely different gospel. Let God be thanked."[126] Kilgore became the first president of the Texas Conference in 1878 and then served as president of the Illinois Conference from 1885 to 1888.[127] He received charge of all of the Southern states east of the Mississippi in 1888. "At the time there were five ordained white ministers and no black. [When the church was organized in 1863, there had been only 22 ordained ministers and eight licensed ministers in all.][128] There were about 500 white church members and 50 black."[129] By 1918 there were 2,500 black Sabbathkeepers.[130] In 1889 the General Conference heard a report from the Southern Field that pointed out some difficulties workers were facing regarding "the peculiar sentiment and prejudices existing in the South ... [and] the difficulty of reaching both whites and blacks in one public meeting ...."[131] Ellen White was in attendance and made note in her diary summarizing Kilgore's presentation: "Elder Kilgore read a lengthy communication in regard to the color line in the South and how to conduct the work there."[132] (The "color line" was their term for segregation.)

Robert M. Kilgore

A. W. Spalding noted the state of matters in the South: "But though there was an interest among Seventh-day Adventists, resources were small, experience was less, and initiative not great. In 1892 the superintendent of the Southern field, R. M. Kilgore, reported that there were no more than fifty colored Sabbathkeepers in the South."[133] "Kilgore lamented the lack of attention to the spiritual needs and conversion of the Negro people. There had been some accessions in the early years, not too stable, when freedmen who still loved their former masters, as in the case of Killen, followed them; or when, with the holdover of antebellum days, Negro attendance at white gatherings was customary, and thus some of the colored people heard the message preached."[134] However, the use of integrated meetings declined after 1871, as white and black churches separated.[135]

Charles M. Kinney, First Ordained African-American Seventh-day Adventist Minister

On October 5, 1889, R. M. Kilgore and J. O. Corliss ordained thirty-four year old African American Charles M. Kinney to the gospel ministry in the Seventh-day Adventist Church, making him the only ordained black minister in the denomination at the time.[136] In recounting his conversion, Kinney described the obstacles he faced in evangelizing other African Americans:

> I FIRST heard of the truths taught by S. D. Adventists under the labors of J. N. Loughborough, in Reno, Nevada, August, 1878, and soon after commenced to keep the Sabbath. Ever since that time I have had a desire to be able to do something for my people, and have done what I could through the efficient means of the tract society. In 1883, by kind assistance of friends in Nevada, and of the California Conference, I was enabled to spend two consecutive years at Healdsburg College, and May 8, 1885, I was sent to Kansas to labor in the interests of the colored people.[137] June 1, I commenced colportage work in Topeka, and have labored up to date as the weather and my health have permitted. A little over a third of the town has thus been canvassed. Number of pages of tracts loaned, 24,647; sold, 2,309; given away, 11,373; visits made, 662. Three ladies have commenced to keep the Sabbath, one of whom united with the Topeka church. ... Unfortunately for my people, three great obstacles stand in the way between them and the truth; namely, ignorance, superstition, and poverty, and besides, they have drank [sic] deep of the wine of Babylon. In view of these difficulties, large accessions of this people cannot be expected, at least not at the present time; but should there be, it would not add to the financial strength of the cause. But these considerations should not deter me or any one else from doing all possible for them. Therefore I earnestly ask the prayers of all who wish to see the truth brought "before many peoples, and nations, and tongues," that I may have strength, physical, mental, and spiritual to do what I can for the colored people.[138]

Elder Charles M. Kinney

Through Kinney's efforts, about two dozen African Americans joined the church. Kinney left Kansas and worked six months in St. Louis, Missouri, where he won a number of African Americans of "a fine class" to the Advent message.[139] Sadly, they received a mixed reception from the 50-member white Seventh-day Adventist church in the city.[140] After having visited the St. Louis church in 1890, Ellen White expressed her concern about conditions she found:

While at St. Louis a year ago, as I knelt in prayer, these words were presented to me as if written with a pen of fire: "All ye are brethren." The Spirit of God rested upon me in a wonderful manner, and matters were opened to me in regard to the church at St. Louis and in other places. The spirit and words of some in regard to members of the church were an offense to God. They were closing the door of their hearts to Jesus. Among those in St. Louis who believe the truth there are colored people who are true and faithful, precious in the sight of the God of heaven, and *they should have just as much respect as any of God's children.* Those who have spoken harshly to them or have despised them have despised the purchase of the blood of Christ, and they need the transforming grace of Christ in their own hearts, that they may have the pitying tenderness of Jesus toward those who love God with all the fervor of which they themselves are capable. The color of the skin does not determine character in the heavenly courts.[141]

After St. Louis, Kinney went to work, by General Conference request, in Louisville, Kentucky.[142] Kinney continued selling books among African Americans living there and reported that the city had a separate black company of nine believers with a Sabbath School attendance of 30.[143] Opposing separate facilities for the two races, Kinney lamented the "separation of the colored people from the white people," calling it "a great sacrifice upon our part; we lose the blessing of learning the truth."[144] Nonetheless, because the members of his congregation were not allowed to attend his ordination at camp meeting, Kinney was the first to recommend the concept of black conferences, thinking that they would provide a way to work more effectively among African Americans and lessen racial tensions in the church.[145] This would be "a viable strategy wherever integration limited or negated church growth." Kinney stressed, at the 1891 General Conference, the importance of spreading the gospel especially in the South through "a distinctly separate work for blacks. . . . More than anything else, Kinney did not want to see the dignity and worth of his people trampled upon." Neither did he want to see whites refuse the gospel because of the presence of blacks in their churches.[146] It was at this same General Conference that Ellen White presented her seminal sermon (written Nov. 4, 1889), "Our Duty to the Colored People."

Slow Progress in the South

Ellen White gave no public counsel regarding the work for the freedmen between 1867 and 1889 (though she did address bigotry privately in 1880).[147] The church needed to discover for itself conditions in the South and adapt methods for work there, recognizing the principle of the dignity of all humanity, which she had already enunciated. While the Seventh-day Adventist Church was turning its mission to the South, it was also ambitiously entering Europe (1874), Scandinavia (1877), Australia (1885), the Pacific Islands (1886), Russia (1886), Africa (1887), Asia (1888), the Near East (1887), the Caribbean islands (1889), and South America (1892).[148] One of the actions of the 1887 session of the General Conference particularly reflected Ellen White's view of humankind. Church representatives affirmed their belief in the equality of all humans. This affirmation was reported in the *San Francisco Chronicle:*

WHEREAS—The Bible says there is neither Jew nor Greek, there is neither bond nor free, but that all are one in Christ Jesus, therefore be it

Resolved: That it is the decided opinion of this conference that when the colored people of the South accept the third angel's message, they should be received into the Church on an equality with the whites, no distinction whatever being made between black and white in church relation.[149]

Nonetheless, this sense of equality did not generally square with the segregation of society at large.[150] Seventh-day Adventists attempted to establish integrated churches, but to "little effect" because Southern blacks "were quite as reluctant to break the social rule as were the white people, and there was but a handful of their race in the churches."[151]

The reports of the 1889 *General Conference Bulletin* regarding the Seventh-day Adventist work in the South detail the difficulties of the period. Work among the freedmen was particularly slow; yet there were bright spots. An African-American Seventh-day Adventist Church was established in Edgefield Junction, Tennessee in 1886.[152] It was pastored by Harry Lowe, who had heard E. B. Lane speak at the railroad station in 1873. At that time, Lowe had been convicted that what Lane was proclaiming about the Sabbath was the truth. Yet rather than joining the Seventh-day Adventists, he became a Baptist minister. Some time later, after reading a tract on the Sabbath, he decided to follow through with his earlier conviction and became a Seventh-day Adventist. The church licensed him as a minister and gave him charge of the Edgefield Junction church.[153] According to Kinney's reckoning, the second black Seventh-day Adventist congregation was organized in Louisville, Kentucky, on February 16, 1890 with Alonzo Barry as its first pastor.[154] Barry had been born under slavery and had accepted the Seventh-day Adventist message through reading the *Advent Review and Sabbath Herald*.[155] His church made up the largest part of the black membership of the Seventh-day Adventist Church at that time. The third black Seventh-day Adventist church to be established was in Bowling Green, Kentucky, in 1891; the fourth was organized by C. M. Kinney in New Orleans in 1892; and the fifth church, having both black and white members, was organized in Nashville, Tennessee, in 1894.[156] Some of its members came from the Edgefield Junction congregation.[157] In 1894, Alonzo Barry also organized a sixth church in Lexington, Kentucky.[158]

Elder Alonzo Barry

Though difficult, in some ways the years between 1865 and 1885, were sometimes called the "mystic years" because they were easier than the ones to come.[159] The treatment of African Americans deteriorated further, as Alfonso Greene, Jr., summarized:

> During this period of the 1880s and 1890s, southern Democrats steadily disenfranchised black voters and began an assault on a wide range of black rights. The first segregation laws involving railroad coaches on passenger trains were passed by the Tennessee legislature in 1881 and the Florida legislature in 1887. In 1887, black farmers formed and participated in the Colored Farmers Alliance and the Populist Party which gave them few, if any, real benefits. Furthermore, the largest numbers of people, 235, mostly blacks, were lynched in the United States in 1892, more than any other year in U.S. history.[160]

It was under these worsening conditions for African Americans that Ellen White vigorously appealed for Seventh-day Adventists to go south and serve among them. Her appeals are our next topic, and they epitomize her conception of the brotherhood of the races while revealing her pragmatic approach to evangelism under prejudice.

Chapter 7

Appeals for Volunteers

Sin rests upon us as a church because we have not made greater effort for the salvation of souls among the colored people. —Ellen White

Recognizing the increasing difficulties ahead, Ellen White issued an urgent appeal for more volunteers to work among the freedmen of the South. This appeal came before she left for Australia in 1891 in the wake of the rancorous 1888 General Conference session, which had the positive effect of renewed focus on Christ our righteousness for the Seventh-day Adventist Church and for Ellen White, evidenced in her books during the 1890s on the life and teachings of Jesus and in her missiology. In her opening remarks at the General Conference session on March 21, 1891 in Battle Creek, Ellen White said:

> I know that that which I now speak will bring me into conflict. This I do not covet, for the conflict has seemed to be continuous of late years; but I do not mean to live a coward or die a coward, leaving my work undone. I must follow in my Master's footsteps.[1]

Then, in the rest of her message, Mrs. White revealed her willingness "to forgo literary and social acceptance by both whites and blacks . . . to set forth views that would provide for the greater good and the long-range advantage of the temporal and eternal ramifications of the race issue."[2] Beginning with the issue of segregation, or the "color line," as it was then termed, she declared:

> There has been much perplexity as to how our laborers in the South shall deal with the "color line." It has been a question to some how far to concede to the prevailing prejudice against the colored people. The Lord has given us light concerning all such matters. There are principles laid down in His Word that should guide us in dealing with these perplexing questions. The Lord Jesus came to our world to save men and women of all nationalities. He died just as much for the colored people as for the white race. . . .

"The incarnation and sacrificial death of Christ," wrote Adventist historian Benjamin Baker, was Ellen White's "motivation for evangelizing African Americans. . . . The message of the incarnation of Christ was a message of identification with marginalized humanity."[3] Linking the humble status of blacks in the post-emancipation South with that of Jesus while He lived on earth, she said:

> The Redeemer of the world was of humble parentage. He, the Majesty of heaven, the King of glory, humbled Himself to accept humanity, and then He chose a life of poverty and toil. . . . He dwelt among the lowly of the earth. To all appearances he was merely a humble man, with few friends. . . .

In her view, commented Baker, "One could not accept 'Christ our Righteousness' while ignoring the suffering of others. The two were inextricably linked. To ignore those in need was to reject Christ Himself. . . . To Ellen White, the only real Christology was an inclusive Christology. Adventists were to consider blacks in the same social stratum as Jesus, to seek them out as Jesus sought out the socially unpromising, and to 'open their hearts' for Jesus to reproduce his earthly life in them." Declared Mrs. White:

> The same price was paid for the salvation of the colored man as for that of the white man, and the slights put upon the colored people by many who claim to be redeemed by the blood of the Lamb, and who therefore acknowledge themselves debtors to Christ, misrepresent Jesus, and reveal that selfishness, tradition, and prejudice pollute the soul. They are not sanctified through the truth. Those who slight a brother because of his color are slighting Christ.
>
> I call upon every church in our land to look well to your own souls. "Examine yourselves, whether ye be in the faith; prove your own selves. Know ye not your own selves, how that Jesus Christ is in you, except ye be reprobates?" God makes no distinction between the North and the South. Whatever may be your prejudices, your wonderful prudence, do not lose sight of this fact, that unless you put on Christ, and His Spirit dwells in you, you are slaves of sin and of Satan. Many who claim to be children of God are children of the wicked one, and have all his passions, his prejudices, his evil spirit, his unlovely traits of character. But the soul that is indeed transformed will not despise anyone whom Christ has purchased with His own blood.

The Birmingham First Seventh-day Adventist Church provides a contemporary example of racial cooperation.

Remembering behavior she had seen while worshipping the year before with the mixed Seventh-day Adventists congregation in St. Louis, Missouri, she commented:

> Men may have both hereditary and cultivated prejudices, but when the love of Jesus fills the heart, and they become one with Christ, they will have the same spirit that He had. *If a colored brother sits by their side, they will not be offended or despise him. They are journeying to the same heaven, and will be seated at the same table to eat bread in the kingdom of God.* If Jesus is abiding in our hearts we cannot despise the colored man who has the same Saviour abiding in his heart. When these unchristian prejudices are broken down, more earnest effort will be put forth to do missionary work among the colored race. . . .

At the 1889 General Conference session, Robert Kilgore had proposed that "separate meetings in places where racial prejudice is strong be endorsed as policy by General Conference resolutions." He believed that among those who " 'know the power of the truth in their own hearts as it is in Christ Jesus, the prejudices that once existed are gone.' It was the prevailing attitudes of 'those from without' that, he believed, necessitated recognition of the color line. Otherwise, Adventism would not even get a hearing among the White population."[4] Commenting on these resolutions, which she considered unnecessary, Ellen White acknowledged that same year that not all prejudices among Adventists were gone:

> Sin rests upon us as a church because we have not made greater effort for the salvation of souls among the colored people. It will always be a difficult matter to deal with the prejudices of the white people in the South and do missionary work for the colored race. But the way this matter has been treated by some is an offense to God. We need not expect that all will be accomplished in the South that God would do until in our missionary efforts we place this question on the ground of principle, and let those who accept the truth be educated to be Bible Christians, working according to Christ's order. *You have no license from God to exclude the colored people from your places of worship. Treat them as Christ's property, which they are, just as much as yourselves. They should hold membership in the church with the white brethren.* Every effort should be made to wipe out the terrible wrong which has been done them. At the same time we must not carry things to extremes and run into fanaticism on this question. Some would think it right to throw down every partition wall and intermarry with the colored people, but this is not the right thing to teach or to practice.
>
> Let us do what we can to send to this class laborers who will work in Christ's name, who will not fail nor be discouraged. We should educate colored men to be missionaries among their own people. We should recognize talent where it exists among the people, and those who have ability should be placed where they may receive an education.
>
> Is it not time for us to live so fully in the light of God's countenance that we who receive so many favors and blessings from Him may know how to treat those less favored, not working from the world's standpoint, but from the Bible standpoint? Is it not right in this line that Christian effort is most needed? Is it not here that our influence should be brought to bear against the customs and practices of the world? Should it not be the work of the white people to elevate the standard of character among the colored race, to teach them how Christians should live, by exemplifying the Spirit of Christ, showing that we are one brotherhood?[5]

The sermon was published as a tract, "Our Duty to the Colored People," and promptly put to one side. Its message would have no noticeable effect until Ellen White's son Edson, who was pursuing commercial ventures, resulting in financial loss and his own spiritual indifference, later learned of the tract and took it as his spiritual marching orders for a intrepid work among the freedmen of Vicksburg, Mississippi.[6]

Once Ellen White was established in Australia, she continued her appeals to the church in a series of ten articles in the *Review and Herald* that began in April 1895. Ciro Sepúlveda characterized their emphasis: "The articles she wrote not only call[ed] the church to task on . . . the 'color line' but also display a very intimate working knowledge of what was happening to African-Americans in the United States."[7] The first article in the series was entitled, "Work among the Colored People." In it, she declared that the freedmen had been neglected out of the same motives as the wounded man in the parable of the Good Samaritan, and she added:

> What should be done for the colored race has long been a vexed question, because professed Christians have not had the Spirit of Christ. They have been called by his name, but they have not imitated his example. Men have thought it necessary to plan in such a way as to meet the prejudice of the white people; and a wall of separation in religious worship has been

built up between the colored people and the white people. The white people have declared themselves willing that the colored people should be converted. They have no objection to this. They were willing that they should be grafted into the same parent stock, Christ, and become branches with themselves of the living Vine; yet they were not willing to sit by the side of their colored brethren, and sing and pray and bear witness to the truth which they had in common. Not for a moment could they tolerate the idea that they should together bear the fruit that should be found on the Christian tree. The image of Christ might be stamped upon the soul; but it still would be necessary to have a separate church and a separate service. But the question is, Is this in harmony with the moving of the Spirit of God? Is it not after the manner in which the Jewish people acted in the days of Christ? Is not this prejudice against the colored people on the part of the white people similar to that which was cherished by the Jews against the Gentiles? . . .

"Le bon-Samaritain" [The Good Samaritan], Aimé Morot, 1880

A year later she would again lament: "How little of the spirit of Christ has been manifested in the treatment given to the colored race in this so-called Christian country. . . . They are often treated as if it were a disgrace to sit by their side, or even to worship in the same congregation."[8] Yet, she knew that methods of labor would need to adapt to changing social circumstances:

> No human mind should seek to draw the line between the colored and the white people. *Let circumstances indicate what shall be done;* for the Lord has his hand on the lever of circumstances.

Some administrators did not catch this principle and injured Adventist influence by attempting to force integration indiscriminately.[9] Nonetheless, Ellen White anticipated Christian post-racialism:

> As the truth is brought to bear upon the minds of both colored and white people, as souls are thoroughly converted, they will become new men and women in Christ Jesus. Christ says, "A new heart also will I give you," and that new heart bears the divine image. Those who are converted among the white people will experience a change in their sentiments. The prejudice which they have inherited and cultivated toward the colored race will die away. They will realize that there is no respect of persons with God. Those who are converted among the colored race will be cleansed from sin, will wear the white robe of Christ's righteousness, which has been woven in the loom of heaven. Both white and colored people must enter into the path of obedience through the same way. The test will come not as regards the outward complexion, but as regards the condition of the heart. Both the white and the colored people have the same Redeemer, who has paid the ransom money with his own life for every member of the human family.[10]

In a letter in July 1895, Ellen White expressed regret over the lack of progress among Southern African Americans:

After the war, if the Northern people had made the South a real missionary field, if they had not left the Negroes to ruin through poverty and ignorance, thousands of souls would have been brought to Christ. But it was an unpromising field, and the Catholics have been more active in it than any other class.[11] ... The colored people might have been helped with much better prospects of success years ago than now. The work is now tenfold harder than it would have been then. ...[12]

In her November article, she outlined practical methods of ministry:

How many have left the colored race to perish by the wayside? Since the slaves gained their freedom at terrible loss of life both to the North and to the South, they have been greatly neglected by those who professed to know God, and as a result thousands of them have failed to gain spiritual freedom. But shall this indifference continue? Shall not decided efforts be made to save them? ...

Why should not Seventh-day Adventists become true laborers together with God in seeking to save the souls of the colored race? Instead of a few, why should not many go forth to labor in this long-neglected field? Where are the families who will become missionaries, and who will engage in labor in this field? Where are the men who have means and experience so that they can go forth to these people, and work for them just where they are? There are men who can educate them in agricultural lines, who can teach the colored people to sow seed and plant orchards. There are others who can teach them to read, and can give them an object lesson from their own life and example. Show them what you yourself can do to gain a livelihood, and it will be an education to them. Are we not called upon to do this very work?[13]

Seventh-day Adventist agriculturalists later took up this challenge in Vicksburg, teaching freedmen better methods of agriculture. In her December 3 article, Ellen White described the benefits for the freedmen's of associating with white Seventh-day Adventists of experience:

Are there not men, women, and youth who will go forth to establish schools, and thus become teachers to instruct the colored people so that they may be enabled to read the word of God? We must teach them to read God's word, or they will become the ready dupes of false shepherds that misinterpret the Scriptures, and that manufacture doctrines and teach traditions which will lead them into the paths of perdition. There are preachers and teachers among the colored people who are addicted to licentious habits; and how can they understand the binding claims of the law of God, when the standard of righteousness is not revealed and exalted before their eyes by the precept and example of their teachers? We must go among them, and show them how to honor and obey God's law, in order that they may be prepared to have a part in the new earth. ... In all your labor let it be apparent that you know Jesus. Present his purity and saving grace, that by beholding, these people may become changed into the divine image. Among most of the colored people we find unseemly practices in their worship of God. They become much excited, and put forth physical exertions that are uncalled for in the solemn worship of God. Their superstitious ideas and uncomely practices cannot at once be dispelled.[14] We must not combat their ideas and treat them with contempt. But let the worker give them an example of what constitutes true heart-service in religious worship. *Let not the colored people be excluded from the religious assemblies of the white people.* They have no chance to exchange their superstitious exercises for a worship that is more sacred and elevating if they are shut out from association with intelligent white people who should give them an example of what they should be and do. Let the white people practice the self-denial necessary, and let them remember that nothing is to be regarded as unimportant which affects the religious life of so vast a number of people as that which composes the colored race. They conduct their worship according to the instruction they have received, and they think that a religion which has no excitement, no noise, no bodily exercises, is not worth the name of religion. These ignorant worshipers need instruction and guidance. They can be won by kindness, and can be confirmed in well-doing. Both old and young will need to be instructed as one would instruct a family of children.[15]

In her December 10 article, Mrs. White remonstrated with influential Seventh-day Adventists for overlooking the needs of the South:

It is not proper to pile building upon building in localities where there are abundant facilities, and neglect fields that are nigh and afar off, where there is need of starting missionary enterprises. Instead of closing our eyes and senses to the wants of those who have nothing, instead of adding more and more facilities to those that are already abundant, let us seek to see what we can do to relieve the distresses of the poor, bruised souls of the colored people.[16]

Ellen White's ideals were radical for the times, yet she was not naive. In her December 17 article, "An Example in History," she again drew parallels from the parable of the Good Samaritan and from the education of the Hebrews after their enslavement in Egypt, recognizing the residual effects of slavery and the prejudice that made working in the South difficult:

Walls of separation have been built up between the whites and the blacks. These walls of prejudice will tumble down of themselves as did the walls of Jericho, when Christians obey the word of God, which enjoins on them supreme love to their maker and impartial love to their neighbors. For Christ's sake, let us *do something now*. Let every church whose members claim to believe the truth for this time, look at this neglected, downtrodden race, that, as a result of slavery, have been deprived of the privilege of thinking and acting for

A young black sharecropper standing in a cotton field in Pulaski County, Arkansas

> themselves. They have been kept at work in the cotton fields, have been driven before the lash *like brute beasts*, and their children have received no enviable heritage. Many of the slaves had noble minds; but the fact that their skin was dark, was sufficient reason for the whites to *treat them as though they were beasts*. When freedom was proclaimed to the captives, a favorable time was given in which to establish schools, and to teach the people to take care of themselves. Much of this kind of work was done by various denominations, and God honored their work.[17] *Those who attempted to work for the black race had to suffer persecution*, and *many were martyrs* to the cause. It was difficult to educate these people in correct ideas, because they had been compelled to do according to the word of their human masters. . . . To show sympathy for the released slaves, was to expose one's self to ridicule, hatred, and persecution. Old-time prejudice still exists, and those who labor in behalf of the colored race will have to encounter difficulties.[18]

In articles in January and February 1896, Ellen White optimistically addressed the additional challenges Seventh-day Adventists would face in uplifting Southern freedmen:

> When they were slaves, they were taught to do the will of those who called them their property. They were kept in ignorance, and today there are thousands among them that cannot read. Many who profess to be teachers among them are corrupt in character, and they interpret the Scriptures in such a way as to fulfill their own purposes, and degrade those who are in their power. The colored people are taught that they must not think or judge for themselves, but that their ministers must be permitted to judge for them.[19] Because of this, the divine plan of salvation has been covered up with a mass of human rubbish and falsehood. The Scripture has been perverted, and the people have been so instructed as to be easily seduced by evil spirits. Mind, as well as body, has been long abused. The whole system of slavery was originated by Satan, who delights in tyrannizing over human beings. Though he has been successful in degrading and corrupting the black race, many are possessed of decided ability, and if they were blessed with opportunities, they would show more intelligence than do many of their more favored brethren among the white people. *Thousands may now be uplifted, and may become agents by which to help those of their own race. There are many who feel the necessity of becoming elevated, and when faithful teachers open the Scriptures, presenting the truth in its native purity to the colored people, the darkness will be dispelled under the bright beams of the Sun of righteousness.* Directed in their search for truth by those who have had advantages enabling them to know the truth, they will become intelligent in the Scriptures.[20]
>
> There are others among the colored people who have quick perceptions and bright minds. Many of the colored race are rich in faith and trust. God sees among them precious jewels that will one day shine out brightly. The colored people deserve more from the hands of the white people than they have received. *There are thousands who have minds capable of cultivation and uplifting*. With proper labor, many who have been looked upon as hopeless will become educators of their race. Through the grace of God the race that the enemy has for generations oppressed may rise to the dignity of God-given manhood and womanhood.[21]

Ellen White's 1891 appeal and the additional articles in the *Review and Herald* are today available in the booklet *The Southern Work*, which was first printed in 1898 by Edson White and was reprinted, beginning in 1966, in facsimile edition.[22] The booklet also includes additional counsels on how to avoid conflict over Sunday labor and the inadvisability of an integrated colony that A. F. Ballenger's proposed (see chapter 8).

Edson White Responds to His Mother's Appeals

Ellen White's recently released letters provide an opportunity to read in context the letters she wrote her son Edson in the early 1890s. Her appeals for her son to let God guide his life were frequent and tender. When Edson renewed his commitment of faith in 1893 and looked for a practical way to serve the gospel cause.[23] Writing his mother, he said: "I have been thinking of going down into Tennessee to work among the colored people. . . . I still hope and trust in God, and am sure He will care for me. I have proved my own way and it is a poor way. I now want God's way, and I know it will be a good way."[24] Conversing with Dr. J. E. Caldwell of Knoxville, Tennessee, he learned about his mother's appeal for workers to go into the South. He became convinced of his mission: to educate and deliver the truths of Scripture to Southern African Americans.[25] He began looking for a printed copy of his mother's appeal. A painter at the Review and Herald Publishing Association office told him of seeing the tract at the former office of the International Tract Society. Anxiously climbing the stairs to the vacated office, he entered the room and found the tract.[26] It included these impressive words: "Not all can go through a long course of education, but if they are consecrated to God, and learn of Him, many can without this do much to bless others. . . . let them be messengers of God's grace, their hearts throbbing in unison with Christ's great heart of love . . ."[27] He began formulating a plan that would take him into the heart of Dixie.

James Edson White

Will Palmer

He shared his plan with his friend Will Palmer, who was also an entrepreneur willing to venture for God.[28] After a brief training course in Battle Creek, the two collaborated in designing

The "Morning Star," as Edson enlarged it in 1896

and directing the construction of the 72-foot *Morning Star* steamboat in Michigan. Then they sailed it down the Mississippi into the heart of Dixie.[29] (Ironically, one of his commercial ventures had been boat construction.[30]) Reaching Memphis in the fall of 1894, they were fined five hundred dollars for operating the steamship without a license. Publicity from their arrest aroused curiosity about Seventh-day Adventists, and they used the opportunity to study the Bible with those who were interested. As a result, some were baptized, like V. O. Cole and his wife. Cole became a life-long literature evangelist.[31]

Then on January 10, 1895, they reached Vicksburg, Mississippi, where White and his staff "found ready access to Negro homes and churches; but as soon as people began to accept their teachings, these avenues closed. When this happened, White and his associates leased a lot and built a small chapel at a cost of

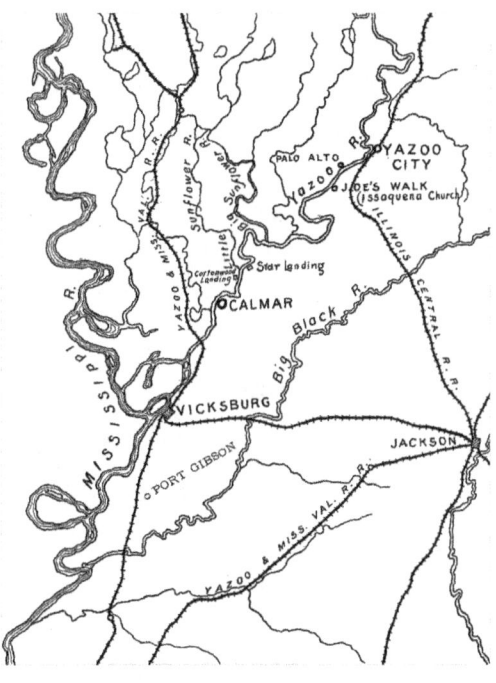

Locations of schools begun through the "Morning Star"

$150. Starting a night school, they soon had 150 attending. During the four years the building was in use, it had to be doubled in size because of the growing interest of the people."[32] White also started a day school for children. In December 1897, White traveled up the Yazoo River, where he established several schools in other locales—Yazoo City, Lintonia and Wilsonia (northern and western suburbs of Yazoo City), Palo Alto, Joe's Walk, and Calmar.[33] The schools had ten teachers, black and white.[34] Adventist lecturers presented the advantages of diversified agriculture and farming techniques to increase crop yield.[35] (Historian Ciro Sepúlveda suggested that these practical Southern schools had a trickle up effect on Seventh-day Adventist schools in the North.[36]) The planter elite in the Delta did not appreciate the Adventists educating their cheap labor force. Local newspapers insinuated that the Adventists did not really care about them. Yet, when Adventists learned from Edson about a lean growing season and a hard winter that limited the people's income, they had sent fifty barrels of clothing along with barrels of flour, meal, grits, molasses and dried apples to distribute to people in the towns on the Yazoo.[37] Ultimately, Edson was instrumental in starting 55 schools in the South, and he wrote several primers and a simplified life of Christ for use in the schools. Sale of these books was a source of income for the Southern Missionary Society.

A selection of Edson White's books

Difficulties in non-segregated work continued to increase. Consequently, Mrs. White gave pragmatic counsel on how to proceed under the reality of prejudice. That is the topic of our next chapter.

1 2 3 4 5 6 7 8 9 10 11 12 13 14

***Morning Star* Southern Missionary Workers**

1. Isaiah Moore, of Pulaski, Iowa, deck hand and teacher in night schools
2. S. W. Trump, printer and pressman
3. Franklin Henry Bryant, stenographer and teacher in night schools
4. J. R. Moore of Vicksburg, boat pilot
5. Dan G. Stephenson, supervisor of the work at Calmar
6. Fred W. Halladay, a public speaker, Bible worker, and teacher in night schools
7. Mrs. Ida C. (Wekell) Halladay, Bible worker and teacher in house-to-house and night schools
8. Fred R. Rogers, principal of Lintonia mission school and night schools
9. Chester Rogers, son of the Rogers
10. Frank H. Schramm, of Grand Rapids, Bible instructor and teacher in house to house and public night schools
11. Mrs. Minnie Rogers, assistant teacher in Lintonia and instructor in music
12. James Edson White
13. Emma McDearmond White (Edson's wife), teacher in the night schools, she also visited with the people
14. Anna Slaughter, assistant in the kitchen

African-American teachers not pictured: Miss Anna Agee and Miss Anna Jensen taught at Vicksburg; J. W. Dancer managed the school in Columbus, Mississippi; M. C. Strachan and W. H. Sebastian taught in the Yazoo area; Franklin G. Warnick (pictured on page 112) taught in Lintonia

White teachers not pictured: Miss M. M. Osborne and Miss Maggie Scott Baptist missionaries to Mississippi who studied the Bible with Will Palmer and became Seventh-day Adventists, taught in Vicksburg; R. T. Nash (pictured on page 112) taught in Lintonia; N. B. King, of Yazoo City, who had been a public school teacher, ministered in Vicksburg, Mississippi.

Chapter 8

Threading the Needle

> Ellen White left no "solution" other than the grace of Christ, but she left no doubt that her position on separation of the races was merely a temporary guideline of expediency to be used "until the Lord shows us a better way." —Ron Graybill[1]

There are ideals, and there is reality. Ellen White promoted ideals in race relations, yet she recognized that the ideals had to be tempered by reality. She warned, "A terrible condition of things is certainly opening before us. According to the light which is given me in regard to the Southern field, the work there must be done as wisely and carefully as possible. . . .The time has not yet come for us to work as though there were no prejudice."[2] Working between the ideal and the reality of the "condition of things," Ellen White "threaded the needle" for ministry within the South. Within the rapidly changing climate of the early twentieth century, Ellen White issued counsels that seem to contradict her earlier ones. In *E. G. White and Church Race Relations*, Ronald D. Graybill addressed the apparent contradiction between Ellen White's statements of the 1890s and those of 1908. Aligning Ellen White's twentieth century counsels regarding race relations with newspaper clippings collected by Clarence C. Crisler from 1903 to 1912 for the book on the history of the Southern efforts, Graybill argued convincingly that deteriorating conditions in the country mandated Ellen White's adapted stance.[3] She astutely avoided fanning controversy, applying her efforts to actually doing good among both races in the South.

Clarence C. Crisler, literary assistant to Ellen G. White

"The Long, Dark Night" in the "Age of Washington"

What was the state of relations between the two races from 1895 to 1910? John Hope Franklin called this period the "long, dark night." Rayford Logan called it the "nadir," or lowest point, of American race relations.[4] Black rights advocate and scholar William E. B. Du Bois put it bluntly: "The Northern people, after freeing the Negro and giving him the right of suffrage, left him high and dry."[5] John Hope Franklin saw the period as lasting until 1923.[6] It was also during this period—on September 18, 1895—that Booker T. Washington delivered his now famous speech at the Cotton States and International Exposition in Atlanta, Georgia. That statement set the tone for race relations in America for years to come. The "Age of Washington" began with that speech, for in it he presented his metaphor

Booker T. Washington

W. E. B. Du Bois

for smooth working relations between the races: "In all things that are purely social we can be as separate as the fingers, yet one as the hand in all things essential to mutual progress."[7] In that same speech, Washington also said: "The wisest among my race understand that the agitation of questions of social equality is the extremist folly and that progress in the enjoyment of all the privileges that will come to us must be the result of severe constant struggle rather than of artificial forcing."[8] He emphasized industrial education for blacks and was considered "sensible" and "progressive," and he was well received by most audiences. Andrew Carnegie supported him, and even the racist Benjamin Tillman admitted that Booker T. Washington was "the greatest colored man of this country."

As Clark Howell, editor of the *Atlanta Constitution*, framed it, the South's message to the North was: "Just let us alone." The people of the South believed that Booker T. Washington had struck the right emphasis. The Battle Creek *Sunday Record* predicted: "[T]he Southern people will give him hearty support in his efforts to keep the Negro out of politics and build up the industrial education of his race."[9] Washington's solution was viewed with greater favor than all other solutions, which fit "into a spectrum ranging from a return to slavery to expatriation to Africa, domestic colonization, and systematic distribution, 'separate but equal'; civil, political, and social equality; and absorption."[10] The biggest challenge to Washington's solution was that of W. E. B. Du Bois, an African American with a doctorate from Harvard. His radical solution was the "abolition of distinctions based on race."[11] (As important as Du Bois was in American civil rights, he was not a prominent figure in Crisler's collection of newspaper clippings until 1909, when Du Bois formed the National Association for the Advancement of Colored People, or NAACP.) The NAACP's demand for "immediate political and social equality" was thwarted by Washington's solution.

Sadly, it was during this period that racial hatred increased dramatically in three main areas: *disenfranchisement* of black voters, the increase of *violence* toward blacks, and the public *segregation* of blacks and whites in public buildings and transportation.[12]

Disenfranchisement of Black Voters

In reality, the good feelings between the North and the South were purchased by the loss of African-American rights in the virtual nullification of the Fifteenth Amendment. The Fifteenth Amendment to the Constitution, which stipulated that race could not be used to deprive a man of the right to vote, was undermined by ingenious methods of disenfranchisement. "Literacy tests" were effective in keeping African Americans from voting due to their lack of education. Illiterate whites could circumvent these tests by passing the "understanding clause," the "good character clause," or the "grandfather clause," which were applied inequitably to disenfranchise black Americans.[13] Between 1895 and 1910, the undermining of this right began with Louisiana in 1898 and spread to North Carolina in 1900, Alabama in 1901, Virginia in 1902, Georgia in 1908, and Oklahoma in 1910.[14]

The Fifteenth Amendment

"The right of citizens of the United States to vote shall not be denied or abridged by the United States or by any state on account of race, color, or previous condition of servitude."

In his inaugural speech, March 4, 1909, William Howard Taft reflected on the Fifteenth Amendment in such a way that it gave many black and white Americans cause for optimism. He declared:

> While the fifteenth amendment has not been generally observed in the past, it ought to be observed, and the tendency of southern legislation to-day is toward the enactment of electoral qualifications which shall square with that amendment. Of course, the mere adoption of a constitutional law is only one step in the right direction. It must be fairly and justly enforced as well. In time both will come.[15]

Taft was either unwilling or unable to enforce the Amendment, and the "tests" were still not applied equally.

William Howard Taft
27th U. S. President

Violence Toward African Americans

There were "bloody mob wars upon the Negro" in North Carolina and Georgia. "Shortly after the red-shirt, white-supremacy election of 1898 in North Carolina a mob of 400 white men led by a former congressman, invaded the colored district of Wilmington, set fire to buildings, killed and wounded many Negroes, and chased hundreds out of town."[16] Following Hoke Smith's 1906 campaign for governor of Georgia, in which he played on white fear of African-American atrocities, four days of anarchy broke out in Atlanta, "in which roving mobs, white and black, freely looted, murdered, and lynched."[17]

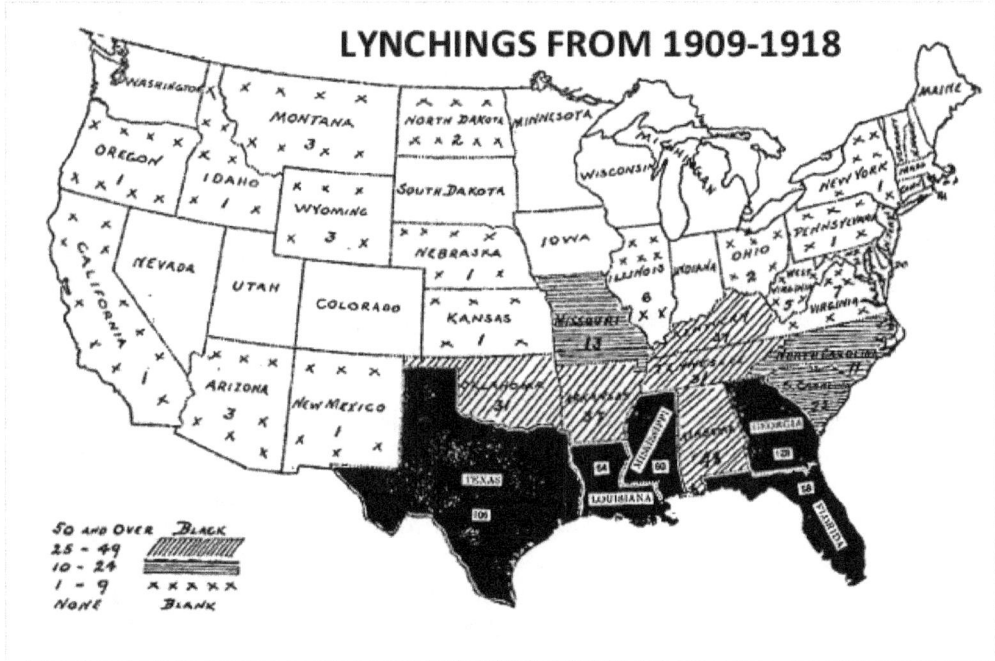

Source: *Thirty Years of Lynching in the United States, 1889-1913*, p. viii

The percentage of black lynchings increased exponentially during this period. C. Van Woodward wrote in *The Strange Career of Jim Crow*: "[O]f the lynchings committed in the first ten years of the present century, 11.4 per cent of the victims were white. In the previous decade 32.2 per cent had been white. " This means that a much greater percentage of lynchings were black for these years. "From 1889 to 1899, 82 per cent of all lynchings occurred in the Southern States. These were the eleven former Confederate States plus Missouri, Kentucky, and Indian Territory, which became Oklahoma in 1907. In the first decade of the twentieth century, 91.1 per cent of all lynchings occurred in these States."[18] This was most definitely racially biased.

Ellen White commented on the increasing violence: "The colored people have had before them the example of commonness and adultery. These evils are all through our world, but when the poor, wretched, ignorant race, who know scarcely anything of purity and righteousness, do commit sin—sin that committed by white people is scarcely condemned—colored people are tortured to death whether proved guilty or not. And the nation that permits this bears the name of Christian. God says, 'Shall I not judge for these things?' "[19]

Public Segregation of Blacks and Whites

Gradually, segregation became institutionalized at the highest level of the United States government. In the Slaughter House Cases (1873), United States v. Reese (1876), and United States v. Cruikshank (1876), the Court "drastically curtailed the privileges and immunities recognized as being under federal protection, thereby removing the protection of the government" for the rights of blacks.[20] In the Civil Rights Case of 1883, "the court held that the Fourteenth Amendment gave Congress power to restrain states but not individuals from the acts of racial discrimination and segregation."[21] In Hall v. deCuir (1877), "the court ruled that a state could not prohibit segregation on a common carrier." At the same time, to get elected, Rutherford B. Hayes brokered a compromise that allowed the whites of the Southern states to work out their own relations with blacks when federal troops were withdrawn.[22] In Louisville, New Orleans and Texas Railroad v. Mississippi (1890), "the court ruled that a state could constitutionally require segregation on carriers."[23] In 1896, the United States Supreme Court "heard Plessy v. Ferguson and decided that the practice of keeping African Americans segregated from the rest of the community did not violate the Constitution. The judges upheld a new legal doctrine, 'separate but equal.' All but one of the judges of the highest court of the land skillfully argued that the Fourteenth Amendment was never intended to abolish distinctions based on color. The 'color line' [or segregation] was given the blessing of the Supreme Court. The decision was carefully calculated to prevent the mingling of the races."[24] In Williams v. Mississippi (1898), "The court completed the opening of the legal road to proscription, segregation and disfranchisement by approving the Mississippi plan for depriving the Negroes of the franchise."[25] Even academics supported the doctrine of the superiority of the Caucasian race. As Woodward put it: "It was not that Southern politicians needed any support from learned circles to sustain their own doctrines, but they found that such intellectual endorsement of their racist theories facilitated

A sign of segregation at a Greyhound Bus station in Rome, Georgia

acceptance of their views and policies."[26] By the end of the first decade of the twentieth century, segregation had gained the status of "the American way of life."[27]

In 1907, Southern lawmakers used fear of "the black peril" to repeal the contract in state constitutions known as "Kirby's Digest." This contract "guaranteed the Negro equal rights with Caucasians in hotels, saloons, theaters, railroads, and other public and quasi-public places."[28] Fear of "the ultimate amalgamation of the races" fueled the undermining of black rights.[29]

Working Under the Dark Cloud of Prejudice

Seventh-day Adventist efforts to educate blacks was at times met with vigorous opposition. In late 1898, Edson White received a telegram while in Vicksburg stating that F. R. Rogers had been ordered to leave Lintonia. Dr. J. A. Crisler, a physician in Yazoo City, sent word that blacks, agitated by local whites, were going to attack the Seventh-day Adventists during the holidays. "We are in trouble," wrote Rogers the next morning. Thankfully, White had taken the *Morning Star* to Vicksburg, so plans to dynamite the steamboat were thwarted.[30] Edson wrote, "On receiving these communications we all felt that great caution and much heavenly wisdom was required to enable us to take the proper course in this matter. The testimonies instruct us that great caution must be exercised so that these evilly disposed persons shall not be aroused and the work closed up as a result.... I am planning now to issue an extra of the *Gospel Herald*. In this we will show our leading denominational institutions.... It will explain that we have nothing whatever to do with politics, that we have not come down to invade the customs of the country, but only to make better men, better citizens, better Christians out of the people."[31] They had done nothing to challenge Southern prejudices. Yet their work and their lives were in danger. They trusted God and docked the *Morning Star* in Yazoo anyway.

By the summer of 1899, new troubles had arisen. White reported to his mother what took place in Calmar, Mississippi, on the evening of May 11, 1899:

Two weeks ago tonight a mob of about 25 white men came to our church at Calmer [sic] at about midnight. They brought out Brother [Dan] Stephenson, our worker, and then looted the church, burning books, maps, charts, etc. They hunted for Brother Casey, our leading colored brother of that place, but he had escaped in time so they did not reach him. They then went to the house of Brother Olvin, called him out, and whipped him with a cow-hide. I think they would have killed him if it had not been for a friendly white man who ordered them to stop whipping after they had struck a few blows. They did not pay any attention to him at first, but he drew his revolver, and said the next man who struck a blow would hear from him, and then they stopped. During the time[,] they shot at Brother Olvin's wife, and struck her in the leg, but did not hurt her seriously.[32] They took Brother Stephenson to the nearest railway station, put him on the cars, and sent him out of the country. They posted notice on

Chapel and parsonage, Calmar, Mississippi

the church forbidding me to return, and forbidding the steamer *Morning Star* to land between Yazoo City and Vicksburg.

The whole difficulty arose from our efforts to aid the colored people. We had given them clothing where in need, and food to those who were hungry, and had taught them some better ideas about farming, introduced different seeds such as peanuts, beans, etc., that bring a high price, . . . and this the whites would not stand.[33]

Seventh-day Adventist historian Arthur W. Spalding described Mrs. Olvin's wound as far more serious—it was "a wound from which she was ever afterwards lame."[34] Edson White added other details in a pamphlet entitled "The Southern Work: Mob Violence." He wrote that Olvin was a marked man for his having given many Bible studies around the area and that Olvin's daughter Mary had seen the whole thing, for, when the men first came to their door, she said: "Well, papa, I suppose you must give your life for the truth!" He also said that Olvin purchased a Winchester rifle to retaliate, yet he was persuaded not to use it because of the effect it would have on the work in Yazoo County and in the South as a whole.[35] Perhaps from concern that legal action might be taken against them, those involved in the attack apologized to Olvin, assuring him that he would be safe to return to their little chapel.[36]

Ellen White recognized that Seventh-day Adventists would have to exercise even greater caution in presenting the Seventh-day Adventist message in a region with marked prejudice. Just a few days after she received Edson's letter about the beating of Brother Olvin, A. F. Ballenger wrote Mrs. White proposing that a number of white Adventist families "purchase a plot of land and develop it while teaching blacks agricultural methods and the Adventist message."[37] On June 5, Mrs. White wrote Ballenger: "The relation of the two races has been a matter hard to deal with, and I fear that it will ever remain a most perplexing problem."[38] Then she cautioned him:

Albion Fox Ballenger

As you say, there is no more fruitful field than the South. It is the prejudice of the white against the black race that makes this field hard, very hard. The whites who have oppressed the colored people still have the same spirit. They did not lose it, although they were conquered in war. They are determined to make it appear that the blacks were better off in slavery than since they were set free. Any provocation from the blacks is met with the greatest cruelty. The field is one that needs to be worked with the greatest discretion. Any mingling of the white people with the colored people, as sleeping in their houses, or showing them friendship as would be shown by the whites to those of their own color, is exasperating to the white people of the South. Yet these same persons employ colored women to nurse their children and further, not a few white men have had children by colored women. . . .

It is from the whites that the greatest opposition may be expected. This is the quarter that we shall need to watch. The white people are prejudiced against the doctrines taught by the Seventh-day Adventists, and a religious opposition is the greatest difficulty. The white people will stir up the blacks by telling them all kinds of stories; and the blacks, who can lie even when it is for their interest to speak the truth, will stir up the whites with falsehoods, and the whites who want an occasion will seize upon any pretext for taking revenge, even upon those of their own color who are presenting the truth. This is the danger. As far as possible, everything that will stir up the race prejudice of the white people should be avoided. There is danger of closing the door so that our white laborers will not be able to work in some places in the South.

Those who undertake work in the South must not enter into any plan for colonizing, for this will place them in perilous circumstances. Some families should be found who for Christ's sake will volunteer to enter the Southern field. At Huntsville there is a building, and something has been done there. Let the proper ones try to make that place different by bringing into it new, live elements. This plant must not become useless. Elements must be brought in which will make the institution self-sustaining. Then if it is necessary, cheap additions can be made. I would not encourage your plan."[39]

Old Plantation Mansion, Huntsville

In this same letter, she predicted: "At the least provocation the poison of prejudice is ready to show its true character, and provocations will be found. It is very hard to make the work run smoothly. Outbreaks will come at any moment and all unexpectedly and there will be destruction of property and even of life itself. Hot-headed people, professing the faith, but without judgment, will think they can do as they please, but they will find themselves in a tight place. I speak that which I know. . . . Parties are already formed and they are waiting, burning with a desire to serve their master, the devil, and do abominable work."[40] Such prejudicial circumstances were precisely the situation in which workers found themselves while laboring in Mississippi. She had expressed the same concern in her original 1891 appeal:

There are able colored ministers who have embraced the truth. Some of these feel unwilling to devote themselves to work for their own race; they wish to preach to the white people. These men are making a great mistake. *They should seek most earnestly to save their own race, and they will not by any means be excluded from the gatherings of the white people.* White men and white women should be qualifying themselves to work among the colored people. There is a large work to be done in educating this ignorant and downtrodden class. We must do more unselfish missionary work than we have done in the Southern states, not picking out merely the most favorable fields. God has children among the colored people all over the land. They need to be enlightened. There are unpromising ones, it is true, but you will find similar degradation among the white people; but even among the lower classes there are souls who will embrace the truth. Some will not be steadfast. Feelings and habits that have been confirmed by lifelong practices will be hard to correct; it will not be easy to implant ideas of purity and holiness, refinement and elevation. But God regards the capacity of every man, He marks the surroundings, and sees how these have formed the *character*, and He pities these souls.[41]

African Americans who wanted to preach to whites were disregarding the great need among their fellow African Americans. Laborers in that grand field were woefully few. Moreover, these black preachers were unmindful of the prejudice that they would face in preaching to whites at that time.

To Ignore Prejudice Would Close Down Prospects

Edson wrote his mother in 1899 about the approach that Mrs. A. S. Steele, the principal and proprietor of the *Colored Orphans' Home* in Chattanooga, was using in dealing with segregation in the South and about Elder N. W. Allee's concerns regarding it:

> He said he realized that the workers among the colored people carried their lives in their hands. This is as true a saying as anything ever spoken. The North MUST realize that the workers coming here will have to be the most careful that it is possible for them to be. If not they will not only imperil their own lives, but will also imperil the lives and bring great distress upon the colored people themselves.[42]

Due to the delay in entering upon the work, Edson wrote his mother in 1899: "I can see that it is far more difficult than it was when we went down five years ago."[43]

Edson believed that Steele's ideas, which were accepted by Dr. John Harvey Kellogg, would place Seventh-day Adventist laborers in the South in grave danger. A few days later, he wrote: "I felt that her work has done much harm in some respects, as she is inclined to disregard all Southern prejudices and customs to be met in the work, which we know to be a dangerous thing."[44]

Ellen White wrote to Frank E. Belden shortly after the confrontation in Yazoo City, Mississippi, telling him how black people had been "deprived of the means of bettering their condition," and "almost every possible avenue to improvement" had been closed to them. God would "judge the nation for their neglect and abuse of His creatures. ... God calls for His workers to consecrate themselves to the cause of justice and reform. . . . . Let the colored people be treated as human beings. *Let them be uplifted.* The youth should be educated to become missionaries among their own people. . . . The age in which we live calls for decided reformatory action; but wisdom must be exercised in dealing with the race that has so long been degraded and abused. That which is now undertaken cannot be carried forward *as it might have been had the white churches at the time of the abolition of slavery acted as Christ would have done in their place.*"[45] Ellen White held the churches responsible for not having acted sooner on the freedmen's behalf.

What about Ellen White's counsels regarding separate schools for African Americans in the South? After the mob violence and the controversy with Kellogg, Edson wrote a woman in Washington, DC, who was planning to work for African Americans there, interpreting the testimonies as he understood them: "Now in regard to the testimonies respecting colored schools unmixed with whites. I understand that this refers to the South only where mixed schools will not be tolerated. God forbid that we should build up color lines where they do not now exist. . . . I think there is a rule that we may safely follow in this color line business. We must regard it only as it affects the outside element in such a way as to close up our work and injure its usefulness."[46] Because he worked more closely with his mother on race relations than anyone else, Edson's understanding of his mother's counsels is most helpful. Her exhortations for black Seventh-day Adventists to teach and preach to those of their own race reflects Edson and Rogers' experience in Yazoo City. Edson wrote his mother in November 1899: "At this place the prejudice was very strong against Bro. Rogers and his wife teaching the colored school, and we felt very sure that it was necessary to put colored teachers into this school and this would allay the prejudice."[47]

Edson wrote Elder Allee about the real danger that Brother Rogers was facing:

> There is a matter of utmost importance that I must write you about. It is Bro. Rogers and the school at Lintonia. It is the settled conviction of the workers here that unless a change is made in the teachers of this school, and colored teachers put in, violence will be done to Bro. Rogers. I tried to talk [present] this when you people were here, but it did not seem to impress you as it did us who are and have been on the ground through it all. Now I feel that the time has come when something MUST BE DONE. I can never consent to keep this faithful man in such a place of danger as he now occupies. I think I shall not favor white teachers coming into Mississippi in the future. I think it will result in nothing but disaster as a rule.[48]

In 1900 and then again in 1904, Ellen White recognized that opportunities were already passing. Writing to her son Edson, she said:

> The Lord is grieved at the indifference manifested by His professed followers toward the ignorant and oppressed colored people. If our people had taken up this work at the close of the Civil War, their faithful labor would have done much to prevent the present condition of suffering and sin.[49]
>
> The work in the Southern field should be fifteen years in advance of what it now is. Warning after warning has been given, saying that the time to work the Southern field was fast passing, and that soon this field would be much more difficult to work. It will be more difficult in the future than it is today.[50]

Nonetheless, she wrote: "It is the purpose of God that His children shall blend in unity. Do they not expect to live together in the same heaven?"[51] Seventh-day Adventists had to work among African Americans in the South with two strikes against them. The first was the prejudice about their working to uplift Southern blacks. Ellen White wrote in 1891: "It is more difficult to labor for the people in the South than it is to labor for the heathen in a foreign land, because of the prejudice existing against the colored people."[52] This prejudice was fueled by opinion pieces in the newspapers that insinuated that Seventh-day Adventists were instructing converts to violate state law and the sensibilities of their neighbors by working on Sunday when they were not. This was the second strike against them, construed from their worshipping on Saturday rather than on Sunday, the more popular day of worship. Ellen White well knew that flaunting Southern sensibilities would win them no favors. She saw the stage being set and wrote the Nashville church: "The attention of statesmen is being called to the condition of the colored people, and by some the national laws are being studied in the light of Bible requirements."[53]

Predictions of Revived Slavery with Race Wars

In "The Armadale Interview" in 1895, Ellen White predicted the return of a sort of slavery: "Slavery will again be revived in the Southern States; *for the spirit of slavery still lives*. Therefore it will not do for those who labor among the colored people to preach the truth as boldly and openly as they would be free to do in other places."[54] Some may think she meant that the literal institution of slavery would return, but she clarified what she meant in a letter she wrote the same day to Elder A. O. Tait: "[T]he colored people everywhere would be placed in a position of surveillance and under cruel treatment by the white people that would be no less than slavery."[55]

In 1907, W. C. White facilitated a meeting between Ellen White and key Seventh-day Adventist educators to carry out what his mother had in mind for the preparation of a book on the history of the educational and evangelistic efforts of the Seventh-day Adventists in the South.[56] This took place Tuesday, April 29, 1907, at Loma Linda, California. Because of Percy T. Magan's experience as the dean of Madison College in Nashville, he was selected to work alongside Dores E. Robinson on the project. During the interview, Ellen White repeated her concern about the resurgence of slavery. For his part, Percy T. Magan described what he hoped they could accomplish through the book. That the book was never published would indicate that, in the end, they deemed it too difficult a task. He said:

W. C. White   Ellen G. White   D. E. Robinson   P. T. Magan

> I had thought we ought, without taking sides or creating a disturbance, [to] tell in a moderate way the conditions in the South. . . . If we could depict the present status somewhat, it would interest our people to go south to work before it is too late. And yet I felt, on the other hand, that we should be very careful in the doing of that, lest we stir up a hornet's nest.

Ellen White responded: "There will be slavery just as verily as it has been, only upon a basis that is more favorable and secure to the white people."[57] Magan elaborated on what "more . . . secure to the white people" might mean and what the penalties might be to those found assisting blacks under such a system:

> More secure, because they do not have to feed the Negroes and care for them. Then if the Negro has got outside that district, or if he is loafing and not working, they can put him on the chain gang for a year. Now they state in their plan that if anyone is caught, whose teachings excite the blacks to foolishness, that he can be taken and put in the chain gang. Senator Tillman has printed that; he has printed it in the leading magazine in the South, that he has spoken it in Chicago and also in Atlanta, Georgia. There are many of the Negroes today who are selling their property and hiding their money in the earth for fear that their land and houses, if they were known to own any, would be taken from them.[58]

It was with this caution in mind that Ellen White brought up the subject of "race war": "That is the danger. That is why I have pleaded, and entreated, entreated, and entreated for the work to be done in the South, because I knew that this very race war would be introduced."[59] She added: "I said that perilous times were coming, and that the sentiments that could then be expressed in regard to what should be done along missionary lines for the colored people could not be expressed in the future without imperiling lives. I said plainly that the work done for the colored people would have to be carried on along lines different from those followed in some sections of the country in former years."[60]

Bloody racial battles did indeed erupt between 1909 and 1921. In many of these incidents, blacks retaliated against white attacks. "The more well known of the acts of violence were against blacks in the [first quarter] of the twentieth century, such as (1) the massacre at East St. Louis, Illinois, in 1917; (2) the multiple lynchings of Brooks and Lowndes Counties in 1918; (3) the Chicago riots in 1919; (4) the Elaine, Arkansas, massacre in 1919." Delbert Baker also cited a fifth, the Eruption of Tulsa, Oklahoma in 1921, just six years after Ellen White's death.[61]

The description of what took place in Tulsa is startling. The precipitating incident was that a nineteen-year old black boy named Dick Rowland had stepped, by accident, on the foot of Sarah Page, a young white woman who operated an elevator. When the young woman yelled, the boy ran. The story of the alleged assault was picked up by the *Tulsa Tribune*. The youth was taken into custody, and the black community got wind of a threatened lynching. Knowing that a white man accused of murdering a taxi driver had been taken by citizens from the jail and lynched, they offered to help protect the jail from attack. A false report that the jail had been stormed by whites drew a band of black men to the jail, but, upon arriving, they discovered that the report was untrue. The sheriff convinced them that they could go home, which they did. Yet they returned later—75 in number. As the sheriff persuaded them to leave once more, "a white man attempted to disarm one of the colored men. A shot was fired, and then—in the words of the sheriff—'all hell broke loose.' There was a fusillade of shots from both sides and twelve men fell dead—two of them colored, ten white. The fighting continued until midnight when the colored men, greatly outnumbered, were forced back to their section of the town."[62] The investigating reporter, Walter F. White, told what happened next:

African Americans taken captive during Tulsa Race Riot, June 1921

> Around five o'clock Wednesday morning the mob, now numbering more than 10,000 made a mass attack on Little Africa. Machine guns were brought into use; eight aeroplanes were employed to spy on the movements of the Negroes and according to some were used in bombing the colored section. All that was lacking to make the scene a replica of modern "Christian" warfare was poison gas. The colored men and women fought gamely in defense of their homes, but the odds were too great. According to the statements of onlookers, men in uniform, either home guards or ex-service men or both, carried cans of oil into Little Africa, and, after looting the homes, set fire to them. Many are the stories of horror told to me—not by colored people—but by the white residents.[63]

According to white Tulsans interviewed by White, one of the principal causes for the unrest was that the whites believed that the blacks had radicalized. By "radicalized," they meant "that Negroes were uncompromisingly denouncing 'Jim-Crow' [railroad] cars, lynching, peonage; in short, were asking that the Federal constitutional guaranties of 'life, liberty, and the pursuit of happiness' be given regardless of color." Such equality was unthinkable to many whites in the thriving city of Tulsa, which then had a population of 90,000 to 100,000.[64]

Graybill's chapter "The Southern Field Is Closing!" describes what Seventh-day Adventists thought was signaling the closing of work in the South. In a pamphlet entitled "An Agitation and an Opportunity" (1907), Seventh-day Adventists predicted restriction of their movements. Ellen White wrote in April 1909:

> The time is coming when we can not easily give them [blacks] the message. Restrictions will be placed about them to such an extent that it will be next to impossible to reach them; but at the present time this is not the case, and we can go to many places where there are colored people, and can open the Scriptures to their understanding.[65]

Quoting Dr. Ira A. Landrith, a Presbyterian of Nashville, Tennessee, the pamphlet said: "The strongest leaders and most upright members of the Negro race are not ambitious for social equality, but are content to be, and to help their people to become, the best examples of what God made of them—Negroes, not white people, nor yet the unwelcome intimates of white people in white homes and schools and churches."[66] Responding to Landrith, the *Atlanta Constitution* stated: "Dr. Landrith . . . shows that the dominant leaders of the Negroes have no thought of social equality—an irrevocable premise upon which the plans of both races must be based. But he also indicates the solemn duty of the ruling race."[67] Black Americans were willing to accept what they could get. Education under white supremacy was better than no education at all.

An Apparent Reversal of Emphasis

As we have noted, Ellen White promoted high ideals in her address to the 1891 General Conference assembly on race relations and the spread of the Seventh-day Adventist message. Before the highest church council she declared:

"There has been much perplexity as to how our laborers in the South shall deal with the 'color line.' It has been a question to some how far to concede to the prevailing prejudice against the colored people."[68] "[T]he black man's name is written in the book of life beside the white man's."[69] "If a colored brother sits by their side, they will not be offended or despise him. They are journeying to the same heaven, and will be seated at the same table to eat bread in the kingdom of God. If Jesus is abiding in our hearts we cannot despise the colored man who has the same Saviour abiding in his heart."[70] "You have no license from God to exclude the colored people from your places of worship. . . . They should hold membership in the church with the white brethren."[71]

As we have also noted, Ellen White's tone remained the same throughout the 1890s. In her articles in the *Review and Herald*, she expounded: "[M]en have thought it necessary . . . to meet the prejudice of the white people; and a wall of separation in religious worship has been built up." Doing so meant that they "have not had the spirit of Christ."[72]

She condemned the actions of those who have not been "willing to sit by the side of their colored brethren and sing and pray and bear witness to the truth which they had in common."[73]

She reminded readers: "There is to be no special heaven for the white man and another heaven for the black man"; "We have no time to build up walls of distinction between the white and the black race."[74] In these testimonies, Ellen White set the high road of race relations. Without these, we would not properly grasp the expediency of her later testimonies, which seem to have a very different tone.

Referring to what she had written from Australia in the 1890s, Ellen White counseled in 1908: "[T]he workers were to make no political speeches, and that the mingling of whites and blacks in social equality was by no means to be encouraged."[75] Her counsel was based on real experiences that led to the closure of the work in Calmar. Their focus was on African Americans' educating and evangelizing other African Americans rather than elevating their own social status. In time, that would take care of itself.

Regarding "equality," she also wrote in 1908: "[T]he colored people should not urge that they be placed on an equality with white people."[76] By this she meant public agitation for equality, which, under the circumstances, would result in prejudice and persecution. Graybill interpreted these statements within their historical and literary contexts.[77] He showed that Ellen White's later stance was in direct response to real changing circumstances that Seventh-day Adventists had met and would have to meet. A June 1900 newspaper response to the work in Yazoo City, Mississippi, illustrates how even a false charge—that they were advocating "social equality"—closed up the work there. The editor of the newspaper issued a warning:

> If these Seventh Day people are here teaching social equality between the races and defiance to a State law, they should be told quietly but firmly to move on. It is easier to put out a spark than it is a conflagration.[78]

One cannot help but understand the word "firmly" to involve threat of bodily harm, as the threats and attacks on Edson White's co-laborers so aptly illustrated.

The Complications of Interracial Marriages

Another of Ellen White's pragmatic counsels has to do with interracial marriage. In a personal letter in 1912 she stated: "In reply to inquiries regarding the advisability of intermarriage between Christian young people of the white and black races, I will say that in my earlier experience this question was brought before me, and the light given me of the Lord was that this step should not be taken; *for it is sure to create controversy and confusion.*"[79] Thus, Ellen White's objection to those of the Negro race marrying Caucasians was that it created controversy within society and confusion for the children of such unions. Her "earlier experience" points back to 1896, when she explained that her concern was for the children of such unions and the treatment that they would receive:

> But there is an objection to the marriage of the white race with the black. All should consider that they have no right to entail upon their offspring that which will place them at a disadvantage; they have no right to give them as a birthright a condition which would subject them to a life of humiliation. The children of these mixed marriages have a feeling of bitterness toward the parents who have given them this lifelong inheritance. For this reason, if there were no other, there should be no intermarriage between the white and the colored race.

Ellen White is clear that this is not because of any inferiority of one race to the other, for she believed that all are equal, as she affirmed just prior to the statement:

> We are one brotherhood. No matter what the gain or the loss, we must act nobly and courageously in the sight of God and our Saviour. Let us as Christians who accept the principle that all men, white and black, are free and equal, adhere to this principle, and not be cowards in the face of the world, and in the face of the heavenly intelligences. We should treat the colored man just as respectfully as we would treat the white man. And we can now, by precept and example, win others to this course.[80]

Her use of the expression, "if there were no other," indicates that the effect on children was for her a most critical consideration in and of itself. In her address to the general assembly in 1891, she had said:

> Then as the children of God are one in Christ, how does Jesus look upon caste, upon society distinctions, upon the division of man from his fellow-man, because of color, race, position, wealth, birth, or attainments? The secret of unity is found in the equality of believers in Christ. ... With God there is no respect of persons.[81]

Working Around Prejudice

Mrs. White continued to appeal for more laborers in "the Southern field." In 1901 she wrote:

> In the eyes of the Lord the Southern field is a most distressing spectacle, a deformity in the midst of a Christian nation, bearing testimony before angels and before men to the neglect of a people who might be helped were it not for the selfishness and covetousness of professing Christians, who will be called to account for their neglect in the day when every man is judged according to his works. The colored people of the South, who have been left in degradation, will then bear witness against the Christian world.[82]

The need for African-American workers only increased. Ellen White told African-American students on June 21, 1904: "We need, O so much, colored workers to labor for their own people, in places where it would not be safe for white people to labor."[83] Rather than thinking about personal advancement, she encouraged young African Americans to use their unique abilities to lead others of their race to Christ and to an understanding of His biblical truth.

However, the editor of the *Yazoo City Herald* misconstrued the Adventists' objective, publicly accusing them of using the carrot of social equality to win converts: "For a time their doctrine did not seem to make much headway. But they have persisted, and by throwing in a large slice of social equality with their Seventh Day observance doctrine, they have influenced a number to join them and to renounce the Sabbath Day, which is and has been observed by every Christian denomination since the morning the Saviour rose from the tomb."[84]

The editor also described Seventh-day Adventists as outside agitators and maligned their motives: "These people are strangers to the negro, and have no real sympathy with his material and religious welfare." Then he went on to say that things were fine the way they were: "The whites and blacks are now living harmoniously together, and it would be the utmost folly for the blacks to listen to any man or woman whose teachings would in the least interfere with this condition."

About the Sabbath, the editor said: "This is a dangerous doctrine for anyone to be teaching in this community—especially among the colored people. No good can result from such a doctrine, and the dangers are only increased when coupled with the practice of social equality." Then he issued a veiled threat: "[T]hey should be told quietly but firmly to move on."

Ellen White had been specific about counseling African Americans *not* to work on Sundays. In 1895, she counseled: "Tell them they need not provoke their neighbors by doing work on Sunday."[85] In 1899, she remarked: "The colored people may work on Sunday as on other days of the week before the Sabbath truth is brought to them, but if they do this after they have accepted the truth, they will be noticed and condemned."[86]

For added effect, the editor connected the work of the Seventh-day Adventists with the events of Reconstruction and raised "the ghost of Reconstruction violence."[87] Then he recounted a little tale built on innuendo and rumor that conflicts with modern standards:

> "It is stated by reliable negroes that he has adopted two negro girls aged about sixteen. Whether or not this is true, we do not know, but we state as an absolute certainty that these negro girls are living with Rogers as members of his family; that they eat at the same table, sleep in the house with his family, sit around the fireside with them, and to all appearances are equal members thereof. Aside from this, which, in itself, is enough to damn him in the eyes of all decent people, the so-called religious doctrine which he teaches is contrary to the law of the land."

The editor went on to say: "We trust that Rogers will have sense enough to understand and respect this sentiment, and seek more congenial fields for the propagation of his noxious social equality ideas before it is too late." This was another veiled threat—a "hint" that Rogers should leave town, if he *knew what was good for him.*

Rogers responded in print: "Understanding the reports that have been circulated about us and our work, I wish to state to the public, in order to right myself on these matters, that we DO NOT believe in social equality, neither do we teach or practice it."[88]

For the local pastors the more upsetting part of the message was the Sabbath, which challenged their hold on the people. It was not difficult for them to produce lies to silence the Adventists. Graybill concluded his contextualizing of Ellen White's counsels with this thought: "The evidence brought to light here supports the contention that the 'segregation' practiced by Adventists in the first decade of this century was motivated, at least in Mississippi, by a desire to reach the Negro and win him to Christ."[89] Alfonzo Greene, Jr., history professor at Oakwood University, wrote in his doctoral dissertation: "Church Historian Arthur W. Spalding indicated it was only at the encouragement of those leaders whose commitment to the black work and those who had seen the problems related to integrated worship services, which were considered to be 'socially unacceptable,' that the church hesitantly agreed to a policy of segregated worship services and facilities."[90] Ellen White was motivated in these statements, Graybill concluded, "by a desire to reach white people, but more importantly, by a desire to maintain the work among Negroes. Even without agitating the color line, race prejudice had served, along with religious prejudice, to actually close some of the work in Mississippi."[91] Later in 1908, Ellen White wrote the church in Washington, DC, admonishing:

Fred Rogers and R. T. Nash with their wives and children, and Franklin G. Warnick at the Day School in Lintonia

> From the light given me, I know that every injudicious movement made in or about Washington, or in other parts of the Southern field, to encourage the sentiment that the white and the colored people are to associate together in social equality, will mean more in retarding our work than any human mind can comprehend.
>
> There is too much at stake for human judgment to be followed in this matter. If the Conference should say that no difference is to be recognized and no separation is to be made in church relationship between the white people and the colored people, our work with both races would be greatly hindered.[92]
>
> In regard to white and colored people worshipping in the same building, this cannot be followed as a general custom with profit to either party—especially in the South. The best thing will be to provide the colored people who accept the truth, with places of worship of their own, in which they can carry on their services by themselves.[93]

Mrs. White had clarified in 1904 what Seventh-day Adventists should publicly advocate:

We are not to take the position that white believers are to worship by themselves and colored believers by themselves. But neither are we to say that they are to worship together. In some places prejudice against the association of the races is so strong in the minds of the whites that they would not attend meeting if colored people were present. Both races must hear the saving truth that we have to present, and in places where the prejudice is so strong, let the colored people be given help to provide themselves with a place for worship in which they may meet together by themselves. *When the mingling of whites and colored believers brings offense to the whites, other plans must be adopted;* for both classes must hear the message that means so much.[94]

Ellen White's apparent reversal of position on segregated places of worship was not a matter of prejudice on her part but of expediency within the circumstances.

Ellen White at a special meeting of educators at the Oakwood Industrial School, June 21, 1904. Edson is first at the left in the front row, and Willy is third from the left. F. R. Rogers is in the third row, far left.

The Heavenly Complexion of the Redeemed

In addressing an African-American church in Vicksburg, Mississippi, on Sabbath March 16, 1901, Mrs. White had said: " 'The Comforter, which is the Holy Ghost, Whom the Father will send in My name, He shall teach you all things, and bring all things to your remembrance.' You are the children of God. He has adopted you, and He desires you to form *characters* here that will give you entrance into the heavenly family. Remembering this, you will be able to bear the trials which you meet here. In heaven there will be no color line; for all will be as white as Christ himself. Let us thank God that we can be members of the royal family."[95] She also wrote: "If Christ makes the colored race clean and white in the blood of the lamb, if He clothes them with the garments of His righteousness, they will be honored in the heavenly kingdom as verily as the white, . . . they will shine forth in the very same complexion that Christ has."[96] Her statements reflect the Scriptural truth: "Beloved, now are we the sons of God, and it doth not yet appear what we shall be: but we know that, when he shall appear, we shall be like him; for we shall see him as he is" (1 John 3:2). Just how white was Christ? He was Mediterranean—not Scandinavian or Irish. He was well within the browner tones of the human race. Since darker pigment protects the skin in equatorial regions, what need will there be in heaven of dark melanin to protect the skin against the rays of the sun?

Strategic Reasons for White Leadership

In a call for more black workers in 1909, Ellen White included a counsel to avoid stirring up "the race prejudice of the white people."[97] She wrote:

> Opportunities are continually presenting themselves *in the Southern States*, and many wise, Christian colored men will be called to the work. But *for several reasons white men must be chosen as leaders*. We are *all members of one body* and are complete only in Christ Jesus, who will uplift His people from the low level to which sin has degraded them and will place them where they shall be acknowledged in the heavenly courts as laborers together with God.
>
> There is work to be done in many hard places, and out of these hard places bright laborers are to come. Let the work be managed so that colored laborers will be educated to work for their own race. Among the Negro race there are many who have talent and ability.[98] Let us search out these men and women, and teach them how to engage in the work of saving souls. God will co-operate with them and give them the victory.[99]

In the same letter, Ellen White delineated what the several reasons were:

> Dear Brethren in Denver: You ask in regard to the wisdom of placing a colored brother as superintendent of your Sabbath school. There are reasons why this would not be advisable. For the spiritual good of the brother this should not be done. And if continued it would prove a detriment to the Sabbath School. In many minds there is a strong prejudice against the colored people, and as a result of such a move, constant difficulties would arise, which would hinder the growth and advancement of the school. From the light that has been given me for years in the past, I know that all would not show to a colored man the respect which for the good of a Sabbath School should be shown to the superintendent. . . .[100]

Not Judged by Color but by Character

The issue of white leadership was a pragmatic matter; it was not a matter of bigotry on Ellen White's part. In the same section of the *Testimonies*, she wrote:

> The religion of the Bible recognizes no caste or color. It ignores rank, wealth, worldly honor. God estimated men as men. With Him, *character* decides their worth. And we are to recognize the Spirit of Christ in whomsoever it is revealed.[101]

This sounds very much like the ideal that Martin Luther King, Jr., promoted in his "I have a dream" speech of August 28, 1963:

Martin Luther King, Jr., delivering his "I have a dream" speech

I have a dream that one day this nation will rise up and live out the true meaning of its creed: "We hold these truths to be self-evident, that all men are created equal."

I have a dream that one day on the red hills of Georgia, the sons of former slaves and the sons of former slave owners will be able to sit down together at the table of brotherhood.

I have a dream that one day even the state of Mississippi, a state sweltering with the heat of injustice, sweltering with the heat of oppression, will be transformed into an oasis of freedom and justice.

I have a dream that my four little children will one day live in a nation where they will not be judged by the color of their skin but by the content of their character.[102]

Booker T. Washington, black America's chief spokesman, continued to exhibit optimism during this "long, dark night." Studiously avoiding mentioning the disenfranchisement and lynchings of African Americans and the escalating segregation of the period, Washington emphasized the progress that African Americans had made in the number of schools and graduates. There was indeed progress in the education and earnings of African Americans during this period. Washington's stated objective was to educate African Americans to prepare skilled, dependable workers. He gave no indication that his view was a temporary expedient; Ellen White, on the other hand, as Graybill has noted, "left no doubt that her position on separation of the races was merely a temporary guideline of expediency to be used 'until the Lord shows us a better way.' "[103] She wrote: "Let the colored believers be provided with neat, tasteful houses of worship. *Let them be shown that this is done not to exclude them from worshiping with white people*, because they are black, *but in order that the progress of the truth may be advanced*. Let them understand that this plan is to be followed *until the Lord shows us a better way*."[104]

In truth, the plan that Booker T. Washington articulated at the Cotton States and International Exposition in Atlanta, Georgia, would be the surest to circumvent white fears and opposition. Then, once African Americans were educated and financially able, who could argue that they were not the social equals of their white counterparts?[105] Seventh-day Adventist educational endeavors are the subject of our next chapter.

Timeline of Ellen G. White's Counsels in the Context of National Events[106]

1850	Fugitive Slave Act
1854	Kansas-Nebraska Act expanded the possible new slave states to the territories north of the 36° 30' line.
1857	Dred Scott Decision identified slaves as "property"; declared the ban of the Missouri Compromise unconstitutional.
1859	*Ellen White advocated civil disobedience to the Fugitive Slave Act and wrote: "[T]he slave is not the property of any man."*
1861, Jan 12	*Ellen White described her vision about war coming with death and suffering.*
1861, Apr 12	Civil War broke out.
1861, Aug 27	*Ellen White reported on her vision of angelic intervention at the Battle of Manassas to curtail further harm, to punish the North and the South, and to call attention to the issue of slavery.*
1862, Feb 18	*Ellen White reported on her vision about Southern preparedness for war. "Slavery," she wrote, "lies at the foundation of the war."*
1863, Jan 1	Emancipation Proclamation
1863, Jan 27	*Ellen White commented on the course of the war and gave counsel on the draft.*
1865	The Thirteenth Amendment made slavery unconstitutional.
1866	Civil Rights Acts (also 1870, 1871, 1875) prohibited discrimination
1877	The Compromise of 1877 and Rutherford B. Hayes' election to the United States presidency.
1883	The Supreme Court ruled that discrimination acts applied to the states and not to individuals.
1891, Mar 20	*Ellen White appealed for volunteers to work with Southern blacks and wrote: "If a colored brother sits by their side, they will not be offended or despise him." "You have no license from God to exclude the colored people from your places of worship. . . . They should hold membership in the church with the white brethren."*
1894	Preacher-martyr Alonzo Parker prophesied: "There will come to you people of Vicksburg just one more chance from God."
1895, Jan 10	Edson began work in Vicksburg, Mississippi.
1895, Apr 2	*Ellen White wrote: "No human mind should seek to draw the line between the colored and the white people. Let circumstances indicate what shall be done; for the Lord has his hand on the lever of circumstances."*
1895, July 24	*Ellen White wrote: "The work is now tenfold harder than it would have been [years ago]."*
1895, Nov 20	*Ellen White wrote: "The time has not yet come for us to work as though there were no prejudice. . . . Slavery will again be revived in the Southern States; for the spirit of slavery still lives. . . . The colored people everywhere would be placed in a position of surveillance and under cruel treatment by the white people that would be no less than slavery."*
1895, Dec 3	*Ellen White wrote: "Let not the colored people be excluded from the religious assemblies of the white people."*
1896	Plessy v. Ferguson defends "separate but equal" facilities for blacks and whites
1898	South Carolina passed a railroad segregation law.
1899, June 5	*Ellen White wrote: "The relation of the two races has been a matter hard to deal with . . . ."*
1899	North Carolina passed a train segregation law.
1899, Oct 22	*Ellen White wrote: "That which is now undertaken cannot be carried forward as it might have been had the white churches at the time of the abolition of slavery acted as Christ would have done in their place. . . . [C]olored people are tortured to death whether proved guilty or not."*
1900–1910	Six major race riots took place in America.
1900–1907	Virginia passed a railroad segregation law. North Carolina, Virginia, Louisiana, Arkansas, South Carolina, Tennessee, Mississippi, Maryland, Florida, and Oklahoma passed streetcar segregation laws.
1901, Mar 16	*Ellen White wrote: "In heaven there will be no color line; for all will be as white as Christ himself."*
1904, Apr 28	*Ellen White approved integrated services in Washington D.C. Seventh-day Adventist Church.*
1907, Apr 29	*Ellen White wrote: "There will be slavery just as verily as it has been, only upon a basis that is more favorable and secure to the white people. . . . That is the danger. That is why I have pleaded, and entreated, entreated, and entreated for the work to be done in the South, because I knew that this very race war would be introduced."*
1907	Kentucky outlawed racially integrated education, affecting Berea College.
1908, Oct 19	*Ellen White wrote: "[W]orkers were to make no political speeches, and that the mingling of whites and blacks in social equality was by no means to be encouraged. . . . the colored people should not urge that they be placed on an equality with white people. . . . In regard to white and colored people worshipping in the same building, this cannot be followed as a general custom with profit to either party—especially in the South. . . . Let the colored believers be provided with neat, tasteful houses of worship. Let them be shown that this is done not to exclude them from worshiping with white people, because they are black, but in order that the progress of the truth may be advanced. Let them understand that this plan is to be followed <u>until the Lord shows us a better way</u>."*
1908, Nov 9	Berea College exceeded Plessy v. Ferguson.
1909	Oklahoma passed segregation laws for schools, trains, and railroad stations.
1909	Supreme Court of Iowa passed laws that businesses could refuse to serve Negroes.
1909	*Ellen White wrote: "[M]any wise, Christian colored men will be called to the work. But for several reasons white men must be chosen as leaders. . . ."*
1912	*Ellen White wrote: "[R]egarding the advisability of intermarriage between Christian young people of the white and black races . . . this step should not be taken; for it is sure to create controversy and confusion." Yet she also said: "We should treat the colored man just as respectfully as we would treat the white man."*

Chapter 9

Education, the Road to Post-Racialism

For many years I have borne a heavy burden in behalf of the Negro race. My heart has ached as I have seen the feeling against this race growing stronger and still stronger, and as I have seen that many Seventh-day Adventists are apparently unable to understand the necessity for an earnest work being done quickly. . . . —Ellen White[1]

Seventh-day Adventists have always taken seriously Christ's commission to go into all the world to *teach* all people about the crucified, risen and soon-coming Savior.[2] By inspiring the heart and educating the mind, changes are made in individuals, in families, and in society at large. This goes for those of the liberated race as well as those of the race of the former slave owners. Immediately after the Civil War, education was one of the greatest needs of the freedmen. They needed to learn to read and write and to plan and provide for their families. When the promises of emancipation left the freedmen discouraged and impoverished, education became even more important. Government agents, Baptists, Methodists, Presbyterians, Episcopalians, and Quakers stepped in to fill the gap, engaging in various educational endeavors for African Americans. In time, so also did Seventh-day Adventists. One of the most helpful histories of these educational efforts is found in Arthur W. Spalding's "Lights and Shades in the Black Belt."[3]

Seventh-day Adventist Mission Schools in the South

Edson White was instrumental in opening many schools for African Americans. The first was in Vicksburg on the corner of Walnut Street and East First Avenue in 1895. Other schools opened in quick succession (see sidebar). The pioneering spirit of Edson White and the workers of the *Morning Star* was responsible for shaping a large part of early Seventh-day Adventist history in Mississippi among African Americans. As a result of the success of the mission schools that Edson White helped to establish, black membership in Mississippi was larger than white membership for a time.[4] Nonetheless, evidence from Edson's letters to his mother demonstrates that he did not build up the "Southern work" among African Americans without competition from other Southern projects.

Opening of Southern Missionary Society Schools

1895	Vicksburg Mission School, Vicksburg, Mississippi
1895	Wilsonia Floating School, Mississippi
1897	Juniata Mission School, Juniata, Mississippi
1899	Yazoo City Mission School, Yazoo City, Mississippi
1901	Jackson Mission School, Jackson, Mississippi
1903	Greenville Mission School, Greenville, Mississippi
	Columbus Mission School, Columbus, Mississippi
1904	Vicksburg Mission School, Vicksburg, Mississippi
1905	Natchez Mission School, Natchez Mississippi
1906	Newellton Mission School, Newellton, Louisiana
	Clarksdale Mission School, Clarksdale, Mississippi
1907	Mobile Mission School, Mobile, Alabama
	Ellisville Mission School, Ellisville, Mississippi
	Day Neighborhood Mission School, Ellisville, Mississippi
	Charity Mission School, Montgomery, Alabama

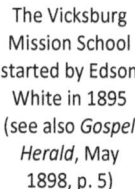

The Vicksburg Mission School started by Edson White in 1895 (see also *Gospel Herald*, May 1898, p. 5)

Agricultural program at the Hillcrest School Farm, Nashville, Tennessee

Anna Knight, the first Black missionary to India, attended the Hillcrest School Farm

Shireman's "Colored" School, Hildebran, North Carolina, c. 1903

In addition to those begun under Edson's influence, there were other schools started for the benefit of African-American young people in the South. Anna Knight opened an industrial school in Mississippi for black and white children, placing it in the hands of a friend when she left for India in 1901 as a medical missionary. Dan T. Shireman's rural school in Hildebran, North Carolina, operated from 1897 until 1903.[5] Part of his work was to minister to the black population in the region, and a young black convert from Yazoo City named Franklin Henry Bryant came in January 1899 to help in the endeavor.[6] At the Hillcrest School, five miles from Nashville, classes began in January 1909.[7]

Schools for African Americans were not just in the South. "Ma Dorsey" operated a school in New York for African Americans from the 1890s to the 1920s, moved it to Tunesassa, New York, when white Seventh-day Adventists abandoned Fernwood Academy in 1921, and continued the school's operation until the Great Depression.[8]

Students at the Lintonia Mission School: (left to right) Robert Walker, Flanigan Wicks, Nettie Williams, Little Walker, Parlee Jones

(left to right) Lelar Knighton, Rosa Jones, Olive Knighton at the Wilsonia Mission School

Larger group of students at the Mission School in Lintonia

Early Christian efforts to educate African Americans were met with vigorous resistance. Ellen White knew about this and wrote:

> One of the difficulties attending the work is that many of the white people living where the colored people are numerous are not willing that special efforts should be put forth to uplift them. When they see schools established for them, when they see them being taught to be self-supporting, to follow trades, to provide themselves with comfortable homes instead of continuing to live in hovels, they see the possibility that selfish plans will be interfered with—that they will no longer be able to hire the Negro for a mere pittance; and their enmity is aroused. They feel that they are injured and abused. Some act as if slavery had never been abolished.[9]

The ire of the planters was directed against the white educators, making their work dangerous. Edson and his mother recognized that the key to circumventing prejudice among Southern whites was for African Americans to educate their own people. They encouraged the church to launch a school to prepare black young people for the task of uplifting their own race.

The Oakwood Industrial Training School

Eighteen years after the closing of the Clarkes' school in Texas, a school for the education of black workers had its start. Of that school, Ellen White would write: "It was the providence of God that the Huntsville School Farm was purchased."[10] Harold L. Lee and Benjamin Baker recounted the humble beginnings of the Oakwood school:

> The General Conference of Seventh-day Adventists had founded Oakwood Industrial School in 1896 as a place of higher education for the increasing number of African American converts to Adventism, then mainly concentrated in the southern region of the United States. The church chose the city of Huntsville, Alabama, for the school site because of its proximity to Nashville and Graysville, Tennessee, then important Adventist centers in the South. Huntsville was also comparatively tolerant in racial matters in the turbulent Jim Crow era, and the low cost of land was an attractive option for Adventist leadership in the North.
>
> The site for the industrial school itself, however, was not so promising. First suggested by veteran Black minister Charles Kinney, the 360-acre plot had been a slave plantation called the Beasley Estate, whose owner was reported to have brutally abused his Black captives. To make matters worse, the Alabama landscape was sloping and uneven. The red clay was hard as granite from being overworked, and dense brush covered the property.
>
> Although pressed for money—and loath to funnel funds into a questionable enterprise in Alabama—the top three church administrators nevertheless surveyed the plot and decided to make the investment. Known unofficially as the "Huntsville School Farm," or just "Huntsville," the school was officially called "Oakwood" for the sixty-five oak trees that stood on the property.

Oakwood Principal Solon M. Jacobs with students and workers, displaying the school's new riding plow, 1897

Oakwood School faculty and students, 1910

Oakwood Industrial School was slow out of the gate after its doors opened on November 16, 1896, with a charter to train Black students to serve humanity through their respective areas of expertise and to spread the good news of Adventism to the world. Challenges with funding, staff, and students—not uncommon during the beginnings of any college—almost extinguished the fledgling school. But through the persistent efforts of Ellen G. White after her return from Australia in 1900, and solid leadership at the school from staff and students, Oakwood survived and even prospered.[11]

In 1909 Oakwood graduated its first class, and the next few years witnessed the establishment of a sanitarium and orphanage, as well as the construction of numerous buildings. The first ministerial student finished his course in 1912, and in 1917 the school officially became Oakwood Junior College.[12]

Ellen White told the students of Oakwood in 1904: "He has given you talents to be improved. He has bestowed on the colored race some of the best and highest talents. He will bless in the work of transforming mind and character."[13] *Talent* certainly is definitely an attribute of the veritable "Who's Who" of past and present notable African-American Seventh-day Adventists with connections to Oakwood—including distinguished faculty and notable alumni. We think of Anna Knight, who studied nursing at Battle Creek Sanitarium and became the first African-American missionary of any denomination, beginning service as a medical missionary in Calcutta, India, in 1901 and continuing to serve in retirement at Oakwood from 1947 to 1972.[14] Then there is Eva B. Dykes, the first African-American woman to complete a doctoral degree in the United States, earning a Ph.D. from Radcliff in English, Latin, German, and Greek language studies, and serving as English professor at Oakwood. Another is Frank Loris Peterson, the first black graduate of Pacific Union College (1916), the first full-time black faculty member at Oakwood, the first black associate secretary of the General Conference of Seventh-

Anna Knight with the star from the *Morning Star*, c. 1960

Barry Black

Calvin Edwin Mosely

day Adventists, and the first black vice president of the General Conference, who also served as president of Oakwood. There is Calvin Edwin Mosely, Jr., the first black chair of the Theology and Religion Department, known as the "Father of Preachers," and the first black pastor of the college church. Singer Wintley Phipps, who has sung for numerous American presidents, and U.S. Senate chaplain Barry Black are also celebrated alumni of Oakwood University.

In *The Ladies of Oakwood*, Ciro Sepúlveda collected the stories of several African-American women connected with Oakwood who have faithfully served God, their church, and humanity. In addition to Eva B. Dykes and Anna Knight, he featured Chessie Harris, who was "Mama Harris" to more than 1,200 black and white boys and girls between 1954 and 1980; C. E. L. Baskerville, who found her calling in teaching; and Inez Booth, "Mama" to the inmates at the Huntsville Penitentiary. Also featured are Jannith Lewis, who became the director of library services at Oakwood and the visionary for their new library; Williemae Erving, campus landscaper and encourager of Oakwood students; Mineola Dixon, who made progress in the business world before returning to Oakwood as the college's first director of student employment, alumni coordinator, and college archivist; Artie Melancon, distinguished teacher in the Department of Education at Oakwood; and Eurydice Osterman, organist and music teacher, with such a breadth of knowledge of music that she conducted workshops for music teachers in many places, including Budapest, Hungary; and Alma Blackman, an educator and musician, who revived the Oakwood elite singing group, the Aeolians. The Aeolians have made a significant name for themselves in performances and competitions.[15]

Eva B. Dykes

Frank Loris Peterson

Chessie Harris

Wintley Phipps

Inez Booth

To these we should add preachers E. E. Cleveland, William C. Scales, C. D. Brooks, C. E. Bradford, Robert Carter, Warren Banfield, R. L. Woodfork, and Maurice Battle, to name just a few.[16] It would fill many volumes to list all the successful and productive alumni of Oakwood and the other early Seventh-day Adventist schools for African Americans, who have served as teachers, pastors, nurses, and other professionals, and who have helped the church and society move beyond segregation and prejudice.

Yet "the struggle" to accomplish their mission was definitely not easy, as our next chapter will illustrate. It is an honest look at what happened when Seventh-day Adventists took Ellen White's pragmatic proposals as rigid rules.

Chapter 10

Calcified Pragmatism

Before long my mother spent much time with the Adventists.... We began to go with my mother to the Adventist meetings that were held further out in the country. For us children, I know it was the good food they served. But we listened, too. There were a handful of Negroes, from small towns in the area, but I would say that it was ninety-nine percent white people. The Adventists felt we were living at the end of time, that the world soon was coming to an end. But they were the friendliest white people I had ever seen." –Malcolm X[1]

Malcolm X referred with fondness in his autobiography to the friendliness of Seventh-day Adventists toward his mother and family in the 1950s. Such positive recollections are certainly due in part to Ellen White's progressive vision for the church and the love of Christ guiding its members. However, as Seventh-day Adventist pastor Eric Walsh has pointed out: "You will find that we have a strong history as a church of racial equality in principle but not always in practice."[2]

Malcolm X

For pragmatic reasons, separate venues for evangelism became necessary in the twentieth century. Yet after Mrs. White's death, the church somehow lost sight of her earlier counsels and hardened her later pragmatic counsels into dogma.[3] Supportive of Woodrow Wilson's segregation policies, the church segregated the General Conference headquarters and other Seventh-day Adventist facilities in Washington, DC.[4] Still, African-American membership grew as a result of the North American Negro Department—from 900 in 1909 to 3,500 in 1918.[5] However, Seventh-day Adventists no longer had the progressive outlook they once had, and, through policies of accommodation, they became generally indifferent to the social needs of black Americans.[6]

A Book That Validated Segregation

The Fruitage of Spiritual Gifts

An example of the calcification of Ellen White's pragmatic counsels into fixed dogma appears in *The Fruitage of Spiritual Gifts* by Lewis H. Christian. The author correctly stated regarding segregation, "National conceits and vain feelings of race supremacy are entirely foreign to the gospel of Christ as set forth in the Spirit of prophecy." He also correctly described her view of the brotherhood of believers, "The ideal for the remnant church of Christ as taught by the messenger of the Lord is one united brotherhood of all true believers without any reference to race, color, or nationality." Yet, he skewed Ellen White's actual views regarding organization and racial equality, recasting Ellen White's race counsels in a light "more acceptable to white Seventh-day Adventists in the United States in the 1940s":[7]

Nevertheless, while ... she warned against building up a "wall of partition," she did not teach the ideas so common today in what is sometimes called race equality. She taught that there should be opportunity for all to advance, but she did not teach that there should be a mingling of the races. She stated very clearly that the colored people should have their own church organization and church buildings. Some at first were opposed to the idea, but experience has proved that the light given us by the Spirit of prophecy was from the Lord. She condemned the idea that there should be mixed marriages between the colored and the white.[8]

Christian mistakenly suggested that Ellen White favored separate organizations for the races. Regarding the advisability of separate ethnic conferences in Europe, Ellen White wrote: "According to the light given me of God, separate organizations, instead of bringing about unity, will create discord."[9] Black regional conferences did not exist during her lifetime.

Christian was also mistaken in asserting that Ellen White did not promote race equality. Her later statements merely avoided the political aspects of equality to avoid thwarting the Seventh-day Adventist mission until God provided "a better way." In her 1891 appeal to church leaders, she most certainly called for equality, as summarized by Benjamin Baker:

1. *Equal love:* Christ died just as much for the black people as for the white people, and the God of the white man is the same God of the black man.
2. *Equal reward:* The black man's name is written next to the white man's name in the book of life.
3. *Equal salvation:* Unless God's Spirit is in your heart, whether you are white or black, you are a slave and need to be freed.
4. *Equal destination:* We are all journeying to the same heaven.
5. *Equal relations:* God makes no distinction between the North and the South; therefore, we must learn to live together here on earth before we can get to heaven.
6. *Equal responsibility:* Let none of Christ's children be cowards in regard to the work for the black race.
7. *Equal priority:* The Seventh-day Adventist Church must give the gospel to African Americans, and it should be at the top of the priority list.[10]

When De-Segregation Was Denied, Separation Ensued

Separation is a natural response of African Americans when efforts to integrate and gain equal rights are thwarted. Oxford lecturer Malcolm Bull and freelance journalist Keith Lockhart described the response this way: "There have always been two poles in the history of the Negro in the United States. One is the push for integration and equal rights. The other, the desire for separation and withdrawal from white society. Integration is perhaps the initial goal, but if competition [between the races] becomes too fierce and the white majority proves too intransigent, blacks are likely to see separation as the best way forward. Segregation is then seen as the answer to discrimination."[11] It was because of the loyalty of African-American Seventh-day Adventists that there has not been a total fracture of the church along racial lines as in other churches. Yet there has been some splintering of African-American leaders and their congregations. Two involved pastors who served during Ellen White's lifetime.

During one of the Sabbaths of the last General Conference sessions that Ellen White attended, she visited the First Church of Seventh-day Adventists on Eighth Street in Washington, DC, a racially mixed congregation. The church was pastored by Elder Lewis C. Sheafe, an African-American minister who also pastored an all-African-American church.[12] With Ellen White as guest speaker, Sheafe's two churches and another all-white church were invited. When the service was over, many came up to shake Mrs. White's hand. She wrote of the experience: "We were surrounded with both white people and colored people so that we could not move."[13] She was delighted by the experience. It was not only an opportunity to encourage Seventh-day Adventists in Washington, DC, but it also gave her an opportunity to experience the unity that she had always envisioned—of men and women of all colors coming together as one in Christ! Unfortunately, "less than positive relationships eventually led Sheafe to leave the Adventist ministry, even though he continued to preach the denomination's beliefs."[14]

Lewis C. Sheafe

Another loss among capable Seventh-day Adventist African-American ministers came in 1917, when John Wesley Manns left the denomination, taking part of the congregation in Savannah, Georgia, with him and establishing the Free Seventh-day Adventist Denomination. Manns explained that his break with the denomination was "because bigoted white leaders among Seventh-day Adventists have failed to consider the necessity of such vital changes, but have fixed a permanent bar against the Negro leadership of the organization."[15]

John W. Manns

Still another loss to the Seventh-day Adventist ministry was that of James Kemuel Humphrey in 1929. Having served as a Baptist minister, Humphrey joined the Seventh-day Adventist Church in 1902 through the efforts of J. N. Loughborough and J. H. Carroll. Humphrey grew the First Harlem Seventh-day Adventist Church to 600 members, baptizing on average 50 people a year. Humphrey's dream was to create a benevolent association and Utopia Park, a parachurch organization that would provide African Americans of New York with "an orphanage, a nursing home, a training school, an industrial area, and health-care facilities."[16] Humphrey pursued the project without involving denominational counsel. He considered the benevolent association "absolutely a problem for the colored people."[17] The president of the Greater New York Conference, Louis Dickson, considered his actions to be insubordinate. Misunderstanding Humphrey's stance and the loyalty of his congregation, Conference officials revoked Humphrey's credentials and disfellowshipped his congregation.[18] Humphrey never fulfilled his dream of a Utopia Park.[19] Had he felt that white conference officials appreciated what he was wanting to accomplish, he could have used experienced counsel in the enterprise.

James K. Humphrey

Peaceful Protest Brings Positive Change

Until the student protest of 1931, Oakwood College in Huntsville, Alabama, had few African-American faculty members and an all-white administration.[20] The students complained that the white teachers showed no interest in black culture or the lives of the students and that the white and African-American teachers had no social interactions. Worse still, during church services and foot washing services, African Americans were kept separate from whites. The students respectfully validated their concerns from the Bible and from Ellen White's writings, and petitioned that relations and student living conditions be improved, that the curriculum be updated, and that the college have more African-American staff, including an African-American president.[21] Each of their petitions was met, including the installment the next year of Oakwood's first African-American president, Professor James L. Moran.[22]

James L. Moran

A Sense of Betrayal That Led to "The Next Best Plan"

The Lucy Byard incident in 1943 showed how arbitrary denominational segregation policies had become.[23] Lucille Lewis Byard was a Virginia-born woman of mixed African-American and European descent. Her pastor, J. Mark Cox, a Seventh-day Adventist pastor since the 1920s, made arrangements for her to receive treatment for illness at the Washington Sanitarium, knowing that black patients had been treated there before.[24]

Lucille Lewis Byard

When Mrs. Byard arrived at the sanitarium, she was cheerful though pneumonia made her breathing difficult. When sanitarium personnel realized that she was a Negro, they told her husband, James, that they could not treat her.[25] Mrs. Byard waited in the hallway without treatment until she could be transported to the Freedman's Hospital, where she died a few days later.[26] Pastor Cox joined J. K. Humphrey and Elder Rowe in conducting her funeral service in Brooklyn.[27] African-American Seventh-day Adventists felt that Washington Sanitarium had turned its back on one of its own. In the wake of this event, Mrs. Ruth Chambers, a close friend of Mrs. Byard, wrote then General Conference president J. L. McElhany:

> Why have the name of Adventist [been] blackened with such doings. If there is no place for us in the buildings, why not make a place where we can go and have a place to die in and not be in the way of the lily whites. . . . Pray for me that this will not turn me bitter. It was a hard blow to Sr. Byard's husband and all her friends. I am trying not to think it was done in a spirit of hatred. But it was done and it has made very hard feelings in all the Negro churches that I have heard talk about it. . . .[28]

Most see this sad event as the stimulus for the creation of regional conferences, though what black Seventh-day Adventists really wanted was equal treatment in Adventist institutions. Church statistician Bert Haloviak summarized: "It seems clear that the momentum from General Conference headquarters for movement toward black conferences sprang from a realization that

SDA institutions were unwilling for integration to occur."[29] General Conference treasurer W. E. Nelson wrote to R. A. Hare, the administrator of the Washington Sanitarium, defending the institution's policy of segregation: "[O]ur institution is not a hospital, primarily it is a sanitarium and as such is entirely different as far as its social standing is concerned.... It would be absolutely disastrous at the present time for the Washington Sanitarium to carry a mixed clientele.... As I view the whole situation, Dr. Hare, it is not a matter of the colored people wanting a little sanitarium of their own where they can receive attention, but what they want is racial and social equality."[30] Black Seventh-day Adventist minister William L. Cheatham polled the black constituency of the Columbia Union and found that all who did not prefer "a colored conference want equality in the present setup. That is in offices, sanitariums, publishing houses and the like. Of course, it is said that the latter will not work. Therefore it seems to me that the next best plan would be the colored conference."[31] Since only white ministers could vote on the proposal, the destiny of the work among African Americans was not in African American hands.

The vote was taken, and what had been rejected in 1929 was now approved. "In April, 1944, the General Conference, at its Spring meeting in Chicago," passed the resolution to form regional conferences, "administered by colored officers and committees," where the black constituency was sufficiently large and where income and territory warranted the organization of separate black regional conferences.[32] These conferences would respond to the unique needs of African Americans, would neutralize racism, facilitate de-segregation, give ownership and self-governance of the work among African Americans, and promote effective evangelism.[33] The conferences included were the Lake Region Conference, the Northeastern Conference, the Allegheny Conference, the South Central Conference, the South Atlantic Conference, the Southwest Region Conference, and the Central States Conference. The first three of these were formed in 1945, the second two in 1946, and the last two in 1947.

The formation of separate overlapping regional conferences was a boon to the advancement of the work among African Americans. It gave African Americans ownership of work previously supervised by white leaders, and black membership grew exponentially. By 1949, the membership of the South Atlantic Conference reached 5,132, with 65 organized churches and nine companies, 19 schools and 30 qualified teachers. This was an additional 2,448 members, 700 of whom joined through the efforts of conference evangelist E. E. Cleveland. The South Central Conference, which covered Kentucky, Tennessee, Alabama, Mississippi, and the northwestern part of Florida, had reached a membership of 2,767, with 42 organized churches and six companies.[34] Having been just nine percent of U. S. membership in 1944, African-American Seventh-day Adventists comprised more than 25 percent in 1995.[35] "Although the church required almost 30 years to acquire 3,000 black members, in less than four years following the restructuring it achieved a growth in excess of 3,500 extra members."[36]

Evangelist E. E. Cleveland

Seventh-day Adventists and the Civil Rights Movement

Regarding segregation, cautiousness and residual unhealthy attitudes held Seventh-day Adventists back from faster progress. General Conference president William Henry Branson wrote a letter in 1954 to union and local conference presidents and managers of Seventh-day Adventist institutions in the North American Division, regarding "Racial Segregation." This comes through in his statement,: "Perhaps no religious group in the United States, or the world, claims so loudly that it is international in its attitudes and services as do the Seventh-day Adventists and yet, in this matter of Negro segregation, we are trailing behind the procession.... Shall we be the last of the Christian bodies to break away from our historic attitudes and chart a new course in our human relationships.... Shall we wait until our hands are forced on this matter, or shall we move forward carefully but surely as men who believe that 'All ye are brethren?' "[37] Just one month after he wrote this, the United States Supreme Court ruled racial segregation in the public schools to be unconstitutional.[38]

Irene Morgan

Suffering from "the comfort of white privilege," white Seventh-day Adventists could afford to be non-interventionists in racial injustice. To this day, many white Seventh-day Adventists are unaware of the involvement of their fellow Adventists in the Civil Rights movement.[39] For example, in 1944, eleven years before Rosa Parks refused to give up her bus seat in Montgomery, Alabama, Seventh-day Adventist Irene Morgan refused to give up her Greyhound bus seat to a white couple in Gloucester County, Virginia, leading to the Supreme Court ruling that segregation in interstate travel was unconstitutional. Also, in 1956, Seventh-day Adventist pastor Warren S. Banfield joined the Tampa, Florida, branch of the NAACP.[40] From 1971 to 1976, he worked as the associate secretary of the Southern Union Conference of Seventh-day Adventists. Afterward, he helped establish the Human Relations Department for the North American Division, dedicated to solving problems of race, class and gender within the Seventh-day Adventist Church. In Tampa, Banfield became involved in civil rights organizations. His skills as a leader and administrator caught the attention of the black community. When the president of the Tampa NAACP resigned, Banfield assisted in the search for a replacement. Before the search was complete, he left to attend a church related function in another city. In his absence, Tampa's Black Interdenominational Ministerial Alliance recommended that Banfield become the next leader of the city's NAACP. Members of the Tampa Branch accepted the nomination and voted on it. When he returned, Banfield learned that he had been elected to fill the presidential vacancy. Initially hesitating to take the job, he weighed the possible conflicts it posed for his relationship with the Seventh-day Adventist Church. Banfield consulted some of his Adventist colleagues about the possibility of serving as president of an NAACP branch, and they all cautioned him against it. They argued that accepting the position would jeopardize the well being of the church, as well as the safety of its members. Furthermore, they told him that the denomination did not believe in getting involved in sociopolitical activity. Not finding their reasons compelling, Banfield accepted the office of president. As a local NAACP official, Banfield kept the city's political

W. S. Banfield, one-time president of the Tampa NAACP

Oakwood students with school sign at the 1965 march

power structure informed of the needs of the black community. In addition, he set the city's civil rights agenda, organized local demonstrations, raised funds and planned community meetings. Banfield also brought in guest speakers to energize the organization.[41]

Seventh-day Adventists Monroe A. Burgess, Randolf P. Stafford, and Alfonso Greene, Sr. also affiliated with the NAACP to work for changes in black civil rights.[42] African-American Seventh-day Adventists also participated in the March on Washington, August 28, 1963, bucking the church's non-interventionist policies on the one hand and enduring the disdain of other African-American Christians for their Sabbath observance on the other. Also, four students from Pacific Union College chose, against the concerns of the school and church authorities, to participate in the March 21, 1965 Civil Rights march in Selma, Alabama. These were Paul Cobb (African-American), Fernando Canales (Hispanic), Will Battles and Milton Hare (white). Six students from Oakwood College likewise shrugged off threats of expulsion to participate in the march. These were Neal Arthur, Harvey Holland, Ben McAdoo, Maceo McGoodwin, Don Monroe, and Russ Nelson.[43] (Interestingly, Oakwood president Garland J. Millet had opened the doors for Martin Luther King, Jr., to speak at Oakwood College on March 19, 1962.[44]) E. E. Cleveland later quipped, "While some of the old saints who had been in the church for years didn't want to get involved (they were the "wait and see'ers") the new believers were an active bunch."[45]

Program autographed for Mervyn Warren by Martin Luther King, Jr., and Ralph Abernathy, March 19, 1962

Seventh-day Adventist Race Relations

Changes in church policy began in the 1960s when lay Seventh-day Adventist and 2010 Ohio Civil Rights Hall of Fame inductee Frank Hale, Jr., invited nine activist-minded laypersons (six women and three men) to meet February 26, 1961, in Columbus, Ohio, to set goals for ending racial inequities.[46] Taking the name "Laymen's Leadership Conference" (LLC), the group of ten set down specific goals for the new organization, which included discontinuing closed admissions policies and quota systems in Seventh-day Adventist schools, hiring teachers based on qualifications, welcoming people of all races and colors to all Seventh-day Adventist churches, establishing institutes to develop techniques and strategies on the improvement of race relations, and following the principles of Scripture and of Ellen G. White on matters of race.

Nelson, Hale, and Holloway at the Layman's Leadership Conference

In a matter of months the LLC was well on its way to being a truly national organization, carrying its message to regional churches across the nation and insisting on a formal meeting with General Conference administrators at the Spring Council of 1962 before the GC session in San Francisco that year. Indeed, the controversial organization had already commanded the attention of the church's top leaders who then sought to respond to Frank Hale, Jr., and Myles Martin (a reporter from Cleveland). At the same time hundreds of letters poured in from faithful black Seventh-day Adventists describing their being denied services from institutions that their tithes and offerings helped to support.[47]

Various instances of racism could be cited, but just two will here be noted. One of the most disturbing was when a white deacon in the 1960s turned a group of black students away from his church with the chilling warning that he had "six bullets for six niggers."[48] Another incident was when a white man elected to serve in the Columbia Union Conference packed up his family and went home to Tennessee because "his wife and children were very upset about being at a party with a Negro family."[49] Though North American Division president Alfred C. McClure formally apologized to African-American members for past mistreatment, the memory of these incidents is still painful.[50]

Yet there were leaders who earnestly sought to rectify racial inequalities. When Neal Wilson became president of the Columbia Union Conference in 1962, he asked evangelist C. D. Brooks to take on a role outside his usual comfort zone. He wanted Brooks to act as field secretary for the Columbia Union, union revivalist, and assistant secretary of stewardship and church development. Wilson believed "a man of Brooks's caliber would show the often-prejudiced white Adventist world the sophistication and refinement of Black Adventism, assuring them that not only could their ministers lead Blacks but could lead whites and other races just as well as their white counterparts."

Neal C. Wilson

C. D. Brooks

"[H]e wanted to obliterate the racial barriers in the church, and he set about to accomplish it with strategic and sure strokes." He also wanted to broaden Brook's ministry, "making him not just a 'regional preacher,' but a global evangelist. But that could never be a reality as long as Brooks pastored only Black churches."[51] At first Brooks turned the request down. However, Wilson's seriousness and utter comfort in working with him and other African Americans led Brooks to pray over the request with his wife and accept the position.[52] "His first assignment in his new post was as keynote speaker on human relations [read "*race* relations"] at four conferences. The audiences were quite large, usually numbering between 2,000 and 2,500 people, and were equally mixed with blacks and whites. Knowing how delicate his topic was . . . Brooks made sure his talks were careful and sensitive, but as usual—and as was his trademark by now—he held no truth back."[53] The seminars worked, and other conferences and unions "replicated them. Invitations poured in for him to train facilitators. The General Conference used Columbia Union's field secretary's program in toto to formulate its own civil rights policies."[54] Wilson's commitment to integration became obvious. At a time when many African-American Seventh-day Adventists wanted to develop black unions, they found no support from Wilson. He wanted "greater rather than less integration." Reported *Spectrum:*

Charles Bradford

"Wilson expressed his passion for racial and ethnic integration through administrative policy and action. Perhaps most obviously, Wilson cleared the path for black administrators to become leaders of the whole church. He invited Charles Bradford to be the secretary of the General Conference for North America. Quickly, delegates to conferences and members in the pew learned that Bradford was one of the denomination's best-read and most powerful speakers."[55] When Charles Bradford was elected vice-president of the North American Division in 1979, it made national news.[56] His appointment to the North American Division presidency was doubly significant in that his mother, Etta Littlejohn, had been a convert under Edson White in Vicksburg, Mississippi, and was one of the first sixteen students to enroll at Oakwood.[57]

In 1985, Wilson wrote: "Racism is among the worst of ingrained prejudices that characterize sinful human beings. . . . Racism is really a heresy and in essence a form of idolatry, for it limits the fatherhood of God by denying the brotherhood of all mankind and by exalting the superiority of one's own race. . . . As a worldwide community of faith, the Seventh-day Adventist Church wishes to witness to and exhibit in her own ranks the unity and love that transcend racial differences and overcomes past alienation between races."[58]

Robert Pierson

Wilson's efforts as North American Division president were multiplied when Robert Pierson became General Conference president. As Lee and Baker noted, with a large share of his ministry having been spent working with blacks in Africa, "it was no surprise that Robert Pierson entered the presidency with an agenda to improve race relations not only in the United States but wherever they were needed. Like Neal Wilson (who would follow him as GC president), Pierson would chip away at the wall of color prejudice in his own way, with well-placed, sure blows."[59]

Dr. Ron Smith, president Southern Union Conference

Such efforts have fostered progress in integrating Seventh-day Adventist institutions as dedicated trendsetters have made it possible for others to break the "color line." More and more churches are integrated; Southern Adventist University is integrated; and the Southern Union Conference has a qualified African-American president—Dr. Ron Smith.[60]

Overlapping Church Organizational Structure

One major issue remains. In a social climate of expanding desegregation, many people are asking why overlapping Seventh-day Adventist structures with separate state and regional conferences is necessary. In his January 17, 2015 sermon, "Why I Believe in the 1,000 Man March after Ferguson," Dwight Nelson, senior pastor of Pioneer Memorial Church, at Andrews University, "called for an end of ethnically separated conferences in the Seventh-day Adventist Church. Shortly afterward, a petition from Pioneer Memorial Church to the North American Division of Seventh-day Adventists went up on Change.org. . . . [and] Dwight Nelson was among those signing the petition. He commented alongside his signature, 'I'm signing this because the time has come at last to live out Jesus' radical command to love one another that we may be one in Him. I hope you will join me.' "[61] The Allegheny East Conference responded to Nelson's sermon in a town hall video conference, facilitated by Frank E. Legette, III, rehearsing the history of the origin of regional conferences with the object of showing their relevance. Their major concern about a unified system of conferences was in who would serve the inner cities.[62] Though the beneficial expedient of the segregation of conferences was conceived as a "threading of the needle" between mission and prejudice until the church found "a better way," today the separate systems of conferences have developed separate constituencies.[63] With the departure of whites from the inner city, the regional conferences increasingly have picked up the responsibility of those areas. As one participant suggested in the chat accompanying the Allegheny East Conference Town Hall meeting, why not have different "brands" to serve different "markets" like Toyota and Lexus? Whether or not the dual system is maintained or reorganized, there needs to be greater interaction between the churches and their members. Ricardo B. Graham, President of the Pacific Union Conference of Seventh-day Adventists, has suggested that there be more cooperation through joint programs and pulpit exchanges.[64] The word from those who recognize the value and sense of belonging of the overlapping organizations is "cooperation, not merger." This also has to do with the integration of the churches themselves. People will always have preferences in worship style, so different cultural experiences will be necessary. However, directing an African-American family to a church on the other side of town must be a thing of the past.

Dwight Nelson, pastor Pioneer Memorial Church, Andrews University

Ricardo B. Graham, president Pacific Union Conference

Baptismal candidates at Fort Myers Shores Church (left to right): Nigel Loney, Roger Johnson, Pedro Nuñez, Jean Paul, Nancy Bartolet, Sarah Noack, and Claudette Loney

A Personal Post Script about the Journey

As a pastor in the Carolina Conference of Seventh-day Adventists, I have enjoyed fellowshipping with church members and laboring with colleagues in ministry from the overlapping South Atlantic Conference churches. I shared a school and assisted H. L. Anderson in tent meetings in Conway, South Carolina. It was our joy to share our baptistery with Elder Jesse West and the newly formed New Life Church of Aiken, South Carolina. Elder P. M. Florence, who followed Elder West, invited me to a weekend of preaching at Oakwood, which was enlightening and memorable. Pastor Steven Brooks and I shared overlapping districts in Wilson, North Carolina, and I volunteered to teach Spanish at the Mount Hebron Adventist Christian School, which Pastor Brooks started. (My home-schooled children, who accompanied me, have fond memories of the experience.) I also enjoyed the camaraderie of pastors from the South Atlantic and South Central Conferences in the masters program at Southern Adventist University. My pastoral colleagues and the African-American members of the churches I have pastored have been my instructors. I learned about dialogical preaching, what it is like to be racially profiled driving in a Southern town (recognizing my own "white privilege"), and the benefit that Regional Conferences have been in the work among African Americans.

Wilhelmina Johnson teaching at Vacation Bible School

Wilhelmina Johnson, who was the first black teacher in the Aiken, South Carolina, High School, was another of my teachers. She became a member of the Aiken Seventh-day Adventist Church as a result of the rediscovery of a long-forgotten Bible lesson enrollment card she had sent in. Pastor Jim Sawtell came across the card and called upon her at her house with Crey Trowell, an African-American member of the church. She was ready to learn many things from the Bible that she had not been taught growing up. What she learned she shared with a fraternity sister Ann Dicks. At the same time, Gloria Curry, another fraternity sister, learned new Bible truth through a seminar conducted by Pastor Sawtell, and the three "sisters" joined the Seventh-day Adventist Church, becoming respected spiritual leaders within the congregation.[65]

Martha Marsh

Long-time friend of my family, native South Carolinian Martha Marsh, knew firsthand the Southern inter-racial experience of the last century. She and her parents were charter members of the Camden Seventh-day Adventist Church in the 1960s, and her parents donated the property upon which the church was built. I had the privilege of visiting with her in September 2014—just after her 90th birthday—and I described my research on Ellen White's counsels on race relations. She recalled with fondness her African-American caregiver Sally and said in her gentle South Carolina accent: "It's a shame that they were looked down on for so long by the white people. . . . Don't you think so? I think it took Martin Luther King to wake the people up."

I agreed and remarked that racial inequality could have been dealt with sooner if the people had been willing. I also mentioned being told, while pastoring in Kingstree, another small South Carolina town, about the lynching of a black man in the 1930s.

"They did?" she said. "Isn't that awful!"

I nodded my head and attempted to correct the negative turn in the conversation I had given it: "A lot of things have happened to get us where we are today, and, in that sense, we have progressed." I then asked her about the percentages of African-American and white members in the Camden Church. She guessed that it was about half and half, and I said, "Now that wouldn't have probably happened when you were a child."

"Oh, I know it," she responded. "No, they'd have pushed them out of the church." She asked what my book was going to be called, and I told her that I was deciding, at the time, between two titles. She didn't seem impressed with the first, but when I mentioned *Journeying to the Same Heaven*, she brightened and said, "That'll catch somebody's eye!" Then, after reflecting on it just a bit, she said, "I kind of like that!"[66]

While in the Aiken-North Augusta district, I had an epiphany regarding race relations. It came to me in the form of an apology as I visited an African-American Baptist church in Augusta, Georgia. I was there to determine whether the work of an artist who painted their baptismal mural would be suitable for the Aiken church's baptistery. After I had waited in their fellowship hall for a few moments, a young lady met me to show me the baptistery painting. Even though, at the time, I did not know whether any of my Southern ancestors had owned slaves, I realized that I was carrying a load of "white guilt" for being part of a race that kept people of another race in slavery. It occurred to me that this was an opportunity to voice what I had been feeling, so I said to the young lady before she took me to see the artwork, "I want to apologize to you for what people of my color did to people of your color." She was surprised by my statement and told me that that was the first time she ever had any white person apologize to her like that.

I do not know what my apology did for the young lady, but I know that it prepared me to be able to consider my family's possible connections with slavery. I knew that the given name of my great grandfather, whom the grandchildren called "Grandpa Jeff," was *Jefferson Davis* Morgan. In researching this book, I learned that Grandpa Jeff was born in February 1861, the very month that Jefferson Davis took office as president of the Confederacy. I also learned that his father, Isham, fought with the 38th Alabama Infantry and died of disease in Mobile, Alabama in 1862. Through a will posted online, I learned that Grandpa Jeff's grandfather, Joseph Morgan, a landowner in Wilcox County, Alabama, had willed several slaves to his children. The will gave their names: "Old Abe," Ell, Net, Washington, Jerry and "Young Abe," Jim, Dan, Henry, Jack, Dave and Tom, "Old Mary," "Old Amy," Lynn, Caroline, Susie, Mass, Let and "Little Net." Knowing their names made slavery much more personal to me. I could not help but wonder how they had been treated. I only hope that it was better than many others. I also pondered how they faired after emancipation. Whatever their experience—and the experience of several million others besides them—we cannot go back and change what happened. Neither can we go back and change past discrimination in the Seventh-day Adventist Church. All that we can do is acknowledge that God has revealed His desire that all people be treated with dignity and that Seventh-day Adventists see all people who accept Jesus' truth as a single brotherhood, "journeying to the same heaven."[67] Seventh-day Adventists have indeed made progress in this regard, but in any journey, the most important step is always the next one.[68]

Ellen White's early vision of the pathway to heaven

Endnotes

PREFACE

[1] John R. McKivigan, *The War against Proslavery Religion*, p. 20. McKivigan's appraisal of the Adventists ignores the many abolitionists who were Adventists, yet it is correct in assessing Miller's view of the world. "Whereas postmillennialism had an optimistic vision of a world tending towards betterment and a bright future, Miller proclaimed that it was heading to destruction" (George R. Knight, *Millennial Fever and the End of the World: A Study of Millerite Adventism*, p. 20).

[2] Completed May 7, 2012. " 'Elephant in the room' is an English metaphorical idiom for an obvious truth that is either being ignored or going unaddressed. The idiomatic expression also applies to an obvious problem or risk no one wants to discuss" (*Cambridge Academic Content Dictionary*, p. 298).

[3] This centered on her statement, "When England does declare war, all nations will have an interest of their own to serve, and there will be general war, general confusion" (*Testimonies for the Church*, vol. 1, p. 259). Dr. Browning felt that this was an example of plausible deniability; I told him that I understood it as a conditional statement about what would occur when England finally did decide to go to war.

[4] Ellen G. White, Ms. 6, 1891 (Nov. 4, 1889), par. 17.

[5] Ellen G. White, "To the Little Remnant Scattered Abroad" (1846), p. 47. Metaphor is from Matt. 7:14.

CHAPTER 1 - What "Elephant"?

[1] Quoted by Wendell Phillips, *Disunion: Two Discourses at Music Hall, on January 20th, and February 17th, 1861*, p. 5.

[2] Darryl G. Hart and John R. Muether, *Seeking a Better Country: 300 Years of American Presbyterianism*, p. 150.

[3] John C. Calhoun, "The Causes by Which the Union Is Endangered," from *The Works of John C. Calhoun*, vol. 1, edited by Richard Kenner Crallé in Edwin C. Rozwenc, *The Causes of the American Civil War*, pp. 9, 10; C. C. Goen, *Broken Churches, Broken Nation: Denominational Schisms and the Coming of the American Civil War*; Allen Garden, "Religious Schism as a Prelude to the American Civil War: Methodists, Baptists, and Slavery," *Andrews University Seminary Studies*, Vol. 24, No. 1 (Spring 1986), p. 17.

[4] C. B. Harrison to Lawrence O'Bryan Branch, Dec. 2, 1860, reprinted in W. Buck Yearns and John G. Barrett, eds., *North Carolina Civil War Documentary*, pp. 11–13, quoted in Stephanie McCurry, *Confederate Reckoning: Power and Politics in the Civil War South*, pp. 41, 43.

[5] James Morton Callahan, *The Diplomatic History of the Southern Confederacy*, pp. 277, 278. Focusing on the tariff was part of a strategy devised by moderate delegates Robert Barnwell Rhett and Maxey Gregg (Don H. Doyle, *Cause of All Nations: An International History of the American Civil War*, p. 31).

[6] Allan Nevins, *The Emergence of Lincoln: Prologue to Civil War, 1859-1861*, p. 465, in Rozwenc, p. 212.

[7] South Carolinian James Henry Hammond declared in 1858: "... you dare not make war on cotton. No power on earth dares to make war upon it. Cotton is king" (Doyle, p. 5). British historian Amanda Foreman dismissed cotton as the cause of British blindness to Southern slavery, citing the bumper crop of cotton in 1859 and 1860 as reason enough for England to not be concerned about future supplies of a raw material that admittedly employed one out of every five Britons. She preferred to interpret British actions as the result of accepting Lincoln's statements about the war being merely to save the Union and accepting Mason and Slidell's obfuscation about the war being about self-governance, leaving them to interpret the North as fighting for "Empire" and the South as fighting for self-determinism (online interview, "Amanda Foreman Part 3 of 4"). Alfred Grant validated that there was a stockpile of cotton in England, yet he acknowledged: "The claim that a Confederate victory would lead to the amelioration and emancipation of the Negro because of the 'moral pressure of Europe' was disingenuous at best. In its coverage of the Civil War in America, the British press simply provided, in the oldest tradition of the Fourth Estate, exactly what its readers demanded" (*The American Civil War and the British Press*, pp. 6, 9). Their blindness to slavery in the South required more than just believing Lincoln; it also required believing Southern obfuscation.

[8] "The American consul in Bristol reported that [William Lowndes] Yancey [Confederate commissioner to Britain and France, 1861–65] had been flagrant in his promises, telling one author of a pro-Confederate article that Richmond had given him 'full powers to pledge gradual emancipation to the governments of Europe on condition of their guaranteeing the independence of the Confederate States.' NARA, M. T-185, roll 7, vol. 7, Zebina Eastman to William Henry Seward, October 20, 1862" (Amanda Foreman, *A World on Fire: Britain's Crucial Role in the American Civil War*, p. 858). An English gentleman with a reputation within the literary world wrote a letter regarding the initial cause of the war and what kept it going. The letter was published in the October 15, 1861 London *Daily News*. In it, the author cited a recent speech by British

Secretary of State for Foreign Affairs Earl Russell: "We now see two parties contending, not upon the question of slavery—though that, I believe, is the original cause of the conflict—not contending with respect to free-trade and protection, but contending, as so many States of the old world have contended, the one side for empire, and the other for power." The one quoting Earl Russell said this appraisal was "inaccurate and misleading," and he went on to assess the divide: "The republican party in the United States elected a President in November last, as representing the principle that slavery should not be extended to the common territories of the Union. Some of the Southern States, incensed at this election, and alarmed at the results to slavery of an executive hostile to its extension, have endeavored by violence—not by legal means, such as the Constitution offered—to establish their independence. The North has gone to war to prevent the dismemberment of the Union by illegal means, a motive which cannot with any precision of thought or language be deemed synonymous with 'empire.' The South has gone to war for immediate independence, with the motive to protect slavery from danger, where it exists, and to ensure its extension hereafter—a purpose very different from the contest of any State in the old world for 'power' " ("Causes and Objects of the War," *Boston Daily Advertiser*, Nov. 18, 1861, p. 2).

It is difficult to assign a single cause for the war since human interactions are complex. Historians have defended various causes. These include industrial versus agrarian economies, a sense of "Southern nationalism" and "Southern rights" (beyond "states' rights"), and the moral issue of slavery. In each scenario, the historian tends to affix blame on either the North or the South. In a final chapter in *The Causes of the American Civil War*, Edwin C. Rozwenc pointed out that recent scholarship on the cause(s) of the war comes down to which apologetic position the historian takes. "... historians writing about the Civil War tend to be apologists for 'geographical, social and other influences' in their personal backgrounds. Thus, for example, Frank L. Owsley becomes a frank apologist for the Southern agrarian tradition; James G. Randall's interpretation may be said to display an overly strong sympathy for moderates like Stephen A. Douglas and James Buchanan; or Arthur M. Schlesinger, Jr., may be characterized as being closely linked in historical thinking to the spirit of Seward's 'irrepressible conflict' ideas as well as to the moral urgency of the abolitionist tradition" (Rozwenc, pp. 226, 227).

[9] Frank Lawrence Owsley, *I'll Take My Stand*, pp. 84, 85, in Rozwenc, p. 130.

[10] Abraham Lincoln, in Michael F. Holt, *The Fate of Their Country*, p. 146. Had the South gained independence there would have been continued battles over whether new territories would belong to the Union or the Confederacy.

[11] "The result of the whole is to give the Northern section a predominance in every department of the Government, and thereby concentrate in it the two elements which constitute the Federal Government,—majority of States, and a majority of their population, estimated in federal numbers. Whatever section concentrates the two in itself possesses the control of the entire Government" (Calhoun, quoted in Rozwenc, p. 3).

[12] Calhoun also noted the North's considering "the relation between the two races in the Southern section" to be a "sin," "a crime," and "a blot and a stain on the character of what they call the Nation" (Calhoun, in Rozwenc, p. 7). For Calhoun's use of "agitation," see Rozwenc, pp. 7–10.

[13] The 1854 Kansas-Nebraska Act, proposed by Stephen A. Douglas, mandated "popular sovereignty." "Popular sovereignty" was "a pre-Civil War doctrine asserting the right of the people living in a newly organized territory to decide by vote of their territorial legislature whether or not slavery would be permitted there" (http://www.merriam-webster.com/dictionary/popular%20sovereignty, accessed 10/16/14). The March 6, 1857 United States Supreme Court Dred Scott decision declared: "(1) Negroes were not citizens, and thus could not sue in federal courts, (2) a slave's residence in a free state did not make him a free man; and (3) the Missouri Compromise of 1820, which had forbidden slavery in that portion of the Louisiana Purchase (except Missouri) lying north of latitude 36° 30´, was an unconstitutional exercise of congressional power" (Joe Wheeler, *Abraham Lincoln: A Man of Faith and Courage*, p. 125).

[14] The imagery of "a house divided" is from Luke 11:17. Uriah Smith published the key statement from the speech, "I do not expect the house to fall; I do not look for a dissolution of the Union; but it will cease to be divided; it will become one thing or the other; for Slavery or against." He prefaced it with: "We print this week an extract from a speech by Abraham Lincoln, at the State Convention of Ills. It will be of interest to the readers of the *Review*, as it shows, on the authority of one who is capable of judging, and whose business it is to watch the design and tendency of legislative action the position which our government at present occupies with regard to the diabolical institution of American Slavery, and the direction in which it is tending on this question. He who looks for good, or hopes for reform in the legislative or executive departments of this government, is doomed, we think, to utter and hopeless disappointment" (*Advent Review and Sabbath Herald*, Sept. 2, 1858, p. 124; hereafter cited as *Review and Herald*). Smith was right. It would take a war costing thousands of Northern and Southern lives to change the national view of slavery.

[15] City University of New York Historian James Oakes argued, with strong evidentiary support, that the Republican party was following an intentional plan in first trying to limit the expansion of slavery and then using military emancipation to fray slavery's edges (Oakes, *Freedom National: The Destruction of Slavery in the United States*, 1861–1865, pp. 51, 52). Nevertheless, the Constitution stipulated that each state would have to vote to limit slavery in its own territories.

[16] "If they are victorious, one Washington editor predicted, the Republicans will 'push their aggressive policy to its legitimate conclusion' by attempting to 'expel slavery from the Union.' The influential Springfield *Daily Illinois State Register*, the editorial voice of Democratic Senator Stephen Douglas, warned that Lincoln 'proposes to legislate so that slavery must soon be extinguished.' Another Douglas paper declared, on the eve of the election, that the Republicans were 'making war upon the Southern people' so as to 'make them ultimately forego that system of labor which they prefer.' See *Constitution* (Washington, DC), Sept. 6, 1860; *Daily Illinois State Register* (Springfield), Sept. 28, 1860; *Daily Ohio Statesman* (Columbus, Ohio), Nov. 2, 1860, in Howard Cecil Perkins, ed., *Northern Editorials on Secession* (American Historical Association), vol. 1, pp. 33, 43, 68" (Oakes, p. 508, fn. 17). "A month before the election, the *Daily True Delta* conceded that Lincoln would not directly 'overthrow' slavery or 'conspire' against southern rights. But 'so far as the south can be dwarfed, cramped and shut in from healthy intercourse with the world ... the abolition president will use the whole power of the country against it.' Lincoln's election, then, would be 'the death knell of the political and social prosperity of the south.'" (Oakes, p. 60).

[17] Doyle, pp. 29, 30. From the founding of the Republican Party in 1854, Democrats labeled its adherents "*Black Republicans*" to identify them as proponents of black equality, which they feared would lead to the blending of the races.

[18] Alexander Stephens, "Cornerstone Address," in Wakelyn, *Southern Pamphlets on Secession*, pp. 405–406.

[19] The framers of the Constitution "did not merely refuse to allow the word *slavery* into the document, they went out of their way to refer to slaves as 'persons held in service' rather than as 'property in man'—a deliberate choice that reflected the influence of antislavery jurisprudence at the time, a choice that would, moreover, become one of the core precepts of all antislavery politics" (Oakes, p. 6).

[20] William J. Cooper, Jr., *Jefferson Davis, American*, pp. 173, 191.

[21] Rozwenc, p. 32.

[22] In 1860, Negroes made up 55% of the population of Davis's home state of Mississippi, 57% of the population of South Carolina, and 37% of the population of the seceding states as a whole ("Results from the 1860 Census," available online at http://www.civil-war.net/pages/1860_census.html, accessed 10/20/14).

[23] According to Davis, Lincoln's announced policy of the exclusion of slavery from new territories would render "property in slaves so insecure as to be comparably worthless, ... thereby annihilating in effect property worth thousands of millions of dollars" (*Jefferson Davis, Constitutionalist: His Letters, Papers, and Speeches*, vol. 5, p. 72, quoted in McPherson, *This Mighty Scourge: Perspectives on the Civil War*, p. 3. See also Jefferson Davis' letter to Congress, from Montgomery, April 29, 1861, in *The War of the Rebellion*, vol. 1, p. 259). "Surrounded by hostile free states, the *Mercury* warned, the 'timid' in the cotton states would begin selling off their own slaves, but there would be no purchasers. The value of slave property would sink to nothing" (Oakes, p. 60). Davis believed "no community should arrogantly assume to interfere with the affairs of another" (Davis, *Speeches of the Honorable Jefferson Davis of Mississippi*, p. 12). In his inaugural address, Davis declared that the Confederacy "illustrates the American idea that governments rest upon the consent of the governed, and that it is the right of the people to alter or abolish governments whenever they become destructive of the ends for which they were established" (Cooper, p. 330).

[24] Rozwenc, p. 30, original spelling retained.

[25] Jefferson Davis, *Papers*, vol. 1, pp. 540, 541, in David Lindsey, *A. Lincoln/Jefferson Davis: The House Divided*, pp. 106–108.

[26] Jefferson Davis, *The Rise and Fall of the Confederate Government*, vol. 1, p. 78, emphasis in original. "For Davis," wrote author William J. Cooper, Jr., "demonstrating that the South had acted constitutionally proved the South was right. Slavery, which in 1861 and before he had regarded as central, he now downplayed as the cause of secession. 'The truth remains intact and incontrovertible,' he proclaimed, 'that the existence of African servitude was in no wise the cause of the conflict, but only an incident.' Davis maintained that the North was wrong not only for refusing to accept the constitutional secession of the southern states, but also for prosecuting a destructive, uncivilized war and imposing an oppressive peace on honorable men who had laid down their arms. [*The Rise and Fall of the Confederate Government*, vol. 1, p. 80]" (Cooper, p. 619). Regarding the South's Constitutional rights, Stephen Douglas declared: "I have said on a former occasion, and I here repeat, that it is neither desirable nor possible to establish uniformity in the local and domestic institution of all the States of the Confederacy. And why? Because the Constitution of the United States rests upon the right of every state to decide all its local and domestic institutions for itself. It is not possible, therefore, to make them conform to each other, unless we subvert the Constitution of the United States" (Rozwenc, p. 22).

[27] "Free labor" described the labor of freemen as distinguished from that of slaves. "The only thing preventing slavery from meeting its appointed destiny was the Slave Power, twisting the meaning of the Constitution to wring from the federal government policies that protected slavery and prolonged its life" (Oakes, p. 30).

[28] Before Lincoln's election, the *Review and Herald* quoted the February 29, 1860 speech of William H. Seward, in which he addressed President Buchanan on the state of the nation: "Mr. President, did ever the annals of any government show a more rapid or more complete departure from the wisdom and virtue of its founders?" ("The Degeneracy of the United States," *Review and Herald*, March 15, 1860, p. 132). In the second year of the war, the *Review and Herald* referred to statements of the founders of the country in support of the ending of slavery. Here are a few of these: " 'There is not a man living who wishes more sincerely than I do to see a plan adopted for the abolition of slavery' (George Washington, Apr. 12th, 1786). 'It is the most earnest wish of America to see an entire stop forever put to the wicked, cruel, and unnatural trade in slaves' (meeting at Fairfax, Va., July 18, 1774, presided over by Washington). 'I tremble for my country, when I reflect that God is just. His justice cannot sleep for ever' (Jefferson's Notes on Slavery in Virginia, 1782). 'The King of Great Britain has waged cruel war against human nature itself, violating its most sacred rights of life and liberty, in the persons of a distant people who never offended him; captivating them and carrying them into slavery in another hemisphere, or to incur miserable death in their transportation hither' (Jefferson's original draft of the Declaration of Independence). 'After the year 1800 of the Christian era, there shall be neither slavery nor involuntary servitude in any of the said states' (Jefferson's Ordinance of 1787, unanimously approved by Congress and signed by Washington). 'We have seen the mere distinction of color made, in the most enlightened period of time, a ground of the most oppressive dominion ever exercised by man over man' (James Madison). 'We have found that this evil has preyed upon the very vitals of the Union, and has been prejudicial to all the States in which it has existed' (James Monroe)' " (U.S., "The Degeneracy of the United States," *Review and Herald*, June 17, 1862, p. 22).

[29] Stephen Douglas was the chief sponsor of the Kansas-Nebraska Act of 1854. "The Kansas-Nebraska Act allowed each territory to decide the issue of slavery on the basis of popular sovereignty. Kansas with slavery would violate the Missouri Compromise, which had kept the Union from falling apart for the last thirty-four years. The long-standing compromise would have to be repealed. Opposition was intense, but ultimately the bill passed in May 1854. Territory north of the sacred 36° 30' line was now open to popular sovereignty. The North was outraged" ("The Kansas-Nebraska Act," found at http://www.ushistory.org/us/31a.asp, accessed 10/16/14).

[30] Quoted in Rozwenc, pp. 25–27. In referring to "other *man's* rights" does he not hint at the emancipation of the slaves since the Constitution calls them "persons held in service" rather than "property in man"?

[31] Avery Craven, "The 1840's and the Democratic Process," *Journal of Southern History*, vol. 16, no. 2 (1950), in Rozwenc, p. 173.

[32] Abraham Lincoln, "Inaugural Address," March 4, 1861. Lincoln was referring to the safeguards for slave owners that had been included in the Constitution to get the Southern colonies to join the Union, according to the rights of the individual states for slavery in their own territories. "Charles Cotesworth Pinckney of South Carolina, one of a handful of slavery's forceful defenders in Philadelphia, had threatened to vote against the proposed Constitution if it 'should fail to insert some security to the southern states against an emancipation of the slave' " (Oakes, p. 2). U.S. Senator Charles Sumner declared: "It is impossible, without violence, at once to the spirit and to the letter of the Constitution, to attribute to Congress any power to legislate, either for its abolition in the States or its support anywhere" (Oakes, p. 5). There was one way that slaves could be emancipated, as John Quincy Adams pointed out: ". . . even though the federal government could not *abolish* slavery in a state, it could *emancipate* the slaves in any state that was in rebellion against the United States" (Oakes p. 41, citing Joseph Story, *Commentaries on the Conflict of Laws*, pp. 92, 93; and David Herbert Donald, *Charles Sumner and the Coming of the Civil War*, p. 388).

[33] David B. Chesebrough, "*God Ordained This War*," p. 85. John Hughes, the archbishop of New York, declared: "Now, we Catholics, and a vast majority of our brave troops in the field, have not the slightest idea of carrying on a war that costs so much blood and treasure just to gratify a clique of Abolitionists in the North. If it were generally known that this is one of the purposes of the war, the drafting of troops would become immediately necessary—volunteers would be few indeed—and the business of recruiting would become even slacker than it is now said to be." Hughes admitted that "our Catholic Dr. Brownson holds that slavery is the cause of the war," yet he countered, "This happens to be simply impossible ... Slavery existed since the Declaration of Independence and before...." (John Hughes, *Metropolitan Record*, in *Bedford Gazette*, Nov. 8, 1861, p. 1). The *Liberator* quoted one source, which it lampooned, as asserting: "This is a war neither for nor against slavery, but for the preservation of the country. This contest has no reference to the institution. The irritating and distracting question of slavery must be kept entirely out of sight." Of course, the *Liberator* went on to declare: "Slavery alone is the cause of all the trouble. It has no other parentage. No good is accomplished by denying the real nature of the disease..." ("The Cause of the War," *Liberator* [Boston], Sept. 6, 1861, p. 141).

[34] "The Emancipation Question. Is Slavery the Cause of the War?" *Newark Advocate* (Newark, Ohio), Dec. 20, 1861.

[35] Abraham Lincoln, Aug. 22, 1862, in the *Reading Times* (Reading, Pennsylvania), Aug. 25, 1862, p. 3, emphasis added. Other newspapers across America picked up the letter. See, for example, *Berkshire County Eagle* (Pittsfield, Massachusetts), Aug. 28, 1862, p. 3; the *Newbern Daily Progress* (New Bern, North Carolina), Aug. 29,

1862, p. 2; and the *Joliet Signal* (Joliet, Illinois), Sept. 2, 1862, p. 3. Lincoln's statement to Greeley was also reported in England ("Current Events," *Home and Foreign Review*, vol. 1 [July 1862], p. 605).

[36] Garden, p. 29.

[37] Harriet Beecher Stowe, "The Church and the Slave Trade," *Review and Herald*, Nov. 20, 1860, p. 2.

[38] Albert Barnes, *The Church and Slavery*, p. 28.

[39] Charles Stearns, *The Way to Abolish Slavery* (1849), pp. 9, 10. Seventh-day Adventist John G. Fee wrote: "And in reference to the colored man in the free States, there are but few churches where he is treated as a brother. ... No wonder that New York has cast her recent vote against the colored man. Some years since a movement was made in the New York Legislature to extend to the colored man equal rights. It was replied, 'It is useless for us to attempt to do so, for the churches will not' " ("The Church, Slavery, and Caste," *Review and Herald*, Feb. 19, 1861, p. 107).

[40] Bertram Wyatt-Brown, "American Abolitionism and Religion," available online at http://nationalhumanitiescenter.org/tserve/nineteen/nkeyinfo/amabrel.htm, accessed 4/25/12. In 1830, there were 23 million Americans, but only 17% attended church (see "The Benevolent Empire," available online at http://www.christianchronicler.com/history1/benevolent_empire.html, accessed 4/25/12). Yet, by 1860, 33% of the nation identified themselves as "Christian" (Richard F. Selcer, *Civil War America, 1850 to 1875*, p. 145).

[41] Tim Stafford, "The Abolitionists," available online at http://www.christianitytoday.com/ch/1992/issue33/3321.html, accessed 4/23/12.

[42] McKivigan, p. 17.

[43] 'Lower judicatories' is a Presbyterian term which refers to "the synods, presbyteries, and sessions in the portion of our country where slavery exists. It was felt that the matter pertained primarily to them; that the proper action should begin with them; that the subject was one in which they had a special interest, and which it was supposed they would be best qualified to understand; and it was presumed that they would take such 'action' in the case as might prevent the necessity of bringing the matter again before the General Assembly, or make it a subject of general agitation in the church." Barnes was careful to point out that the matter was remanded to this level of church government, with the assumption that officials would "devise some efficient method for detaching the church from all connection with slavery," and, in the words of the 1839 resolution, "take such action as, in their judgment, would be most judicious and best adapted *to* REMOVE THE EVIL" (Barnes, p. 74).

[44] McKivigan, p. 33.

[45] The *Review and Herald* quoted a news item reprimanding the American Tract Society for having a slaveholder on its executive committee and the American Bible Society for electing a slaveholder to its vice-presidency. It also quoted from the *Golden Rule:* "A religion that dares not rebuke stealing, adultery, and blasphemy, under the general name of slavery, is a whited sepulchre, and is in alliance with the bitterest foes of Christ. If the American Tract Society, through a squeamish conservatism, a most unmartyr-like fear and liberalism has been betrayed into this sin, let it repent, and bring forth works meet for repentance" ("How to Make Infidels," *Review and Herald*, May 21, 1857, p. 19).

[46] Garden, p. 17. Some of the better known Abolitionists were William Lloyd Garrison and his newspaper the *Liberator*, eloquent former slaves Sojourner Truth and Frederick Douglass, women's rights advocate Elizabeth Cady Stanton and Abby Kelley, Quaker Lucretia Mott, and South Carolina Quakers Angelina and Sarah Grimké. As a side note, Louis B. Reynolds noted that Frederick Douglass's daughter, Rosetta Douglass Sprague, joined the First Seventh-day Adventist Church on Eighth Street NE, in Washington, DC (*We Have Tomorrow*, p. 23).

[47] Mennonites are credited with staging America's first public protest against slavery. Quakers threatened any of their members who imported slaves with expulsion from the denomination ("Christianity and Slavery: Movement Towards Abolitionism," available online at www.religioustolerance.org/chr_slav3.htm, accessed 1/4/15). However, there are isolated cases of slaveholding among the Quakers. See, for example, Ashley Ellen Humphries, "The Migration of Westfield Quakers from Surry County, North Carolina, 1786-1828."

[48] The *Review and Herald* added: "Nothing is said of the Episcopal Convention. Nor does it change, in its general aspect, the position of the churches in their silent complicity with the evil of slavery" ("The American Board and Slave Trade," *Review and Herald*, Dec. 11, 1860, p. 32, quoting Mrs. Harriet Beecher Stowe, from the New York *Independent*).

[49] Lester B. Scherer, *Slavery and the Churches*, pp. 132-135, quoted in McKivigan, p. 26.

[50] Jonathan Grant, "Heaven Bound, Earthly Good," p. 49; Alfonzo Greene, "[Black] Regional Conferences in the Seventh-Day Adventists (SDA) Church Compared with United Methodist [Black] Central Jurisdiction/Annual Conferences with White SDA Conferences, From 1940-2001," *Dissertations*, Paper 160, pp. 11, 24. A splinter of the Methodist Church, the Wesleyan Methodist Connection of America, "saw slavery as a moral evil" and "refused to admit into membership anyone who owned slaves or sanctioned the existence of slavery in America" (Brian Strayer, "John Byington: First General Conference President, Circuit-Riding Preacher, and Radical Reformer," book manuscript at Pacific Press, forthcoming).

[51] Ronald L. Numbers and Jonathan M. Butler, *The Disappointed: Millerism and Millenarianism in the Nineteenth Century*, p. 140, quoted in Peter K. Chung, "Rise of the Remnant: The Formation of the Seventh-day Adventist Church from the Era of Slavery and the Civil War," p. 20.

[52] Jonathan M. Butler, "From Millerism to Seventh-day Adventism: Boundlessness to Consolidation," *Church History*, vol. 55, no. 1 (March 1986), p. 54, cited by Chung, p. 19.

[53] William Miller to Truman Hendryx, Feb. 25, 1834, reconstructed from Numbers and Butler, p. 140, cited by Chung, p. 20, and David L. Rowe, *God's Strange Work: William Miller and the End of the World*, p. 154, original spelling retained, bracketed wording supplied by Rowe.

[54] A "piquet" (properly spelled "picket") is "a guard posted in front of an army to give notice of the approach of the enemy" (Webster's 1828 *Dictionary*, available online at www.christiantech.com).

[55] Numbers and Butler, p. 141, in Chung, p. 22.

[56] Jonathan Grant, p. 82.

[57] Numbers and Butler, p. 149.

[58] Chung, p. 21.

[59] The most fundamental of Seventh-day Adventist beliefs are: faith in Jesus (Rom. 5:1, 2; Eph. 2:8–10), His imminent return (Rev. 22:12; John 14:1–3), His heavenly priesthood (Heb. 8:1, 2), the perpetuity of the law of God (Rom. 3:31; 7:22, 25; 8:4, 7; 1 Cor. 7:19; 1 Tim 1:8–11; Heb. 8:10; 10:16) including the seventh-day Sabbath (Acts 13:27, 42, 44; 16:13; 17:2), and the bodily resurrection at Jesus' return of those who "sleep in Jesus" (Job 19:26; 1 Thess. 4:14; 1 Cor. 15:53, 54).

[60] John Byington and U. Smith, "Report of General Conference of Seventh-day Adventists," *Review and Herald*, May 26, 1863, pp. 204–206.

[61] Jonathan Grant, p. 55.

[62] "The war itself and its long, sordid aftermath of so-called reconstruction—considered even worse than the war itself—permitted little, if any, thought of entering the Southland in an organized manner. Only a few widely scattered believers lived in the entire section" (Louis A. Hansen, *From So Small a Dream*, p. 21). "Seventh-day Adventists made no progress in the South before the Civil War. A stray member or two in Maryland and Virginia and a scattered company in Missouri marked the limits of their advance" (Arthur W. Spalding, *Captains of the Host*, p. 488).

[63] Mrs. White did this through her published works and private correspondence. She wrote to the church in Roosevelt, New York, about a Seventh-day Adventist elder who was in favor of slavery: "I saw that Brother A. Ross must be cautious of his words. He has not regarded slavery in a Bible light. He does not see it as God sees it. Brother Ross has expressed himself unguardedly and has exerted a wrong influence. He is watched, and he will surely be in a dangerous position unless he strives to counteract the influence His words have carried. As a people we must use great caution. As we do not engage in the war and pray for union and preach in regard to union, suspicions are aroused. If one like Brother Ross expresses sentiments not fully comprehended, but taken that he favors the South, this people will be branded as Secessionists, and in this excited state of the people but a word would set them on fire and destroy our safety. Brother Ross's views are not correct in regard to the institution of slavery" (Letter 16 [Aug. 3], 1861, in *Manuscript Releases*, vol. 5, p. 60). The text of the letter is in Letter 24, 1862 (*Testimonies for the Church*, vol. 1, p. 359), which is "a copy of a letter written to Bro. A[lexander M.] R[oss], Oswego, New York" in preparation for "Testimony for the Church, no. 9" (Jan. 1863). Ross publicly confessed his wrong ("From Bro. Ross," *Review and Herald*, April 21, 1863, p. 167). Ellen White also addressed an Adventist woman who was surrounded by secessionists. "You speak of living among secesh. I am sorry that it is so. It is so strange that Northern men can sympathize with this terrible rebellion and the institution of slavery" ("An Extract from a Letter Written to a Distant Female Friend," *Review and Herald*, Sept. 16, 1862, p. 126). Regarding the content of her vision at Rochester, New York, December 25, 1865, Mrs. White wrote that the "political views" of Sabbath-keepers lacking in sympathy for the "oppressed colored race" were "not right before God" (*Testimonies for the Church*, vol. 1, pp. 533, 534).

[64] This number is a broad estimate, not a careful calculation of recorded listings of visions.

[65] Ministerial Association of Seventh-day Adventists, *Seventh-day Adventists Believe: An Exposition of the Fundamental Beliefs of the Seventh-day Adventist Church* (1988, 2005), p. 258.

[66] Ellen G. White, *The Great Controversy*, p. vii. Arthur L. White, "Ellen G. White: A Brief Biography," available online at http://www.whiteestate.org/about/egwbio.asp, accessed 2/16/15, quoting White, *The Great Controversy* (1888), p. "d."

[67] Sources are noted for Old Testament historical works, Solomon's proverbs, and Luke's Gospel.

[68] W. C. White to L. E. Froom, Jan. 8, 1928, in *Selected Messages*, bk. 3, pp. 459, 460; W. C. White to L. E. Froom, Dec. 13, 1934.

[69] White, *The Great Controversy* (1888), p. "h."

[70] Ciro Sepúlveda, *Ellen White on the Color Line: The Idea of Race in a Christian Community*, Preface. We should note that Robert M. Kilgore's father, John Lindsay Kilgore, and John Byington, first president of the General Conference of

Seventh-day Adventists, helped slaves escape to freedom in Canada (G. Tom Carter, *The 19th Century Odyssey of John and Judith*, pp. 74, 134). Before joining the Adventists, Byington had left the Methodist Episcopal Church because it did not oppose slavery (Southwestern Adventist College. Alumni Association, *Lest We Forget, The Heritage of Southwestern Adventist College*, p. 2; Leslie N. Pollard, "The Cross-Culture Challenging a Church as it Begins a New Millennium" *Adventist Review*, Feb. 2000, cited by Roy Branson, "Ellen G. White: Racist or Champion of Equality?" available online at http://www.oakwood.edu/goldmine/hdoc/blacksda/champ). Byington "frequently chaired meetings of the St. Lawrence County Anti-Slavery Society, participated in abolitionist conventions, and—along with several other Byingtons and their Hilliard cousins—signed petitions in the 1850s demanding that the U.S. Congress abolish slavery, which he called 'an outrage [on humanity]' and 'a sin [under all circumstances]' " (Brian Strayer, "Remembering the Radical Politics of the Pioneers: John Byington," January 25, 2015, available online at https://adventistpeace.wordpress.com/2015/01/25/john-byingtons-radical-abolitionism-by-brian-strayer, accessed 2/8/15, and Strayer, "John Byington").

[71] Ellen G. White, "Testimony No. 5," *Testimonies for the Church*, vol. 1, p. 202, emphasis added. The closing article of Testimony No. 5 (in its entirety in *Testimonies for the Church*, vol. 1, pp. 185–209) was printed in June 1859 (see "Testimony for the Church, No. 5," *Review and Herald*, June 16, 1859, p. 32), yet it has the dateline "Mannsville, New York, October 21, 1858" (*Testimonies for the Church*, vol. 1, p. 209). One extreme example of the return of a slave, in response to the Fugitive Slave Act, was a free black man who faced punishment for harboring his own son, even though he did so with the knowledge of the boy's master (*Independent*, "The Mortara Case at Washington," *Review and Herald*, May 5, 1859, pp. 186, 187).

[72] White, *Testimonies for the Church*, vol. 1, p. 266; "Lift Up Your Eyes and Look on the Field," *Review and Herald*, Jan. 28, 1896, p. 50; adapted from Letter 80a (Aug. 16), 1895, par. 28. We should note that slavery based on race was a new type of slavery. In the ancient world, the enslaved were criminals, debtors, and prisoners of war. The similarity of the enslavement of the Israelites to the Egyptians before the Exodus to the slavery of American Negroes made the freeing of Israel under Moses a fit symbol of the freedom about which Southern slaves dreamed Winthrop D. Jordan's *White Over Black: American Attitudes Towards the Negro 1550–1812* delineates the evolution of white perceptions of difference between whites and blacks and the whites' use of the supposed difference in justifying race-based slavery. Jordan's book continues to be the definitive work on the subject.

[73] Uriah Smith, "The Warning Voice of Time and Prophecy," *Review and Herald*, June 23, 1853, p. 18. Smith prefaced this, declaring: "Let the united cry of millions tell,—Millions that groan beneath oppression's rod, Beneath the sin-forged chains of slavery, Robbed of their rights, to brutes degraded down."

[74] E. R. Seaman, "The Days of Noah and the Sons of Man," *Review and Herald*, June 13, 1854, p. 157. James White wrote: "It was thought that by the compromise of 1850, known as the 'Fugitive Slave Law,' the agitation of the slavery question was settled; but it is now revived again in its worst form. The greatest excitement prevails in regard to it, throughout the country. Politicians speak of it as an act which 'menaces the freedom of our institutions and the permanency of our Union.' They speak of it as 'well calculated to awaken the worst apprehensions, and the most fearful forebodings of future calamity.' They warn the people 'that the dearest interests of Freedom and the Union are in imminent peril.' Certain it is, that it is a question which will not be easily settled" ([James White], "The Nebraska Bill," *Review and Herald*, March 7, 1854, p. 56).

[75] J. N. Andrews, "Three Angels of Rev. XIV," *Review and Herald*, April 3, 1855, pp. 202, 203.

[76] Joshua R. Giddings, letter to T. W. Higgins, Jan. 7, 1857, in *Proceedings of the State Disunion Convention Held at Worcester, Massachusetts, January 15, 1857*, Appendix, pp. 6, 7, emphasis in original, quoted in [Uriah Smith], "The Dragon Voice," *Review and Herald*, Feb. 5, 1857, p. 106. Giddings was an attorney from Ohio who served as a U.S. representative for two decades and was an influential voice in establishing the Republican platform in 1856 (see Walter Buell, *Joshua R. Giddings: A Sketch*, Cleveland, Ohio: William W. Williams, 1882, pp. 9, 25, 204, 209).

[77] Douglas Morgan, *Adventism and the American Republic: The Public Involvement of a Major Apocalyptic Movement*, p. 26. Morgan made this assertion based on Ellen White's first printed statement on slavery: "Then commenced the jubilee, when the land should rest. I saw the pious slave rise in triumph and victory, and shake off the chains that bound him, while his wicked master was in confusion, and knew not what to do; for the wicked could not understand the words of the voice of God. Soon appeared the great white cloud. It looked more lovely than ever before. On it sat the S̲o̲n̲ of man" (Letter 1 [April 7], 1847 to Joseph Bates, published in her first book, *A Sketch of the Christian Experience and Views of Ellen G. White* [1851], p. 18). Just because slavery ended in America in 1865 does not mean that it no longer exists in the world at large. Estimates regarding the number of slaves at the present time range from almost 21 million to 29 million ("Forced labour, human trafficking and slavery," available online at http://www.ilo.org/global/topics/forced-labour/lang--en/index.htm, accessed 2/8/15; Oliver Milman, "Andrew Forrest signs up religious forces to fight slavery and trafficking," available online at http://www.theguardian.com/world/2014/mar/18/andrew-forrest-signs-up-religious-forces-to-fight-slavery-and-trafficking, accessed 2/8/15). Sabbatarian Adventists also saw the upholding of slavery as evidence that the United States was the false

prophet of Revelation 13. Methodist-minister-turned-Adventist Joseph B. Frisbie wrote: "... a government which will keep in abject slavery three millions of human beings, will not hesitate in the time of trouble, with its dragon voice, to make a decree to put to death all that will not worship, or obey..." ("From Bro. Frisbie," *Review and Herald*, Nov. 8, 1853, p. 142).

[78] Joseph Bates, *The Autobiography of Elder Joseph Bates* (1868), p. 236.

[79] Bates, p. 261. Bates and his companion, Heman S. Gurney, took the advent message to the slaveholding state of Maryland. Adventist "George Storrs, an ardent abolitionist, had been mobbed that same month in Virginia." Josiah Litch identified Adventists S. C. Chandler and S. S. Brewer as taking the Advent message to Virginia and North and South Carolina ("The Rise and Progress of Adventism," *Review and Herald*, May 8, 1856, p. 27). While there, Bates spoke with slaves along the way, and the slaves listened intently to their preaching from the gallery of a Methodist meeting-house. One slave came and offered to buy some literature, and Gurney made a copy of his last piece (Bates, pp. 277, 280–285, 290, 291). "The General Conference of May 1843 in New York sympathized with the need but decided to send only literature and not preachers" (Jonathan Grant, pp. 84, 85, based on George R. Knight, *Joseph Bates: The Real Founder of Seventh-day Adventism*, p. 63). Few blacks could read, and it was against the law in much of the South to teach blacks to read. In North Carolina, the legislature enacted, in 1830, "A Bill to Prevent All Persons from Teaching Slaves to Read or Write, the Use of Figures Excepted." Violation of such laws resulted in steep fines, imprisonment, or whipping. The Virginia Revised Code of 1819 stipulated: "That all meetings or assemblages of slaves, or free negroes or mulattoes mixing and associating with such slaves at any meeting-house or houses, &c., in the night; or at any SCHOOL OR SCHOOLS for teaching them READING OR WRITING, either in the day or night, under whatsoever pretext, shall be deemed and considered an UNLAWFUL ASSEMBLY; and any justice of a county, &c., wherein such assemblage shall be, either from his own knowledge or the information of others, of such unlawful assemblage, &c., may issue his warrant, directed to any sworn officer or officers, authorizing him or them to enter the house or houses where such unlawful assemblages, &c., may be, for the purpose of apprehending or dispersing such slaves, and to inflict corporal punishment on the offender or offenders, at the discretion of any justice of the peace, not exceeding twenty lashes" ("The Slave Experience: Education, Arts, & Culture. Original Documents," available online at http://www.pbs.org/wnet/slavery/experience/education/docs1.html, accessed 12/18/15). "Although every southern state had outlawed the teaching of reading and writing to enslaved blacks (and in some cases, free blacks as well), there is considerable evidence that some whites defied the law" ("The Case of Mrs. Margaret Douglass," available online at http://www.pbs.org/wgbh/aia/part4/4h2945.html, accessed 2/8/15).

[80] [Uriah Smith], "Politics," *Review and Herald*, Sept. 11, 1856, p. 152.

[81] Morgan, *Adventism and the American Republic*, p. 28. Anson Byington wrote: "Bro. Smith: I have taken the *Review* some six or seven years and have been much edified with its contents. Having been engaged for the last twenty-five years in the antislavery cause, I have regarded the *Review* as an auxiliary until the last two or three years, in which it has failed to aid the cause of abolition. And as I want my money for abolition purposes, I must discontinue the paper when the three dollars herein enclosed are expended" ("From A Byington," *Review and Herald*, Mar. 10, 1859, p. 124). Anson Byington was an active abolitionist. In the 1830s and 1840s he "was president of the Chittenden County, Vermont Anti-Slavery Society" and "had been expelled from the Congregational Church in 1849 for his abolitionist views" (Strayer, "Remembering the Radical Politics of the Pioneers: John Byington"). "According to the abolitionist publisher Joseph P. Poland ... three different routes were used for conveying 'scores and hundreds' of escaped slaves on from Montpelier, Vermont, to their final destination of Canada. One of these routes ran through Williston, where Anson Byington and William H. French were 'agents' for the Underground Railroad" (Douglas Morgan, "Peacemaking Heritage Series: An Abolitionist Urges Adventist Action," Feb. 29, 2008, available online at http://spectrummagazine.org/blog/2008/02/29/peacemaking-heritage-series-abolitionist-urges-adventist-action, accessed 8/3/14). "New evidence indicates that Anson and John Byington actively assisted fugitive slaves in escaping to Canada along the famous Underground Railroad which ran through Bucks Bridge in St. Lawrence County" (Strayer). "It is not known how involved the Byington family was in the 'Underground Railway,' but [it is reported that] they would not turn those away who they knew needed assistance. The old slave, Sojourner Truth, was much esteemed in the Byington family, as well as Will Locket, another colored slave. John and Catharine always had a warm place in their hearts and homes for these people and others in need" ("John Byington's Family," *Lest We Forget*, vol. 2, no. 1). Sojourner Truth (formerly Isabella Van Wagener) died at approximately 100 years of age and was buried in the Oak Hill Cemetery near the grave of Ellen G. White (Benjamin J. Baker, compiler, "Black Seventh-day Adventist Timeline," available online at http://www.blacksdahistory.org/timelines.html, accessed 5/13/15).

[82] "From A. Byington," *Review and Herald*, March 10, 1859, p. 124.

[83] See Bill Knott, "Writing Against Wrongs: Early Adventists Blistered Their Culture for Tolerating Human Slavery," *Adventist Review*, Feb. 28, 2002, pp. 8–13. Byington wrote back to Smith on March 28, 1859: "I admit that the legislation, not only of the slave States, but also of the nation, is dragonic enough to warrant the application of the prophecy of the two-horned beast to our government, but I deny that our Federal constitution any where speaks as a

dragon; but on the contrary, I maintain that its prohibitions and provisions are ample to nullify all Sunday laws, as well as slave laws, and to fulfill its promises in the preamble to establish justice, and secure liberty, the great ends for which it was ordained of God through the people of the United States, and that 'we the people' are morally responsible for its just and faithful administration, whatever may be the meaning of the prophecies, or however near the second advent.

"Need we go to the South to find the proper subjects of this reform? not at all. There is no one State in our whole thirty-three, that has given the fugitive slave the full benefit of her constitutional State sovereignty, in protecting him from the prowling kidnapper, nor has any one of them ever sent a delegation to Congress, by whom the slave's constitutional right to liberty and citizenship has been manfully maintained. So that there are men enough about our doors under the dominion and bondage of this political sin, of which they must repent or perish, on whom reformers might afford to expend some little effort.

"So long as I shall remain firm in my views of the constitution of our country, as expressed above, I shall feel my obligation to spend time, and breath, and money, for their promulgation and maintenance. Nor can I well afford to patronize any pulpit or periodical professing to be a moral reformer, which denies or ignores this obligation. But if you can prove those views to be incorrect, and show that our constitution is a 'covenant with hell, and an agreement with death,' if its alleged pro-slavery guarantees can be fairly made out—if its guarantees of liberty, and prohibitions of slavery can be fairly and fully explained away, then will your obligation cease to act under it. But if human government be an ordinance of God, you cannot claim our confidence as a true and available reformer, until you put forth your efforts and influence for positive revolution, or for dissolution of our national compact, and re-organization on the basis of the Declaration of Independence. Or, if it be admitted that all human government is of the Devil, there will be no difficulty in believing that the Prince of darkness will hold his dominion to the end" ("Communication from Bro. A. Byington," *Review and Herald*, April 21, 1859 p. 174). Smith commented: "We have no strictures to offer on the above. Our brother has made a declaration of his position, as we have of ours. Time will shortly determine the best policy" (*Review and Herald*, April 21, 1859, pp. 174, 175). Byington also responded on April 19, 1860, to Joseph H. Waggoner about whether he would countenance killing in defense of the nation and whether he would uphold the fugitive slave law. On the first question, he responded that such defense was equivalent to self-defense, quoting: "In a war of defense, I would find means immense, And fight till all are exhausted." With his previous vocal avowal of Abolitionism, he was surprised that such a question should be asked about the Fugitive Slave Law. He affirmed his stance: "... whenever a fair opportunity offers, I would hazard much in aiding the slave to escape; for I regard not only the fugitive slave law, but also all slave laws, whether State or national, as not only against the divine law, but also unconstitutional" ("Reply to Bro. Waggoner," *Review and Herald*, May 3, 1860, p. 190). Less confrontational, sabbatarian Adventist William S. Foote wrote: "So far as I have to do with the subject of slavery as an individual member of the body of Christ, I have no right to let it occupy my mind to the exclusion of things of greater import. I have no right to enter into the political field and get into discussion with pro-slavery men." He also wrote that the nation should "take care of his own business; I should mind my own; I can pray for the oppressed and down trodden; if opportunity offers I can assist them otherwise, but to do anything towards the abolition of slavery, I cannot, for several reasons. One is, that I consider our country hopelessly in the hands of Satan, and that it will continue to be until he who is stronger than the strong man armed shall come and take from him all the armor wherein he trusts, and with him shall divide the spoils [Matt. 12:29; Mark 3:27]. Another reason is, judging from passing events and the present mould of the public mind, I am positive that there will not be time enough to revolutionize public sentiment; consequently the ameliorating of the condition of our slave population is entirely out of our reach. Another reason. The Apocalyptic Babylon is to be destroyed when in the very height of her temporal prosperity and glory. She is then to be dealing in 'gold, silver, precious stones,' etc., '*slaves and souls of men*,' and consequently human slavery will continue until the advent of our King [Rev. 18:12, 13]. Lord hasten the day, for our souls are sick with every day's report of wrong and outrage with which the earth is filled" (Wm. S. Foote, "Slavery," *Review and Herald*, March 1, 1860, p. 114, emphasis in original).

[84] U. Smith, "The National Sin," *Review and Herald*, Aug. 20, 1861, p. 94. Some Seventh-day Adventists saw laws supporting slavery as evidence of America's dragon-like voice (see Rev. 13:11). J. H. Waggoner decried the "union of *democratic* professions and *slaveocratic* practices" ("National Degeneracy," *Review and Herald*, Aug. 12, 1858, p. 100). J. N. Loughborough wrote: "While the civil power declares in its declaration of independence that all men are entitled to liberty, by its voice, or laws, it holds about four millions of beings in slavery. The ecclesiastical power of the government, which is Protestant, claims to grant to all, toleration and freedom of faith. Yet at the same time it joins in with the voice of civil authority in enforcing slavery, while the measures by which it does so may gall the consciences of men" ("Image of the Beast," *Review and Herald*, Jan. 15, 1861, p. 69). James White accurately summarized the Seventh-day Adventist position: "For the past ten years the *Review* has taught that the United States of America were a subject of prophecy, and that slavery is pointed out in the prophetic word as the darkest and most damning sin upon this nation...." Regarding the general Adventist view of the war, he added: "The hope which stimulates others, that the war will soon terminate with the freedom of the millions of 'bond-men and bond-women' of North America, and that a period of peace and millennial glory is to follow, we do not cherish." Because

of the lack of progress in the war and biblical indications of human servitude at Christ's return (Rev. 6:15; 18:12, 13), he wrote somewhat tentatively, "We think we see, through the prophetic word, the continuation of slavery down to the end of all earthly governments" ([James White], "The Nation," *Review and Herald*, Aug. 12, 1862, p. 84). Of course, slavery does still exist.

[85] U.S., "The War, and Its Cause," *Review and Herald*, Nov. 12, 1861, p. 188, emphasis added.

[86] In answering the question "Is Slavery Sanctioned by the Bible?" James White gave front-page coverage, in 1861, to a "Premium Tract" treating the subject (*Review and Herald*, Oct. 1, 1861, pp. 137–139; Oct. 8, 1861, pp. 145–147). When war was in full swing, the *Review and Herald* published a sermon entitled, "The Cause and Cure of the Present Civil War," by F. H. Callagher of Michigan (*Review and Herald*, Aug. 19, 1862, pp. 89–91). Callagher had declared: "Slavery has been again and again, in an especial manner, highly favored by this government" (*Review and Herald*, Aug. 19, 1862, p. 90). In 1863, James White ran another series on the topic, entitled "The Bible No Refuge for Slavery" (*Review and Herald*, Feb. 3–May 5, 1863), extracting from Rev. Luther Lee's book, *Slavery Examined in the Light of the Bible* (1855). Interestingly, Lee "had been instrumental in John Byington's conversion" as a Methodist and became the first president of the Wesleyan Methodist Connection of America as well as editor of the *True Wesleyan* and of the *Juvenile Wesleyan* (Strayer, John Byington manuscript).

[87] "... the anti-slavery teachings of several of our publications based upon certain prophecies have been such that their circulation has been positively forbidden in the slave States" ([James White], "The Nation," *Review and Herald*, Aug. 12, 1862, p. 84). "... the South will only receive or listen to their publications on condition of their refraining from putting forth any thing with respect to Slavery" (*New-York Tribune*, "The Tract Society," *Review and Herald*, Oct. 15, 1856, p. 185).

[88] William C. White, Dores E. Robinson, and Arthur L. White, "The Spirit of Prophecy and Military Service" (June 15, 1956), p. 1. James White succinctly affirmed: "We know of not one man among Seventh-day Adventists who has the least sympathy for secession" ([James White], "The Nation," *Review and Herald*, Aug. 12, 1862, p. 84). Mrs. White later stated the case more accurately, writing in a chapter entitled "Rebellion" in "Testimony for the church, No. 9": "*There are a few in the ranks of Sabbathkeepers who sympathize with the slaveholder. When they embraced the truth, they did not leave behind them all the errors they should have left*" (*Testimonies for the Church*, vol. 1, p. 358, emphasis added). Eric Anderson summarized: "Even as they despaired of the future of the United States' experiment in democracy, they did not embrace an ideology that saw the nation as flawed from the start or inherently oppressive. Even in the darkest days of the Civil War, they believed that America had 'the best government under heaven,' and that, 'with the exception of those enactments pressed upon it by the slave power, its laws are good.' " (Eric Anderson, "War, Slavery, and Race," *Ellen Harmon White: American Prophet*, p. 265, quoting from White, "The Nation," *Review and Herald*, Aug. 12, 1862, p. 84). For a more complete bibliography of works on the Seventh-day Adventist Church and the Civil War, see "American Civil War and SDA Church," available online at http://www.blacksdahistory.org/files/43902760.pdf, accessed 2/3/15.

CHAPTER 2 - "Great Distress Coming"

[1] Eric Anderson makes this same point: "Her strictly predictive writings turn out to be remarkably secondary to another objective—namely, instructing Adventist believers in their duty" (Anderson, *Ellen Harmon White*, p. 262).

[2] The first vision is the second chapter in Testimony No. 7, "Great Distress Coming" (White, *Testimonies for the Church*, vol. 1, pp. 260–263). *The Comprehensive Index of Ellen G. White's Writings* assumes that this chapter was part of the vision in chapter one, which Ellen White received on Jan. 4, 1862 (*Testimonies for the Church*, vol. 1, pp. 253–260).

[3] Northerners tended to name a battle after a body of water (hence the North called this battle "the Battle of Bull Run") and Southerners, after a town (hence the South called it "the Battle of Manassas").

[4] First published in "Communication from Sister White: Slavery and the War," *Review and Herald*, Aug. 27, 1861, pp. 100–102, it was subsequently published as the third chapter in Testimony No. 7, "Slavery and the War" (White, *Testimonies for the Church*, vol. 1, pp. 264–268). Mrs. White had published only one other article in 1861. Pre-war articles were rare, with two in 1854, one in 1855, two in 1856, two in 1857, one in 1858, and one in 1859. Not one of these was a front-page article.

[5] The first chapter in Testimony No. 7, "The North and the South" (*Testimonies for the Church*, vol. 1, pp. 253–260).

[6] "Testimony for the church, No. 7, is now ready," *Review and Herald*, Feb. 18, 1862, p. 96. In reprinting testimony number 7 in 1864 in *Spiritual Gifts*, vol. 4b, pp. 58–63, the second and third visions were omitted. This was likely because the focus on slavery as the legitimate reason for the war and on conflicting motivations for the war, in the second and third visions, was not relevant. When President Lincoln having issued his Emancipation Proclamation on Jan. 1, 1863, both matters had become irrelevant ("Publications," *Review and Herald*, Aug. 23, 1864, p. 104). (The Thirteenth Amendment was ratified by the Senate on April 8, 1864, by Congress on Jan. 31, 1865, and by the states on Dec. 6, 1865.) Yet, the "greater distress" in the first vision was still quite relevant. In her introduction to the reprint of the testimonies, Ellen White explained: "The first edition of most of these pamphlets being exhausted, and there being an increasing demand for them, it has been thought best to re-print them, as given in the following pages, omitting local and personal matters, and giving those portions only which are of practical and

general interest and importance. Most of Testimony No. 4 may be found in the second volume of *Spiritual Gifts*, hence, it is omitted in this volume" (*Spiritual Gifts*, vol. 4b, p. ii). She also omitted portions of many other testimonies that were included.

[7] In January 1863, Ellen White published the 48-page pamphlet "Testimony for the church, No. 9." In it she gave guidance on the war and the believers' duty with regard to it, the influence of Spiritualism in battle through leading generals, as well as other non-war-related topics ("Testimony for the Church No. 9, is now ready," *Review and Herald*, Jan. 27, 1863, p. 72, quoted in Arthur L. White, *Ellen G. White, Volume 2: The Progressive Years, 1863–1876*, p. 45).

[8] "Whether the article was based on a single vision or on several, we do not know, but Ellen White's repeated reference to what she was shown or what she saw makes it clear that a vision or visions formed the immediate background" (Arthur L. White, *Ellen G. White, Volume 2: The Progressive Years, 1863–1876*, p. 46).

[9] *New-York Daily Tribune*, Oct. 17, 1851, quoted in Jeter Allen Isely, *Horace Greeley and the Republican Party 1853–1861: A Study of the New York Tribune*, pp. 305, 306. The date 1851 is in the original source and is corroborated by H. Von Holst, *The Constitutional and Political History of the United States* (1885), vol. 4, p. 40.

[10] Oakes, p. 68.

[11] "Compromises for the Crisis," *New York Times*, Jan. 10, 1861, p. 4. Perhaps referring to General Scott's Anaconda Plan, which had as its first step the blocking of Southern ports to cut off Confederate support from other countries.

[12] Quoted by William Henry Gregory (Galway County) in *House of Commons Debate*, July 18, 1862, vol. 168, c. 550; also quoted in the *Times-Picayune* (New Orleans, Louisiana), June 15, 1861, p. 2, col. 2. Clay had joined the anti-slavery movement as a result of hearing William Lloyd Garrison speak. Serving three terms in the Kentucky House of Representatives, becoming a Republican, and publishing an anti-slavery newspaper, Clay gained many enemies. He successfully fended off attacks on his life in 1845 and 1849. Clay was responsible for granting land to abolitionist John G. Fee, who started the progressive Berea College, which accepted students from all races. Clay served as Minister to the Russian Court at St. Petersburg during the Civil War. When Lincoln recalled Clay to serve as a general in the Union Army, Clay accepted the post on the condition that Lincoln emancipate slaves under Confederate control. After sending Clay to the border states to evaluate their willingness to accept emancipation, Lincoln issued the proclamation.

[13] "Approximately 620,000 soldiers died from combat, accident, starvation, and disease during the Civil War. This number comes from an 1889 study of the war performed by William F. Fox and Thomas Leonard Livermore. Both men fought for the Union. Their estimate is derived from an exhaustive study of the combat and casualty records generated by the armies over five years of fighting" ("Civil War Facts: Answers to Your Civil War Questions," available online at http://www.civilwar.org/education/history/faq, accessed 2/8/15). "For 110 years, the numbers stood as gospel: 618,222 men died in the Civil War, 360,222 from the North and 258,000 from the South—by far the greatest toll of any war in American history. But new research shows that the numbers were far too low. By combing through newly digitized census data from the 19th century, J. David Hacker, a demographic historian from Binghamton University in New York, has recalculated the death toll and increased it by more than 20 percent—to 750,000" (Guy Gugliotta, "New Estimate Raises Civil War Death Toll," available online at http://www.nytimes.com/2012/04/03/science/civil-war-toll-up-by-20-percent-in-new-estimate.html?pagewanted=all&_r=0, accessed 2/8/15). Faust pointed out: "By the midpoint of the conflict, it seemed that in the South, 'nearly every household mourns some loved one lost' " (Drew Gilpin Faust, *This Republic of Suffering*, p. xiii).

[14] A. B., "Peaceful Disunion," *New-York Tribune*, Jan. 11, 1861, p. 6. The columnist went on to say: "It is the stronger party; let it act calmly, dispassionately, and kindly, for it says to the South: 'If you wish to go out of the Union, do so quietly, and we will settle our National affairs on an equitable basis; we desire no coerced association, and if the Union is not a voluntary one, let us dissolve it; but let us do it wisely and in a dignified manner; let us fix on a certain time, say the 4th of March, 1865, when Mr. Lincoln's term will expire, or, if you cannot wait so long, then the 4th of March, 1863. In the mean time, let us carry on all our industrial and commercial operations as heretofore, so as to avoid useless revulsions; let us establish a treaty of commerce and a custom-union mutually advantageous; let us arrange for the payment of the national debt, and the division of the public property, and settle all matters so as to promote the interests of both parties; two years are a short time to do this.' " Ardent Unionist Jacob Engelbrecht of Frederick, Maryland wrote in his diary: ". . . the South Carolinians & Allabamians were ready to secede from the Union of the u. States, and at this time They are making Wonderful preperation to leave this Glorious Union for my o[w]npart I say go as quick as you please,—they have been Domone[ering] long enough—the sooner they go the better for the peace & quiet of our country" (*The Diary of Jacob Engelbrecht, 1818-1878*, William R. Quynn, editor, vol. 3, p. 33, original spelling retained).

[15] Horace Greeley, *The American Conflict: A History of the Great Rebellion in the United States of America, 1860–1864*, vol. 1, p. 438.

[16] "The War," *Harper's Weekly*, May 4, 1861, p. 274, col. 1.

[17] Allan Nevins, *War for the Union: War Becomes Revolution, 1862–1863* (1959), vol. 2, p. 5.

[18] A. Lincoln, letter to Congress, July 4, 1861, *Messages and Papers*, vol. VI, pp. 20–26, in Frank Williams Prescott, *Tariff Legislation 1859–1862: Its Relation to Protection and Political Activities*, master's thesis, University of Wisconsin, p. 68.

[19] This is the title of Testimony for the Church No. 7 in *Spiritual Gifts*, vol. 4b, p. 58.

[20] Loughborough reported that it was the dedication of the meeting-house ("The Study of the Testimonies.–No. 4," *General Conference Daily Bulletin*, Jan. 31, 1893, p. 61). Church representatives, farmer Harvey Keeney and cabinetmaker Andrew Hafer, had invited Loughborough, Waggoner, James White, and Byington to attend ("Appointments," *Review and Herald*, Jan. 1, 1861, p. 56). The church had first met in the house of Harvey and Sarah Keeney with about twenty-six in attendance ("Appointments," *Review and Herald*, Dec. 29, 1859, p. 48; *Review and Herald*, Jan. 5, 1860, p. 56; George Busk, *Review and Herald*, Jan. 26, 1860, pp. 78, 79) and later in the Stony-Ridge schoolhouse ("Note from Bro. Byington," *Review and Herald*, March 29, 1860, p. 152; J. N. Loughborough, "Appointments, *Review and Herald*, May 10, 1860, p. 200). On May 13, 1860, before purchasing property and erecting a place of worship, the church legally incorporated as the "Parkville Church of Christ's second advent" (J. N. Loughborough, "Meetings in Parkville, Mich.," *Review and Herald*, May 29, 1860, p. 9). On August 2, 1862, Byington met with Parkville members to "organize a church there under the name of Seventh-day Adventist" ("Appointments," *Review and Herald*, July 22, 1862, p. 64). Parkville had 24 members in mid–1863 ("State of the Cause in Michigan," *Review and Herald*, June 2, 1863, p. 6). In 1867 Byington wrote: "Sabbath and first-day, Dec. 22, I was with the church in Parkville. By removal and deaths, their number is quite reduced and the few much scattered, which makes it difficult for them to sustain meetings at their pleasant house of worship. They attended to their legal appointment of Trustees, and we hope some faithful brethren will be raised up or move to Parkville to aid them in spiritual things" ("Sketch of Meetings," *Review and Herald*, Feb. 5, 1867, p. 108). By 1877 the church had disbanded: "The village now contains three stores, three churches—denominationally classified as follows: One Presbyterian, one Methodist Episcopal, and one Advent. (The latter was erected [dedicated] in 1861, the first members being Harvey Kinney [Keeney] and wife, Andrew Hafer, Oran Bovee, J. H. Alrich [Aldrich ("Extracts from Letters," *Review and Herald*, March 15, 1860, p. 135)], Aaron H. Adams and Mary Sidler [Mary and Daniel Sedler are in the 1860 U.S. Census]. No church organization now exists.)" (*History of St. Joseph County, Michigan* [1877], p. 217). Sister M. Bovee of Mendon, just east of Parkville, died in May 1861 ("Extracts from Letters," *Review and Herald*, April 19, 1860, p. 175; John Byington, "Appointments," *Review and Herald*, May 28, 1861, p. 16).

[21] Isaac F. Ulrich diary for Saturday, January 12, 1861, Western Michigan University interlibrary loan.

[22] J. N. Loughborough, "Sketches of the Past—No. 121," *Pacific Union Recorder*, March 7, 1912, p. 1. James White reported briefly: "We have just returned from the Conferences at Monterey, Wright and Parkville, in unusual health, and greatly revived and encouraged" ("Brief Report," *Review and Herald*, Jan. 15, 1861, p. 72). He mentioned presenting Systematic Benevolence—planned support of the ministry through tithing. Ellen White referred to counsel for an individual she received in vision at Parkville (Letter 2 [Feb. 23], 1861; see Arthur L. White, letter to Hedwig Jemison, Nov. 2, 1964).

[23] J. N. Loughborough, *The Great Second Advent Movement: Its Rise and Progress* (1905), p. 337; *Pacific Union Recorder*, March 7, 1912. Eric Anderson noted: "... there is no contemporary confirmation of this dramatic prediction" (*Ellen Harmon White*, p. 276). Nonetheless, M. E. Cornell does provide indirect corroboration of the impact of Ellen White's visions by the next year: "Several testified that their doubts in regard to sister White's visions were now all removed. Bro. [Charles Smith] Glover [of Newton] said his name had been paraded in the public print, by our enemies, as a "vision lover," but he was not ashamed of the visions, nor to own that he loved them" ("Report of Meetings," *Review and Herald*, Feb. 11, 1862, p. 85). Loughborough based his accounts on diaries he had kept since "November 1853" (Loughborough, *Rise and Progress of the Seventh-day Adventists*, p. iii). Unfortunately, his diaries for 1860 to 1867 are missing (Heidi Magesa, e-mail, April 14, 2005). On Jan. 30, 1891, former resident of St. Joseph County, Mrs. Martha V. Ensign, of Wild Flower, Fresno County, California, provided testimony corroborating the Parkville vision: "This certifies that I was living in St. Joseph Co., Mich., in January, 1861, about six miles from Parkville. I was not an Adventist. On the 12th day of that month, a number of my neighbors went to Parkville to attend meetings. When they came home, they told me that there was a woman at the meeting that was in a trance, and who said that there was a terrible war coming on the United States; that large armies were going to be raised on both sides, in the South as well as in the North, and there would be many who would suffer in prisons; and pinching want would be felt in many families in consequence of losing husbands, sons, and brothers in the war; and that there were men in the house who would lose sons in that war" (Loughborough, *Rise and Progress of the Seventh-day Adventists*, p. 237). The 1860 and 1870 U.S. Censuses list Martha and her husband, Lucius, and their children living in Lockport, Michigan (just south of Parkville); the 1875 Kansas Census shows them living in Bala, Kansas; the 1900 U.S. Census shows her and her husband living in Fresno, California. John Byington's daughter, Martha D. Byington-Amadon, remembered a similar dramatic announcement in a tent meeting regarding coming bloodshed in the nation: "Sister White was taken in vision. After coming out, she walked up and down in the tent, appearing in great perplexity, and repeating these words several times: 'This country is to be deluged with blood' " (*Notebook Leaflets from the Elmshaven Library*, vol. 1, p. 59).

[24] J. N. Loughborough, "Remarkable Fulfillments of the Visions," *Review and Herald*, Dec. 25, 1866, p. 30.

[25] The *Scioto Gazette* suggested: "A good many well meaning but very nervous people profess to be not a little alarmed just now, lest the country should be plunged into civil war by the acts of the democratic traitors down South, and the imbecility and indecision of the democratic administration at Washington. . . . The civil war will extend no further than the re-taking of such of the government property as the rebels may get possession of, and the holding of the other property against their attacks. Nervous people can continue to go about their business in peace, and rest quietly in their beds; their slumbers will not be disturbed yet awhile by the booming of cannon, the rattle of the musketry, the clashing of swords nor the horrors of the 'fratricidal and patricidal strife' about which some of the speakers last Saturday appeared so alarmed" ("Civil War," *Scioto Gazette* [Chillicothe, Ohio], Jan. 8, 1861, p. 2).

Word of the secession of Mississippi, Florida, and Alabama had not reached Michigan before Ellen White's vision. The day of her vision, the *New-York Tribune* reported, from electro magnetic telegraph, that Florida and Alabama had seceded the day previous at 2:30 p.m. (*New-York Tribune*, Jan. 12, 1861, p. 4). The last *Kalamazoo Gazette* available to Ellen White before she spoke in Parkville, Michigan, on Sabbath, January 12, still held out hope that the Crittenden Compromise would stave off armed conflict: "Tallahassee, Fla., Jan. 2. A large number of the State Convention have arrived here. Resolutions will be adopted declaring the right of Florida to secede, and the Convention will then proceed deliberately to determine the ordinance of secession. . . . Jan. 5. The Crittenden compromise seems to be gaining friends, who entertain the opinion that if it were fairly presented to the people, it would be accepted by them as a basis of agreement. The main difficulty, however, in the way, is that parties are at present indisposed to offer it without assurance that others will receive it in a mutual spirit of accommodation for both North and South. The Alabama and Mississippi delegations held a conference last night, and afterwards telegraphed to the Conventions of their respective States advising them to secede immediately, saying there is no prospect of a satisfactory adjustment. They resolved to remain here, awaiting the action of their States" ("Secession Movement," *Kalamazoo Gazette*, Jan. 11, 1861, p. 3). Other newspapers held out similar hope. The Crittenden compromise, issued in late 1860 by Kentucky Congressman John J. Crittenden, "would have recognized a constitutional right to slave property in the territories south of the old Missouri Compromise line, guaranteed the admission of new slave states organized south of the line, prevented Congress from abolishing slavery in Washington, and banned federal regulation of the domestic slave trade. Additional resolutions called for vigorous federal enforcement of the Fugitive Slave Act and the repeal of northern personal liberty laws. Taken together, these proposals would very nearly make slavery national" (Oakes, p. 73). The Crittenden Compromise was killed in the U.S. Senate on January 16 (*Marshall Statesman* [Marshall, Michigan], Jan. 23, 1861, p. 2).

[26] Quoted by J. N. Loughborough, *Rise and Progress* (1892), pp. 236–237, emphasis added for wording that corresponds to Testimony No. 7: "*I saw* greater distress in the land than we have yet witnessed. I heard groans and cries of distress, and saw large companies in active *battle*. *I heard the booming of the cannon*, the clash of arms, the *hand-to-hand fight*, and the groans and prayers of the *dying*. The ground was *covered with* the wounded and *the dead*. I saw desolate, despairing families, and pinching want in many dwellings. Even now many families are *suffering want*, but this will increase. The faces of many looked haggard, pale, and pinched with hunger" (White, *Testimonies for the Church*, vol. 1, p. 260). ("*The dead and dying were on every* side" appears on page 266 and those who "have been taken prisoners by the rebels," on page 255. That she did not include the prediction about the loss of Parkville sons would indicate that she did not wish to capitalize on people's loss to promote her prophetic gift.) The corresponding wording validates Loughborough's summary. Regarding his mother's view of *Rise and Progress*, W. C. White wrote: "I can say that I have often heard her speak of this book. . . . I have heard her say that she was sorry that you had made her so prominent in the work" (Letter to J. N. Loughborough, Nov. 20, 1899, p. 2). She wrote: "I certainly think that it would be well if Elder Loughborough's book could be given a larger circulation" (Letter 141 [July 12], 1903, par. 1). "Elder Loughborough's book should receive attention. Our leading men should see what can be done for the circulation of this book" (Letter 105 [June 1], 1903, par. 4). Loughborough reviewed "the manuscript for his new book" with Mrs. White (Letter 87 [Feb. 15], 1904, par. 7), yet she apparently found nothing to correct in his description of the 1861 vision. His quoting of her words remained virtually unchanged from *Rise and Progress*, pp. 236–237, to the *General Conference Daily Bulletin*, Jan. 31, 1893, p. 61, to *The Great Second Advent Movement* (1905), p. 338, to *The Prophetic Gift in the Gospel Church* (1911), pp. 79. Apparently unaware of this vision, former Seventh-day Adventist ministers B. F. Snook and W. H. Brinkerhoff asserted: "But she could not foresee the terrible rebellion in our government, nor that slavery would be abolished, nor when peace would be made, and that her visions would be rejected by many good brethren. But, after these things have happened she can see them all" ("The Visions of E. G. White, Not of God," p. 26). The evidence shows that she did foresee the war, its length, that the North would win, and that its end would be linked with the emancipation of the slaves.

[27] *Free Press*, "Union Resolutions by the State Agricultural Society," *Western Chronicle* (Three Rivers, Michigan), Jan. 10, 1861, p. 2: "*Whereas*, A crisis has arisen in the affairs of the national government, threatening the most serious injury to the present Confederacy of States, if not an actual dissolution of our beloved Union, under which we have grown and prospered, by the blessing of Divine Providence, more than any other nation known in history; . . . Resolved. That we urge upon the people of this State the importance of cherishing a spirit of conciliation and fraternal feeling towards our brethren

of other sections of the country, and the employment of all proper means to avert so great a calamity as that which at present threatens the fairest fabric of human government—the Union of the United States."

[28] "Near the stand sat Judge Osborne [sic], whose wife was a Sabbath-keeper. By his side sat Mr. Shelhouse [sic], owner of a large woolen factory, both leading men in the Republican party. When Mrs. White told what was coming, they looked at me and shook their heads. One year from that time when I spoke in the same church, these two men sat together again. My subject was spiritual gifts. In illustration of the gift as manifest by Sister White, I referred to the vision of Jan. 12, 1861. . . . One had lost his only adopted son in the war . . ." (Loughborough, "Sketches of the Past—No. 122," *Pacific Union Recorder*, March 14, 1912, p. 1). Earlier Loughborough had written:". . . both of those men buried their faces in their hands, and one of them began to sob aloud. And no wonder. Six weeks before he had buried his only son, brought home from the war a corpse, and the man beside him had lost one son in the war and had another one in a rebel prison. Brother Kinne [sic] said there were at least five persons in the house that day of the dedication who afterward lost sons in the war" (*General Conference Daily Bulletin*, Jan. 31, 1893, p. 61). Loughborough later added: "Before the war was over, ten men who were in that meeting lost twelve sons in the war" ("Daily Reading Course on the Spirit of Prophecy: Things Which We Have Seen and Heard," *Atlantic Union Gleaner*, Nov. 7, 1917, p. 1). Many St. Joseph sons did die in the war (see *History of St. Joseph County, Michigan*, pp. 58, 59, 70, 71, 80–82, 89, 106, 107, 125–127, 133, 134, 148, 149, 163, 164, 176, 177, 186, 187, 192, 197, 198, 203, 204, 211, 212, 218, 226, 227). However some details in Loughborough's account do not align with other historical sources. Though Schellhous was likely a Republican, since his son Charles served as chairman of the St. Joseph County Republican committee (*State of Michigan Proceedings of the Public Domain Commission*, vol. 6, p. 259). However, according to *History of St. Joseph County, Michigan* (1877), p. 231, Osborn was "a staunch Democrat in politics." Osborn had two adopted sons who were soldiers—Frank and George, born to Rebecca and her first husband William Foster (*1850 United States Federal Census, Illinois, LaSalle, Ottawa*). Frank (named "Walter" at birth, for his paternal grandfather) died from wounds at the Battle of South Mountain but was not brought home. George's pension file does *not* reveal time in a rebel prison (National Archives). Schellhous had no sons old enough to serve. The only son may have been John A. Troy, whose body was brought home to South Park Cemetery. He died Sept. 14, 1862 at South Mountain, serving in the 17th Infantry, Company C. Another Parkville son who died before November 1862 was Henry M. Woodward, who died of typhoid fever April 16, 1862, serving in the Eleventh Infantry, Company C (Cutler, *History of St. Joseph County, Michigan* [1877], p. 251; L. H. Everts, p. 218).

[29] Such was also the opinion of the columnist for the *Western Chronicle* (Three Rivers, Michigan), when he wrote on December 13 from Washington: "But we will weather the storm—the finances will come out right—the men of the North will execute the requirements of the Constitution, Fugitive Slave and all: the South will return to her senses, and the stars and stripes will still flicker in the breeze" (SHELL BARK, "Our Washington Correspondence," *Western Chronicle*, Dec. 20, 1860, p. 2). Gen. John E. Wool believed: "The Union can be preserved, but it requires firm, decided, prompt and energetic measures on the part of the President. He has only to exert the power conferred upon him by the Constitution and laws of Congress, and all will be safe, and he will prevent a civil war, which never fails to call forth all the baser passions of the human heart. If a separation should take place, you may rest assured blood would flow in torrents, followed by pestilence, famine and desolation" (*Clinton Republican* [Wilmington, OH], Jan. 11, 1861, p. 1).

[30] J. N. Loughborough, "Remarkable Fulfillments of the Visions," *Review and Herald*, Dec. 25, 1866, p. 30. Years later, Loughborough recounted that, after the church got started in 1859, "a physician had moved into the place who was a spirit medium" (*Pacific Union Recorder*, March 14, 1912, p. 1). Loughborough called the physician "Dr. Brown" (p. 2). No physician named "Brown" is listed in St. Joseph County during this period, though Loughborough referred to a Methodist minister named "Brown" who spoke against Adventist teachings ("Report of Meetings," *Review and Herald*, Dec. 22, 1859, p. 37). Two of Parkville's physicians do not seem to fit his description. Dr. Robert McElrath was an established physician and landowner in Parkville. Dr. Isaac D. Howard moved to Parkville in 1857 but was a member in good standing of the Methodist Episcopal Church (Chapman Brothers, *Portrait and Biographical Album of St. Joseph County, Michigan*, pp. 451, 452). A third physician, Dr. Anson Lovejoy, lived with his family in Parkville and Flowerfield during this period (*1860 United States Federal Census, Michigan, St Joseph, Flowerfield*, p. 24; the *Michigan State Gazetteer and Business Directory for 1863-4*, p. 436). That he was an "eclectic physician" (Clarence E. Lovejoy, *The Lovejoy Genealogy with Biographies and History, 1460–1930*, p. 412) allows that he may have used alternative healing methods. Eclectic physician Joseph Rodes Buchanan used phrenology and mesmerism (Carol Trowbridge, *Andrew Taylor Still*, p. 111). Loughborough described the doctor who examined Ellen White as being a "mesmerizer" ("Remarkable Fulfillments of the Visions," *Review and Herald*, Dec. 25, 1866, p. 30). However, there is no direct evidence that Lovejoy used mesmerism or that he was a spiritualist. In a later account, Loughborough wrote about Judge Osborn's description of the doctor's actions: "It was evident to all of us that the spirit that controlled the doctor as a medium, and the Spirit that controlled Mrs. White in vision, had no sympathy with each other. The doctor's actions made us think of the evil spirits that wanted to know if the Lord had come to torment them before their time" ("Sketches of the Past—No. 122," *Pacific Union Recorder*, March 14, 1912, p. 2).

[31] Moses Hull, then an Adventist minister, announced a follow-up meeting at Parkville in which the subject of the prophetic gift was revisited: "THERE will be a conference at Parkville, Mich., on Sabbath and first-day, Jan. 25 and 26. Bro. and Sr. White may be expected. I will try to be there the 23d. Will the brethren from Colon, Flowerfield, and Brady attend?" (M. Hull, "Appointments," *Review and Herald*, Jan. 14, 1862, p. 56). Hull did not go, but M. E. Cornell did—accompanied by J. N. Loughborough. Cornell reported: "As Bro. Waggoner was going to Indiana, and we to Ohio, it was thought best for us to attend the conference at Parkville, as Bro. Hull's duty called him another way. We found a representation from Monterey, Newton, Colon, Union City, Burr Oak, Flowerfield, and Vicksburgh. They were evidently disappointed in not seeing Bro. and sister White, but appeared satisfied with an explanation, and gladly received the word preached by us. The subjects presented were the Christian's hope, *spiritual gifts*, necessity of the whole armor, the three [angels'] messages, and the signs of the times. Several testified that their doubts in regard to *sister White's visions* were now all removed" ("Report of Meetings," *Review and Herald*, Feb. 11, 1862, p. 85, emphasis added). J. H. Waggoner, who also attended because illness slowed his journey to Indiana, reported that Cornell made two presentations "on the perpetuity of the gifts of the Spirit" ("Trip to Indiana," *Review and Herald*, Feb. 11, 1862, p. 85, emphasis added).

[32] Loughborough reported: "Sabbath and first-day, Nov. 1 & 2, in company with Bro. Byington, visited the brethren at Parkville. Organized a church there of seventeen members. Two were baptized during this meeting. Good attention was given to the word spoken" ("Report from Bro. Loughborough," *Review and Herald*, Dec. 23, 1862, p. 29).

[33] See death certificates for Frank A. Osborn and George A. Osborn at "U.S. Civil War Soldier Records and Profiles, 1861-1865." Their parents got married June 8, 1843, so Frank was not yet 19 when they enlisted (Michigan, County Marriages).

[34] *History of St. Joseph County, Michigan* (1877), p. 218, lists him as Frank H. Osborn; his enlistment papers, as Frank A. Osborn; the 1860 US Census, as Francis Osborn; and the 1850 US Census, as Walter Foster.

[35] John Robertson, *Michigan in the War* (1882), p. 376; George H. Turner, *Record of Service of Michigan Volunteers in the Civil War, 1861–1865*, vol. 17, p. 79.

[36] See *History of St. Joseph County, Michigan* (1877), p. 231, and Rebecca B. Osborn Find A Grave Memorial #70539378, http://www.findagrave.com/cgi-bin/fg.cgi?page=pv&GRid=70539378&Pipi=43143097. Loughborough identified Rebecca as a "sabbath-keeper," by which he likely meant a Seventh-day Adventist, and Leonard E. Schellhous's father, Lorancie Schellhous, as a Seventh-day Adventist ("Sketches of the Past—No. 122," *Pacific Union Recorder*, March 14, 1912, p. 1). Lorancie wrote many letters to the *Review and Herald* ("From Bro. Schellhous," *Review and Herald*, July 22, 1858, p. 79; Jan. 13, 1859, p. 63; Dec. 8, 1859, p. 23; *Review and Herald*, Dec. 11, 1860, p. 31; July 16, 1861, p. 55; Jan. 17, 1865, p. 63; July 3, 1866, p. 39; March 3, 1868, p. 187; and Aug. 25, 1868, p. 155; "A Request," *Review and Herald*, Feb. 25, 1862, p. 104). He also mentioned his son Leonard E. Schellhous in his autobiography, and ended it saying: "And now being eighty years old lacking a few weeks and my wife a little over eighty years, waiting for our deliverance, trusting in the Lord, thinking it is better to trust in him and keep his commandments, than to follow the traditions of men, finally to heed the instruction of Solomon, hear the conclusion of the whole matter. Fear God and keep his commandments which is the whole duty of man" (*Life of Lorancie Schellhous*, p. 13).

[37] Loughborough, *Rise and Progress*, p. 239. Loughborough reported that Keeney gave him five names and added, "... if I were at home, where I could talk with my people, I could give you more names." This would indicate that the conversation did not take place at Parkville but elsewhere, likely Battle Creek, during the General Conference session the year before Keeney's death ("Obituary Notices: Keeney," *Review and Herald*, Oct. 21, 1884, p. 671). Loughborough's 1883 diary indicates that he returned from England to attend the General Conference session in Battle Creek from Oct. 21–Nov. 20, 1883.

[38] The *New York Herald*, in Greeley, pp. 201, 202. In the same issue of the *Tribune*, another columnist submitted "What Congress Might and Should Do to Save the Union." The first thing was to "Stop agitating the N– question," and the second was to completely support "the Union, the Constitution, and the enforcement of the laws," which meant the laws that supported slavery in the South (*New-York Tribune*, Jan. 11, 1861, p. 4).

[39] Ronald C. White, *A. Lincoln: A Biography* (2009), p. 413; Loughborough, *Rise and Progress*, pp. 237, 238.

[40] Rozwenc, p. 28.

[41] Doyle, p. 29.

[42] Ronald C. White, pp. 413, 417, 418.

[43] The popularity of "John Brown's Body" (also called "John Brown's Song") among Northern soldiers dates back to May 1861 (James J. Fuld, *The Book of World-Famous Music: Classical, Popular, and Folk Courier Dover*, pp. 132, 133). Thus, on some level, Northern soldiers must have known that one object of the war was the abolition of slavery.

[44] Benjamin R. Tubb, "Civil War Music: The Battle Hymn of the Republic," available online at http://www.civilwar.org/education/history/on-the-homefront/culture/music/the-battle-hymn-of-the-republic/the-battle-hymn-of-the.html, accessed 12/16/15. The contrast between Julia Ward Howe's view of God's "terrible swift sword" and Ellen White's view of a protracted war was inspired by Jud Lake's Civil War manuscript.

CHAPTER 3 - "Slavery and the War"

[1] Jackson got his nickname "Stonewall" in this very battle.

[2] Henry Kyd Douglas, *I Rode with Stonewall*, p. 11.

[3] William Willis Blackford, *War Years with Jeb Stuart*, p. 34, emphasis added.

[4] Louis Morris Starr, *Bohemian Brigade: Civil War Newsmen in Action*, pp. 43, 44, 46, 47.

[5] Quoted in "The Battle at Bull's Run," *Harper's Weekly*, Aug. 3, 1861, pp. 491, 492. Veteran British military correspondent William Howard Russell, who was also returning from Centreville toward the bridge over Cub Run, described a similar surprise and the cry of those retreating, "Turn back! Turn back! We are whipped!" (Richard Wheeler, *A Rising Thunder: From Lincoln's Election to the Battle of Bull Run: An Eyewitness History*, p. 383).

[6] Edwin S. Barrett, *What I Saw at Bull Run*, pp. 24, 25.

[7] Ellen G. White, Letter 6a (July 26), 1861. She would have read: "In the utter confusion prevailing, it is wholly impossible to get reliable news"; "it probable that if our men had stood their ground even fifteen minutes longer, they would have had undisputed possession of the field" (*Detroit Free Press*, July 26, 1861, p. 3). In receiving Henry J. Raymond's telegraphed account, the *New York Times* took McDowell's victory for granted and prematurely printed the headline, "Crushing Rebellion. The Greatest Battle Ever Fought on the Continent.... The Rebels Routed and Driven Behind the Manassas Lines"—a headline that was corrected the following morning (*New York Times*, July 22, 1861, p. 1, in Horace H. Cunningham, *Field Medical Services at the Battles of Manassas [Bull Run]*, p. 13). The August 1 *Circular* (Oneida, New York) reported: "The loss of the Northern troops is not so great, as first reported.... The retreat as a whole was less disorderly than at first reported." The July 23 *New York Herald* headline read: "Rebel Account of the First Skirmish at Bull's Run." It was hardly a "skirmish." The *Detroit Free Press* reported: "Jeff Davis Says His Loss at Bull Run was Three Thousand" and "The Rebel Loss Nearly Four Thousand" (*Detroit Free Press*, July 26, 1861, p. 1). Confederate casualties were almost 2,000 and Union casualties, about 2,700. One newspaper called attention to the Confederate troops' "diabolical deeds" toward the wounded in throwing "hot shot" into their hospital buildings (*New York Herald*, July 24, 1861, col. D). British reporter William Howard Russell, who came late to the Battle of Bull Run, did not minimize the chaotic retreat of the Union soldiers. After his account, no other British journalist reported on the war from the Northern perspective ("Amanda Foreman Part 3 of 4," available online at https://www.youtube.com/watch?v=8Ezlz8uGjwA, marker 5:00, accessed 1/22/15).

[8] White, *Testimonies for the Church*, vol. 1, p. 266. The article that Ellen White read (*Detroit Free Press*, Jan. 26, 1861, p. 4), does not mention exhaustion from the march to the battle, though it does mention later exhaustion as did Blackford, p. 33.

[9] Webster's 1828 *Dictionary*, available online at http://www.christiantech.com.

[10] White, *Testimonies for the Church*, vol. 1, p. 267, written August 3, 1861, emphasis added. After the war, Uriah Smith reminded Seventh-day Adventists of this prediction, commenting: "For its complicity with this great crime the North has had to endure the terrible pressure of this bloody struggle for four weary years; but the most direful results of the war seem to be falling upon the South for the sin of slavery itself" ("Destitution and Suffering at the South," *Review and Herald*, May 16, 1865, p. 189).

[11] White, *Testimonies for the Church*, vol. 1, p. 267.

[12] Orville Victor, *Incidents and Anecdotes of the War* (1862), p. 185. "Union soldiers... ran past the ["startled"] spectators" ("Senate History. 1851-1877. July 21, 1861. Senators Witness the First Battle of Bull Run," available online at http://www.senate.gov/artandhistory/history/minute/Witness_Bull_Run.htm, accessed 12/27/15.

[13] Jim Murphy, *The Boys' War: Confederate and Union Soldiers Talk about the Civil War* (1993), p. 16.

[14] James Longstreet, *From Manassas to Appomattox*, p. 30. "With this order came a message to me, saying that the Federals were pressing severely on our left, and to the limit of its tension, that reinforcements were in sight, approaching their right, which might prove too heavy for our brave men, and force us back, for which emergency our brigades should be held ready to cover retreat. These anxious moments were soon relieved by the approach of General Kirby Smith's command, that had been mistaken as reinforcements for the enemy.... McDowell made a gallant effort to recover his lost power, . . . but our convex line, that he was just now pressing back upon itself, was changed.... Although his renewed efforts were brave, his men seemed to have given confidence over to despair. Still a show of battle was made until General Johnston directed the brigades of Holmes and Early to good positions for attack, when fight was abandoned and flight ensued" (Longstreet, pp. 26, 27).

[15] Orville James Victor, editor, *The History, Civil, Political and Military, of the Southern Rebellion*, vol. 2, (1861), p. 258. So confused was the retreat that McDowell apologized for not submitting his report until August 4 because of "the inability of the subordinate commanders to get earlier a true account of the state of their commands" (Victor, p. 254).

[16] Wheeler, *A Rising Thunder*, p. 380, with an allusion to 2 Cor. 5:8.

[17] John W. Urban, *My Experiences Mid Shot and Shell and in Rebel Den*, p. 55.

[18] Urban, pp. 51, 53, 56.
[19] Andrew Ward, *The Slaves' War: the Civil War in the Words of Former Slaves* (2009), p. 42.
[20] E.g., *Sam Richards's Civil War Diary: A Chronicle of the Atlanta Home Front* (2009), p. 32; Samuel Boykin, "The Late Victory at Manassas," *Christian Index*, July 31, 1861, at http://www.civilwarbaptists.com/thisdayinhistory/1861-july-31, accessed 4/25/12.
[21] Anderson, *Ellen Harmon White*, p. 266. Cf. [James White], "Sunday Battles," *Review and Herald*, Feb. 9, 1864, p. 84.
[22] Faust, p. 190.
[23] White, *Testimonies for the Church*, vol. 1, p. 264.
[24] Wheeler, *A Rising Thunder*, p. 390.
[25] White, *Testimonies for the Church*, vol. 1, p. 266.
[26] "The War," *Harper's Weekly*, May 4, 1861, p. 274, col. 2.
[27] "With such support, and such resources, if this war be not brought to a speedy close, and the supremacy of the Government forcibly asserted throughout the country, it will be the fault of ABRAHAM LINCOLN" ("The War," *Harper's Weekly*, May 4, 1861, p. 274, col. 1).
[28] White, *Testimonies for the Church*, vol. 1, p. 266; with minor change in *Review and Herald*, Aug. 27, 1861, p. 101.
[29] Nathan and David (2 Sam. 12:7); Micaiah et al. (2 Chron. 18:4–17; Hosea 4:12; Amos 9:10; and Micah 2:8, 9; 3:5).
[30] "The Emancipation Question. Is Slavery the Cause of the War?" *Newark Advocate* (Newark, Ohio), Dec. 20, 1861.
[31] U.S., "Traitors in Power," *Review and Herald*, Feb. 4, 1862, p. 78. Without the war having as its purpose the ending of slavery, Eric Anderson's appraisal of Smith's view is correct: "In his [Smith's] thinking, a clear victory for the Union was simply not a possibility" (Anderson, *Ellen Harmon White*, p. 264).

CHAPTER 4 - "The North and the South"

[1] Sympathetic to the South, Buchanan recommended in December 1860 that Congress pass "a constitutional amendment to recognize the South's right of property in slaves, the duty of the Federal Government to protect this right in all common territories, the validity of the Fugitive Slave Law, and the nullification of state laws which interfered with the recovery of slaves" (Helen F. Mount, "Education of the Negro in the Military Department of the South, 1861–1865"). Buchanan's collusion with the South was in what he did *not* do. "By the winter months of December and January, Southerners had taken advantage of Buchanan's hands-off policy and had begun what he predicted would never happen—their assaults on federal property, not just in South Carolina but throughout the South. Buchanan did not try to block the takeovers of Fort Moultrie and Castle Pinckney in Charleston harbor; nor did he comment on the surrender by a naval officer of the revenue cutter *Aiken*. He said nothing when, on January 3, 1861, Georgia troops captured Fort Pulaski, and nothing about the successful assaults by Louisiana militia forces on Forts Jackson, St. Phillips, and Pike or the seizure of the New Orleans or Baton Rouge customhouses. Nor did he respond a few days later when Florida militia seized the Pensacola navy yard along with Fort Barrancas and Fort McRae, or in February when secessionists seized the Little Rock arsenal in Arkansas. Perhaps most egregiously, he said nothing when a general of the U.S. Army, David Twiggs, simply surrendered his military units without any struggle to a local militia before Texas had even seceded. Most of these aggressive actions were prompted by the false statements and threatening propaganda, fostered by Southern governors, that the United States was about to send federal reinforcements" (John W. Birkner and Michael J. Quest, editors, *James Buchanan and the Coming of the Civil War*, p. 173).

[2] White, *Testimonies for the Church*, vol. 1, p. 253. "Before the junction of the army of Virginia with the army of the Potomac could be effected, the Confederates had completed the concentration of their forces at the decisive point. The object of their operations during a whole month was to gain time for this collecting of their armies. From the moment when it was accomplished, their tactics changed, and they passed from the defensive to the offensive, and gathered by bold and rapid movements the harvest which had ripened by delay" ("Current Events," *Home and Foreign Review*, vol. 1 [July 1862], p. 599).

[3] In McCurry, p. 55. On Davis's activities in Dec. 1860, see *The Papers of Jefferson Davis*, vol. 6, p. 374. On Edmund W. Pettus's efforts, see William L. Barney, *Secessionist Impulse: Alabama and Mississippi in 1860*, pp. 189, 201–204, and John K. Bettersworth, *Confederate Mississippi: The People and Policies of a Cotton State in Wartime*, pp. 1–21.

[4] McCurry, p. 55, citing G. P. Whittington, "Thomas O. Moore, Governor of Louisiana, 1860–1864," *The Louisiana Historical Quarterly*, vol. 13 (Jan. 1930), no. 1.

[5] "Secession Movement," *Kalamazoo Gazette*, Jan. 11, 1861, p. 3.

[6] Brinkmanship—running up to the edge of a precipice to get one's way—seems to have been a favorite tactic of South Carolina. Its use began under Calhoun. "Jackson met head-on the challenge of John C. Calhoun, leader of forces trying to rid themselves of a high protective tariff. When South Carolina undertook to nullify the tariff, Jackson ordered armed forces to Charleston and privately threatened to hang Calhoun. Violence seemed imminent until Clay negotiated a

compromise: tariffs were lowered and South Carolina dropped nullification" ("Andrew Jackson," available online at https://www.whitehouse.gov/1600/presidents/andrewjackson, accessed 4/13/15). "Published after his death, Calhoun's two treatises on political theory and American constitutionalism, the *Disquisition* and *Discourse*, demonstrate his hope that America could avoid the pending conflict.... His last years were spent attempting to unify the South and avoid strife. On March 31, 1850, Calhoun died in Washington, D.C. In death, Calhoun became a source of inspiration for the Confederate government, its leaders, and the South" (H. Lee Cheek, *John C. Calhoun: Selected Writings and Speeches*, p. xv). "The responsibility for the actual secession does not rest in an especial degree on any individual leader. Secession began rather with the spontaneous movement of the whole community of South Carolina, and in the States which followed leading politicians expressed rather than inspired the general will. The guilt which any of us can venture to attribute for this action of a whole deluded society must rest on men like Calhoun, who in a previous generation, while opinion in the South was still to some extent unformed, stifled all thought of reform and gave the semblance of moral and intellectual justification to a system only susceptible of a historical excuse" (Charnwood, *Abraham Lincoln*, pp. 181, 182).

[7] *Boston Daily Advertiser*, Jan. 25, 1861, p. 2.

[8] *Philadelphia Inquirer*, Jan. 29, 1861, p. 2.

[9] White, *Testimonies for the Church*, vol. 1, p. 253. For the merchandising of "slaves and souls of men," see Rev. 18:13.

[10] White, *Testimonies for the Church*, vol. 1, p. 254. In the June 27, 1865 *Review and Herald*, Uriah Smith responded to G. N. Sappington of Lynxville, Wisconsin, "it was not then, at the time the testimony was given, its object" (Uriah Smith, "Explanation Wanted," *Review and Herald*, June 27, 1895, p. 30).

[11] John Beatty and Harrison Caroll Hobart, *The Citizen-Soldier: The Memoirs of a Civil War Volunteer*, p. 20.

[12] McPherson, *For Cause and Comrades*, p. 19.

[13] Bell Irvin Wiley, *The Life of Billy Yank*, p. 40, quoted in McPherson, p. 117.

[14] McPherson, p. 118.

[15] McPherson, p. 117. For the sentiments of other soldiers, see Chandra Manning, *What This Cruel War Was Over* (2008).

[16] "Baptists and the American Civil War: July 24, 1861," available online at http://www.civilwarbaptists.com/thisdayinhistory/1861-july-24, accessed 4/25/12.

[17] Under the Constitution, the federal powers could not end slavery. That was a state's right. Yet ultimately, the voting in of the Fifteenth Amendment to the Constitution ended slavery.

[18] White, *Testimonies for the Church*, vol. 1, p. 254.

[19] Spoken at the celebration of the emancipation of the slaves of the West Indies, at Abington, Massachusetts, and reported in *New York Times*, Aug. 6, 1862.

[20] "Current Events," *Home and Foreign Review*, vol. 1 (July 1862), p. 604; see the abbreviated form of the article in the *New York Herald*, "Wendell Phillips Spouting Foul Treason," reprinted in the *Liberator* (Boston), Aug. 15, 1862, p. 129, available online at http://fair-use.org/the-liberator/1862/08/15/the-liberator-32-33.pdf, accessed 1/23/15.

[21] White, *Testimonies for the Church*, vol. 1, p. 255.

[22] White, *Testimonies for the Church*, vol. 1, pp. 256, 257.

[23] White, *Testimonies for the Church*, vol. 1, p. 258.

[24] "But, infamous as it is, it finds an advocate in the Abolition press. The slaves are to be indiscriminately slaughtered, and when the last one is butchered, then it is thought the institution will cease to exist. The soul recoils in horror at the idea of an unscrupulous war upon the innocent and defenceless slave" (Mobile *Register*, quoted in "The Slaves to Be Murdered," *Liberator* [Boston], July 5, 1861, p. 106; also in "Stimulants for the Rebels," *Springfield* [Massachusetts] *Daily Republican*, June 3, 1861, p. 2).

[25] White, *Testimonies for the Church*, vol. 1, p. 258.

[26] White, *Testimonies for the Church*, vol. 1, p. 258. Snook and Brinkerhoff asserted: "What was the corner stone of the Confederacy: Slavery. Thus England was willing to aid where slavery was not intended to be done away" ("The Visions of E. G. White, Not of God,'" p. 22). Snook and Brinkerhoff were apparently unaware of England's deliberations about entering the war and Confederate assurances that the incidental matter of slavery would be dealt with once the South gained independence from the North. Because of her business ties with the South, England was willing to ignore Southern slavery until Lincoln made the war about ending slavery by his Emancipation Proclamation of January 1, 1863.

[27] William Schaw Lindsay, *House of Commons Debate*, July 18, 1862, vol. 168, cols. 515, 516.

[28] "It was the fear of democracy that most influenced the ruling class of Britain in its relationship with America during the middle Victorian period.... In May 1861, Queen Victoria had issued a Proclamation of Neutrality, which was all shadow and little substance. The press continued to enjoy and build upon the message, but it had little meaning.... British newspapers and journals portrayed the Confederacy not only as a land of virtuous aristocrats, but also as a homogeneous and patriotic entity" (Alfred Grant, *The American Civil War and the British Press*, pp. 6–8).

²⁹ Taken from the book description available online at http://books.google.com/books/about/English_Public_Opinion_and_the_American.html?id=WMUXggOQ7ZsC, accessed 2/16/15.

³⁰ Richard I. Lester, *Confederate Finance and Purchasing in Great Britain*, p. x. The success of the Confederacy would have required contradictory objectives. It would require the abolition of slavery because England had been staunchly anti-slavery since the Slavery Abolition Act of 1833. Yet it would also require the continuance of slavery so that the South could maintain her economy and pay back war loans made by English financiers, based on an undervalued appraisal of her cotton (Eugene R. Dattel, *Cotton and Race in the Making of America: The Human Costs of Economic Power*, p. 188).

³¹ John D. Bennett, *The London Confederates*, p. 143.

³² William H. Aspinwall, letter to the editor of *New York Times*, Oct. 14, 1868, in *The Nation*, Oct. 14, 1875, p. 245.

³³ Bruce Catton and James M. McPherson, *The Civil War*, p. 101. In his review of *The Trent Affair: A Diplomatic Crisis*, Charles S. Campbell cited author Norman B. Ferris to explain "why a relatively trivial maritime incident threatened to touch off a trans-Atlantic war at the end of the year 1861." One option that Campbell pondered is: "... did they want to seize the opportunity to ensure the breakup of the United States?" (*American Historical Review*, vol. 82, no. 5 [Dec. 1977], pp. 1331–1332). Seven weeks of deliberation ensued. In relation to Britain's ultimatum, Abraham Lincoln is famously quoted as telling Secretary of State Seward, "One war at a time."

³⁴ Amanda Foreman, ("A World on Fire: A Saga of the Civil War, at Home and Abroad," available online at http://www.youtube.com/watch?v=-zHHPmiqa9s, 31:12, accessed 1/10/15).

³⁵ White, *Testimonies for the Church*, vol. 1, p. 258, emphasis added.

³⁶ Lindsay, *House of Commons Debate*, July 18, 1862, vol. 168, col. 520.

³⁷ PRO FO/5/189, in Foreman, *A World on Fire*, p. 856.

³⁸ "The Address of the Southern Independence Association, Upon Its Establishment in London, Dec., 1863," in Goddard, *The American Rebellion*, p. 398. Amanda Foreman maintained that England preferred a single American nation, citing Gladstone's view: "Two years after the conclusion of the war, in 1867, Gladstone admitted in a letter to the American author and abolitionist Charles Edwards Lester: 'I had imbibed, conscientiously if erroneously, an opinion that 20 or 24 millions of the North would be happier, and would be stronger ... without the South than with it, and also that the negroes would be nearer to emancipation under a Southern Government than under the old system of the Union, that had not at that date [August 1862] been abandoned.... As far as regards the special or separate interest of England in the matter, I ... had always contended that it was best for our interest that the Union should be kept entire" (Foreman, *A World on Fire*, p. 321). Yet on December 6, 1860, the *New York Times* reported: "We learn from a well known English capitalist, just arrived here, that every Englishman that he had conversed with on the subject of disunion was in ecstasies over the impending ruin which overhangs the Union, and they hope to God it will eventually occur" (*Western Chronicle* [Three Rivers, Michigan], Dec. 13, 1860, p. 2).

³⁹ John W. Raimo, *A Guide to Manuscripts Relating to America in Great Britain and Ireland*, p. 58, in Bennett, p. 137.

⁴⁰ *Times* (London), Jan. 16, 1863, in Bennett, p. 137. Regarding his role as financial agent, see Bennett, p. 59. The London *Examiner* (Sept. 26, 1863) expressed similar faith that slavery would dissolve once the Confederacy gained independence. British capitalists were willing to set up bonds to loan the Confederacy money, with cotton as collateral, though highly undervalued. Amanda Foreman cited two letters as evidence that British dignitaries naively accepted slavery as only a side issue in the war. One was written in September 1862 by the pro-Southern Earl of Shaftesbury to John Slidell, the Confederate Ambassador to France, innocently asking him "if the [Confederate] President could not in some way present the prospect of gradual emancipation. Such a declaration coming from him unsolicited would have the happiest effect in Europe" (Foreman, *A World on Fire*, p. 294). Slidell avoided a direct response, stating that abolition was for each state to decide and that the President could not speak for them. The other letter was written to Jefferson Davis by the British *Southern Independence Association* after Lincoln's Emancipation Proclamation, asking the president of the Confederacy when he was going to make his own statement about emancipation of the slaves. In his book of letters written to educate the British people about the true views of the Confederate states, Goddard quoted the Association's goal: "The Association will also devote itself to the cultivation of friendly feelings between the people of Great Britain and of the Confederate States; and it will, in particular, steadily but kindly represent to the Southern States, that recognition by Europe must necessarily lead to a revision of the system of servile labour unhappily bequeathed to them by England, in accordance with the spirit of the age, so as to combine the gradual extinction of slavery with the preservation of property, the maintenance of the civil polity, and the true civilisation of the negro race" (Samuel Aspinwall Goddard, *The American Rebellion: Letters on the American Rebellion*, p. 399). In "Reply to the Southern Independence Association," written to the editor of the *Daily Post*, Goddard exhorted: "... the attempt to cajole the people of Great Britain into aiding the establishment of a slave empire, by the hope, that when established, and seeing the wickedness of slavery, it would emancipate the slaves, is an insult to common sense" (Goddard, p. 402).

[41] France and Russia were powers that sought revenge. Albert A. Woldman wrote: "... the visit by a Russian naval squadron to New York represented the high point of Russian-American cooperation; this, he says, was due to a number of factors: Russia's intention to prevent British and French military interference in the affairs of the United States; Russia's need to restore its international position, which had been undermined by the Crimean War; and Russia's desire to take revenge on Britain for its defeat in the Crimean War. Woldman suggests, however, that the significance of this friendly act was greatly exaggerated by the Americans, who were to remember it as one of the events that saved their country" (Albert A. Woldman, *Lincoln and the Russians*, pp. viii, 131, 135–136, 149, cited by Norman E. Saul and Richard D. McKinzie, *Russian-American Dialogue on Cultural Relations, 1776–1914*, p. 95). Russia's interest was revealed in minister to Russia George V. N. Lothrop's June 4, 1885 "speech before the legislature of Michigan." In it he recalled "the friendship shown by that power towards us during our civil war" and revealed "that when France and England were threatening to intervene the czar sent a 'large fleet' into American waters under sealed orders. Subsequently, the danger of intervention having passed, the 'sealed orders' were opened, and it was found that they directed that, upon the first hostile demonstration against us by other powers, 'the batteries of the Russian fleet should open on the enemies of the Union" (*Sentinel* [Milwaukee, Wisconsin], June 10, 1885, p. 4. The same exchange was reported in "The New American Minister to Russia," *Nevada State Journal*, June 6, 1885, p. 1; "Honoring Minister Lothrop," *New York Times*, June 5, 1885; and "Our Russian Minister," *Salt Lake Evening Democrat*, June 5, 1885, p. 2.) The value of the presence of Russian ships at this point in the war (in Sept. 1863) has been debated (see James Morton Callahan, *Russo-American Relations During the American Civil War*; and Willis Fletcher Johnson, *America's Foreign Relations*, vol. 2).

[42] White, *Testimonies for the Church*, vol. 1, pp. 258, 259, emphasis added. Regarding "foreign governments or people," the late confidential agent of the Confederate Department of State in Europe, Edwin de Leon, wrote in his memoir: "Why should they be expected to sympathize or affiliate with a government antagonistic to their own, and with a people who loudly proclaimed their superiority over the subjects of 'European despotism'[?]" (Edwin De Leon, *Secret History of Confederate Diplomacy Abroad*, p. 9).

[43] Yet neither England nor France officially acknowledged the Confederacy as an independent nation. "Only the Pope of Rome, of all the rulers of the earth, acting as a temporal prince, officially recognized Jefferson Davis as the head of a real Government.... In the autumn of 1862, Pope Pius the Ninth addressed a letter to the Archbishops of New York and New Orleans, enjoining them to employ their prayers and influence for the restoration of peace. These were published, and on the 23d of September, 1863, Jefferson Davis, in his official capacity, addressed a letter to 'The Most Venerable Chief of the Holy See, and Sovereign Pontiff of the Roman Catholic Church,' thanking him, in his own name and that of the Confederate States, for his 'Christian charity and love,' declaring that they then were and ever had been earnestly desirous that the 'wicked war should cease.' To this the Pope replied on the 3d of December, in a letter 'To the Illustrious and Honorable Jefferson Davis, President of the Confederate States of America,' expressing his gratification that Davis appreciated his letter to the archbishops, and to recognize that he and his people were animated by the same desire as himself 'for peace and tranquility.' This was the only official recognition the Chief Conspirator ever received by the head of any Government" (Benson John Lossing, *The Pictorial Field Book of the Civil War in the United States of America*, vol. 3, p. 47).

[44] "The cabinet agreed to form a six-member war committee. Military experts were called in, and at the War Office, strategic plans drawn up during previous periods of tension were taken out for revision. Maine was to be the first target, with simultaneous actions by the Royal Navy to blockade Boston, New Bedford, Newport, Long Island, New York, and the Delaware River. If necessary, these ports would be bombarded into submission. 'War has no doubt its honours and its evils,' Admiral Milne reminded the [British] secretary of state for the navy, who deprecated such wanton destruction, 'but to make war felt it must be carried out against the Enemy with energy, and every place made to feel what war really is.' ... Their best option was to launch the first strike and capture Maine" (Amanda Foreman, *A World on Fire*, pp. 183, 184).

[45] William Henry Gregory quoted the question of another member of Parliament: "... will recognition give you one bale of cotton, and will it not entail war?" (*House of Commons Debate*, July 18, 1862, vol. 168, col. 566).

[46] "The Conversion of Lord Palmerston in Belligerent Rights," *Spectator*, March 15, 1862, available online at http://archive.spectator.co.uk/article/15th-march-1862/8/the-conversion-of-lord-palmerston-on-from-the-risk, accessed 5/2/14.

[47] Peter Alfred Taylor, *House of Commons Debate*, 18 July 1862, vol. 168, cols. 524, 525.

[48] Ellen White's only other published use of the term "general confusion" is in a letter to her son Edson and daughter-in-law Emma, in which she compared a busy train depot to the day of judgment: "I never beheld such a scene as this before—men and women rushing frantically this way and that, crowding one another and treading upon one another. I thought of the day when the wrath of God unmixed with mercy shall fall upon the heads of the wicked. The *general confusion*, the imprecations, the fear expressed in countenances, the pale faces, the weary, distressed looks, the angry looks and oaths, reminded us of a day far more exciting which will be general. I thought, Shall we be then among the peaceful and holy who have made God and heaven our trust, or shall we be among the fearful, terror-stricken, hopeless, despairing

ones? You, my dear children, with us may be among that number who shall calmly lean upon an Arm that is mighty to save to the utmost, an Arm we have sought after and relied upon when the evil day was not upon us" (Letter 24 [Sept.] 1870, in *Manuscript Releases*, vol. 20, pp. 331, 332, emphasis added).

[49] Francis D. Nichol, *Ellen G. White and Her Critics*, pp. 122, 123; Herbert E. Douglass, *Messenger of the Lord*, p. 487. The prophecies about Christ's imminent return are likewise conditional. Mrs. White wrote: "The angels of God in their messages to men represent time as very short. Thus it has always been presented to me. It is true that time has continued longer than we expected in the early days of this message. Our Saviour did not appear as soon as we hoped. But has the word of the Lord failed? Never! It should be remembered that the promises and threatenings of God are alike conditional" (Ms. 4, 1883, in *Selected Messages*, bk. 1, p. 67). Scripture also contains prophecies with an imminent quality, though time has indeed been prolonged (1 Thess. 4:15, 17; Rev. 3:11; 22:7, 12, 20).

[50] The planned attack would have been either to protect their territories in Canada or to aid in the division of the country so that they could enjoy a weaker competitor in the United States and a dependent ally in the Confederacy.

[51] At the end of the testimony on "Slavery and the War" is a description that fits the two ensuing World Wars of the twentieth century. Notice that this is not a description of war in America. Ellen White wrote: "I was shown *the inhabitants of the earth* in the utmost confusion. War, bloodshed, privation, want, famine, and pestilence were abroad in the land. As these things surrounded God's people, they began to press together, and to cast aside their little difficulties. Self-dignity no longer controlled them; deep humility took its place. Suffering, perplexity, and privation caused reason to resume its throne, and the passionate and unreasonable man became sane, and acted with discretion and wisdom. My attention was then called from the scene. There seemed to be *a little time of peace. Once more the inhabitants of the earth* were presented before me; and again everything was in the utmost confusion. Strife, war, and bloodshed, with famine and pestilence, raged everywhere. Other nations were engaged in this war and confusion. War caused famine. Want and bloodshed caused pestilence. And then men's hearts failed them for fear, 'and for looking after those things which are coming on the earth' " (White, *Testimonies for the Church*, vol. 1, p. 268, emphasis added).

[52] Abraham Lincoln, "Second Inaugural Address," in *Speeches and Writings*, pp. 686–687, quoted in Faust, p. 189.

[53] Peter Brock, *Pacifism in the United States: From the Colonial Era to the First World War*, p. 845.

[54] Drew Gilpin Faust, *A Sacred Circle*, p. 140, quoted in Bertram Wyatt-Brown, *Religion and the American Civil War*, Randall M. Miller, Harry S. Stout, and Charles Reagan Wilson, eds., pp. 93, 94.

[55] Wyatt-Brown, p. 10.

[56] From Daniel Stowell, " 'We Have Sinned and God Has Smitten Us!' John H. Caldwell and the Religious Meaning of Confederate Defeat," *Georgia Historical Quarterly* 78 (Spring 1994): pp. 1–38, in Wyatt-Brown, p. 32.

[57] Wyatt-Brown, p. 81.

[58] What Ellen White declared in Testimony number seven is: "This nation will yet be humbled into the dust" (White, *Testimonies for the Church*, vol. 1, p. 259). D. M. Canright failed to grasp this fact in *Life of Mrs. E. G. White, Seventh-day Adventist Prophet: Her False Claims Refuted*, p. 133: "She says: 'Jan. 4, 1862, I was shown some things in regard to our nation.' (p. 253.) It is all a bitter denunciation of Lincoln's administration and his management of the war. Every move had been wrong, and only defeat was prophesied. . . . her whole message was one of opposition, faultfinding, condemnation, and a prophecy of defeat and final failure—exactly that of the opponents of Lincoln and his management of the war." However, Eric Anderson wrote: "Her private correspondence yields not a single reference to the name of Lincoln, a leader about whom the historian expects her to have definite and quotable opinions" (Anderson, *Ellen Harmon White*, pp. 262, 263). In other words, Ellen White could not have criticized Lincoln when she did not mention his name except in her January 4, 1862 statement, "Before President Lincoln's administration commenced, great advantage was taken by the South" (White, *Testimonies for the Church*, vol. 1, p. 253). Drawing from "Testimony for the church, No. 9," Douglas Morgan described her concerns about the northern forces (and not Abraham Lincoln's administration) as "collusion with the rebels, racial bigotry, reliance on spiritualism for guidance, and the treachery of pro-slavery generals combined to sabotage the Union cause" (Douglas Morgan, "Civil War," *The Ellen G. White Encyclopedia*, p. 721). Ultimately, the policy that won the war was that which Ellen White had always upheld—the emancipation of the slaves. Lincoln was wise enough to know that he did not have support for the emancipation of the slaves until Northerners had become sick of the war.

[59] "Testimony for the church, No. 9" was announced as available at the end of January 1863 ("Testimony for the Church No. 9, is now ready," *Review and Herald*, Jan. 27, 1863, p. 72). The Battle of Gettysburg was fought July 1–3, 1863.

[60] White, *Testimonies for the Church*, vol. 1, p. 359, published in "Testimony for the church, No. 9," in January 1863, but first included in Letter 24, 1862, written to Ross Alexander. After the war, Uriah Smith reminded Seventh-day Adventists of

this prediction, citing descriptions of Southern destitution in the *New York Express* and in the *New-York Daily Tribune*. This destitution included the decimation of crops, major cities, railroads, and the economy, and the death of most able-bodied men ("Destitution and Suffering at the South," *Review and Herald*, May 16, 1865, p. 189). The London *Times* of Oct. 13, 1865, set the Confederacy's debt at $3,450,766,000 (Richard I. Lester, "An Aspect of Confederate Finance During the American Civil War: the Erlanger Loan and the Plan of 1864," *Business History*, July 1, 1974, pp. 130–144).

[61] White, "Testimony for the church, No. 9," *Testimonies for the Church*, vol. 1, p. 365.

[62] J. H. W., "Questions," *Review and Herald*, May 6, 1862, p. 182.

[63] New Bedford, Massachusetts *Republican Standard*, "The War," *Review and Herald*, June 10, 1862, p. 11, 12.

[64] This included Arkansas, Texas, Louisiana, Mississippi, Alabama, Florida, Georgia, South Carolina, North Carolina, and Virginia, except for a few counties and parishes occupied by Federal troops.

[65] Forbes was in England on a secret mission for the Federal government (Douglas H. Maynard, "The Forbes-Aspinwall Mission," *Mississippi Valley Historical Review*, vol. 45, 1958, p. 73). The *Spectator* of January 31, 1863, reported: "The week has been full of signs of a coming change in public opinion. The civil war in America has become an anti-slavery struggle, and slowly but certainly English opinion is swinging round to its true position—a passive but unqualified dislike of all who contend for human bondage. Last week a public meeting in Liverpool, the stronghold of slavish principles and slaveowning prejudices, endorsed Mr. Lincoln's proclamation" ("News of the Week," *Spectator*, Jan. 31, 1863).

[66] Collie to Wharncliffe, Jan. 23, 1865, *Wharncliffe Muniments*, p. 461, cited by Bennett, p. 142.

[67] Her statement was that the Southern forces did not have "the valor and the power of endurance that Northern men have" (*Testimonies for the Church*, vol. 1, p. 266).

[68] Loughborough heard and reported on the speech ("All This Came," *Review and Herald*, Nov. 14, 1899, p. 730; *Rise and Progress*, p. 242). Loughborough had been president of the Illinois Conference since March 1891 ("Special Notices: Ottawa, Illinois Camp-Meeting," *Review and Herald*, Aug. 2, 1892, p. 493). Most of St. John's two-hour Ottawa speech was not recorded; however, the *InterOcean* mentioned it ("St. John Amuses His Audience," *InterOcean* [Chicago, IL], June 30, 1891, p. 1). "St. John never used a prepared speech but delivered his message extemporaneously and ensured no doubt that his agenda was on religious and moral grounds as well being a political statement. 'Our covenant touching this matter is with the Lord,' he said, 'and we propose to complete the good work.' " As governor, he had opened Kansas to the "exodus" of former slaves from the South beginning in 1875 ("Governor Records - St. John, 1879-1883").

[69] Chesebrough, p. 86.

[70] In his book on James White, Gerald Wheeler discussed military service and James White's efforts to enable service-age Seventh-day Adventists to keep the commandments of God. He described White's controversial article "The Nation," in which he placed responsibility on the government for causing soldiers to violate the fourth and sixth commandments. He also described James White's work with John P. Kellogg to solicit funds for signing bonuses for volunteers and his urging of all church members to share the burden of raising $300 commutation fees that Adventists might forego military service and keep God's law (Wheeler, *James White: Innovator and Overcomer*, pp. 143, 144). The chapter "Adventists and the Civil War" ends saying: "James White feared that the war might destroy the new church. He suggested that the General Conference committee appoint the second Sabbath in February 1865 as a day of fasting and prayer both for Adventist soldiers and for a quick conclusion to the war. Shortly afterward the church leadership called for its members to set aside March 1–4 for 'earnest and importunate prayer' about the situation. Within six weeks General Lee surrendered his army, and many Adventists felt that God had directly answered their prayers [Byington et al, "Day of Fasting and Prayer," *Review and Herald*, Jan. 31, 1865, p. 80; "Humiliation and Prayer," *Review and Herald*, Feb. 21, 1865, p. 100, republished in *Review and Herald*, April 25, 1865, pp. 164, 165]. The Adventist Church could now devote itself more fully to its mission" (Wheeler, p. 145).

[71] The actual last battle of the war was fought at Palmito Ranch, Texas, on May 13, 1865.

[72] "Though many Northern preachers pushed and attempted to pressure Lincoln into issuing a statement on emancipation, often criticizing him for not acting swiftly on that subject, they were generally supportive of the president throughout the war. Henry Ward Beecher was one of those who had publicly chastened Lincoln for his failure to act rapidly on emancipation, yet on most everything else Beecher was a staunch supporter of the nation's leader" (Chesebrough, p. 87). "Like her, some unwise hot-heads urged Lincoln to immediately declare slavery abolished. General Fremont had to be removed from his command because he began that very thing in the West" (Canright, p. 133). Yet Canright acknowledged that, unlike the "unwise hot-heads," Ellen White did not direct her testimony to Lincoln: "It was all directed to us, a little handful of about ten thousand, half women, none of any influence in the Government or in the war. Bible prophets went directly to the king and told him how to conduct the war, and what the end would be. Our prophet had no such message" (Canright, p. 133). These statements about the war were included in "Testimonies for the Church," not testimonies for the United States president. She gave their object: "The scenes which are passing before us are of sufficient magnitude to cause us to arouse...." (*Spiritual Gifts*, vol. 4b, p. 59).

[73] The event was also reported in the *New York Times* ("The Jubilee among the Freedmen. How the Slaves Celebrated Their Emancipation," *New York Times*, April 4, 1865).

[74] "A Jubilee at Charleston," *Review and Herald*, April 25, 1865, p. 166.

[75] "Freedmen's Jubilee," *Charleston Daily Courier*, March 22, 1865; "From South Carolina: Grand Procession of Colored Loyalists," *New-York Daily Tribune*, April 4, 1865, p. 6.

[76] Nancy F. Elkins contended that Seventh-day Adventists did not enter the South to increase their influence but as "part of their larger missionary endeavors. . . . Maintaining health of body, mind, and soul was the motivation of their ministry" (Nancy F. Elkins, "Seventh-Day Adventists: A Study of Home Mission Work in Western North Carolina," *Appalachian Journal*, Winter 1981, p. 119).

CHAPTER 5 - Answering a Prejudicial Charge

[1] Recycled at Dirk Anderson, "Ellen White Supremacist," http://www.nonsda.org/egw/egw62.shtml, accessed 1/10/15. See also Carol Putnam, "AMALGAMATION: The Racist Doctrine Seventh-Day Adventists Don't Want You to Know," available online at http://new.exchristian.net/2010/09/amalgamation-racist-doctrine-seventh.html, accessed 4/12/15.

[2] Ellen G. White, *Spiritual Gifts*, vol. 3 (1864), p. 64; *The Spirit of Prophecy*, vol. 1, p. 69, emphasis added.

[3] *Spiritual Gifts*, vol. 3, p. 75; *The Spirit of Prophecy*, vol. 1, p. 78, emphasis added.

[4] *The Spirit of Prophecy*, vol. 1, pp. 69, 78, emphasis added.

[5] Michael W. Campbell and Timothy G. Standish, "Amalgamation," *The Ellen G. White Encyclopedia*, p. 590. Jud Lake and Jerry Moon prepared a general article, "Current Science and Ellen White: Twelve Controversial Statements," in the *Ellen G. White Encyclopedia*, pp. 231–233, which also deals with her amalgamation statements.

[6] Webster's 1828 *Dictionary*, available online at www.christiantech.com. In an updated version of his article "A Beast in the Garden," sent to the author in 2009, Willey read the 1889 *Century Dictionary* definition of "amalgamation," which refers to intermarriage between blacks and whites, into Ellen White's 1864 statement.

[7] List compiled by Alfredo Vergel at the Heritage Center, Southwestern Adventist University, Sept. 5, 2012.

[8] Herman Merivale, *Lectures on Colonization and Colonies* (1842), v. 2, p. 180.

[9] Benjamin Parham Aydelott, *Incidental Benefits of Denominational Division* (1846), p. 105.

[10] Samuel George Morton, *Types of Mankind* (1854), p. 67. Significantly, Morton's book *Crania Americana* helped justify the claim of Negro inferiority.

[11] Robert Dale Owen, *The Wrong of Slavery* (1864), p. 219.

[12] Louis Agassiz, *A Journey in Brazil* (1869), p. 293.

[13] Arthur Mapletoft Curteis, *Rise of the Macedonian Empire* (1890), p. 194.

[14] James Ford Rhodes, *History of the United States from the Compromise of 1850* (1892), vol. 1, p. 335.

[15] E. B. Lane, "The South," *Review and Herald*, Sept. 26, 1871, pp. 118, 119.

[16] C. H. Spurgeon, "The World on Fire," quoted in *Review and Herald*, Aug. 21, 1879, p. 65.

[17] Martin Luther; Jaroslav Jan Pelikan, Hilton C. Oswald, Helmut T. Lehmann, translators, *Luther's Works*, Vol. 2: Lectures on Genesis: Chapters 6–14, sect. 2, p. 29, emphasis added.

[18] "Amalgamation of Man and Beast: Solving the Riddle," a presentation by Dr. T. Joe Willey at the San Diego Chapter of the Association of Adventist Forums, Oct. 13, 2007, transcribed by Kevin L. Morgan, with a copy sent to the speaker. Willey asserted that Ellen White believed that the Negro is inherently inferior because of amalgamation, but her statement about the responsibility of the Master who treated his slave like a "brute beast" implies that it was not their inherent nature or ability but the slaves' lack of opportunity that limited their moral development.

[19] Snook and Brinkerhoff came to a similar conclusion in the 27-page pamphlet, "The Visions of E. G. White, Not of God," p. 9—a conclusion that Uriah Smith rebutted. Willey also accused Ellen White of being a quasi-polygynist, asserting that she believed that blacks were "another beast . . . created outside of God's creative works in Genesis" (Willey, "Amalgamation of Man and Beast: Solving the Riddle," a presentation at the San Diego Adventist Forum, Oct. 13, 2007). On the contrary, Ellen White emphasized "their common relationship to [whites] by creation and by redemption and their rights to the blessings of freedom" (White, *Testimonies for the Church*, vol. 1, pp. 201, 202).

[20] Willey, emphasis added.

[21] "Ariel" (Buckner H. Payne), *The Negro: What Is His Ethnological Status?* (1867) pp. 21–28, emphasis from Willey. Archive.org has a 48-page pamphlet entitled, "The Negro: What Is His Ethnological Status? Is he the progeny of Ham? Is he a descendent of Adam and Eve? Has he a soul? Or is he a beast in God's nomenclature? What is his status as fixed by God in creation? What is his relation to the white race?" Second edition. The date, July 1840, is attached at the end. A 67-page pamphlet with the same content was printed by the Harpoon, edited by John S. Bonner. The pamphlet is entitled *The negro, his ethnological status; or, Is the negro a beast?* Its Introduction states: "Written as early as July, 1840, but . . . not printed until

after the close of the civil war ... To the last chapter a 'conclusion' was added, but the main article had been written 25 years before." Robert A. Young responded almost immediately with *The Negro: A Reply to Ariel* (1867). A much later book with a similar view is Charles Carroll's *The Negro a Beast: Or In the Image of God* (1900). Responses to Carroll's book came from William G. Schell, *Is the Negro a Beast?* (1901), and W. S. Armistead, *The Negro is a Man* (1903). A slightly later book supporting the supposed inherent inferiority of Negroes states: "Time nor circumstance nor climate affect not the negro race, all nature forbids an amalgamation between them and the Caucasians. Nature tolerates not hybrids, or mules, or mulattoes. It is clearly proven that a race between the three typical stocks, can only be maintained by a continual drain upon a parent stock" (John Campbell, *Negro-mania: being an examination of the falsely assumed equality of the various races of men*, pp. 11, 12, cited by Michael Campbell, " 'Amalgamation': Ellen White's Most Controversial Statement," March 25, 2014, available online at http://www.adventisthistory.org/2014/03/25/amalgamation-ellen-whites-most-controversial-statement, accessed 7/12/14). Modern science has demonstrated that pure breeds tend to have more physical problems than mutts do.

[22] White, *Spiritual Gifts*, vol. 1 (1858), p. 193, emphasis added; quoted in T. Joe Willey in "Amalgamation of Man and Beast: Solving the Riddle," a presentation at the San Diego Chapter of the Association of Adventist Forums, Oct. 13, 2007. Interestingly, the concept "as though they had not been" is from Obadiah 16. She published her earliest written statement about slavery in her first book in 1851: "Then commenced the jubilee, when the land should rest. I saw the pious slave rise in triumph and victory, and shake off the chains that bound him, while his wicked master was in confusion, and knew not what to do; for the wicked could not understand the words of the voice of God" (Ellen G. White, *A Sketch of the Christian Experience and Views of Ellen G. White*, p. 18). This statement reflects the biblical description of those who are afraid to see Jesus when He returns: "And the kings of the earth, and the great men, and the rich men, and the chief captains, and the mighty men, and every bondman, and every free man, hid themselves in the dens and in the rocks of the mountains; and said to the mountains and rocks, Fall on us, and hide us from the face of him that sitteth on the throne, and from the wrath of the Lamb: for the great day of his wrath is come; and who shall be able to stand?" (Rev. 6:15).

[23] In quoting this passage, Eric Anderson changed the statement to past perfect tense: "the slave-master would have to answer for the soul of his slave whom he *had* kept in ignorance" ("War, Slavery, and Race," *Ellen Harmon White*, p. 266). However, the statement, written in present tense, was an indictment of their then current practice.

[24] White, *Spiritual Gifts*, vol. 1 (1858), p. 193.

[25] "Communication from Sister White: Slavery and the War," *Review and Herald*, Aug. 27, 1861, pp. 100–102, emphasis added; with minor variations in *Testimonies for the Church*, vol. 1, p. 266. She did not reprint this statement in *Spiritual Gifts*, vol. 4b. However, in 1866, J. N. Loughborough called attention to the prediction, citing the recently published letter of a Southerner in the *New York Independent* (see "Scuds in the Political Heavens," *Review and Herald*, April 24, 1866, p. 164): "Slavery in the South is as much a fact now as it was five years ago; and, having lost nothing but the name—with the increased ratio in which the 'peculiar institution' is gaining ground—if the Southern States are reconstructed on the principles enunciated by the President and his copperhead coadjutors of the North, we may say, with the disorganizers of the Chicago Convention, 'The war is a failure' " (J. N. Loughborough, "Little Time of Peace," *Review and Herald*, May 1, 1866, p. 173).

[26] The concept of using a bottle as a record of suffering comes from Psalm 56:8: "Thou tellest my wanderings: put thou my tears into thy bottle: are they not in thy book?"

[27] White, *Spiritual Gifts*, vol. 1 (1858), pp. 191, 192, emphasis added (except for the emphasis in "*Such* are Christ's followers!"), recycled in *Review and Herald*, Aug. 27, 1861, p. 100. See also White, *Testimonies for the Church*, vol. 1 (1859), p. 202: "The law of our land requiring us to deliver a slave to his master, we are not to obey; and we must abide the consequences of violating this law. The slave is not the property of any man. God is his rightful master, and man has no right to take God's workmanship into his hands, and claim him as his own."

[28] White, *Testimonies for the Church*, vol. 1, p. 358 (published in "Testimony no. 9" in January 1863), emphasis added.

[29] Mrs. E. G. White, "The Good Shepherd's Estimate of a Lost Sheep," *Signs of the Times*, Nov. 20, 1893.

[30] In her 1890 book, Ellen White described the origin of the races as springing from the sons of Noah (*Patriarchs and Prophets*, p. 117). For those who take the Genesis account at face value, the races could have come from no one else, for Noah's three sons were the bottleneck through which all the races of humanity came to be.

[31] Payne's book is not listed in the online inventory of Ellen White's libraries, compiled by Johns, Poirier, and Graybill.

[32] Campbell and Standish explained the omission of the amalgamation statements from Ellen White's later telling of the Flood story because of the more general nature of the book's target audience and "the hostile use made of these quotations by 'Southern authors' " ("Amalgamation," *The Ellen G. White Encyclopedia*, p. 593, citing W. C. White, "Some Early Statements—Why Not Reprinted?" DF 316). See also Ronald Osborn, "True Blood: Race, Science, and Early Adventist Amalgamation Theory Revisited," *Spectrum Magazine*, vol. 38, no. 4 (Fall 2010), and the earlier article of Gordon Shigley, "Amalgamation of Man and Beast: What Did Ellen White Mean?" *Spectrum*, June 1982, pp. 10–19.

[33] Ronald Osborn, p. 4.

[34] Smith also answered objections from Gilbert Cranmer who, like Snook and Brinkerhoff, rejected Mrs. White's visions. Regarding Snook's disaffection, the Ellen G. White Estate has on file a letter from Snook, dated May 31, 1865 and addressed to Elder W. S. Ingraham, in which he proposed: "How would you like to strike out on the old doctrine of the independence of the churches? Please answer by return mail." (Ingraham had abstained in voting on the name of the church and was slow to accept organization. See his confession about his independence in "Note from Bro Ingraham," *Review and Herald*, March 19, 1861, p. 144.) After James and Ellen White visited Iowa in July 1865 and supplied answers to their objections, Snook and Brinkerhoff experienced a reversal of attitude (U. Smith, G. W. Amadon, and J. M. Aldrich, "Remarks," *Review and Herald*, Jan. 23, 1866, p. 63), and they wrote letters of confession ("From Bro. Snook," and "From Bro. Brinkerhoff," *Review and Herald*, July 25, 1865, pp. 62, 63). Snook's confession reveals their difficulty: "I now feel that I have been led by the wicked one in my movements of late, especially in my opposition to the body. Apparent difficulties in relation to Sister White's visions have been accumulating in my mind for some time. These were magnified by the enemy until doubts resulted in unbelief and rebellion" (*Review and Herald*, July 25, 1865, p. 62). Though church officials accepted their confessions, they could not restore them to leadership. The church at Battle Creek wrote: "... when they have shown themselves by their future course, true to the principles of Christianity, we shall be happy to see them again in our midst" (E. S. Walker, "Response of the Battle Creek Church," *Review and Herald*, July 25, 1865, p. 63). Toward the end of 1865, Snook and Brinkerhoff "relapsed into a new state of doubts and criticism" (Levterov, "Marion Party," *The Ellen G. White Encyclopedia*, p. 959), leaving the church with the "Marion Party." From May 1866 to 1868, Brinkerhoff edited the *Hope of Israel;* Snook edited it from 1868 to 1870 (*The History of Linn County, Iowa*, p. 449). By 1869, he was a Universalist (*Waterloo* [Iowa] *Courier*, July 22, 1869, p. 4) and was working as an attorney, notary public (*Waterloo Courier*, July 28, 1870, p. 1), and "minister" (*1870 United States Federal Census, Iowa, Black Hawk, Big Creek*). He later served as a "Public Principal" (Iowa State Census, 1885) and a Universalist minister (Iowa State Census, 1895). Snook, who was still an "Adventist," debated other ministers about the Sabbath—including Brinkerhoff (*Waterloo Courier*, July 22, 1869, p. 4). After a disastrous defeat in 1870 ("The Lisbon Debate," *Cambridge City* [Indiana] *Tribune*, Jan. 13, 1870, p. 1), he became a Universalist clergyman (*Cambridge City Tribune*, March 17, 1870, p. 15; *1870 United States Federal Census, Iowa, Marion Township*).

[35] The series ran from June 12 to July 31, 1866, with the response on amalgamation in the July 31 issue. Uriah Smith published a statement of leadership approval in the June 12 installment: " 'Resolved, That we, the members of the General and Mich. State Conference, having *heard a portion of the manuscript* which has been prepared by Bro. U. Smith, in response to certain objections recently brought against the visions of Sister White, do hereby express our hearty approval of the same. Resolved, That we tender our thanks to Bro. Smith for his able defense of the visions against the attacks of their opponents.' " ([Uriah Smith], "Objections to the Visions," *Review and Herald*, June 12, 1866, p. 16, emphasis added). The entire rebuttal was published two years later as *The Visions of Mrs. E. G. White: A Manifestation of Spiritual Gifts According to the Scriptures*. A second and shorter response to assertions about the impossibility of the amalgamation of man and beast came from 26-year-old George Vincent Kilgore of Washington, Iowa ("Blind Guides," *Review and Herald*, Nov. 28, 1878, p. 170). Kilgore described his response: "I referred him to *Johnson's New Cyclopedia*, pp. 1040, 1042, that he might learn for the first time, if he never knew it before, that 'Allied species are capable, as a rule, of pairing and producing offspring;' and that, 'under the influence of man, mongrel races readily arise and are indefinitely sustained,'—just exactly what Sister White says. . . . I showed that her teachings were correct (Lev. 18:23, 24) . . ." His rebuttal does not support the amalgamation of *non*-allied species of animals, nor the crossing of humans and animals. "Mongrel races" are the result of the crossing of races of *humans*.

[36] Snook and Brinkerhoff, "The Visions of E. G. White, Not of God," p. 9, italics supplied (notice that they had "varieties of species" without "of animals"). The pamphlet was printed in May 1866, when Snook was 30 and Brinkerhoff was 28. In understanding how Snook and Brinkerhoff could acknowledge that the charge was denied by Seventh-day Adventists yet still insist that it was true, one should consider the animosity that occasioned the pamphlet. Issue 21 in the same chapter of the pamphlet echoed Snook's smarting from the reprimand he received from Ellen White. She described their error in "Testimony for the church, No. 9": "They mistook zeal and fanaticism for conscientiousness. Instead of being guided by reason and sound judgment, they allowed their feelings to take the lead. They were ready to become martyrs for their faith. . . . Instead of making their petitions to the God of heaven and relying solely upon His power, they petitioned the legislature and were refused" (*Testimonies for the Church*, vol. 1, p. 356). Brinkerhoff retorted that this was precisely what the brethren of Michigan had done, and they did not receive any reprimand. Ellen White's point was that, because of Seventh-day Adventists' refusal to pray and fast for the Union until slavery should be acknowledged as the cause of the war, *timing* and *approach* in response to God's leading made all the difference. The issue of military service was a difficult one, and the Iowans' actions had put them under suspicion of sympathizing with the "rebellion" and vocally opposing any conscription law (Ronald D. Graybill, "This Perplexing War: Why Adventists Avoided Military Service in the Civil War," *Insight*, Oct. 10, 1978, p. 4). James White wrote: "The object of our article entitled, The Nation, in No. 11, was to briefly state the views our people entertain of slavery, and to check that spirit of fanaticism which would recklessly proclaim abroad that we should resist a military draft" ("The War

Question," *Review and Herald*, Oct. 14, 1862, p. 159). Graybill described Snook's petition: "In Iowa, B. F. Snook, president of the Iowa Conference, decided to strike out on his own, and immediately led out in a petition to the Iowa legislature for special exemptions from service in the State militia. Henry Carver, an Adventist farmer in Iowa, had previously refused to sign this petition, but now, feeling 'shorn of my strength' by James White's editorial, he capitulated [Henry E. Carver, "The War," *Review and Herald*, Oct. 21, 1862, p. 166]. Both of these men left the church in 1866 and were instrumental in founding the Church of God (Adventist)" (Graybill, p. 5). Snook confessed: "I have opposed Bro. White's position on 'The Nation' to some extent. However I did so in all sincerity, believing him to be wrong. I now am sorry that I have been so hasty and inconsiderate, and ask forgiveness, and herein disclaim all that I have said against his views, and declare myself in full confidence and sympathy with him in his present move. ... To kill in war, when defending our government and our rights, is no violation of the sixth commandment" (White, p. 159). Snook later asked forgiveness of the brethren for "rushing them into that act of petitioning" (B. F. Snook, "Testimony No. 9," *Review and Herald*, March 3, 1863, p. 109). Snook's draft registration, dated July 23, 1863, when he was 28, lists him as living in Ohio, married, and a "minister of the Gospel."

Writing to Uriah Smith about his responsibility under greater knowledge, Ellen White cut Snook and Brinkerhoff some slack over Smith: "Brinkerhoof [sic] and Snook, had they had the light and knowledge you have had of the work God has given me to do, might have stood to this day and you are far more guilty in the position you have taken with the testimonies sounding in your ears for the last two years, and unheeded" (Letter 73 [Nov. 25], 1890, in *The Ellen G. White 1888 Materials*, p. 732).

[37] "Confusion" is a key word used in Scripture. See discussion on Leviticus 18:23 and 20:12.

[38] Smith, *The Visions of Mrs. E. G. White: A Manifestation of Spiritual Gifts According to the Scriptures*, pp. 102–105.

[39] In 1901, Seventh-day Adventist minister Sheridan Sidney Smith of Mauston, Wisconsin, queried: "... in 'Spiritual Gifts,' Vol. III, page 75, it says: 'Since the flood, there has been amalgamation of man and beast, as may be seen in the almost endless varieties of species of animals and in certain races of men.' But in Acts 17:26 we read that God 'hath made of one blood all nations of men for to dwell on all the face of the earth,' etc. Can amalgamated blood be saved? I would like a little light on this subject." Uriah Smith responded: "As to statements in 'Spiritual Gifts,' page 75, it is not difficult to believe that there have been attempts at amalgamation between man and beast. The difficulty is to believe that the results of such attempts could be perpetuated; and we do not understand the statement to affirm that it could be carried to such an extent as to violate or invalidate physiological law. Thus, if *amalgamation* could be carried to such an extent as that a human being should beget a beast, such beasts could not perpetuate their species; but might it not be that sufficient results of bestiality [Lev. 18:23, 24] would appear as to leave a *trace of amalgamation*, without destroying the power of generation? The horse and jackass can produce the mule; but mules cannot perpetuate their own species. But the *amalgamation* of which 'Spiritual Gifts' speaks is seen in what is called certain 'races of men.' This shows that deterioration, was not recognized to such a degree as to eliminate the human, and transform any such offspring into beasts. That objection therefore may not be raised against any class of human beings" (Uriah Smith, "In the Question Chair," *Review and Herald*, Nov. 5, 1901, p. 721, emphasis added). It is hard to imagine what "trace of amalgamation" could be transferred by bestiality between unrelated species.

[40] As one assignment in a master's class on British History, I surveyed articles and letters published in response to Darwin's *Origin of Species* and concluded: "Germans were more inclined than the French to accept the views of Lyell and Darwin. Fritz Müller wrote *Facts and Arguments for Darwin* (1869). Thomas Huxley, 'Darwin's bulldog,' led the intellectual charge. Yet in the first ten to twenty years from *Origin's* publication, most of the popular literature was against it." Many British writers thoughtfully took exception with various aspects of Darwin's inferential theory: "[Mr. Darwin] recognises very distinctly the variability of species; who does not? But *he does not see the limits of this variability;* and this is precisely what he ought to see" (Charles Robert Bree, *An Exposition of the Fallacies in the Hypothesis of Mr. Darwin*, 1872, pp. 395, 404, emphasis added). "If the theory of Natural Selection is true, Geology ought to furnish the most valuable and complete evidence in its support. But Mr. Darwin acknowledges that some of the facts of Geology are nearly fatal to his theory; and in order to surmount these difficulties, he lays great stress on the imperfection of the geological record" (Samuel Davey, *Darwin, Carlyle, Dickens: the Fools, Jesters, and Comic Characters in Shakspeare, with Other Essays, &c*, 1879, pp. 24, 25). I also wrote: "Little by little, the handful of British scientists who supported Darwin's new views grew in number. In *More Criticism on Darwin* (1872), Huxley wrote: '... as time has slipped by, a happy change has come over Mr. Darwin's critics. The mixture of ignorance and insolence which, at first, characterized a large proportion of the attacks with which he was assailed, is no longer the sad distinction of anti-Darwinian criticism. Instead of abusive nonsense, which merely discredited its writers, we read essays, which are, at worst, more or less intelligent and appreciative; while, sometimes, like that which appeared in the *North British Review* for 1867, they have a real and permanent value' (Thomas Huxley, *More Criticism on Darwin and Administrative Nihilism*, 1872, pp. 5, 6)" (Kevin L. Morgan, "Scientific Research and Discovery Stimulate Controversy in Victorian Britain," HIS 5106, Dr. Michael J. Turner, Oct. 11, 2011, pp. 6, 8, 12, 13). Notice that the

timeframe for these responses is *later* than Uriah Smith's response to Snook and Brinkerhoff. Regarding naturalists, hybridization, and the species, Carl Linnaeus believed that hybridization between the original "species produced the wide variety of species we see today" (Todd Charles Wood, "Species Variability and Creationism," *Origins*, 2008, no. 62, p. 9).

[41] Frank Lewis Marsh, *Fundamental Biology*, p. 50, reproduced in *Creationism in Twentieth-century America: The Early Writings of Harold W. Clark and Frank Lewis Marsh*, Ronald L. Numbers, editor, p. 450, emphasis in the original. Smith may have gotten his notions of the blurring of lines between human and animal from speculative Victorian reports regarding the copulation of apes with humans, but the amalgamation to which Smith referred was "within a few years after the flood." He asked, "What has *the ancient sin* of amalgamation to do with any race or people at the present time?" (Smith, *The Visions of Mrs. E. G. White: A Manifestation of Spiritual Gifts According to the Scriptures*, pp. 102, 104, emphasis added).

[42] "Amalgamation," *The Ellen G. White Encyclopedia*, p. 591. James White's endorsement reads: "The Association has just published a pamphlet entitled, 'The Visions of Mrs. E. G. White, a Manifestation of Spiritual Gifts According to the Scriptures.' It is written by the editor of the REVIEW. While carefully reading the manuscript I felt very grateful to God that our people could have this able defense of those views which they so much love and prize, and which others despise and oppose. This book is designed for a very wide circulation. There will be 2000 copies upon the camp ground. Price 20 cents. Postage 2 cents. JAMES WHITE" ("New and Important Work," *Review and Herald*, Aug. 25, 1868, p. 160). D. E. Robinson's 1931 statement about amalgamation is entitled, "Amalgamation Versus Evolution." In it, Robinson wrote: "Granting these valuable contributions to the study of the scientific aspect of Mrs. White's statement, yet in his insertion of the word 'of' to elucidate his understanding of the passage in question, he has, it seems to many, done violence to the text, and has not given to it the meaning which it seems certain was intended by the author herself. The insertion of this word, making it read 'amalgamation of man and (of) beast,' and interpreted to mean only that 'there has been hybridizing among animals, and also among distinct types or kinds of men which the Lord desired to keep separate and distinct,' would not be doing violence to the language used perhaps, if it were not evident that the author herself did intend the reader to understand it in its most obvious meaning" (Robinson, "Amalgamation Versus Evolution," p. 2). (Her statements after 1870 do not support this assertion about her intent.) Nichol countered: "At no time did Mrs. White offer any comment on the matter. James White spoke approvingly of Smith's book defending Mrs. White against fifty-two objections. But it would be a bold assumption to conclude from this that he agreed with every detail of every explanation and defense that Smith presented. (See James White's approving paragraph in "New and Important Work," *Review and Herald*, Aug. 25, 1868, p. 160.) In the chapter 'The Image Beast and 666' we noted that James White approved, with apparently no qualification, a certain prophetic chart. But later, and in another connection, he gently ridiculed a point of prophetic interpretation that is reflected in one statement in the chart. Now, if we are not warranted in drawing from James White's approval of Smith's book the conclusion that he specifically endorsed Smith's statement on amalgamation, we are even less warranted in concluding from James White's approval that Mrs. White approved. Mrs. White's silence proves nothing. Only rarely did she make a statement regarding the accuracy or inaccuracy of explanations made by others concerning her writings" (Francis D. Nichol, *Ellen G. White and Her Critics*, p. 322, fn. 103). Arthur L. White endorsed Froom's treatment of the subject of amalgamation, which is dependent on Marsh (A. L. White to Dr. Donald R. Gibbs, Cortland, New York, July 20, 1971, available online at http://drc.whiteestate.org/read.php?id=114464, accessed 1/20/15). Robinson's assumption is that in the distant past it was easier for species to combine and produce a fertile hybrid. He expressed this view in a letter to George McCready Price, dated April 29, 1931 (DF 31D8, egw_4563.pdf, available online at http://drc.whiteestate.org/read.php?id=134960, accessed 1/20/15). Robinson cited the extinct archaeopteryx as a bird/reptilian hybrid, and the platypus, echidna, hyena, and wildebeest, as examples of living hybrids (Robinson, p. 4).

[43] "Objections to the Visions," *Review and Herald*, June 12, 1866, p. 16.

[44] The pertinent portion of the letter reads: "Dear Brother: In your letter of Dec. 26, 1923, you refer to a statement found in 'Spirit of Prophecy', Vol. 1, page 78, which reads 'Since the flood there has been amalgamation of man and beast, as may be seen in the almost endless varieties of species of animals and in certain races of man.' ... Then you ask the following questions [regarding Uriah Smith's statement that Ellen White's description "referred to the Hottentots and Digger Indians"]. 1. Did your mother ever endorse this statement? Answer. She did not. 2. Has she ever in her writings or otherwise applied this statement in the above mentioned book, to the African or Negro race? Answer. Neither in her published books or her manuscripts has she applied this statement to the African or Negro Race...." (DF 316, William C. White to Pastor Warren George Kneeland, Jan. 18, 1924, obtained from the Ellen G. White Estate, Inc.; referenced by T. Joe Willey, "A Beast in the Garden: Amalgamation of Man and Beast Challenges the Unity of Mankind," p. 6, available online at http://www.docin.com/p-412350824.html, accessed 6/8/14.).

[45] Marsh, *Fundamental Biology*, pp. 50, 51, reproduced in Numbers, pp. 450, 451. For a delineation of the 1947 debate between Frank Lewis Marsh and Harold Clark about the meaning of "amalgamation," see David C. Read, *Dinosaurs: An Adventist View*, pp. 483–490, in which Read summarized the debate: "Clark was correct that amalgamation means the

mixing of very different kinds of creatures, and Marsh was correct that this cannot be done by means of sexual reproduction. How then could it have been accomplished? This was an insoluble problem in Ellen White's time, and it appeared even farther from a solution in 1947. But the scientific advances we reviewed in the previous chapter suggest a solution. Clark and Marsh both made one assumption that, in retrospect, was unwarranted. They both assumed, along with most other commentators, that 'amalgamation' was accomplished by means of *sexual reproduction*. But Ellen White never said that 'amalgamation' had anything to do with sexual reproduction" (Read, p. 490).

[46] "Sola scriptura," available online at https://en.wikipedia.org/wiki/Sola_scriptura, accessed 1/4/16.

[47] *Spiritual Gifts*, vol. 3 (1864), pp. 63, 64, emphasis added; *The Spirit of Prophecy*, vol. 1, p. 68. Not all preflood amalgamation defaced the image of God. It was only that which involved human beings.

[48] White, *Patriarchs and Prophets* (1890), p. 82.

[49] Jubilees 5:2, 3, in Robert Henry Charles, *The Apocrypha and Pseudepigrapha of the Old Testament in English*, vol. 2, p. 20, emphasis added.

[50] Jubilees 7:23, 24, in Charles, p. 24; see also James H. Charlesworth, *The Old Testament Pseudepigrapha*, vol. 2, p. 70.

[51] *Spiritual Gifts*, vol. 3, pp. 60, 61, emphasis added; *The Spirit of Prophecy*, vol. 1, p. 66.

[52] The *flesh* of beasts is different from the flesh of men. 1 Cor. 15:39 says: "All flesh is not the same flesh: but there is one kind of flesh of men, another flesh of beasts, another of fishes, and another of birds."

[53] Mrs. Ellen G. White, "Am I My Brother's Keeper?" *Review and Herald*, Jan. 21, 1896.

[54] Remember too how the children of Israel "*corrupted* themselves" by worshipping the calf god (Exod. 32:7).

[55] Credit is due Will Futs for locating the corresponding Scriptures in his study, "The Days of Noah: Understanding Ellen White's Amalgamation Statements," available online at http://willfults.com/ellen-white-amalgamation, accessed 6/6/2014.

[56] *Spiritual Gifts*, vol. 3, p. 143, emphasis added; *The Spirit of Prophecy*, vol. 1, p. 131. She later used "base crime" to describe the sin which Joseph was falsely accused of committing ("Joseph in Egypt," *The Signs of the Times*, Jan. 8, 1880).

[57] E. G. White, "Duty of Parents to Their Children," *Review and Herald*, Sept. 19, 1854, p. 46, emphasis added.

[58] White, *The Spirit of Prophecy*, vol. 1 (1870), pp. 69, 78.

[59] *Spiritual Gifts*, vol. 3, p. 70; *The Spirit of Prophecy*, vol. 1, p. 74, emphasis added.

[60] *Spiritual Gifts*, vol. 3, pp. 75, 76; with minor variations, in *The Spirit of Prophecy*, vol. 1, p. 78.

[61] Mrs. E. G. White, "A Living Church," *Review and Herald*, June 3, 1880, emphasis added.

[62] White, *Patriarchs and Prophets*, p. 338, emphasis added.

[63] Ellen G. White, *Testimonies for the Church*, vol. 2 (1868), p. 252.

[64] "Seth and Enoch," *The Signs of the Times*, Feb. 20, 1879; from *Spiritual Gifts*, vol. 3 (1864), p. 60; *The Spirit of Prophecy*, vol. 3, p. 65, which had "the descendents of Seth."

[65] Ellen G. White, *Testimonies for the Church*, vol. 5, p. 93, from "Testimony for the Battle Creek Church" (PH117), read Dec. 1881 before conference delegates and leading workers in the Review and Herald office, sanitarium, and college.

[66] Mrs. E. G. White, "Among the Churches: Freshwater," *The Signs of the Times*, Feb. 16, 1882.

[67] Mrs. E. G. White, "Marrying and Giving in Marriage," *Review and Herald*, Sept. 25, 1888, p. 609.

[68] White, *Patriarchs and Prophets*, pp. 81, 82, emphasis added.

[69] Mrs. E. G. White, "Lessons From the Life of Solomon—No. 20: 'Be Ye Separate,' " *Review and Herald*, Feb. 1, 1906, p. 8, emphasis added.

[70] Ronald Osborn, p. 4.

[71] White, *Testimonies for the Church*, vol. 5, p. 93.

[72] W. C. White, "Some Early Statements—Why Not Reprinted?" DF 316.

[73] Letters between Dr. David Paulson and Ellen White answer the matter of infallibility in her writing. Paulson wrote Mrs. White: "I was led to conclude and most firmly believe that *every* word that you ever spoke in public or private, that every letter you wrote under *any* and *all* circumstances, was as inspired as the ten commandments. I held that view with absolute tenacity against innumerable objections raised to it by many who were occupying prominent positions in the [Adventist] cause" (Letter to Ellen White, April 19, 1906, in "Correct Views Concerning the Testimonies: A Reply to an Inquirer," *Review and Herald*, Aug. 30, 1906, p. 8, emphasis in original). She responded: "My brother, you have studied my writings diligently, and you have never found that I have made any such claims. Neither will you find that the pioneers in our cause ever made such claims" (Letter 206 [June 14], 1906, published in "Correct Views Concerning the Testimonies: A Reply to an Inquirer," *Review and Herald*, Aug. 30, 1906, p. 8).

[74] Ellen G. White, *Spiritual Gifts*, vol. 4a, p. 121.

[75] Nicknamed "Dinosaur Bob," amateur paleontologist Robert Correia had the largest private collection of dinosaur bones in the United States. He co-operated with professional paleontologists in locating several major finds of pre-historic bones (Steve Toloken, "Creationist Joins Forces With Scientists: Fossil Discoveries Help 2 Theories," *Daily Press*, Nov. 27, 1994).

[76] Arthur Chadwick commented: "The dinosaurs comprise a whole ecosystem (small, medium and large herbivores and carnivores, etc). It is hard to rationalize making them all the results of amalgamation" (e-mail, Jan. 12, 2016).

[77] Dirk Anderson, "Amalgamation: A Denominational Embarrassment," available online at http://nonsda.org/egw/critica.shtml, accessed 9/14/14. The *pseudepigrapha* are extra-biblical Jewish religious works falsely attributed to earlier writers, likely written between 300 BC and AD 300. A book of Jasher is mentioned in Joshua 10:13 and 2 Samuel 1:18.

[78] Ellen White used "races of men" in the following statement, quoted in three books and one periodical article: " 'I will put enmity between thee and the woman, and between thy seed and her seed; it shall bruise thy head, and thou shalt bruise his heel.' [Genesis 3:15.] The divine sentence pronounced against Satan after the fall of man, was also a prophecy, embracing all the ages to the close of time, and foreshadowing the great conflict to engage all the *races of men* who should live upon the earth" (White, *The Spirit of Prophecy*, vol. 4, p. 324; *The Great Controversy*, 1888 and 1911 editions, p. 505; "The Enmity," *The Signs of the Times*, Feb. 17, 1909, p. 3, emphasis added).

[79] Ellen White referred to more than the "three great races" (*Patriarchs and Prophets*, p. 117) of Negro, Caucasian, and Mongoloid: "Among Jews, Turks, Parsees, Hindus, and many other nationalities and races he distributed the word of God in these various tongues and everywhere heralded the approaching reign of the Messiah" (*The Great Controversy*, p. 361).

[80] "The original TOL hypothesis has failed but a new 'statistical TOL hypothesis' is promising" (Maureen A. O'Malley and Eugene V. Koonin, "How stands the Tree of Life a Century and a Half after The Origin?" available online at http://www.ncbi.nlm.nih.gov/pmc/articles/PMC3158114, accessed 7/16/14). "Life scientists once thought that trees based on anatomy and on the molecular sequences of proteins and DNA would be the same ... [that] there would be consistency among the trees based on the DNA sequences of different genes .... that if they used the whole genome instead of individual genes, the data might average out and things would be better ...." Evidence shows that each of these notions was wrong (Lee M. Spetner, "Reviewing *The Evolution Revolution*, the NCSE Offers Uninformed Criticism that Misses the Point," available online at http://www.evolutionnews.org/2016/01/reviewing_the_e102281.html, accessed 1/13/16; see original article for references).

[81] Graham Lawton, "Why Darwin was wrong about the tree of life," *New Scientist*, Jan. 21, 2009. "... lateral, or horizontal, gene transfer ... involves the delivery of single genes, or whole suites of them, not from a parent cell to its offspring but across species barriers" (W. Ford Doolittle, quoted by Graham Coulter-Smith, "Viral Creativity: Crossing the Boundary between Life and Nonlife," Feb. 4, 2009, available online at http://artintelligence.net/review/?p=840, accessed 1/21/15). "... evolutionary trees from different genes often have conflicting branching patterns. ... A major challenge for incorporating such large amounts of data into inference of species trees is that conflicting genealogical histories often exist in different genes throughout the genome" (Degnan and Rosenberg, "Gene tree discordance, phylogenetic inference and the multispecies coalescent," *Trends in Ecology and Evolution*, Vol. 24 [2009], pp. 332–340). "Phylogenetic incongruities can be seen everywhere in the universal tree, from its root to the major branchings within and among the various taxa to the makeup of the primary groupings themselves" (Carl Woese, "The Universal Ancestor," *Proceedings of the National Academy of Sciences USA*, vol. 95, no. 12 [June 1998], pp. 6854-6859). "... different proteins generate different phylogenetic tree[s]" (Arcady R. Mushegian et al., "Large-Scale Taxonomic Profiling of Eukaryotic Model Organisms: A Comparison of Orthologous Proteins Encoded by the Human, Fly, Nematode, and Yeast Genomes," *Genome Research*, Vol. 8 [1998], pp. 590–598).

[82] "Hybridisation isn't the only force undermining the multicellular tree: it is becoming increasingly apparent that HGT plays an unexpectedly big role in animals too. As ever more multicellular genomes are sequenced, ever more incongruous bits of DNA are turning up. Last year, for example, a team at the University of Texas at Arlington found a peculiar chunk of DNA in the genomes of eight animals—the mouse, rat, bushbaby, little brown bat, tenrec, opossum, anole lizard and African clawed frog—but not in 25 others, including humans, elephants, chickens and fish. This patchy distribution suggests that the sequence must have entered each genome independently by horizontal transfer. [John K. Pace, II, Clement Gilbert, Marlena S. Clark, and Cedric Feschotte, "Repeated horizontal transfer of a DNA transposon in mammals and other tetrapods," *Proceedings of the National Academy of Sciences*, vol. 105, no. 44 (Nov. 4, 2008), p. 17023].

"Other cases of HGT in multicellular organisms are coming in thick and fast. HGT has been documented in insects, fish and plants, and a few years ago a piece of snake DNA was found in cows. The most likely agents of this genetic shuffling are viruses, which constantly cut and paste DNA from one genome into another, often across great taxonomic distances. In fact, by some reckonings, 40 to 50 per cent of the human genome consists of DNA imported horizontally by viruses, some of which has taken on vital biological functions" ([Garry Hamilton, "Viruses: The unsung heroes of evolution,"] *New Scientist*, Aug. 27, 2008, p. 38). [For foreign DNA to be co-opted for integrated biological functions would be remarkable.] The same is probably true of the genomes of other big animals. 'The number of horizontal transfers in animals is not as high as in microbes, but it can be evolutionarily significant,' says Bapteste.

"Biologist Michael Syvanen of the University of California, Davis ... recently compared 2000 genes that are common to humans, frogs, sea squirts, sea urchins, fruit flies and nematodes. In theory, he should have been able to use the gene sequences to construct an evolutionary tree showing the relationships between the six animals. He failed. The problem was that different genes told contradictory evolutionary stories. This was especially true of sea-squirt genes. Conventionally, sea squirts—also known as tunicates—are lumped together with frogs, humans and other vertebrates in the phylum Chordata, but the genes were sending mixed signals. Some genes did indeed cluster within the chordates, but others indicated that tunicates should be placed with sea urchins, which aren't chordates. 'Roughly 50 per cent of its genes have one evolutionary history and 50 per cent another,' Syvanen says. The most likely explanation for this, he argues, is that tunicates are chimeras. . . . 'We've just annihilated the tree of life. It's not a tree any more, it's a different topology entirely,' says Syvanen. 'What would Darwin have made of that?' " (Graham Lawton, "Why Darwin was wrong about the tree of life," *New Scientist*, Jan. 21, 2009).

[83] See Ben Smith, "Georgia Geneticist Challenges Evolution, Links Humans to Pigs," July 29, 2013, available online at http://saportareport.com/blog/2013/07/mccarthy_human_pig_chimp_evolution/, accessed 9/14/14). See also "Pigs and Humans Share 112 DNA Mutations, Say Scientists," available online at http://tech.firstpost.com/news-analysis/pigs-and-humans-share-112-dna-mutations-say-scientists-212100.html, accessed 9/14/14. Kangaroos are said to share major portions of DNA with humans as well. The director of the Center of Excellence for Kangaroo Genomics, Jenny Graves, told reporters: "There are a few differences, we have a few more of this, a few less of that, but they are the same genes and a lot of them are in the same order. . . . We thought they'd be completely scrambled, but they're not. There is [*sic*] great chunks of the human genome which is sitting right there in the kangaroo genome" (Rob Taylor, "Kangaroo genes close to humans," Nov. 18, 2008, available online at http://www.reuters.com/article/2008/11/18/us-australia-kangaroos-idUSTRE4AH1P020081118, accessed 4/5/15). "Phylogenetic incongruities can be seen everywhere in the universal tree, from its root to the major branchings within and among the various taxa to the makeup of the primary groupings themselves" (Carl Woese, "The Universal Ancestor," *Proceedings of the National Academy of Sciences USA*, vol. 95, no. 12, pp. 6854-6859 [June 1998].

[84] Quoting material from Lawton's article, Paul Giem commented: "This is particularly fascinating when one considers that most of the genetic manipulation done by humans (a subset of ID) is in fact guided horizontal gene transfer. That bit about 'The most likely agents of this genetic shuffling are viruses' is, barring studies on the probability of viruses accounting for such massive HGT in a reasonable timeframe, simply whistling past the graveyard. HGT by an intelligent agent would be expected to be much more efficient than unguided HGT, as we have seen during the last 20 years. It remains to be seen how efficient natural viral or other unguided HGT is, but it is a reasonable bet that it is orders of magnitude too small to reasonably account for the facts as known. This would make excellent research material for someone wishing to do ID-related research" (Jan. 22, 2009, available online at http://www.uncommondescent.com/intelligent-design/darwins-big-mistake-gradualism, accessed 7/19/14). "Most of these elements represent ancient retroviral infections, as evidenced by their wide distribution in primate species, and no infectious counterparts of human endogenous retroviruses (HERVs) are known to exist today" (Jennifer F. Hughes and John M. Coffin, "Human endogenous retrovirus K solo-LTR formation and insertional polymorphisms: Implications for human and viral evolution," PNAS Feb. 10, 2004, vol. 101, no. 6, quoted in Sean D. Pitman, M.D., "Pseudogenes and Other Forms of 'Junk' DNA."

[85] Molecular palaeobiologist Kevin L. Peterson said: "I've looked at thousands of microRNA genes, and I can't find a single example that would support the traditional tree. . . . The microRNAs are totally unambiguous, . . . but they give a totally different tree from what everyone else wants. . . . a radically different diagram for mammals: one that aligns humans more closely with elephants than with rodents" (Elie Dolgin, "Phylogeny: Rewriting Evolution," *Nature*, vol. 486 [June 28, 2012], pp. 460-462).

[86] Ellen G. White, Ms. 16 (Feb. 10), 1898, par. 3; edited in "Whole-hearted Service," *The Signs of the Times*, Feb. 1, 1899, p. 82.

[87] Ellen G. White, Ms. 65 (April 25), 1899, in *Selected Messages*, bk. 2, p. 288, emphasis added.

[88] Marsh took Ellen White's statement "the base crime of amalgamation of man and beast . . . defaced the image of God, and caused confusion everywhere" to mean "that before the flood man amalgamating with man 'defaced the image of God', and beast amalgamating with beast 'caused confusion everywhere' " (Frank Lewis Marsh, *The Early Writings of Harold W. Clark and Frank Lewis Marsh*, p. 48).

[89] "[Harold] Clark defended the view that Ellen White taught [that] hybridization between humans and animals had taken place before and after the Flood. Marsh argued for his modified view, derived from [George McCready] Price, that hybridization can only take place within the limits of the created kind" (Wood, p. 20).

[90] "Kind" (Heb. *miyn*) is mentioned in the early chapters of Genesis (Gen. 1:24, 25; 6:20; 7:14; 8:19). The term *baramin*, coined by Frank Lewis Marsh, combines the word *bara* "create" with *miyn* "kind" (Wood, p. 19).

[91] Charles E. Dudley, *The Genealogy of Ellen Gould Harmon White*, p. 23.

[92] Joslyn's full report is included in "THE GENEALOGY OF ELLEN G. WHITE: An Update," available online at http://www.whiteestate.org/issues/genealogy.html, accessed 11/18/15.

CHAPTER 6 - Early Seventh-day Adventist Ministry to the Freedmen

[1] "Report of the Third Annual Session of the General Conference of S. D. Adventists," *Review and Herald*, May 23, 1865, p. 197. In October, a similar statement was issued: "*Resolved*. That we feel a deep interest in the case of the freedmen, and an earnest desire that the message of the third angel may be sent to those in the South from whom it has been hitherto excluded by the horrid tyranny of the institution of slavery" ("Fourth Annual Report of the N. Y. State Conference," *Review and Herald*, Oct. 31, 1865, p. 173, signed A. Lanphear, *President*, and R. F. Cottrell, *Secretary*).

[2] Stephanie D. Johnson, "Reading, Writing, Arithmetic ... Our Early Beginnings," *North American Regional Voice*, Sept. 1979, p. 6. Edson White, who launched many schools in the South, was one of the first twelve students under Goodloe Harper Bell in the first Seventh-day Adventist school (Jonathan Grant, p. 56).

[3] R. K. McCune, "Progress of the Cause: Tennessee," *Review and Herald*, July 1, 1873, p. 22.

[4] Hansen, p. 257.

[5] Hansen, p. 33.

[6] In [Uriah Smith], "Is Slavery Dead?" *Review and Herald*, June 20, 1865, p. 20. Another *Review and Herald* article concluded with the statement of a prominent Tennessean: "What it required a great army to destroy can easily be restored by the people when that army is removed" (*New York Sun*, "Not Cured Yet," *Review and Herald*, Aug. 8, 1865, p. 79).

[7] The Thirteenth Amendment to the U.S. Constitution abolished slavery and involuntary servitude, except as punishment for a crime; the Fourteenth Amendment granted the rights of citizenship to all persons born in the United States; and the Fifteenth Amendment stipulated that race could not be used to deprive a man of the right to vote. The last was undermined in the South by poll taxes, literacy tests, and grandfather clauses (Darlene Clark Hine, William C. Hine, and Stanley Harrold, *The African-American Odyssey*, pp. 310, 313, 314, 316, 318, 331, cited by Greene, pp. 38, 39).

[8] "Civil War," available online at http://en.wikipedia.org/wiki/American_Civil_War, accessed 5/3/14. Its formal title was the U.S. Bureau of Refugees, Freedmen and Abandoned Lands. The Freedmen's Bureau also assisted poor Southern whites.

[9] "News and Miscellany," *Review and Herald*, Jan. 15, 1867, p. 68. Immediately after announcing this gain for the freedmen, the paper noted: "Information comes from North Carolina that a new crusade against the freedmen in that state has been inaugurated. All manner of charges are brought against them, and whipping and selling them into slavery is quite general; one planter near Wilmington having boasted that he has purchased hands enough to restock his plantation. By an existing State law, a man convicted of a crime and punished at the whipping-post is forever disfranchised; and it is hoped by this means they will be able in the future to thwart any action of the Congress giving suffrage to the freedmen."

[10] "News and Miscellany," *Review and Herald*, April 16, 1867, p. 224.

[11] "Exclusion of Free Blacks," available online at http://slavenorth.com/exclusion.htm, accessed 10/22/14.

[12] "News and Miscellany: The Tennessee Election," *Review and Herald*, July 9, 1867, p. 61. See also *Detroit Daily Post*, "Outrages in the South," *Review and Herald*, Jan. 31, 1871, p. 51; *Detroit Tribune*, "Report on Southern Outrages," *Review and Herald*, April 4, 1871, p. 128; and Seilhamer, *Leslie's History of the Republican Party*, vol. 1 (1903).

[13] Kessia Reyne Bennett, "Resistance and Accommodation to Racism Among Early Seventh-day Adventist Missionaries in the American South: A Case Study in Relating to Cultural Oppression in Missions" (April 2011), p. 33, quoting Spalding, *Captains of the Host*, p. 488.

[14] "The Scheme to Exterminate the Colored Race," *Southern Christian Intelligencer*, Aug. 5, 1965, quoted in *Review and Herald*, Sept. 5, 1865, p. 107.

[15] W. B. Stickney, "Links in the chain of Violence—the Maltreatment of Women, and the Murder of whites and blacks," *Review and Herald*, Aug. 28, 1866, p. 102. Stickney was an Episcopal priest who had ministered to blacks in the South during the war and became an agent of the Freedmen's Bureau in Shreveport, Louisiana after the war.

[16] *The American Missionary*, "Mississippi: Assault Upon Rev. J. P. Bradwell. Murder of Liet. Blanding," *Review and Herald*, Aug. 14, 1866, p. 83.

[17] *Review and Herald*, Feb. 27, 1866, p. 104.

[18] John Putnam Gulliver, "The President and Congress: A Word with the Congregational Clergy," *Caledonian* (St. Johnsbury, VT), March 30, 1866, p. 1. The misspelling of "Freedman's" exists in the original. Gulliver had delivered a sermon on slavery, "The lioness and her whelps," Dec. 18, 1859, dealing with John Brown's Harpers Ferry raid.

[19] *Testimonies for the Church*, vol. 1, p. 266.

[20] [Uriah Smith], *Review and Herald*, March 27, 1866, p. 136.

[21] *The Review and Herald* reported on the formation of the Ku Klux Klan in Giles County, quoting from the *Cincinnati Gazette* of July 12, 1868. It went on to describe their activities: "One day they take out a white school-teacher, strip him and beat him into a jelly. Another night they warn a radical citizen that his presence in the community is not desired—that, in fact, his political opinions have rendered him odious, and that, if he does not leave the community within so many days,

he will be visited. Again, they go to a negro's house, take the man out, put a chain about his neck, mount their horses, and lead him about the neighborhood, and when he is exhausted with fatigue and fright, compel him to dance and sing before them. The next night they take a white man—an officer of the State—drag him from his affrighted wife and children, take him into the woods, tie him to a tree, and then riddle him with bullets, as they did to James L. Frances, of Overton County, a few nights since, poor Mrs. Frances following the scoundrels who had her husband in charge, and finding him tied to a tree, a cold corpse, riddled with twenty bullets. It is folly to deny these things, for they are vouched for by the members of the various churches from the North engaged in the Freedman's Mission, and show the determination of the late rebels to control the institutions of the South in, if they cannot do it out of, the Union, and also their determination to rule the colored people as serfs, if they cannot do so as slaves. The *Lost Cause* is as dear to them as ever, and what is still more to wondered at, and what calls for increased vigilance, is the fact that so many in the North now, as at the beginning of the war, are urging them on in their unholy work. …" ("Eternal Vigilance," *Review and Herald*, Aug. 11, 1868, p. 124).

[22] The *Review and Herald* described the treatment of freedmen in Carroll County, Tennessee, a scene of later Seventh-day Adventist persecution: "Colored men coming to town fifty miles on foot, leaving their little crops and possessions, and fleeing in dread of their lives, report parties of masked horsemen visiting the negro cabins in search of arms, and, in many cases, forcing the blacks to pledge themselves to vote for Seymour and Blair, or flee in terror from their homes, leaving their growing crops and their little all behind. Nor is this by far the worst. At Huntington, in Carroll county, a short time since, a negro woman was taken out and so unmercifully whipped by the Ku-Klux, that for days her back bore bloody testimony to their fiendish cruelty. In the same neighborhood, at about the same time, a white man was also taken out and severely beaten at their hands. On a Sunday in the same county, a dozen or so colored men, going home from church, were stopped by a gang of such hopeful Democracy, and all whipped; the blasphemous wretches telling the negroes they were spirits of Shiloh battle-field, but five hours from h—ll" ("The Reign of Terror in the South," *Review and Herald*, Aug. 25, 1868, p. 157).

[23] *Religious Telescope*, "The Wicked Go Unpunished." *Review and Herald*, Oct. 23, 1866, p. 163.

[24] *The Independent* (New York), "The Terrible Condition of the South," *Review and Herald*, Dec. 11, 1866, p. 9.

[25] "Home News: Texas," *Review and Herald*, Dec. 25, 1866, p. 32.

[26] *The American Missionary*, "Outrages on the Freedmen," *Review and Herald*, March 19, 1867, p. 177. In an earlier article, "Wages Kept Back by Fraud," Uriah Smith reported the words of a teacher of the freedmen in Georgia: "There has seemed lately to be an unusual influx of poor, destitute people from the country. 'Soon as we made de crop, dey run us off, and gib us nothin,' is the pitiful story they tell of their cruel masters, too well confirmed by their wretched appearance and tattered dress" (*Review and Herald*, April 10, 1866, p. 148).

[27] "Prosperity of the Freedmen," *Review and Herald*, Nov. 28, 1871, p. 192. The *Review and Herald* continued reporting on the mistreatment of the freedmen: "In April, 1865, the military power of the Rebellion was finally broken, after a four years' struggle. In the six years following, how far have we carried the greater work of restoring order and peace to one half of the nation? The contradictions of the partisan press can no longer obscure the existence of the gravest evils throughout the South. It is established, past all reasonable question, that there prevails an uncontrolled spirit of lawlessness, which continually breaks out into, the worst violence and outrage. By floggings, expulsions, and murders, a large part of the community in the South are kept in constant terror. These outrages are not the occasional and incidental outbreaks of an imperfectly civilized section. Their vast number, the character of their victims, and the tolerance or concealment given to them by a very large class, mark them as belonging to a political persecution. Nor, further, is it to be denied that at some times and in some sections—as Tennessee and North Carolina—the persecuted party, gaining power, have retaliated with almost equal lawlessness and bitterness upon their foes. But far the greater burden of these sins of violence falls on the enemies of the negro" (*Christian Union*, "Where are We?" *Review and Herald*, April 18, 1871, p. 139).

[28] Samuel Eliot Morison, *The Oxford History of the American People* (New York: Oxford University Press, 1965), p. 707. See also John Hope Franklin, *Reconstruction: After the Civil War*, pp. 48–53; Horace Mann Bond, *Negro Education in Alabama: A Study in Cotton and Steel* (Tuscaloosa, AL: The University of Alabama Press, 1994).

[29] David Burner, Eugene D. Genovese, and Forrest McDonald, *The American People*, vol. 1, p. 481.

[30] John Hope Franklin, *Reconstruction: After the Civil War*, pp. 179, 180. The Black Codes were laws passed by Southern states from 1865 to 1866 that restricted African Americans' freedom, compelling them to work under low wages or debt.

[31] *1860 United States Federal Census, Minnesota, Benton, Princeton*, p. 3; "Receipts. For Review and Herald," *Review and Herald*, Feb. 6, 1866, p. 80.

[32] "L. Morris (50 cts. each for Mrs. M. Thompson and Mrs. L. M. Gates)" ("Receipts. For Review and Herald," *Review and Herald*, Oct. 1, 1857, p. 176). Lucia Morris, Marcella Thompson (of Omro, Wisconsin), and Louisa M. Gates (of Trenton, Wisconsin), were daughters of Samuel and Betsey Horr of Trenton, Wisconsin, the mother being a member of the Mackford, Wisconsin Seventh-day Adventist Church ("Obituary Notices: Horr," *Review and Herald*, Oct. 29, 1895, p.

703). "Lucia Morris: The paper has been sent regularly to Mrs. L. M. Gates, Beaver Dam, Wis., from the time her name was sent, up to the present number" ("Business Items," *Review and Herald*, Oct. 14, 1858, p. 168). By 1859, Mrs. Gates had accepted the Seventh-day Adventist faith (L. M. Gates, "A New Year's Address to Those Engaged in Proclaiming the 'Present Truth,'" *Review and Herald*, Jan. 20, 1859, p. 70; "From Sister Gates," *Review and Herald*, Aug. 25, 1859, p. 111; L. M. Gates, "The Messages," *Review and Herald*, July 31, 1860, p. 81).

[33] "Books Sent by Mail," *Review and Herald*, May 26, 1868, p. 368.

[34] "Receipts. For Review and Herald" and "Books Sent By Mail," *Review and Herald*, July 14, 1868, p. 64.

[35] The 1870 U.S. Census lists McCune as having been born in Ohio and puts him and his wife and four children in Davidson County, Tennessee (*1870 United States Federal Census, Tennessee, Davidson, District 20*, p. 31). The *Nashville City Directory* of 1873 listed Edgefield Junction as "A Station in Davidson County, Tennessee, on the Louisville & Nashville Railroad, at the Junction of the St. Louis & South-Eastern Railroad, 175 miles from Louisville, and 10 miles from Nashville," and it listed "R. K. McCune" as a carpenter (*The Nashville City Directory*, March 1873, pp. 169, 170).

[36] A. W. Spalding, *Captains of the Host*, p. 489; *Origin and History of Seventh-day Adventists*, vol. 2, p. 169.

[37] E. B. Lane, "Progress of the Cause: Report of Labor: Tennessee," *Review and Herald*, May 2, 1871, p. 158.

[38] "Here are a few keeping the Sabbath who desire baptism. They embraced the truth from reading publications, having never heard a discourse from one of our ministers. There is but one Church (Catholic) in the place, and, as the schoolhouse was small, we accepted an invitation to occupy the station and telegraph rooms in the depot building, the white people occupying one room, the colored the other. These, however, soon became insufficient to accommodate the people. Accordingly the freight room was prepared, and the platform outside also seated before all could be comfortably entertained. I have now given thirteen discourses which brought me to the Sabbath question, which seems to be received without unusual opposition, and I look for some to embrace and keep it, with all God's commands. I will before long give my views in another article of the South as a field of labor" (Lane, p. 158).

[39] R. K. McCune, and others, "Progress of the Cause: From Brethren in Tennessee," *Review and Herald*, Aug. 8, 1871, p. 63. Interestingly, it is in this same issue of the paper that Joseph Clarke contributed the article, "Is the Rebellion Quelled?" which is quoted later in this chapter.

[40] R. K. McCune, "Progress of the Cause: From Bro. McCune," *Review and Herald*, Dec. 5, 1871, p. 198.

[41] R. K. McCune, *Review and Herald*, May 7, 1872, p. 166.

[42] "We have had a very refreshing visit from Bro. E. B. Lane, and a great reviving in our midst, considering the short stay he made with us. Seven were baptized, a little church of thirteen members organized, and some others are willing to join, but circumstances at present hinder them from so doing. We have organized S. B. [systematic benevolence] to the amount of thirty-three dollars, which would have been more but for the fearful work the cholera is making around us. It is said to be the most destructive malady that ever visited Nashville, and all kinds of business is sadly deranged. We beg the prayers of our people, that the destroying angel may pass us by, and God's mercy be extended to the community at large" (R. K. McCune, "Progress of the Cause: Tennessee," *Review and Herald*, July 1, 1873, p. 22). Thirteen was frequently cited as the number of baptized believers when a church was organized.

[43] R. K. McCune, "Progress of the Cause: Tennessee," *Review and Herald*, Sept. 30, 1873, p. 126.

[44] R. K. McCune, "Progress of the Cause: Tennessee," *Review and Herald*, May 19, 1874, p. 182. Mary A. Remley mentioned his move in 1875 ("Progress of the Cause: Tennessee," *Review and Herald*, July 15, 1875, p. 22).

[45] *1880 United States Federal Census, Wisconsin, Green Lake, Mackford, 068*, p. 15.

[46] Subsequent quarterly meetings would be held in Edgefield Junction. On the separate black congregation, see R. Steven Norman, III, "The Early History of South Central Conference, 1863–1945," p. 12. On its contribution to the Nashville church, see Hansen, p. 48. Before leaving in 1874, McCune made one last appeal for a minister—"Our prayer is that God in his mercy will soon send us a preacher for this State" (R. K. McCune, "Progress of the Cause: Tennessee," *Review and Herald*, May 19, 1874, p. 182).

[47] Hansen, p. 30. Squire Osborne is listed as a "Boat man," married to Mary E., and living with Charlton Brown in Greenup County, Kentucky (*1850 United States Federal Census, Kentucky, Greenup, District 1*, p. 449). This was the year he married his wife, Mary Ellen Pickens ("Squire Osborn in the U.S. and International Marriage Records, 1560-1900," available at: http://search.ancestry.com/cgi-bin/sse.dll?indiv=1&db=WorldMarr_ga&gss=angs-d&pcat=34&h=911069&ml_rpos=1, accessed 2/15/15). Osborne is listed as a farmer living in Lime Creek, Iowa, with his wife Mary E. in the 1856 Iowa census (*Iowa, State Census Collection, 1836-1925, 1856, Washington, Lime Creek*, p. 18, available online at http://interactive.ancestry.com/1084/IA_67-0749/5041544, accessed 2/15/15). He is listed as a merchant and living with his wife and four children in Lime Creek, Washington County, Iowa, in the 1860 U.S. Census (*1860 United States Federal Census, Iowa, Washington, Lime Creek*, p. 7).

[48] "Died, near Lynn, Greenup Co., Kentucky. Dec. 2, 1871, Bro. James Osborn, in his eighty-first year. A little over a year since, he became interested in present truth, through the labors of his son, S. Osborn, of Iowa, who was at his house on a visit" (J. Hare, "Obituary Notices," *Review and Herald*, Feb. 27, 1872, p. 87).

[49] Arthur W. Spalding, "Lights and Shades in the Black Belt," pp. 137, 138. A nine-part series of articles under the name "Lights and Shades in the Black Belt" was described as consisting "of advance chapters of Mr. Spaulding's forthcoming book bearing the name used as the title of this series of articles. This book contains a brief history of the Negro race in America, and the story of our denominational work for the Negro, including the story of the Southern Missionary Society and the Negro schools" ("A New Series of Articles—A New Book," *The Youth's Instructor*, April 6, 1915, p. 16). Yet the articles, published from April to June, dealt with topics preceding those in the manuscript. The *Youth's Instructor* announced: "'Lights and Shades in the Black Belt,' with its companion volume, 'The Men of the Mountains,' will be issued within a few weeks by the publishers, the Southern Publishing Association, Nashville, Tenn" ("From Here and There," *The Youth's Instructor*, July 20, 1915, p. 2). *The Southern Union Worker* later projected that *The Men of the Mountains* would come out in November, and the "manuscript for another book by Professor Spaulding, entitled 'Lights and Shades in the Black Belt' is nearly ready" ("Publishing House Notes," *The Southern Union Worker*, Oct. 14, 1915, p. 329). Though available online in unpublished form, "Lights and Shades in the Black Belt" was never published, R. W. Schwarz wrote: "The unpublished manuscript 'Light [sic] and Shades in the Black Belt' (1913) prepared by A. Spalding for Ellen White's office contains much valuable material, but is marred by the racial stereotypes of the period" (R. W. Schwarz, *Light Bearers to the Remnant*, p. 248).

[50] Hansen, p. 30.

[51] J. Hare, "From Kentucky," *Review and Herald*, Jan. 30, 1872, p. 55.

[52] S. Osborne, "Progress of the Cause: Greenup Co., Kentucky," *Review and Herald*, April 23, 1872, p. 150. Osborne consistently identified himself in the *Review and Herald* as "S. Osborne." In "Lights and Shades in the Black Belt," p. 137, Spalding misidentified him as "Silas" (a younger brother's name). The mistake has been carried on ever since. In *Captains of the Host*, p. 492, and *Origin and History of Seventh-day Adventists*, p. 173, Spalding identified him as "Squier [sic] Osborne." The 1900 U.S. Federal Census, his transit permit, and his tombstone identify him as "Squire Osborne" (*1900 United States Federal Census, Kentucky, Bullitt, Shepersville, District 0014*, p. 31; *Kentucky Death Records, Fayetteville, 1903, Transit Permit 623*; "Squire Osborne," Find A Grave Memorial #90198607, available online at http://www.findagrave.com/cgi-bin/fg.cgi?page=gr&GRid=90198607&ref=acom, accessed 2/12/15).

[53] S. Osborne, "Greenup Co., Ky," *Review and Herald*, March 4, 1873, p. 94; "Tennessee Conference Proceedings," *Review and Herald*, Nov. 12, 1889, p. 716.

[54] S. Osborne, "Progress of the Cause: Green Co., Ky," *Review and Herald*, Jan. 1, 1875, p. 6.

[55] S. Osborne, "Progress of the Cause: Kentucky," *Review and Herald*, April 1, 1875, p. 110.

[56] S. Osborne, "Progress of the Cause: Kentucky," *Review and Herald*, Sept. 30, 1875, p. 102. January 20, 1876, he again wrote: "May the Lord work upon minds to turn them South" (S. Osborne, "Progress of the Cause: Present View, Tenn.," *Review and Herald*, Sept. 30, 1875).

[57] S. Osborne, "Progress of the Cause: Kentucky," *Review and Herald*, Feb. 10, 1876, p. 46.

[58] "Special Session of the General Conference," *Review and Herald*, April 6, 1876, p. 108.

[59] U.S., "The Conference," *Review and Herald*, April 13, 1876, p. 116.

[60] D. M. Canright, "Progress of the Cause: The Kentucky and Tennessee Conference," *Review and Herald*, June 1, 1876, p. 174.

[61] "When it was decided to hold a camp-meeting in eastern Kentucky, his heart leaped for joy, and he came to the meeting full of thanksgiving that he could see the work begin to advance, and something definite being done" (Otho C. Godsmark, "Fell With the Armor On," *Review and Herald*, Aug. 4, 1903, p. 23).

[62] "'We shall soon know how all these things are,' said the aged Rev. Squire Osborne, of Salt River, Bullitt county, Ky., at the noon meeting of the Seventh Day Adventists in London Park, Lexington, Sunday. An instant later he lay cold in death from apoplexy" (*The Bourbon News* [Paris, KY], July 21, 1903, p. 5). "Squire Osborne, the oldest member in the United States of the Seventh Day Adventists, died suddenly in Lexington" (*Richmond Climax* [Richmond, KY], July 29, 1903, p. 4; see also *Arlington Journal* [Arlington, Texas], July 30, 1903).

[63] See Hansen, pp. 30, 31. S. N. Haskell reported on a connection to freedmen in Florida: "Within the last six months, quite an intelligent colored man from Florida, who was a preacher there among his own people, came North with a view of remaining. He was prevailed upon to investigate the claims of the seventh-day Sabbath, and the doctrine of the second coming of Christ. He saw the harmony of the Scriptures upon these points, embraced these truths, and then felt that he must immediately return to his people with them" ("The Cause is Onward," *Review and Herald*, May 26, 1874, p. 190).

[64] Charles O. Taylor, "Progress of the Cause: Georgia," *Review and Herald*, Jan. 4, 1877, p. 7.

[65] Charles O. Taylor, "Quitman, GA," *Review and Herald*, Sept. 20, 1877, p. 101.

[66] C. O. Taylor, "Progress of the Cause: Georgia," *Review and Herald*, Oct. 18, 1877, p. 126.

[67] C. O. Taylor, "Progress of the Cause: Reynolds, GA," *Review and Herald*, April 18, 1878, p. 127.

[68] C. O. Taylor, "Progress of the Cause: Georgia," *Review and Herald*, April 10, 1879, p. 118. "Taylor C. O. Rev. Adventist" is listed in Reynolds, Georgia, in *Shole's Georgia State Gazetteer, 1879-80*, p. 648, available online at http://interactive.ancestry.com/2469/41199_1220706242_4012-00673/1401226991, accessed 2/15/15.

[69] "Interesting Extracts from Letters," *Review and Herald*, April 5, 1877, supplement, p. 4, from the assistant secretary of the New England Tract Society, which was originally organized in 1868 as the "Vigilant Missionary Society" (Jonathan Grant, p. 56).

[70] "Interesting Extracts from Letters."

[71] "Interesting Extracts from Letters."

[72] "Interesting Extracts from Letters."

[73] "Interesting Extracts from Letters."

[74] Spalding, *Origin and History of Seventh-day Adventists*, vol. 1, p. 181; A. W. Spalding, *Footprints of the Pioneers*, p. 215; Ruby Clark Demyen, *The First Valle Crucis Seventh-day Adventist Church and Church School and other Mountain Stories*, p. 2. Although frequently identified as the first meetinghouse built south of the Mason Dixon Line, there were earlier church buildings constructed. R. Steven Norman, III, identified its date of construction: "The Valle Crucis Church, originally called the Bethel Church, was organized by L. P. Hodges in the home of Larkin Townsend on May 15, 1881, with 11 charter members.... Realizing the need for a meeting house in which to worship, Townsend donated the land, and the believers walked as far as 10 miles to help build their church on Dutch Creek in 1882" ("Southern Union Trail of Adventists," *Southern Tidings*, Oct. 2010, p. 16). Before this, in 1878, Squire Osborne reported that the Powder Mills, Kentucky "church has a small house of worship inclosed, and an effort is making to have it finished in time for the Conference" ("Kentucky and Tennessee," *Review and Herald*, Aug. 8, 1878, p. 51). Robert M. Kilgore reported earlier about a church building in Cleburne: "Although the friends are poor, they have nearly inclosed a very neat little house of worship" (R. M. Kilgore, "Progress of the Cause: Texas," *Review and Herald*, April 18, 1878, p. 126).

[75] Regarding D. T. Bourdeau in Kentucky, see D. T. Bourdeau, "Progress of the Cause: Kentucky," *Review and Herald*, Jan. 23, 1872, p. 46; May 28, 1872, p. 191. He specifically labored in Nolin and Locust Grove and mentioned interacting with Baptists and Disciples of Christ ministers, and noted that there was a large population of Catholics. He did not mention seeing or interacting with blacks (D. T. Bourdeau, "Progress of the Cause: Locust Grove, Kentucky," *Review and Herald*, Feb. 20, 1872, p. 78).

[76] E. B. Lane and J. O. Corliss, "Progress of the Cause, New Market, Virginia," *Review and Herald*, March 9, 1876, p. 78.

[77] This included Kentucky, Tennessee, North Carolina, Georgia, and Alabama (J. W., "The South," *Review and Herald*, Dec. 9, 1880, p. 376). In 1880, White was finally able to remark that "not a few laborers are being raised up in the South."

[78] Spalding, *Origin and History of Seventh-day Adventists*, vol. 2, p. 171. "Brother Soule is laboring in Bledsoe County, about one hundred miles east of Nashville" (D. M. Canright, "Progress of the Cause: East Tennessee," *Review and Herald*, June 15, 1876, p. 190).

[79] Spalding, *Captains of the Host*, p. 490.

[80] "Mo. T. & M. Society," *Review and Herald*, Oct. 12, 1876, p. 118.

[81] Mrs. Van Slyke moved from Hamilton, Caldwell County, Missouri, to Taitsville, Ray County, Missouri, in November ("Please Notice," *Review and Herald*, Nov. 30, 1876, p. 176).

[82] Mrs. H. M. Van Slyke, "Among the Freedmen," *Review and Herald*, Feb. 22, 1877, p. 59.

[83] In July, John Snyder gave notice that Mrs. Van Slyke was still secretary of the District 1, Missouri Missionary and Tract Society and that she was once again in Hamilton ("Notice," *Review and Herald*, July 12, 1877, p. 24). In October, Emma B. Evans gave notice of thankfulness to God for His restoration of Mrs. Van Slyke's health in answer to prayer ("A Card," *Review and Herald*, Oct. 18, 1877, p. 127). Mrs. Van Slyke died April 14, 1887 and is buried in Hamilton, Missouri. Three months earlier, she had contributed the poem "Coming" about Christ's return, which she had first submitted to the *Review and Herald* (The *Golden Sickle*, Jan. 15, 1887, p. 9; *Review and Herald*, Aug. 12, 1875, p. 49).

[84] The correctness of Canright's observation depended upon the timeframe and the region of the South considered. Both Charles O. Taylor and Squire Osborne reported preaching to white congregations with blacks in attendance—Taylor in Georgia and Osborne in Kentucky. Otho C. Godsmark described meetings in Georgia in 1888 in which segregating blacks from whites cost him his audience ("Lights and Shades in the Black Belt," pp. 143–146).

[85] D. M. Canright, "Progress of the Cause: Texas," *Review and Herald*, May 25, 1876, p. 166. D. M. Canright visited the South in 1876, encouraging the organization of the Kentucky and Tennessee Conference (Albert Dittes, *A Struggle Against Great Odds: Seventh-day Adventist Origins in Post Civil War Kentucky and Tennessee*, p. 3). Canright

described the 100 members who met at Mammoth Cave, Kentucky: "Almost all of them were Southern people; some of them had been slaveholders and rebels during the war, with strong feelings against the Northern people. But now they have laid all these things aside. We found them just as warm-hearted, confiding, and true as our Northern people. So far as I can see, they are as ready to hear us and learn the truth from us as though we were Southerners" (D. M. Canright, "The Kentucky and Tennessee Conference," *Review and Herald*, May 4, 1876, p. 174).

[86] For their endorsement for their mission by the Bowling Green, Ohio, Seventh-day Adventist Church (H. A. St. John and J. B. Craw, "Testimonial," *Review and Herald*, Dec. 14, 1876, p. 192). For their work in Texas, see Jos. Clarke, "Our Field," *Review and Herald*, March 1, 1877, p. 72; J. and S. Clarke, "Progress of the Cause: Texas: Deckman, Dallas Co.," *Review and Herald*, March 22, 1877, p. 94; R. M. Kilgore, "Progress of the Cause: Texas" *Review and Herald*, May 17, 1877, p. 158; and Jos. Clarke, "Progress of the Cause: Texas: Deckman, Dallas Co.," *Review and Herald*, May 24, 1877, p. 166.

[87] Schwarz, p. 233; A. B. Rust, E. G. Rust, and Jos. Clarke, "Progress of the Cause: Texas," *Review and Herald*, April 5, 1877, p. 111. See also Spalding, *Origin and History of Seventh-day Adventists*, vol. 2, p. 184.

[88] Joseph Clarke, "Spiritual Gifts," *Review and Herald*, Nov. 26, 1867, p. 381.

[89] Clarke makes the same point about the Constitution supporting slavery in "Two Baals: Which is the Best?" *Review and Herald*, June 4, 1857, p. 37.

[90] Joseph Clarke, "You Will Vote at Our Spring Election, Won't You," *Review and Herald*, April 23, 1857, p. 198.

[91] Dred Scott was born a slave to the Peter Blow family in 1799. When the Blow family moved to St. Louis, Missouri, they sold Scott to his new master, Dr. John Emerson, who carried him to posts in Illinois and the Wisconsin Territory where slavery had been prohibited by the 1820 Missouri Compromise. When Emerson's widow hired him out in St. Louis, in violation of the Missouri Compromise, Scott sued for his family's freedom in lower courts. Then, on March 6, 1857, he filed suit for their freedom in the courts of St. Louis. The case worked its way up to the U.S. Supreme Court, and the Supreme Court ruled that persons of African descent cannot be, nor ever were intended to be, citizens under the United States Constitution and that the Missouri Compromise of 1820, which prohibited slavery in northern territories, was unconstitutional. After Dred Scott's death from tuberculosis, his family was given back to the Blow family, who granted them their freedom in May 1857 ("The *revised* Dred Scott Case Collection: History of Dred Scott," available online at http://digital.wustl.edu/dredscott/history.html, accessed 2/17/15).

[92] Light came in "Testimony for the church, No. 9."

[93] Joseph Clarke, "The War! The War!!" *Review and Herald*, Sept. 23, 1862, p. 134. Clarke described his joining the Congregational church of Gorham, Maine, on September 4, 1831, at the age of thirteen (Joseph Clarke, "The Judgment," *Review and Herald*, May 20, 1875, p. 166). This is significant because slaves from Gorham that served in the military in the Revolutionary War were liberated in 1783 after "the Massachusetts Supreme Court ruled that a clause in the state constitution that regarded all men as 'free and equal' made slavery illegal" (Hugh D. McLellan, *History of Gorham*, pp. 133, 299; Noah Bruce, "Maine History X," *The Portland Phoenix*, Aug. 30, 2001), Maine entered the Union in 1820 as a free state, and, insistent on independence of local bodies, Congregationalists became important in many social reform movements, including abolitionism. "Congregationalists such as Lewis Tappan, Joshua Leavitt, Amos A. Phelps, and Jonathan Blanchard were important figures in the American and Foreign Anti-Slavery Society and in later religious abolitionist projects. Abolitionist comeouters from the New School Presbyterians and from other denominations often joined the Congregationalists and strengthened their antislavery commitment. In interdenominational abolitionist projects, Congregationalists were among the most active members of the Christian Anti-Slavery Conventions and the Church Anti-Slavery Society" (McKivigan, p. 175).

[94] J. Clarke, "Our Country," *Review and Herald*, July 21, 1863, p. 61.

[95] J. Clarke, "The Punishment of the South," *Review and Herald*, Jan. 23, 1866, pp. 61, 62. In a personal letter, Ellen White encouraged Joseph Clarke to do personal evangelism and write more for Seventh-day Adventist periodicals: "Dear Brother Clarke: While at Lovett's Grove, I was shown some individual cases. I saw that you and your Brother John should improve the talents committed to you, for God would soon require what He has lent you with usury. I saw that fireside preachers were needed: I was shown that as individuals are investigating the evidences of our position, they can be much helped by your visiting them in their family, praying with them, and imparting instruction to them from the Word of God. There are many ways in which our different talents can be improved. I was shown, Brother Clarke, that it was not duty for you to give to others your property; much of your time, I was shown, would be occupied in writing, and improving opportunities of doing good to others, by leading them to the truth" (Ellen G. White, Letter 9 [March 22], 1868, pars. 1, 2). Clarke submitted over 721 articles for *The Review and Herald*, with additional articles for *The Signs of the Times*, *The Youth's Instructor*, *The Health Reformer*, *The Gospel Sickle*, and *The American Sentinel*. For his support of the denominational name "Seventh-day Adventist," see B. F. Snook, "Report from Bro. Snook," *Review and Herald*, April 23, 1861, p. 181.

[96] The *Raleigh Daily Telegram*, May 13, 1871, p. 3, states that he was from North Carolina and that he was shot.

[97] "Suffrage" is "the right to vote in political elections" (*The New Lexicon Webster's Dictionary*, p. 989).

[98] Jos. Clarke, "Is the Rebellion Quelled?" *Review and Herald*, Aug. 8, 1871, p. 63. Spalding had a more conciliatory view, believing that loyalty to the Republican party was an extreme ("Lights and Shades in the Black Belt," p. 45).

[99] Greene, p. 42.

[100] Jos. Clarke, "The Slave," *Review and Herald*, Dec. 2, 1875, p. 175.

[101] Jos. Clarke, "The Freedmen," *Review and Herald*, Sept. 14, 1876, p. 91.

[102] Joseph Clarke (and his brother John) studied at Western Reserve College in Ohio (*Catalogue of the officers and students at the Western Reserve College*, 1844-45, p. 14). He taught winter school in Liberty, Ohio in 1849-1850 (Michael A. Leeson, *Commemorative Historical and Biographical Record of Wood County, Ohio*, p. 394).

[103] Joseph Clarke, "Notes by the Way," *Review and Herald*, Sept. 26, 1878, p. 111. Clarke also paired up with A. B. and E. G. Rust and "did considerable speaking in the country between Dallas and Cleburne."

[104] "Their labor among the freedmen, standing, as it does, aloof and separate from party and political objects and influences, is sure to result in good, the fruit of which will be realized in the kingdom of God" (R. M. Kilgore, "Progress of the Cause: Texas," *Review and Herald*, May 17, 1877, p. 158).

[105] Joseph Clarke, letter to Uriah Smith, Feb. 24, 1878, Archives, General Conference of Seventh-day Adventists.

[106] Carter, *The 19th Century Odyssey of John and Judith: From the Battlefields of the Civil War to Spiritual Battlefields on the Texas Frontier*, p. 74.

[107] Carter, p. 76.

[108] The *Times-Picayune* (New Orleans, Louisiana), Sept. 25, 1877, p. 2, reported: "The Seventh Day Adventists have secured a solid foothold and a number of followers in Johnson county. One of their preachers, Mr. Kilgore, has been preaching at Cleburne several weeks, and secured over forty converts, the majority of whom had formerly been members of other Protestant denominations." The Austin *Weekly Democratic Statesman* reported: "The first campmeeting of the Seventh Day Adventists was in session at Rockwall from the ninth to the thirteenth of August. Six counties were represented. Says a correspondent in the Fort Worth *Democrat* from their midst: 'Their work is but two years old, but there are 250 adherents. They are ardent Bible students, holding for a simple natural interpretation. They expect the soon advent of the Saviour, but set no time. They keep the seventh day to obey the fourth commandment, teaching that Sunday is a heathen Catholic day, for which there is no scripture. They teach that the dead are unconsciously awaiting the judgment and that the wicked will be finally destroyed or burnt up. They publish largely, in eight languages, with offices in California, Michigan and Switzerland. Missionaries are in many foreign lands, and others to be sent to every nation. They expect to warn the world of the soon advent of the duty of keeping the seventh day. They are zealous, temperate and devoted to their work. The leading [e]lder is the one who "wound up" Elder Caskey at Terrell in June last' " (*Weekly Democratic Statesman* [Austin, Texas], Aug. 22, 1878, p. 2). The *Statesman* also reported: "The Seventh Day Adventists, now kicking up a stir in Dallas, differ from the Second Day Adventists in this, that they set no particular time for the coming of the Lord; they believe in translation—that the elect will journey to Heaven as Elijah did [1 Thess. 4:17], and that the wicked will be annihilated [2 Thess. 2:8; John 3:16], or, perhaps, not raised until one thousand years after the righteous [Rev. 20:5]. During this time, some of them contend that Christ will reign upon earth, and his reign will be a period of happiness for the righteous and one of torture for the wicked. They observe the seventh day as a holy day [Isa. 58:13], and usually resort to immersion as a mode of baptism [John 3:23; Acts 8:38]. Strict temperance views prevail among them [Gal. 5:23; Rom. 13:13], and abstinence from the use of tobacco, coffee and port is recommended. There are several sects of Adventists, which differ in a portion of their tenets, but in the main entertain similar views. The Seventh Day Adventists originated in 1844, and their belief shows that variety is the spice even of Christian life" (*Weekly Democratic Statesman* [Austin, Texas], Nov. 25, 1880, p. 1).

[109] For Killen's profession, see Taylor, "Progress of the Cause: Reynolds, GA," April 18, 1878, p. 127. Since 1872, Dr. J. A. Killingsworth and his family had been the only Sabbath-observers in Spaulding County, Georgia. Killen described his first contact with Taylor: "Not long ago, a Mr. Taylor, living in Brooks Co., in this State, passed through our county; and I had the privilege of hearing him talk privately on the Lord's Sabbath, and other Bible subjects that were new to me, or at least were very different from what I had been taught to believe. I told him I would investigate these subjects, and gave him twenty cents with which to send me some tracts that I selected from his list. I received them, and others besides. Bro. Taylor left with me a few tracts and papers, old numbers of the REVIEW and SIGNS. I have read them all with a great deal of interest, and am anxious to know more about these great subjects. I have handed them around to others, but find the people generally very slow to listen to anything new. A great many are ready to confess that we have the wrong Sabbath, but seem to think it makes but very little difference. I have been a missionary Baptist for twenty years, and if I have been keeping a day for the Lord's Sabbath which is not the Sabbath, I pray God that from this time I may obey him. I told the pastor of the church to which I belong (B. F. Thorp, one of the big preachers of our denomination in this State) of my investigations, and in his first sermon afterward, he said the Sabbath was changed to Sunday in honor of the resurrection; and yesterday he sent me a New York paper, *The Examiner and Chronicle*, of Oct. 4, containing an article headed, 'Yes, We Have a Christian Sabbath.' The only

argument I see in it is that Sunday is the Sabbath on account of the 'fitness of things.' I thought we Baptists always had Bible reasons for our belief. I know I am not sufficiently posted to defend myself; and I intend to take your paper and send for more tracts before long." (W. F. Killen in "Progress of the Cause: Letters from the Southern Field," *Review and Herald*, Oct. 25, 1877, p. 135). See also C. O. Taylor, "Progress of the Cause: Reynolds, GA," *Review and Herald*, Jan. 3, 1878, pp. 6, 7; C. O. Taylor, "Progress of the Cause: Reynolds, GA," *Review and Herald*, April 18, 1878, p. 127. Identified as the county school superintendent in the 1880 U.S. Census (*1880 United States Federal Census, Georgia, Houston, Lower 5th, 030*, p. 11). Killen inherited the "Chastain Place" plantation from his father, John Killen ("Will of John Killen 11 Feb 1869 Houston County, GA," available online at http://files.usgwarchives.net/ga/houston/wills/k4500002.txt, accessed 2/10/15). Killen had enlisted in Company A, Georgia Co. A, 14th Light Artillery Battery, serving under the Confederacy in the Civil War, and had mustered out of service as a corporal ("William F Killen in the U.S. Civil War Soldier Records and Profiles, 1861-1865"). Spalding mistakenly identified him as "J. S. Killen" in *Captains of the Host*, p. 499, and *Origin and History of Seventh-day Adventists*, vol. 2, p. 182, but correctly identified him as "W. F. Killen" in "Lights and Shades in the Black Belt," p. 138.

[110] "Lights and Shades in the Black Belt," p. 138. Killen wrote: "I spent the holy Sabbath in reading the Bible and the papers you sent me. I have kept three Sabbaths, blessed be the name of the Lord. Before I got through reading 'The Three [Angels'] Messages,' God opened my eyes, and I was in a great hurry to obey him. My wife and children, and my mother-in-law [Zelpha Lane], all cheerfully keep the Sabbath with me, and I have no trouble in getting my laborers (colored people) to keep it. I feel like 'lifting up my voice like a trumpet,' and showing the professed followers of God their transgressions. How gladly would I preach to this people if they would let me; but I trust that God will yet open the way for me, and grant me what I have been a long time praying for, that is, to be a humble, faithful preacher of the pure gospel of the Son of God. Dear Bro. Taylor, I am with you, mind and soul. I have counted the cost, and do not intend to look back" (W. F. Killen, quoted in C. O. Taylor, "Progress of the Cause: Reynolds, GA," *Review and Herald*, Jan. 3, 1878, p. 7).

[111] On the same page in the 1880 U.S. Census are listed William F. Killen (age 43)—with his wife Martha [Ann Permelia] and children Charles S., Eva, William F., Jr. (actually "William Lane"), Robert, Herbert, Susie, Mattie, and John—and Edmund Killen (age 39)—with his wife Leah and children Mattie, Madison, Eddie, Leah, Rachel, and Annie (*1880 United States Federal Census, Georgia, Houston, Lower 5th, 030*, p. 36).

[112] C. O. Taylor, "Progress of the Cause: Reynolds, Georgia," *Review and Herald*, March 14, 1878, p. 86. "Edmund Killen, already a preacher, proclaimed the message among his people, resulting in a number of adherents" (Spalding, *Origin and History of Seventh-day Adventists*, vol. 2, p. 343). W. F. Killen wrote of him: "The colored man, Edmund Killen, is holding on firmly to the truth. I believe he will do right just as far as he knows. I would be glad if he were licensed to preach the truth among those of his race. He is certainly doing a good work among them. I baptized his wife [Leah] the second Sunday in last June" (W. F. Killen, "Progress of the Cause: Georgia," *Review and Herald*, Aug. 30, 1881, p. 155.

[113] J. O. Corliss, "The Work in the South: Georgia," *Review and Herald*, Dec. 16, 1880, p. 397; "Lights and Shades in the Black Belt," p. 138; Reynolds, *We Have Tomorrow* (1984), p. 50. "The Killen family later furnished a number of workers, four of the boys and two or three of the girls entering the colporteur work, two of them becoming ministers and passing on their faith and work to the third generation" (Spalding, *Origin and History*, vol. 2, p. 182). Will L. Killen, state agent for North Carolina, wrote about the results of book sales and Bible readings: "The colored people are taking hold more rapidly than the whites. About fifteen of them have begun keeping the Sabbath" (*Review and Herald*, May 2, 1893, p. 283).

[114] W. F. Killen, "Progress of the Cause: Georgia," *Review and Herald*, March 29, 1881, p. 202.

[115] Otho and Cora married on Sept. 20, 1886 (Alger, "The Lane-Godsmark Family," p. 9). Otho Godsmark's father, Richard Godsmark, was stepfather to Sands and Elbert Lane (Spalding, *Origin and History of Seventh-day Adventists*, vol. 2, pp. 84, 85).

[116] S. H. Lane wrote in March 1888 about laboring with O. C. Godsmark and C. F. Curtis in Austell, Senoia, Reynolds, and Quitman, Georgia, and he told of plans for a "camp meeting" in the summer ("Progress of the Cause: The Work in Several States," *Review and Herald*, March 13, 1888, p. 172). Godsmark wrote about meetings in Reynolds, Georgia, with two baptized and a group of 25 organized into a Sabbath school (O. C. Godsmark, "Progress of the Cause: Georgia," *Review and Herald*, April 10, 1888, p. 235). The first camp meeting of Seventh-day Adventists was held in Reynolds, Georgia, July 18–25, 1888. S. H. Lane and O. C. Godsmark spoke. W. H. Killen baptized four (Chas. F. Curtis, "The Georgia Camp Meeting," *Review and Herald*, Aug. 21, 1888, p. 541). The next notice about Godsmark and Lane is at the General Conference, with Godsmark being reassigned to Illinois and Lane to New York ("S. D. Adventist General Conference," *Review and Herald*, Nov. 6, 1888, p. 698).

[117] Former slaves Prince Johnson, Calline Brown, Maria White, and Susan Jones all used the term "poor white-trash" to refer to lower class whites (Andrew Waters, *Prayin' to Be Set Free*, pp. 19, 28, 151, 191). Ruben Fox said: "Master sure didn't 'low no poor-white trash around there. It's them kind of folks what's got things so tore up now" (Waters, p. 174).

" 'When I was a boy,' recalled Waters McIntosh, 'we used to sing, 'Rather be a Negro than a poor white man.' 'I think I'm better than a certain class of white folks,' declared a Tennessee slave who had known 'white folks from the cradle up,' and he didn't 'mind telling them so, neither' " (Andrew Ward, *The Slaves' War*, p. 14).

[118] "Lights and Shades in the Black Belt," pp. 143–146.

[119] For example, see "Lights and Shades in the Black Belt," p. 50.

[120] "Lights and Shades in the Black Belt," p. 76.

[121] Both men had difficulty gaining converts at times. G. G. Rupert wrote of Killen: "After closing the tent meeting, I went to Perry, Ga. On my way to Alabama, where I spent a day with Eld. Killen and family. This family have kept the Sabbath in this place eight years alone. We baptized the two sons, who are of an age to become useful laborers in the cause" (G. G. Rupert, "Progress of the Cause: Georgia," *Review and Herald*, Sept. 7, 1886, p. 571). *The Portsmouth Daily Times* (Portsmouth, Ohio) reported: "Rev. Squire Osborne, Adventist, *en route* for the lower part of Kentucky, stopped a few days in Springville, and delivered several lectures explanatory of his doctrine. He has made some converts in this county, but as a general thing he has found pork eaters wedded to their idols" ("Springville Items," *The Portsmouth Times* [Portsmouth, Ohio], March 18, 1876, p. 3).

[122] Regarding Osborne's visit to Battle Creek, see J. W[hite]., "The Work in the South," *Review and Herald*, May 31, 1877, p. 172. Regarding their agreement, see Godsmark in "Lights and Shades in the Black Belt," p. 139.

[123] "Lights and Shades in the Black Belt," p. 139.

[124] D. Downer, "Need of Laborers," *Review and Herald*, April 28, 1874, p. 158. Downer is listed in the 1880 U.S. Federal Census as a "Minister Advent," living in Arkansaw, Wisconsin (*1880 United States Federal Census, Wisconsin, Pepin, Arkansaw, 108*, p. 4). Born Oct. 14, 1844, Downer was well-known in Wisconsin as an advent preacher, naturalist, and taxidermist. He was a merchant, and, at the time of his death (Feb. 9, 1894), he was the postmaster at Cable, Wisconsin. He was a Civil War veteran, serving under the noted Eagle Regiment, the 8th Wisconsin Infantry, from August 29, 1862, to the end of the war, sharing in his noble regiment's sacrifices and triumphs (David R. Downer, *The Downers of America: With Genealogical Record*, p. 176).

[125] "For eight years Elder Kilgore labored mightily in Texas, enduring much opposition from free-swinging Texan ministers and their boisterous following, and receiving much support from independent-minded citizens and officials, who jokingly charged, because of his easy reference to supporting texts, that he had 'springs in his Bible.' He endured floods, tent burnings, [and] threats of lynch law. In Peoria he was given notice to leave the State within twenty-four hours, or suffer the consequences; but the audience, led by a lawyer, stood solidly in his defense, and the sheriff sent him word to stick by and he would be protected. [R. M. Kilgore, "Texas Tent: Peoria, Oct. 11," *Review and Herald*, Oct. 25, 1877, p. 134.] At Cleburne, after gales, a destructive flood, and vociferous, tumultuous opposition, he brought out a large church, and made it one of the strongholds of the cause in the State. In the end he left a strong conference of eight hundred members, imbued with missionary zeal, which gave it a steady growth" (Spalding, *Origin and History*, vol. 2, pp. 184, 185).

[126] R. M. Kilgore, "Texas Tent," *Review and Herald*, Sept. 6, 1877, p. 86.

[127] Greene, p. 44.

[128] John Byington and U. Smith, "Report of General Conference of Seventh-day Adventists," *Review and Herald*, May 26, 1863, p. 206.

[129] Jeff Crocombe, "The Beginning of Regional Conferences in the US," available online at http://h0bbes.wordpress.com/2006/08/07/the-beginning-of-regional-conferences-in-the-us, accessed 5/9/14.

[130] Hansen, p. 152.

[131] R. M. Kilgore, "Report of the Southern Field," *General Conference Bulletin*, Oct. 21, 1889, p. 26.

[132] Ellen G. White, "Diary, October 1889," Ms. 22 (Oct. 20), 1889, par. 12.

[133] Spalding, *Captains of the Host*, p. 635.

[134] Spalding, *Captains of the Host*, p. 502.

[135] " 'Joint worship was the predominant pattern for Christians in the American South before the Civil War.' ... By 1871, a huge majority of southern Blacks were worshipping in denominations distinct from their White brethren, a pattern that persisted into the twentieth century" (Bennett, "Resistance and Accommodation," p. 19, citing Katherine L. Dvorak, *An African-American Exodus: The Segregation of Southern Churches*, pp. 1, 2, 4, 5).

[136] Benjamin Baker, "A Look in the Mirror: Ellen White, Blacks, and the Adventist Church," p. 1. Harold D. Singleton, "A Short History of the Work of Seventh-day Adventists among the Negroes of North America before 1909, submitted for Social Science Seminary and World Politics" (1932), p. 2, in Delbert Baker, *Telling the Story*, p. 142. "It was decided by the council that Bro. C. M. Kinney, of Louisville, should be ordained and set apart to the work of the ministry among his own people, which was done at the close of the meeting" (R. M. Kilgore, "Tennessee Camp-Meeting and Nashville Institute," *Review and Herald*, Oct. 29, 1889, p. 683).

[137] Many African Americans had fled to Kansas when Governor John P. St. John opened the doors to them.

[138] Charles M. Kinn[e]y, "Progress of the Cause: Labor Among the Colored People of Topeka, Kansas," *Review and Herald*, Oct. 27, 1885, p. 668.

[139] The expression "fine class" is from a letter, reflecting on conditions in the church, from D. T. Jones to C. M. Kinny, March 6, 1889, GC Archives, RG 11, Box 3059, cited by Baker, "A Look in the Mirror," p. 1.

[140] Baker, "A Look in the Mirror," p. 1.

[141] Ms. 6 (prepared for a tract March 20), 1891, p. 7, written Nov. 4, 1889; *The Southern Work*, p. 11, emphasis added.

[142] Dan. T. Jones, "Synopsis of the Proceedings of the General Conference Committee," *Review and Herald*, April 9, 1889, p. 235.

[143] C. M. Kinney, "Progress of the Cause: Labor Among the Colored People," *Review and Herald*, Nov. 12, 1889, p. 716.

[144] Calvin Rock, *Institutional Loyalty Versus Racial Freedom: The Dilemma of Black Seventh-day Adventists*, p. 228.

[145] Jonathan Grant, p. 96.

[146] R. Clifford Jones, *James K. Humphrey and the Sabbath Day Adventists*, p. 92.

[147] Ms. 6 (March 20), 1891, was written November 4, 1889 (*Manuscript Releases*, vol. 4, p. 100, par. 2). Before this, Ellen White's last statement on race was published in September 1867 in a chapter entitled, "Political Sentiments." There she addressed church members, "These brethren cannot receive the approval of God while they lack sympathy for *the oppressed colored race* and are at variance with the pure, republican principles of our Government. God has no more sympathy with rebellion upon earth than with the rebellion in heaven, when the great rebel questioned the foundation of God's government and was thrust out with all who sympathized with him in his rebellion" (White, *Testimonies for the Church*, vol. 1, p. 534, emphasis added). Her use of "race" between 1867 and 1889 referred to the *human* race. In 1882 and 1884, she made vague references to that which divides, in statements in which she upheld the Bible as providing a history of "the human race," "unsullied" and "unmarred by human prejudice or human pride" ("The Primal Object of Education," *Review and Herald*, July 11, 1882; "Importance of Education," *Review and Herald*, Aug. 19, 1884). Her next use of "race," in terms of that which divides humanity, was in "No Caste in Christ," *Review and Herald*, Dec. 22, 1891.

She wrote the church in Woodland, California: "Every species of slavery is not in accordance with the Word of God. The evils are too great to be enumerated. And if men and women have embraced the solemn truth for these last days that sanctifies the soul, the old political sentiments that sustain the old system of slavery will be, before they are translated, purged from them. ... God's Spirit has been grieved by the feelings cherished by some in the Woodland Church. What these souls need is conversion to God. The light shines so clearly now none need to walk in darkness. My testimonies have gone all through the Southern states. These testimonies speak decidedly and positively in regard to the subject of slavery. It was a system unbalanced and unjust. While we do not and will not dabble in politics, we will be colaborers with Jesus Christ" (Letter 36 [July], 1880, pars. 4, 5).

[148] During this period, Ellen White developed other branches of ministry, including health ministry, traveled to new fields of labor in California and Texas, and published on the life of Christ and the patriarchs.

[149] "The Adventists. First Day of Their Annual Conference," *San Francisco Chronicle*, Nov. 14, 1887, p. 3. General Conference sessions were held for the first time outside Michigan—in Oakland, California.

[150] Significantly, this statement was not included in the *General Conference Bulletin*.

[151] Spalding, *Captains of the Host*, p. 504. Nonetheless, the fact that C. M. Kinney studied at Healdsburg College "would seem to indicate that a color line, which would become a major issue in the Nation in the twentieth century, was not as visible in the Seventh-day Adventist church in the 1870s and 1880s as it was in the larger society where white and black students were unable to mingle" (Sepúlveda, p. 128, citing Reynolds, *We Have Tomorrow*, and "Lights and Shades in the Black Belt").

[152] It had become a separate company three years before. "In 1883 the blacks in the Edgefield Junction Church were organized into a separate company called the First Colored Seventh-day Adventist Church by Elder Samuel Fulton. It officially became a church on November 9, 1886. Some were disappointed with the separation and left [the] church" (R. Steven Norman, III, "The Early History of South Central Conference, 1863–1945," p. 12).

[153] Jacob Justiss, "A Remarkable Century of Progress," *North American Informant*, November-December 1971, p. 1.

[154] R. Steven Norman, III, "Edson White's Southern Work Remembered," *Southern Tidings*, Oct. 1995, p. 2. T. B. Buckner of Selma, Alabama was another early ordained black minister (Spalding, *Origin and History of Seventh-day Adventists*, vol. 2, p. 343; taken from a facsimile in C. M. Kinney's own handwriting, "The First Official Effort for the Colored People," in Baker, *Telling the Story*, p. 4/79 [425]).

[155] "S.D.A. Accomplishments in Interracial Relations—1934," p. 4, available online at http://documents.adventistarchives.org/Resources/RegionalConf/RCO-01.pdf, accessed 1/12/15.

[156] Delbert W. Baker, "In Search of Adventist African-American Roots: Exploring the History of Adventist African-Americans in the United States," *Adventist Review*, Feb. 4, 1993, p. 13.

[157] Hansen, p. 48.

[158] Two of the Lexington Church's charter members were Attorney J. Alexander Chiles and Dr. Mary A. Britton. Dr. Britton was the first black female physician in Lexington and was a Civil Rights activist, fighting the "Separate Coach Bill." Her great nephew, Dr. Benjamin Hooks, is a former national president of the NAACP (R. Steven Norman, III, "The Early History of South Central Conference, 1863–1945," pp. 17, 42).

[159] Delbert Baker, "A Statement on Ellen G. White's Use of the Term 'Race War' and Other Related Insights," p. 29.

[160] Greene, p. 38.

CHAPTER 7 - An Appeal for Volunteers

[1] Ellen G. White, *The Southern Work*, p. 10. She promoted missions for "colored people" in Letter 18, 1890, par. 25.

[2] Delbert Baker, "A Statement on Ellen G. White's Use of the Term 'Race War' and Other Related Insights," pp. 2, 3.

[3] Benjamin Baker, "Ellen White, 1888, and Black People."

[4] Douglas Morgan, *Lewis C. Sheafe: Apostle to Black America*, p. 118.

[5] Ellen G. White, Ms. 6, 1891, written Nov. 4, 1889, in *The Southern Work*, pp. 9–17, emphasis added. "Christ came to this earth with a message of mercy and forgiveness. He laid the foundation for a religion by which Jew and Gentile, black and white, free and bond, are linked together in one common brotherhood, recognized as equal in the sight of God. The Saviour has a boundless love for every human being. In each one He sees capacity for improvement. With divine energy and hope He greets those for whom He has given His life. In His *strength* they can live a life rich in good works, filled with the power of the Spirit" (White, *Testimonies for the Church*, vol. 7 [1902], p. 225). Rilla Eubanks, a thirteen-year-old student at the Lintonia school wrote: "As we know[,] we have a great and awful responsibility resting upon us: we hold the destiny of a race in our hands" ("Why Should We Elevate," *Gospel Herald*, Dec. 1900, p. 103).

[6] Edson wrote: "And while I have no religious inclinations now in the least, I shall make a business of studying and getting into line" (Letter, May 18, 1893). Ellen White's concern for her son through this period comes through in her letters to him: "You write in Willie's letter that you are now about to engage in a new enterprise which will get us all out of debt in a short time. My son, I say, Don't do this. I see in this only another infatuating delusion of the enemy. Did you not have the same glowing prospects before you in your late plans and enterprises? Were you not lured on by the hope of great profits to come? And yet what have these amounted to? Why, there would be such a success in your business if you could have just a little more means for present emergencies, and I knew that if I did not consent to sign the notes you presented, you would say that it would have been a success if you could have had just the amount at the right time. Thus one enterprise has been entered into after another with the same result—disappointment. . . ." (Letter 94 [May 5], 1892, par. 1). "I have not lost my love and interest for you, although so far separated from you. But without positive evidence of a decided change in your spiritual condition, I cannot respond as you desire. I know that unless you do surrender to God I could not put trust and confidence in you to be connected with me, as you have been, in business relations, asnd we so far away that we can have no direct influence over your plans and course of action" (Letter 57 [Oct.] 1892, par. 4). Ron Graybill tells the story in *Mission to Black America*.

[7] Sepúlveda, p. 49.

[8] Ellen G. White, "The Treatment of the Colored Race," Ms. 7 (Feb. 3), 1896, par. 1, in *Manuscript Releases*, vol. 4, p. 8.

[9] See "Lights and Shades in the Black Belt," p. 139.

[10] Mrs. E. G. White, "Work Among the Colored People," *Review and Herald*, April 2, 1895, pp. 209, 210.

[11] Corroboration of this statement is found in a news article of the day: "The Catholics among the Freedmen. The Protestant sects are alarmed at the efforts to be made by the Catholics among the Freedmen. The New York *Observer* says: 'The colored men are coming under the influence of the Roman Catholics, and one of the objects of the present Romanist Council in Baltimore has been to devise measures for the conversion to [the] Papacy of the black race on this continent. The negroes have a natural tendency to fanaticism; they are also easily influenced by the shows and pomps of Romanism. Bishop [Martin J.] Spalding publicly declared in Baltimore that the Roman Catholic Church was the only church in which neither color nor caste were recognized, and urged the propagation of Romanism among the blacks, especially in Maryland, where there are already some religious houses devoted to the black race.'" ("News and Miscellany: Home News: The Catholics Among the Freemen," *Review and Herald*, Dec. 18, 1866, p. 20). A *Signs* article declared: "WE have occasionally referred to the efforts being made by the Roman Catholic Church to win the colored people to their communion. They are meeting with no little success. Dr. Fulton writes from the South of the progress of their work: 'Black nuns are beginning to abound; schools for the education of Romish priests are beginning to appear. Churches decorated with the choicest products of art, and flaming with tinselry and show, are seen in most of our large cities crowded with colored people. Black people are welcomed to the Romish churches, because Rome intends to increase her power by the colored vote, and appreciates the magnitude of her opportunity. In Baltimore there are fourteen colored schools. The Douglas Institute has a fine hall, a library and readingroom, owned by colored people.'—Sel." ("Papists among the Freedmen," *Signs of the Times*, April 8, 1875, p. 176). A *Review* article declared:

"In the Watch Tower department, this week, is, given a significant article on the Southern Problem, showing how the Roman Catholic Church, as soon as the ballot was given to the colored people, set herself assiduously at work to absorb into herself all that element, to secure their power. She . . . wants the political power which they will wield, when brought under her control" ("A Growing Danger," *Review and Herald*, Dec. 6, 1877, p. 180). Another *Review* article, which cited the Nashville *Christian Advocate* as not being "alarmist," discussed "the spread of Romanism among our colored population: It seems to be generally understood that the Romish Church will in future devote special attention to the spiritual welfare of the colored people in the South, regarding them as eligible subjects for missionary work. In Alabama and Georgia the priests have already established churches, and the colored communicants can be counted by thousands" ("The Watch Tower," *Review and Herald*, Feb. 28, 1878, p. 65). Yet, as black suffrage diminished, so did Catholic interest in them.

[12] Ellen G. White, Letter 5 (July 24), 1895, to "Brethren in Responsible Positions in America."

[13] Mrs. E. G. White, "An Appeal for the Southern Field," *Review and Herald*, Nov. 26, 1895, pp. 753, 754.

[14] ". . . the emotional side of religion was certainly the most attractive to the freedman, who, largely abandoning his dances and festivals of slave times, poured into his church his wealth of emotion . . ." (Spalding, "Lights and Shades in the Black Belt," p. 75). Spalding also described the use of poetic fictions in black preaching (Spalding, pp. 81, 82).

[15] White, "An Appeal for the South—2," *Review and Herald*, Dec. 3, 1895, emphasis added

[16] White, "An Appeal for the South—3," *Review and Herald*, Dec. 10, 1895, p. 38.

[17] Spalding's unpublished manuscript "Lights and Shades in the Black Belt" deals with more than the progress within Seventh-day Adventist work. It also surveys the efforts of other denominations in educating the freedmen.

[18] White, "An Example in History," *Review and Herald*, Dec. 17, 1895, emphasis added.

[19] Illustrated by reports from the ministers of Vicksburg, which are depicted in Samuel G. London, Jr., *Seventh-day Adventists and the Civil Rights Movement*, p. 47.

[20] White, "Lift Up Your Eyes and Look on the Field," *Review and Herald*, Jan. 28, 1896.

[21] Ellen G. White, *Testimonies for the Church*, vol. 7 (1902), p. 229, emphasis added. Similar counsel was in Ellen G. White, "Volunteers Wanted for the Southern Field," *Review and Herald*, February 4, 1896, p. 65.

[22] Arthur L. White explained why *The Southern Work* went out of print: ". . . there are today proportionately a larger number of colored Seventh-day Adventists per million population of Negroes in the United States than there are white Seventh-day Adventists per million population of white people in the United States. This makes it very clear that denominational work among the colored race is not now neglected." (Letter, Nov. 8, 1861, Q&A File Number 43-C-49).

[23] Edson wrote his mother: "I have surrendered fully and completely, and never enjoyed life before as I am now. I have for years been under a strain, with so much to accomplish, and it has stood right in my way. Now, I have left it all with my Saviour, and the burden does not bear me down any longer" (Letter, Aug. 10, 1893).

[24] Arthur L. White, *Ellen G. White: The Australian Years*, 1891–1900, p. 97; letter in latter part of August, 1893.

[25] Benjamin Baker, *Crucial Moments: Twelve Defining Events in Black Adventist History*, p. 54. Ron Graybill points also to an earlier conversation with C. C. Lewis (Graybill, *Mission to Black America*, p. 14).

[26] Graybill describes the tract as being found scattered on the floor (*Mission to Black America*, p. 17).

[27] Ellen G. White, *The Southern Work*, p. 16.

[28] Edson wrote about Will Palmer's conversion in his letter to his mother, Oct. 31, 1893.

[29] "Beginning Work. Steamer Morning Star," *Gospel Herald*, June 1900, p. 37.

[30] Ellen White wrote him: "The last trial, in the building of the last boat, and all the circumstances connected with it, nearly cost me my life. You can never know how I have waited for you to see your wrong in this matter, and repent and confess before God, that He might forgive and heal you. I have carried the burden on my soul ever since, for I knew that unless you should see how cruel it was for you to pursue the course you did, in the face of warnings, entreaties, and of positive promises on your part, you would never come to the right position before God" (Letter 94 [May 5], 1892, par. 6).

[31] Hansen, pp. 192, 193.

[32] Hansen, p. 193.

[33] In the June 1900 issue of the *Gospel Herald*, Edson White summarized the progress of the educational and evangelistic work accomplished on the Yazoo River from 1894 to mid–1900. A caption in the *Gospel Herald* indicates that there were 194 students at the Lintonia School (*Gospel Herald*, May 1899, p. 75).

[34] See "Lights and Shades in the Black Belt," pp. 245, 250, 252, 254, 255, 262, and "Morning Star Group of Southern Missionary Workers," *Gospel Herald*, March 1899, pp. 68, 69. Three other black converts from the area who deserve mention are Thomas Murphy, William J. Astrap, and Franklin Henry Bryant ("Lights and Shades," p. 254).

[35] Samuel G. London, p. 51.

[36] See Ciro Sepúlveda, "Booker T. Washington, Ellen G. White, and Adventists Manual Training Schools."

[37] See also Hansen, p. 196; Arthur L. White, *Ellen G. White: The Early Elmshaven Years 1900–1905*, vol. 5, p. 62.

CHAPTER 8 - Threading the Needle

[1] Ronald D. Graybill, *E. G. White and Church Race Relations*, p. 52, referencing Ellen White's statement, "Let them understand that this plan is to be followed *until the Lord shows us a better way*" (*Testimonies for the Church*, vol. 9, pp. 206, 207, emphasis added).

[2] Manuscript 22a (Nov. 20), 1895, in *The Southern Work*, pp. 69, 71.

[3] Crisler collected seven scrapbooks of newspaper clippings between 1903 and 1912 and entitled them "The Negro Problem." They are in the possession of the library at Oakwood College in Huntsville, Alabama. (Graybill, p. 9). Crisler was Ellen White's private secretary from 1901 to her death in 1915. After her death, he went on to serve as a missionary in the Orient.

[4] Rayford Whittingham Logan, *The Betrayal of the Negro from Rutherford B. Hayes to Woodrow Wilson* (New York: Da Capo Press, 1997), p. xiv.

[5] *New York Age*, Feb. 28, 1907, Sc. 1, p. 20, quoted in Graybill, p. 20.

[6] From his Sidney Hillman Lectures at Howard University in 1961, cited by Logan, p. xxi. Graybill set the limits of the period as between 1895 and 1910 because these were the years that Ellen White wrote most about the work in the South, and it was the period during which Edson worked among blacks in communities along the Mississippi (Graybill, pp. 17, 18). Coincidentally, Booker T. Washington and Ellen G. White both died in 1915.

[7] Logan, p. 279.

[8] Logan, p. 280.

[9] *Sunday Record* (Battle Creek), Jan. 31, 1904, Sc. 2.

[10] Graybill, p. 49.

[11] John Hope Franklin, *From Slavery to Freedom* (1969), p. 445.

[12] Segregated public transportation would not be challenged until the 1950s and 1960s.

[13] Whites could circumvent literacy tests in one of three ways: the 'understanding clause' excepted the candidate if he understood the Constitution when read to him; the 'good character clause' excepted the candidate if he was of a good character and understood the duties and obligations of citizenship; the 'grandfather clause' exempted the candidate "if his father or grandfather had been eligible to vote on January 1, 1860, or if he or an ancestor had served with either the United States or Confederate States military forces during the Civil War.... In 1915 the Supreme Court ruled the grandfather clauses unconstitutional, but by that time the Black electorate in the South had been almost completely decimated. In Louisiana there were 130,344 registered Black voters in 1896, but only 5,320 in 1900. In New Orleans there were 14,000 Black voters in 1896, but only 408 in 1908. In Alabama only 3,000 of the 181,471 previously registered Black voters were registered by 1900. In Virginia the ranks of Black voters shrank from 147,000 prior to 1902 to 21,000 after 1905" (Norman K. Miles, "Tensions Between the Races," *The World of Ellen G. White*, p. 55; J. W. Sumners, "The 'Grandfather Clause,'" *Lawyer and Banker and Southern Bench and Bar Review*, February 1914, p. 39).

[14] Woodward, *The Strange Career of Jim Crow*, p. 84.

[15] William Howard Taft, *Presidential addresses and state papers, from March 4, 1909 to March 4, 1910* (1910), vol. 1, p. 64.

[16] United States Congress, *Congressional Record: Proceedings and Debates of the 85th Congress*, Vol. 103, Part 10 (U.S. Government Printing Office, 1957), p. 12913.

[17] Woodward, pp. 86, 87.

[18] Graybill, p. 23.

[19] Ellen G. White, Letter 165 (Oct. 22), 1899, to F. E. Belden, in *Manuscript Releases*, vol. 4, p. 15.

[20] Baker, "A Statement on Ellen G. White's Use of the Term 'Race War' and Other Related Insights," p. 16.

[21] Woodward, p. 71.

[22] "The 1876 presidential election that put Rutherford B. Hayes in the White House, by [a] very close margin, came with conditions: an agreement with the Democrats that the Republicans would discontinue federal troop occupation in the South and allow the advancement of radical Reconstruction policy promoting African American voting rights, employment, and equality in accommodations. Not surprisingly, the latter was never realized" ("Governor Records - St. John, 1879-1883").

[23] Baker, p. 16.

[24] Sepúlveda, *Ellen White on the Color Line*, p. 55; Franklin, *From Slavery to Freedom*, p. 339.

[25] Woodward, p. 71.

[26] Woodward, p. 79.

[27] Baker, p. 18.

[28] *New York Age*, May 16, 1907, section 3, p. 8.

[29] *New York Age*, May 23, 1907, section 3, p. 10, quoted in Graybill, p. 28.

[30] James Edson White, Letter to Ellen G. White, May 25, 1899, quoted in Graybill, pp. 56, 57; Hansen, pp. 195, 196.

[31] Graybill, pp. 54, 55.

[32] Nathan W. Olvin was a black sharecropper who was converted in late 1898 in tent meetings held at Bliss's Landing, Mississippi. Olvin had assisted in the distribution of food and clothing to the needy of Calmar (Samuel G. London, p. 51; Edson White, "Relief for the Suffering," *Gospel Herald*, March 1899, pp. 61, 62). He lived with his wife Catharine and nine-year-old daughter Mary (*1900 United States Federal Census, Mississippi, Issaquena, Beat 01, District 0030*).

[33] James Edson White to Ellen G. White, May 25, 1899. For a dramatic recounting of the event, see Samuel G. London, pp. 50–52. In 1971, Graybill interviewed 95-year old B. N. Simrall who told him the story had survived that the attack was because Edson and his helpers had given away provisions to get converts, causing few to be willing to work on Saturdays (Ronald D. Graybill, "They're Coming to Get You, Nate," *Insight*, Aug. 10, 1971, p. 6).

[34] "Lights and Shades in the Black Belt," p. 253.

[35] Edson White, "The Southern Work: Mob Violence" (Battle Creek, Michigan: June 9, 1899), excerpted in James R. Nix, *The Spirit of Sacrifice & Commitment: Experiences of Seventh-day Adventist Pioneers*, p. 177.

[36] Olvin endured much. He was falsely accused of murdering John Carter, an orphan boy that he and his wife took in (*1900 U.S. Census, Mississippi, Issaquena, Beat 01, District 0030*). The boy, who had been weakened and dizzy from dysentery, accidentally fell from a porch and fractured his skull on a washtub below. Ten-year-old Mary saw the boy fall and cried out, waking Olvin. The boy died that night. Edson defended Olvin in print and by legal representation ("False Accusation," *Gospel Herald*, Oct. 1900, pp. 89, 90). Olvin waited in jail until his bond was allowed and then stayed on the *Morning Star* until his trial in February ("Sick and in Prison," *Gospel Herald*, January 1901, p. 2). He changed his plea from "not guilty" to "guilty," knowing the jury was stacked against him. Olvin's wife Catharine died of tuberculosis while he served his sentence ("Obituaries: Olvin," *Review and Herald*, March 31, 1904, p. 23; Graybill, *Mission to Black America*, pp. 140, 141).

[37] See Graybill, *E. G. White and Church Race Relations*, p. 58; Benjamin J. Baker, *A Place Called Oakwood*, pp. 11–13.

[38] White, *The Southern Work*, pp. 83.

[39] Ellen G. White, Letter 90 (June 5), 1899, to A. F. Ballenger, in *The Southern Work*, pp. 84–86.

[40] White, *The Southern Work*, pp. 86, 87.

[41] Ellen G. White, Sermon, "Our Duty to the Colored People," March 20, 1891, emphasis added.

[42] James Edson White, Letter to Ellen G. White, May 14, 1899.

[43] James Edson White, Letter to Ellen G. White, Aug. 19, 1899.

[44] James Edson White, Letter to Ellen G. White, Aug. 24, 1899.

[45] Ellen G. White, Letter 165 (Oct. 22) 1899, to F. E. Belden, in *Manuscript Releases*, vol. 4, pp. 13, 14, emphasis added.

[46] James Edson White, Letter to M. A. Cornwell, Oct. 10, 1899, quoted in Graybill, pp. 64, 65.

[47] James Edson White, Letter to Ellen G. White, Nov. 20, 1899.

[48] James Edson White, Letter to N. W. Allee, Feb. 16, 1900.

[49] Graybill, p. 21.

[50] Ellen G. White, Letter 99 (Feb. 23), 1904.

[51] Ellen G. White, *Testimonies for the Church*, vol. 8 (1904), p. 240.

[52] Ellen G. White, Ms. 24, 1891, "The Work in the Southern Field."

[53] Ellen G. White, Letter 317 (Sept. 24), 1907.

[54] Ellen G. White, "Interview re Work Among the Colored People," Ms. 22a (Nov. 20), 1895, in *Spalding and Magan Collection*, p. 21, emphasis added. This counsel was in harmony with her prediction first published in 1884, "As the defenders of truth refuse to honor the Sunday-Sabbath, some of them will be thrust into prison, some will be exiled, some will be treated as slaves. To human wisdom, all this now seems impossible; but as the restraining Spirit of God shall be withdrawn from men, and they shall be under the control of Satan, who hates the divine precepts, there will be strange developments" (White, *The Spirit of Prophecy*, vol. 4, p. 425). Such slavery will not be based on race: "But many of all nations, and all classes, high and low, rich and poor, black and white, will be cast into the most unjust and cruel bondage" (White, *The Spirit of Prophecy*, vol. 4, p. 445).

[55] Ellen G. White, Letter 73 (Nov. 20), 1895, to Elder Tait, p. 2. The letter was published in its entirety in *The Southern Work*, pp. 72–79. See also the Ellen G. White Estate document "Comments on the Ellen G. White Statements Relative to the Revival of Slavery," available online at http://drc.whiteestate.org/files/6785.pdf, accessed 1/25/15).

[56] Ellen White wrote: "I realize that the first thing I ought to do is to prepare matter for the books that should be brought out; but there are other things that I must do. The attitude of some of my brethren in regard to the Southern field, and the reports that are being circulated—reports that I know to be untrue—make it necessary for me to take up this matter. I can no longer allow false impressions to be made, without saying what I know to be the truth. I shall publish in book form what I have

written in regard to the work in the Southern field. I shall no longer handle this matter with the tips of my fingers. Our people shall have in book form the facts of the history of the work in the South. When this book is out, I shall know that I have done my part to undeceive minds" (Ellen G. White, Letter 206, 1902, to W. C. White, December 13, 1902, quoted in Graybill, p. 93). The Ellen G. White Estate has an unpublished manuscript of just over one hundred pages entitled, "The Southern Work: A Historical Sketch of the Evangelical Work of the Seventh-day Adventists in the Southern States of America" (Roy E. Graham, *Ellen G. White, Co-Founder of the Seventh-day Adventist Church*, p. 268; Tim Poirier, e-mail to Kevin L. Morgan, April 13, 2015). Graybill wrote: "The book was never carried through to its final form. The work later prepared by Spalding ["Lights and Shades in the Black Belt"] was an attempt to fulfill Ellen White's desires in this line.... Ellen White's age and the press of other duties probably delayed its publication, and when she died the matter was not carried further. Nevertheless, her repeated testimonies to denominational leaders urging greater interest and activity in evangelism and education for Negroes were many during the period from 1891 until her death" (Graybill, p. 93). The articles in the *Youth's Instructor* of 1915 taken from introductory chapters for "Lights and Shades in the Black Belt" are not in the manuscript by the same name at the Ellen G. White Estate. Though the book was announced as nearing its publication, it never was published.

[57] Ellen G. White, Ms. 196 (April 29), 1907, Interview DF 151, p. 5. Ellen White added: "I am instructed to say to our people throughout the cities of the South, let everything be done under the direction of the Lord. The work is nearing its close. We are nearer the end than when we first believed. Satan is doing his best to block the way to the progress of the message. He is putting forth efforts to bring about the enactment of a Sunday law, which will result in *slavery* in the Southern field, and will close the door to the observance of the true Sabbath which God has given to men to keep holy" (White, Ms. 196, 1907, p. 8, emphasis added). In the A. O. Tait letter, she counseled: "If the colored people are in any way educated to work on Sunday, there will be unsparing, *merciless oppression* brought upon them" (*The Southern Work*, p. 74). Popular regard for Sunday did bring Seventh-day Adventists under increased scrutiny at this time. W. C. White and other Seventh-day Adventists were arrested for minor activities on Sunday at Pacific Press in Oakland, California (Julius Nam, "Adventists in American Courts—The Sunday Law Cases," *Spectrum Forum*, January 11, 2013).

[58] White, Ms. 196, 1907, p. 5.
[59] White, Ms. 196, 1907.
[60] Ellen G. White, *Testimonies for the Church*, vol. 9, p. 206.
[61] Delbert Baker, "A Statement on Ellen G. White's Use of the Term 'Race War' and Other Related Insights," p. 36.
[62] Walter F. White, "The Eruption of Tulsa," *Nation*, vol. 112, no. 292 (June 29, 1921), pp. 909, 910.
[63] Aptheker, *A Documentary History of the Negro People in the United States, 1910-1932*, p. 331, in White, p. 910.
[64] Walter F. White, p. 909.
[65] Ellen G. White, Ms. 15 (April 26), 1909, "Words of Encouragement to Self-Supporting Workers."
[66] "An Agitation and an Opportunity," p. 7.
[67] "An Agitation and an Opportunity," pp. 8, 9.
[68] White, *The Southern Work*, p. 9.
[69] White, *The Southern Work*, p. 12.
[70] White, *The Southern Work*, p. 14.
[71] White, *The Southern Work*, p. 15.
[72] White, *The Southern Work*, p. 19.
[73] White, *The Southern Work*, p. 20.
[74] White, *The Southern Work*, p. 55.
[75] White, *Testimonies for the Church*, vol. 9, p. 206.
[76] White, *Testimonies for the Church*, vol. 9, p. 214.
[77] Graybill, p. 15.
[78] "A Word to the Colored People. Danger in Following the Seventh-day Adventists," *Yazoo City Herald*, June 1, 1900, quoted in *Gospel Herald*, Oct. 1900, p. 89, in Graybill, p. 72.
[79] Ellen G. White, Letter 36, 1912, in *Selected Messages*, bk. 2, p. 344, emphasis added.
[80] Ellen G. White, Ms. 7 (Feb. 3), 1896, in *Selected Messages*, bk. 2, p. 343.
[81] Mrs. E. G. White, "No Caste in Christ," *Review and Herald*, Dec. 22, 1891, p. 785.
[82] Ellen G. White, Letter 113 (Aug. 13), 1901, pg. 2.
[83] Ellen G. White, Ms. 60 (June 21), 1904, par. 14, in *Manuscript Releases*, vol. 4, p. 24; vol. 6, p. 210.
[84] *Yazoo City Herald*, June 1, 1900, quoted in *Gospel Herald*, Oct. 1900, p. 88. Scripture and history do not validate their claim about the Sunday-Sabbath beginning the morning of the Resurrection.
[85] White, *The Southern Work*, p. 73. This presentation was at the Oakwood Industrial School.
[86] Ellen G. White, Ms. 118 (Aug. 21, copied), 1899, in Graybill, pp. 75, 76.

[87] Graybill, pp. 76, 77, citing "Seventh-day Adventists," *Yazoo Sentinel*, June 7, 1900, quoted in "The Southern Field Closing to the Message," *Gospel Herald*, Oct. 1900, p. 86.

[88] Graybill, pp. 79, 80. There are subtle clues in the photographs chronicling their efforts that validate Roger's statement. White leaders are at the center of the picture while black workers and students are off to the side.

[89] Graybill, p. 85.

[90] Greene, p. 39.

[91] Graybill, pp. 87, 88.

[92] Ellen G. White, Letter 304 (Oct. 19), 1908, in *Manuscript Releases*, vol. 4, p. 32.

[93] White, *Testimonies for the Church*, vol. 9, p. 206.

[94] Ellen G. White, Ms. 114 (Sept. 17), 1904, in Baker, *A Place Called Oakwood*, pp. 125, 126, emphasis added.

[95] Ellen G. White, "Trust in God," *Gospel Herald*, March 1901, p. 22.

[96] Ellen G. White, Letter 304 (Oct. 19), 1903.

[97] Ellen G. White, Letter 90 (June 5), 1899, in *The Southern Work*, pp. 84–86.

[98] Earlier she wrote: "There are among the negro race those who have *superior natural intelligence*, and who, if converted to Christ, could do a good work for their own people. Many should be given the opportunity of learning trades. And others are to be trained to labor as evangelists, Bible workers, teachers, nurses, hygienic cooks, and colporteurs. Many can be taught to be home missionaries" ("The Collection for the Colored Work," *Review and Herald*, Sept. 28, 1905, emphasis added).

[99] Ellen G. White, "Among the Colored People," *Testimonies for the Church*, vol. 9, p. 202, emphasis added.

[100] Ellen G. White, Letter 84 (July 16), 1901, in *Manuscript Releases*, vol. 4, p. 18.

[101] White, *Testimonies for the Church*, vol. 9, p. 223, emphasis added.

[102] See Benjamin J. Baker, "Who's That Adventist Woman Beside Martin Luther King Jr.?" for an interesting connection between King's speech and Seventh-day Adventist Yolanda Clarke.

[103] Graybill, p. 52.

[104] White, *Testimonies for the Church*, vol. 9, pp. 206, 207, emphasis added.

[105] Changing mindsets requires educating both the minority group and enlightening the majority group. To his credit, the Moody Bible president Paul Nyquist issued the following statement after the vandalization of notices for a meeting, led by a white student, on "white privilege": "People who are white, such as myself, because we are of the majority culture, often fail to understand the privileges we enjoy due to our skin color, for it is all we have ever known. Therefore, the conversation hosted on our campus last week is part of an ongoing effort to bring greater campus-wide understanding to the issue and I applaud and affirm its purpose" ("The Church Is Not Post-Racial," available online at http://www.relevantmagazine.com/reject-apathy/worldview/church-not-post-racial, accessed 4/27/15).

[106] The concept for this exhibit came from reading Ron Graybill, *E. G. White and Race Relations*, and G. Tom Carter, *The 19th Century Odyssey of John and Judith*, Appendix C.

CHAPTER 9 - Education, the Road to Post-Racialism

[1] White, *Testimonies for the Church*, vol. 9, p. 204.

[2] Matthew 28:19, 20.

[3] Both the manuscript and the introductory chapters in the *Youth's Instructor* are available online (see bibliography). Spalding devoted much of the first part of the manuscript for "Lights and Shades in the Black Belt" to the educational and philanthropic work of other denominations.

[4] Hansen, p. 251.

[5] Facts on Anna Knight are from Hansen, p. 251. For more on the Hillcrest School, see "Lights and Shades in the Black Belt," pp. 309–314, 317, 320, 325, 326, 330; Schwarz, p. 248. Facts on Daniel T. Shireman are from Hansen, pp. 145, 146. Other schools besides Hildebran that were started upon Ellen White's urgings were Eufola, in 1908, Fletcher in 1909, Glen Alpine and Cowee Mountains in 1910, and Pisgah in 1914 (Elkins, p. 121).

[6] "At Hickory, N.C.," *Gospel Herald*, June 1900, p. 46; "Explanations of Financial Report. Field Expense and Aid," *Gospel Herald*, June 1900, p. 52. Bryant ended up leaving for more education and graduated in 1907 as the first black student with a law degree from Colorado University (Colorado University, *General catalogue of the officers and graduates of the University of Colorado, 1877-1910*, p. 127). Bryant's book, *Black Smiles*, was first published in 1903 and became a nostalgic reminder of daily life under slavery. Edson White purchased the book from the copyright holder (Peter J. Rennings) and published it for the Southern Missionary Society in 1909 (Letter, Edson White to W. C. White, March 7, 1909, p. 6).

⁷ "A Madison-type school for colored people started in 1908 on a farm on Whites Creek Pike about five miles from Nashville, made possible by the generosity of Mrs. Nellie H. Druillard, whose missionary service in Africa had given her a sympathetic interest in the colored race" (Hansen, p. 174).

⁸ Brian E. Strayer, *Where the Pine Trees Softly Whisper: the History of Union Springs Academy*, chapter 1.

⁹ White, *Testimonies for the Church*, vol. 9, pp. 204, 205. Ellen White contended with "apologists of slavery" (J. H. Waggoner, "Modern Spiritualism," *Signs of the Times*, Sept. 4, 1879, p. 267) as late as 1880 (see Letter 36 [July], 1880).

¹⁰ Ellen G. White, Letter 313 (Nov. 2), 1904; Ms. 123, 1908, par. 27; "The Oakwood Manual Training School" [SpTB12] (1908), p. 11.

¹¹ Details of early agriculture and class work are in "Lights and Shades in the Black Belt," pp. 229–244.

¹² Lee with Baker, *C. D. Brooks: The Man Behind the Message*, pp. 44, 45. For more on the Oakwood Industrial School, see "Sixty-five Oak Trees," in Benjamin Baker, *Crucial Moments*, pp. 85–95. There are other books on the development and influence of Oakwood, such as *A Place Called Oakwood: Inspired Counsel. A Comprehensive Compilation of Ellen G. White Statements on the Oakwood Educational Institution*, Benjamin J. Baker, compiler; and *Telling the Story* (articles on the development of the Seventh-day Adventist work in black America by Louis B. Reynolds, Arthur W. Spalding, Malcom Bull and Keith Lockhart, Roy Branson, Roy E. Graham, Harold D. Singleton, James Edson White, Fred R. Rogers, and George I. Butler), Delbert Baker, compiler; and Mervyn A. Warren, *Oakwood! A Vision Splendid*; *Adventist Heritage*, special Oakwood edition, March 1996.

¹³ Ellen G. White, Ms. 60 (June 21), 1904, talk at Oakwood Industrial School, in Manuscript Releases, vol. 6, p. 215.

¹⁴ Summaries of Anna Knight's life can be found in Josephine Benton, "Innovative Administrator: Anna Knight: 1874 to 1972," *Called by God*, pp. 61–73; and in Anna Knight, *Mississippi Girl: An Autobiography*.

¹⁵ See Roy E. Malcolm, *The Aeolians: Directors Recall Precious Memories* (1999).

¹⁶ Louis B. Reynolds provided biographical information about these and others in *We Have Tomorrow*.

CHAPTER 10 - Calcified Pragmatism

¹ Malcolm Little, *The Autobiography of Malcolm X* (1965), p. 17.

² Eric Walsh, "Who Stopped the Movement?" Feb. 28, 2009, 7:22. Walsh is the former director of public health and health officer for the city of Pasadena, California, and the associate pastor at the Altadena Seventh-day Adventist Church. Douglas Morgan quoted Arna Bontemps, who was raised in the Seventh-day Adventist Church and taught in its schools for nearly fifteen years in the 1920s and 1930s, as saying in 1950: "In race relations Adventists are retarded ... In their early years, Adventists were solid on the race question," however, their present backward condition was the result of "compromise to appease the South" (Douglas Morgan, "The Significance of a Solid Start: Adventism and Race Relations, 1880-1920," presented at the Seventh Triennial Association of Seventh-day Adventist Historians Conference, March 22, 2013, p. 1).

³ See Kessia Reyne Bennett's insightful dissertation showing how the liberation of the slaves disrupted Southern society, which had been built upon the maintenance of a stable but "unspeakably inhumane" system of "White enfranchisement and Black disenfranchisement" (Bennett, pp. 7, 8). Bennett also summarized the stages of Adventist relation to racist beliefs: "Early Adventist missionaries first resisted the racist beliefs and practices of the South. Then, pressured by custom and escalating violence, they began to accommodate the racism by racially segregating, yet continuing to resist the oppression of Blacks. Over time, however, the segregation which began as accommodation was normalized and institutionalized. In effect, it became part of the Adventist culture in America" (Bennett, p. 4).

⁴ "The first Black person to work at the General Conference was the director of the Negro Department. Neither he nor Black visitors to the General Conference were permitted to eat in the Review and Herald cafeteria (the eating place for the General Conference workers at the time). Segregation was the norm for the first half of the 1900s" (Delbert Baker, "Regional Conferences: 50 Years of Progress," *Adventist Review*, Nov. 2, 1995, p. 12). William H. Green was that first African-American secretary of the Negro Department. He held the position from 1918 until his sudden death from extreme fatigue October 31, 1928 (Charles E. Dudley, Sr., *Thou Who Hast Brought Us*, book 3, vol. 3, p. 116; Carrie L. Stringer, "Death of Elder W. H. Green," *Field Tidings*, Jan. 2, 1929, p. 5).

⁵ Greene, p. 62.

⁶ Alven Makapela argued that "white Seventh-day Adventist leaders were unwilling, even at this early stage, to eradicate racism from their organization" (*The Problem with Africanity in the Seventh Day Adventist Church*, p. 220, quoted in Jonathan Grant, pp. 23, 24).

⁷ Lewis Harrison Christian, *The Fruitage of Spiritual Gifts: The Influence and Guidance of Ellen G. White in the Advent Movement*, p. 183; Sepúlveda, p. 129.

⁸ Christian, p. 182.

⁹ Ellen G. White, Ms. 94 (Sept. 1), 1905, from Loma Linda, in *Testimonies for the Church*, vol. 9, p. 195.

[10] *The Southern Work*, pp. 9–12, rephrased by Benjamin Baker, "The Woman Who Wouldn't Be Quiet," *Adventist Review*, Feb. 21, 2002, p. 28.

[11] Malcolm Bull and Keith Lockhart, *Seeking A Sanctuary: Seventh-day Adventism and the American Dream*, pp. 202, 203.

[12] "Lewis Sheafe (1859–1938) was born just before the Civil War and died just before World War II" (Douglas Morgan, *Lewis C. Sheafe: Apostle to Black America*, p. 18).

[13] Ellen G. White, Ms. 45 (May 14), 1904.

[14] Morgan, *Lewis C. Sheafe*, p. 12.

[15] Charles E. Bradford, "Black Seventh-day Adventists and Church Loyalty," in *Perspectives: Black Seventh-day Adventists Face the Twenty-first Century*, Calvin Rock, editor, p. 16, quoted in "Free Seventh-day Adventists: A Brief Historical Sketch," available online at http://freesda.weebly.com/our-history.html, accessed 4/1/15. The photo in this book is from Manns' passport (which states that he had blue eyes). The photo in *Thou Who Hast Brought Us*, book 3, vol. 3, p. 39, is not Manns.

[16] Jonathan Grant, p. 63; Delbert, Susan, and Benjamin Baker, editors, *People of Providence: Selected Quotations on Black People from the Writings of Ellen G. White* (2010), p. 309.

[17] Greene, p. 386.

[18] R. Clifford Jones, p. 15.

[19] R. Clifford Jones, p. 182.

[20] Holly Fisher, "Oakwood College Students' Quest for Social Justice Before and During the Civil Rights Era," *Journal of African American History*, Spring 2003, p. 110, cited by Jonathan Grant, p. 29.

[21] Walter W. Fordham, *Righteous Rebel: An Autobiography*, p. 26. Lee and Baker point out that it was Walter Fordham, the father of C. D. Brook's wife Walterene, who led the "student strike" in 1931 (Lee with Baker, p. 136).

[22] A much more nuanced account of the student strike can be found in Jacob Justiss, *Angels in Ebony*, pp. 74–79.

[23] See Baker, *Crucial Moments*, pp. 118–125.

[24] Bert Haloviak, "Impact of SDA Eschatological Assumptions on Certain Issues of Social Policy," p. 13.

[25] *1930 United States Federal Census, New York, Queens, Queens (Districts 251-500), District 336* and *1940 United States Federal Census, New York, Queens, New York, 41-1216*. They were married on Sept. 23, 1928, according to the New York Marriage Index.

[26] See Schwarz, p. 143; Greene, p. 103; and Reynolds, pp. 300–302; "Obituary Notices: Byard," *Atlantic Union Gleaner*, Dec. 17, 1943, p. 6.

[27] Hattie W. Brown, "Brooklyn Social Notes: Brooklyn Deaths," *New York Age*, Dec. 4, 1943, p. 8.

[28] Mrs. Ruth Chambers to J. L. McElhany, Jan. 21, 1944, in Haloviak, p. 14.

[29] Haloviak, p. 15. Details on the formation of the regional conferences are in Justiss, *Angels in Ebony*, pp. 43–51.

[30] Nelson to Hare, April 9, 1944, in Haloviak, p. 16. A group of laymen formed on October 16, 1964 as the National Association for the Advancement of Worldwide Work Among Colored Seventh-day Adventists and met on October 31, 1943 with the president of the General Conference, J. L. McElhany. "In response, the General Conference president voted to call in all of the Black Departmental men and pastors of the leading Black churches from all over America in order to discuss the race problem at a special meeting during Spring Council, April 8–19, 1944. The agenda called for the integration of White conferences. But during the meeting, the idea of Black conferences evolved as a new type of organization for the Black worker" (Koranteng-Pipim, "Separate Black And White Conferences—Part 1: The Sin We Don't Want To Overcome," p. 3).

[31] William L. Cheatham to J. L. McElhany, Nov. 26, 1944, in Haloviak, p. 16.

[32] Hansen, p. 206.

[33] Baker, *Crucial Moments*, p. 135.

[34] Hansen, pp. 206, 207.

[35] Delbert W. Baker, "Regional Conferences: 50 Years of Progress," *Adventist Review*, Nov. 2, 1995, p. 14.

[36] Greene, pp. 107, 108.

[37] W. H. Branson, Letter, April 13, 1954, in Haloviak, pp. 17, 18, referring to Ellen White's 1891 and 1896 statements.

[38] Haloviak, p. 18.

[39] Jonathan Grant, p. 3.

[40] Jonathan Grant, p. 120.

[41] Samuel G. London, Jr., "The Sociopolitical Activism of Warren S. Banfield," pp. 1–3.

[42] Samuel G. London, Jr., *Seventh-day Adventists and the Civil Rights Movement*, pp. 105, 109.

[43] Stephen T. Porter, "The Mighty Walk," *Liberty*, May/June 2013.

[44] Mervyn A. Warren described the speech that he delivered at Oakwood, for its similar elements, as practice for his "I have a dream" speech (Warren, "Oakwood? Oh, Yes . . .," *Southern Tidings*, February 2016, p. 9). The text of his speech is included as an appendix in Warren's book, *King Came Preaching* (2001), pp. 170–181.

⁴⁵ "ANN Perspective: Rosa Parks, Civil Rights Pioneer, Touched Adventist Lives in Her City," *Adventist News Network*, available online at http://news.adventist.org/all-news/news/go/2005-10-31/ann-perspective-rosa-parks-civil-rights-pioneer-touched-adventist-lives-in-her-city, accessed 2/5/15. See Cleveland's autobiography for more.

⁴⁶ A catalyst for this invitation was Burrell and Bonnie Scott's 13-year-old daughter's denial of admission by Mt. Vernon Academy ("Mount Vernon Academy Center of Race Issue," *Lancaster Eagle-Gazette* [Lancaster, Ohio)] July 31, 1962, p. 8).

⁴⁷ Lee with Baker, p. 120.

⁴⁸ Samuel G. London, Jr., *Seventh-day Adventists and the Civil Rights Movement*, p. 124.

⁴⁹ Lee with Baker, p. 136. The Negro family at the party was C. D. Brooks and his family.

⁵⁰ "An Expression of Sorrow and Apology," *Adventist Review*, December 1999, North American Division edition, p. 12.

⁵¹ Lee with Baker, p. 133.

⁵² Lee with Baker, p. 129.

⁵³ Lee with Baker, p. 133.

⁵⁴ Lee with Baker, p. 135.

⁵⁵ "Five Most Influential SDAs—1969–1994," *Spectrum*, Dec. 1994, p. 10.

⁵⁶ See George Vecsey, "7th Day Adventists Elect Black Chief," *New York Times*, Jan. 12, 1979, p. A20, and Marjorie Hyer Washington, "Seventh-Day Adventists Elect a Black President," *Washington Post*, Jan. 13, 1979, p. A8.

⁵⁷ Charles E. Bradford, "MORNING STAR riverboat," available online at http://www.modelshipmaster.com/products/riverboats/Morning-Star-riverboat.htm, accessed 12/13/15.

⁵⁸ Neal C. Wilson, June 27, 1985, in Haloviak, p. 18.

⁵⁹ Lee with Baker, p. 153.

⁶⁰ Stephen Richardson, Ministerial Director of the Allegheny East Conference of Seventh-day Adventists, described this as "Black Flight," and Henry J. Fordham, III, President of the Allegheny East Conference, expressed concern that young African Americans are losing an understanding of their Adventist African-American history and are abandoning African-American solidarity and African-American causes ("Are We Still Relevant? Town Hall Meeting," sponsored by the Allegheny East Conference of Seventh-day Adventists, Feb. 28, 2015, available online at https://www.youtube.com/watch?v=Rm64ppLIvGs, accessed 2/28/2015). Upwardly mobile young African Americans are not returning to the inner city. Even students at Oakwood University, who were interviewed, were unaware of the history of Lucy Byard and the formation of regional conferences. Post racialism is a double-edged sword. Forgetting the pains of the past enables racism to be forgotten, yet it also erases a certain sense of identity and motivation that results from what the president of the Allegheny East Conference, Henry J. Fordham, III, described as "the struggle."

⁶¹ Jared Wright and Alisa Williams, "Dwight Nelson's MLK-Weekend Sermon Spurs Petition to Eradicate Ethnic Conferences," available online at http://spectrummagazine.org/article/2015/01/22/dwight-nelsons-mlk-weekend-sermon-spurs-petition-eradicate-ethnic-conferences, accessed 1/27/15.

⁶² "Are We Still Relevant? Town Hall Meeting," Feb. 28, 2015. The North American Division Administration voted on March 25, 2015 an affirmation of Regional Conferences, which said, in part: "We vote, to affirm that the historical establishment and current role and function of Regional Conferences are structurally essential, mission effective, and relevant in reaching the diverse populations and urban centers within our division" ("Affirmation of the Mission Role of North American Division Regional Conferences," available online at http://www.nadadventist.org/article/1073742907/news/archived-news-stories/2015-news-archives/3-25-15-affirmation-of-the-mission-role-of-north-american-division-regional-conferences, accessed 3/27/15).

⁶³ White, *Testimonies for the Church*, vol. 9, p. 207.

⁶⁴ Ricardo B. Graham, "Black Seventh-day Adventists and Racial Reconciliation," *Perspectives: Black Seventh-Day Adventists Face the Twenty-first Century*, pp. 132, 137.

⁶⁵ Wilhelmina Johnson, interview with Kevin L. Morgan, Aug. 27, 2014.

⁶⁶ Martha Marsh, interview with Kevin L. Morgan, Sept. 9, 2014.

⁶⁷ When I went to Ethiopia to conduct evangelistic meetings in 2007, church workers there insisted on carrying everything for me wherever we went. This made me feel a bit uncomfortable, so I spoke to a group of them through my interpreter Maphesa (whom I gratefully called "my voice"), asking if they knew that we used to have slavery in the United States and that we finally put an end to it. They said that they did. I then said, "Now blacks and whites have racial equality in my country. If Maphesa can carry a chair to put on the platform, I can too."

⁶⁸ When asked what that next step is, I have answered that it is to see the death of all divisions based on prejudice.

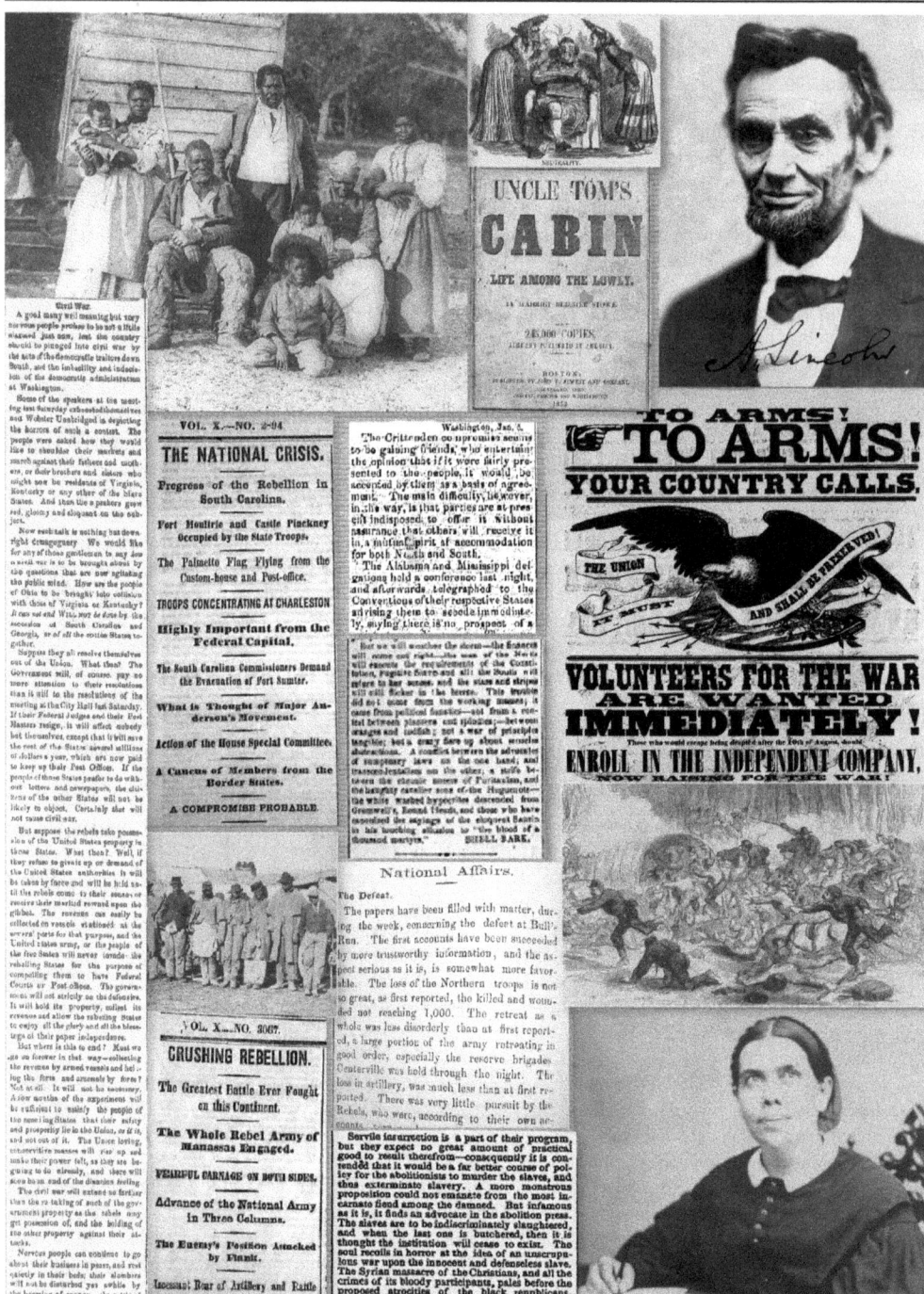
Photographs and newspaper clippings about slavery and the beginning of the American Civil War

Bibliographical Index

1850 United States Federal Census, Illinois, LaSalle, Ottawa. Available online at http://interactive.ancestry.com/8054/4193364-00062/19197419, accessed 12/31/15. **148**

1850 United States Federal Census, Kentucky, Greenup, District 1. Available online at http://interactive.ancestry.com/8054/4192492_00455/17167611, accessed 2/15/15. **167**

1860 United States Federal Census, Iowa, Washington, Lime Creek, p. 7. Available online at http://interactive.ancestry.com/7667/4230556_00007/5800351, accessed 2/15/15. **167**

1860 United States Federal Census, Michigan, St Joseph, Flowerfield. Available online at http://interactive.ancestry.com/7667/4232714_00514/45347337, accessed 2/8/15. **148**

1860 United States Federal Census, Minnesota, Benton, Princeton. Available online at http://interactive.ancestry.com/7667/4232720_00087/45453283, accessed 2/10/15. **166**

1870 United States Federal Census, Iowa, Black Hawk, Big Creek. Available online at http://interactive.ancestry.com/7163/4263523_00045/21159500, accessed 4/17/15. **159**

1870 United States Federal Census, Iowa, Marion Township. Available online at http://interactive.ancestry.com/7163/4263636_00585/35545330. **159**

1870 United States Federal Census, Tennessee, Davidson, District 20. Available online at http://interactive.ancestry.com/7163/4276591_00224/4477755, accessed 2/10/15. **167**

1880 United States Federal Census, Georgia, Houston, Lower 5th, 030. Available online at http://interactive.ancestry.com/6742/4240146-00692/8710259, accessed 2/10/15. **172**

1880 United States Federal Census, Wisconsin, Green Lake, Mackford, 068. Available online at http://interactive.ancestry.com/6742/4244751-00672/46145515, accessed 2/10/15. **167**

1880 United States Federal Census, Wisconsin, Pepin, Arkansaw, 108. Available online at http://interactive.ancestry.com/6742/4244769-00512/28898647, accessed 2/10/15. **173**

1900 United States Federal Census, Kentucky, Bullitt, Shepersville, District 0014. Available online at http://interactive.ancestry.com/7602/004118899_00036/37742842, accessed 2/12/15. **168**

1900 United States Federal Census, Mississippi, Issaquena, Beat 01, District 0030. Available online at http://interactive.ancestry.com/7602/004119874_00466/27835619, accessed 4/23/15. **178**

1930 United States Federal Census, New York, Queens, Queens (Districts 251-500), District 336. Available online at http://interactive.ancestry.com/6224/4639147_00869/45034979, accessed 2/24/15. **182**

1940 United States Federal Census, New York, Queens, New York, 41-1216. Available online at http://interactive.ancestry.com/2442/m-t0627-02743-00759/12059520, accessed 2/24/15. **182**

Aamodt, Terrie Dopp; Eric Anderson; Gary Land; Ronald L. Numbers. *Ellen Harmon White: American Prophet.* Oxford; New York: Oxford University Press, 2014. **144, 146, 151, 155, 158**

A. B. "Peaceful Disunion." *New-York Tribune,* Jan. 11, 1861, p. 6. Available online at http://www.newspapers.com/image/85338427, accessed 2/25/15. **145**

"A Bill to Prevent All Persons from Teaching Slaves to Read or Write, the Use of Figures Excepted (1830)." Available online at http://www.learnnc.org/lp/editions/nchist-newnation/4384, accessed 1/5/15. **142**

"The Adventists. First Day of Their Annual Conference." *San Francisco Chronicle,* Nov. 14, 1887, p. 3. **174**

"Affirmation of the Mission Role of North American Division Regional Conferences." Available online at http://www.nadadventist.org/article/1073742907/news/archived-news-stories/2015-news-archives/3-25-15-affirmation-of-the-mission-role-of-north-american-division-regional-conferences, accessed 3/27/15. **183**

"A Growing Danger." *Review and Herald,* Dec. 6, 1877, p. 180. **176**

"A Jubilee at Charleston." *Review and Herald,* April 25, 1865, pp. 166, 167. **156**

Alger, Linda Andrews. "The Lane-Godsmark Family, a term paper presented in partial fulfillment for the course Denominational History (Hi 300)." Available online at http://www.andrews.edu/library/car/cardigital/digitized/documents/b12208693.pdf, accessed 2/10/15. **172**

Allegheny East Conference. "Are We Still Relevant? Town Hall Meeting." Feb. 28, 2015. Available online at https://www.youtube.com/watch?v=Rm64ppLIvGs, accessed 2/28/2015. **183**

"Amalgamation." Available online at http://www.merriam-webster.com/thesaurus/amalgamation, accessed 6/11/14. **157**

"American Civil War and SDA Church." Available online at http://www.blacksdahistory.org/files/43902760.pdf, accessed 2/3/15. **144**

American Missionary. "Mississippi: Assault Upon Rev. J. P. Bradwell. Murder of Liet. Blanding." *Review and Herald,* Aug. 14, 1866, p. 83. **165**

———. "Outrages on the Freedmen." *Review and Herald,* March 19, 1867, pp. 176, 177. **166**

"An Agitation and an Opportunity." Mountain View, CA: Pacific Press Publishing Assoc., 1907. Available online at http://library.ellenwhite.org/content/file/agitation-and-opportunity-df-3#document, accessed 4/26/15. **179**

Anderson, Dirk. "Amalgamation: A Denominational Embarrassment." Available online at http://nonsda.org/egw/critica.shtml, accessed 9/14/14. **163**

———. "Ellen White Supremacist." Available online at http://www.nonsda.org/egw/egw62.shtml, accessed 1/10/15. **157**

Anderson, Eric. "War, Slavery, and Race." *Ellen Harmon White: American Prophet.* Oxford; New York: Oxford University Press, 2014, pp. 262–278. **144, 146, 151, 155, 158**

"Andrew Jackson." Available online at https://www.whitehouse.gov/1600/presidents/andrewjackson, accessed 4/13/15. **152**

Andrews, John Nevins. "Three Angels of Rev. XIV." *Review and Herald,* April 3, 1855, pp. 202, 203. **141**

"A New Series of Articles—A New Book." *The Youth's Instructor,* April 6, 1915, p. 16. **168**

"ANN Perspective: Rosa Parks, Civil Rights Pioneer, Touched Adventist Lives in Her City." *Adventist News Network.* Available online at http://news.adventist.org/all-news/news/go/2005-10-31/ann-perspective-rosa-parks-civil-rights-pioneer-touched-adventist-lives-in-her-city, accessed 1/8/15. **183**

"Appointments." *Review and Herald,* Dec. 29, 1859, p. 48; Jan. 5, 1860, p. 56; Jan. 1, 1861, p. 56; July 22, 1862, p. 64. **146**

Aptheker, Herbert. *A Documentary History of the Negro People in the United States, 1910-1932*. Secaucus, NJ: Citadel Press, 1973. **179**

Arlington Journal [Arlington, Texas], July 30, 1903. Available online at https://www.arlingtonlibrary.org/files/journal1903.pdf, accessed 12/17/15. **168**

Armistead, W. S. *The Negro is a Man*. Trenton, GA: Armistead and Vickers, 1903. **158**

Aspinwall, William H. Letter to the editor of the *New York Times*, Oct. 14, 1868, in *The Nation*, Oct. 14, 1875, p. 245. Available online at http://books.google.com/books?id=i_0xAQAAIAAJ&pg=PA245, accessed 4/17/12. **153**

"A Word to the Colored People. Danger in Following the Seventh-day Adventists." *Yazoo City Herald*, June 1, 1900, quoted in *The Gospel Herald*, Oct. 1900, p. 88. **179**

Baker, Benjamin J. "A Look in the Mirror: Ellen White, Blacks, and the Adventist Church." Adventism and Adventist History: Sesquicentennial Reflections. January 6, 2014. **173, 174**

———. *A Place Called Oakwood: Inspired Counsel. A Comprehensive Compilation of Ellen G. White Statements on the Oakwood Educational Institution*. Huntsville, AL: Oakwood College Press, 2007. Available online at http://www.blacksdahistory.org/files/39518148.pdf, accessed 4/16/15. **178, 180, 181**

———. "Black Seventh-day Adventist Timeline." Available online at http://www.blacksdahistory.org/timelines.html, accessed 5/13/15. **142**

———. *Crucial Moments: Twelve Defining Events in Black Adventist History*. Hagerstown, MD: Review and Herald Publishing Assoc., 2005. **176, 181, 182**

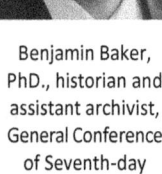

Benjamin Baker, PhD., historian and assistant archivist, General Conference of Seventh-day Adventists

———. "Ellen White, 1888, and Black People." available online at http://archives.adventistreview.org/article/6713/archives/issue-2013-1528/ellen-white-1888-and-black-people, accessed 11/30/15. **175**

———. " 'I Do Not Mean to Live a Coward or Die a Coward' An Examination of Ellen G. White's Lifelong Relationship to Black People" (2011). Doctoral dissertation. Howard University, Washington, DC. **3**

———. *People of Providence: Selected Quotations on Black People from the Writings of Ellen G. White*. Huntsville, AL: Oakwood University Publishing Office, 2010. **182**

———. "The Woman Who Wouldn't Be Quiet." *Adventist Review*, Feb. 21, 2002, pp. 26–28. **182**

———. "Who's That Adventist Woman Beside Martin Luther King Jr.?" Available online at http://www.adventistreview.org/church-news/story2267-whos-that-adventist-woman-beside-martin-luther-king-jr, accessed 4/16/15. **180**

Baker, Delbert W. "A Statement on Ellen G. White's Use of the Term 'Race War' and Other Related Insights." Takoma Park, MD: Ellen G. White Estate, 1984. Available online at http://drc.whiteestate.org/read.php?id=36792, accessed 1/10/15. **175, 177, 179**

———. "In Search of Adventist African-American Roots: Exploring the History of Adventist African-Americans in the United States." *Adventist Review*, Feb. 4, 1993, p. 13. **174**

———. "Regional Conferences: 50 Years of Progress." *Adventist Review*, Nov. 2, 1995, pp. 11–15. **181, 182**

———. *Telling the Story: An Anthology on the Development of the Black SDA Work: A Collection of Historical Documents, Articles, and Visuals on Selected Topics Relevant to the Black SDA Work*. Loma Linda, CA: Loma Linda University Printing Services, 1996. Available online at http://documents.adventistarchives.org/Books/EthnAdv1996.pdf, accessed 1/8/15. **173, 174, 181**

Delbert Baker, PhD., vice chancellor Adventist University of Africa, Kenya

"Baptists and the American Civil War: July 24, 1861." Available online at http://www.civilwarbaptists.com/thisdayinhistory/1861-july-24, accessed 4/25/12. **152**

Barnes, Albert. *The Church and Slavery*, 2nd ed. Philadelphia: Parry & McMillan, 1857. **139**

Barney, William L. *Secessionist Impulse: Alabama and Mississippi in 1860*. Princeton, NJ: Princeton University Press, 1974; repr., Tuscaloosa, 2004. **151**

Barrett, Edwin S. *What I Saw at Bull Run*. Boston: Beacon Press, Thomas Todd, Printer, 1886. **150**

Bates, Joseph. *The Autobiography of Elder Joseph Bates*. Battle Creek, MI: Press of the Seventh-day Adventist Publishing Assoc., 1868. **142**

"The Battle at Bull's Run." *Harper's Weekly*, Aug. 3, 1861, pp. 491, 492. **150**

Beatty, John, and Harrison Carroll Hobart. *The Citizen-Soldier: The Memoirs of a Civil War Volunteer*. Cincinnati: Wilstach, Baldwin & Co., 1879. **152**

"The Benevolent Empire." Available online at http://www.christianchronicler.com/history1/benevolent_empire.html, accessed 4/25/12. **139**

Bennett, John D. *The London Confederates*. Jefferson, NC: McFarland & Co., Inc., Publishers, 2008. **153, 156**

Bennett, Kessia Reyne. "Resistance and Accommodation to Racism Among Early Seventh-day Adventist Missionaries in the American South: A Case Study in Relating to Cultural Oppression in Missions." April 2011. Master's dissertation. Andrews University, Berrien Springs, MI. Available online at http://digitalcommons.andrews.edu/theses/29, accessed 11/19/15. **165, 173, 181**

Benton, Josephine. *Called by God: Stories of Seventh-day Adventist Women Ministers*. Lincoln, NE: AdventSource, 2002. Available online at https://drive.google.com/file/d/0Bxa-xjkVWScYWHpTN2lfMGxLOE0/view, accessed 1/12/16. **181**

Berkshire County Eagle (Pittsfield, MA), Aug. 28, 1862, p. 3. **138**

Bettersworth, John K. *Confederate Mississippi: The People and Policies of a Cotton State in Wartime*. Baton Rouge: Louisiana State University Press, 1943. **151**

Birkner, John W., and Michael J. Quest, editors. *James Buchanan and the Coming of the Civil War*. Tallahassee, FL: University Press of Florida, 2013. **151**

Blackford, William Willis. *War Years with Jeb Stuart*. New York: Charles Scribner's Sons, 1945. **150**

"Books Sent By Mail." *Review and Herald*, July 14, 1868, p. 64. **167**

"Books Sent by Mail." *Review and Herald*, May 26, 1868, p. 368. **167**

Bond, Horace Mann. *Negro Education in Alabama: A Study in Cotton and Steel*. Tuscaloosa, AL: The University of Alabama Press, 1994. **166**

Boston Daily Advertiser, Jan. 25, 1861, p. 2. **152**

Bourdeau, Daniel T. "Progress of the Cause: Kentucky." *Review and Herald*, Jan. 23, 1872, p. 46. **169**

———. "Progress of the Cause: Kentucky." *Review and Herald*, May 28, 1872, p. 191. **169**

———. "Progress of the Cause: Locust Grove, Kentucky." *Review and Herald*, Feb. 20, 1872, p. 78. **169**

Boykin, Samuel. "The Late Victory at Manassas." *Christian Index*, July 31, 1861. Available online at http://www.civilwarbaptists.com/thisdayinhistory/1861-july-31, accessed 4/25/12. **151**

Bradford, Charles E. "Black Seventh-day Adventists and Church Loyalty." *Perspectives: Black Seventh-day Adventists Face the Twenty-first Century*. Calvin B. Rock, ed. Hagerstown, MD: Review and Herald Publishing Assoc., 1996, pp. 11–19. **182**

———. "MORNING STAR riverboat." Available online at http://www.modelshipmaster.com/products/riverboats/Morning-Star-riverboat.htm, accessed 12/13/15. **183**

Branson, Roy. "Ellen G. White: Racist or Champion of Equality?" Available online at http://www.oakwood.edu/goldmine/hdoc/blacksda/champ/, accessed 1/4/15. **141**

Branson, W. H. Letter, April 13, 1954, in Bert Haloviak. "Impact of SDA Eschatological Assumptions on Certain Issues of Social Policy." Oct. 27, 1999, pp. 17, 18. **182**

Bree, Charles Robert. *An Exposition of the Fallacies in the Hypothesis of Mr. Darwin*. London: Longmans, Green, and Co., 1872. **160**

Brinkerhoff, William Henry. "From Bro. Brinkerhoff." *Review and Herald*, July 25, 1865, p. 63. **159**

Brock, Peter. *Pacifism in the United States: From the Colonial Era to the First World War*. Princeton, NJ: Princeton University Press, 1968. **155**

Brown, Hattie W. "Brooklyn Social Notes: Brooklyn Deaths." *The New York Age*, Dec. 4, 1943, p. 8. **182**

Bruce, Noah. "Maine History X." *The Portland Phoenix*, Aug. 30, 2001. Available online at http://www.portlandphoenix.com/archive/features/01/08/31/feat_slaves.html, accessed 1/11/16. **170**

Bryant, Franklin Henry. *Black Smiles; or, The Sunny Side of Sable Life*. Nashville, TN: Blackfoot Studio, 1903; Southern Missionary Society, 1909. **180**

Buell, Walter. *Joshua R. Giddings: A Sketch*. Cleveland, Ohio: William W. Williams, 1882. **141**

Bull, Malcolm, and Keith Lockhart. *Seeking A Sanctuary: Seventh-day Adventism and the American Dream*. Bloomington, Indiana University Press, 2007. **182**

Burner, David, Eugene D. Genovese, and Forrest McDonald. *The American People*. 3 vols. New York: Revisionary Press, 1980. **166**

"Business Items." *Review and Herald*, Oct. 14, 1858, p. 168. **167**

Busk, George. *Review and Herald*, Jan. 26, 1860, pp. 78, 79. **146**

Butler, Jonathan M. "From Millerism to Seventh-day Adventism: Boundlessness to Consolidation." *Church History*, vol. 55, no. 1 (March 1986), pp. 50–64. Available online at http://www.jstor.org/stable/3165422?loginSuccess=true&seq=1#page_scan_tab_contents, accessed 11/18/15. **140**

Byington, Anson. "Communication from Bro. A. Byington." *Review and Herald*, April 21, 1859, pp. 174, 175. **143**

———. "From A. Byington." *Review and Herald*, March 10, 1859, p. 124. **142**

———. "Reply to Bro. Waggoner." *Review and Herald*, May 3, 1860, p. 190. **143**

Byington, John, James White, J. N. Loughborough, George W. Amazon. "Humiliation and Prayer." *Review and Herald*, Feb. 21, 1865, p. 100; April 25, 1865, pp. 164, 165. **156**

Byington, John, John N. Loughborough, and George W. Amadon. "Day of Fasting and Prayer." *Review and Herald*, Jan. 31, 1865, p. 80. **156**

Byington, John, and Uriah Smith. "Report of General Conference of Seventh-day Adventists." *Review and Herald*, May 26, 1863, pp. 204–206. **140, 173**

Byington, John. "Appointments." *Review and Herald*, May 28, 1861, p. 16. **146**

———. "Note from Bro. Byington." *Review and Herald*, March 29, 1860, p. 152. **146**

———. "Sketch of Meetings." *Review and Herald*, Feb. 5, 1867, p. 108. **146**

Calhoun, John Caldwell. *The Works of John C. Calhoun*. 6 vols. Edited by Richard Kenner Crallé. New York: D. Appleton and Co., 1854. **135**

———. *John C. Calhoun: Selected Writings and Speeches*. Edited by H. Lee Cheek. Washington, DC: Regnery Pub., 2003. **152**

Callagher, F. H. "The Cause and Cure of the Present Civil War." *Review and Herald*, Aug. 19, 1862, pp. 89–91. **144**

Callahan, James Morton. *The Diplomatic History of the Southern Confederacy*. Springfield, MS: The Walden Press, 1957. **135**

———. *Russo-American Relations During the American Civil War*. Morgantown, WV: Dept. of History and Political Science, 1908. Available online at https://books.google.com/books?id=SbgJAAAAIAAJ, accessed 1/25/15. **154**

Cambridge Academic Content Dictionary Cambridge: Cambridge University Press, 2009. **135**

Cambridge City Tribune (Cambridge City, Indiana), March 17, 1870, p. 15. **159**

Campbell, Charles S. Review of *The Trent Affair: A Diplomatic Crisis* by Norman B. Ferris. *The American Historical Review*, vol. 82, no. 5, Dec. 1977, pp. 1331, 1332. **153**

Campbell, Duncan Andrew. *English Public Opinion and the American Civil War*. Woodbridge, Suffolk, UK; Rochester, NY: Royal Historical Society/Boydell Press, 2003. **35**

Campbell, John. *Negro-mania: being an examination of the falsely assumed equality of the various races of men, Demonstrated by the Investigations of Champollion, Wilkinson, Rosellini, Van Amringe, Gliddon, Young, Morton, Knox, Lawrence, Gen. J. H. Hammond, Murray, Smith, W. Gilmore Simms, English, Conrad, Elder, Prichard, Blumenbach, Cuvier, Brown, Le vaillant, Carlyle, Cardinal Wiseman, Burchhardt, and Jefferson, Together with a Concluding Chapter Presenting a Comparative Statement of the Condition of the Negroes* in the West Indies Before and Since Emancipation. Philadelphia: Campbell and Power, 1851. **158**

Campbell, Michael. " 'Amalgamation': Ellen White's Most Controversial Statement." March 25, 2014. Available online at http://www.adventisthistory.org/2014/03/25/amalgamation-ellen-whites-most-controversial-statement, accessed 7/12/14. **158**

Campbell, Michael, and Timothy G. Standish. "Amalgamation." *The Ellen G. White Encyclopedia.* Hagerstown, MD: Review and Herald Publishing Assoc., 2013, pp. 590–594. **157, 158**

Canright, Dudley M. *Life of Mrs. E. G. White, Seventh-day Adventist Prophet: Her False Claims Refuted.* Cincinnati, OH: Standard, 1919. Available online at http://www.ellenwhiteexposed.com/canright/egw16.htm, accessed 5/14/14. **155, 156**

———. "Progress of the Cause: East Tennessee." *Review and Herald,* June 15, 1876, p. 190. **169**

———. "Progress of the Cause: Texas." *Review and Herald,* May 25, 1876, p. 166. **169**

———. "Progress of the Cause: The Kentucky and Tennessee Conference." *Review and Herald,* June 1, 1876, p. 174. **168**

Carroll, Charles. *The Negro a Beast: Or In the Image of God The Reasoner of the Age, the Revelator of the Century! The Bible as it is! The Negro and His Relation to the Human Family! The Negro a beast, but created with articulate speech, and hands, that he may be of service to his master—the White man. The Negro not the Son of Ham, Neither can it be proven by the Bible, and the argument of the theologian who would claim such, melts to mist before the thunderous and convincing arguments of this masterful book.* St. Louis, MO: American Book and Bible House, 1900. Available online at http://www.biblical-truth.info/In%20the%20Image%20of%20God%20-%20by%20Charles%20Carroll.pdf, accessed 7/9/14. **158**

Carter, G. Tom. *The 19th Century Odyssey of John and Judith: From the Battlefields of the Civil War to Spiritual Battlefields on the Texas Frontier.* Silver Spring, MD: General Conference of Seventh-day Adventists, Ministerial Association, 2007. **141, 171, 180**

Carver, Henry E. "The War." *Review and Herald,* Oct. 21, 1862, pp. 166, 167. **160**

"The Case of Mrs. Margaret Douglass." Available online at http://www.pbs.org/wgbh/aia/part4/4h2945.html, accessed 2/8/15. **142**

Catalogue of the officers and students at the Western Reserve College, 1844-45. Hudson, Ohio: The Ohio Observer, 1844. Available online at http://interactive.ancestry.com/2207/32217_632606_0426-00014/761722, accessed 2/6/15. **171**

Catton, Bruce and James M. McPherson. *The Civil War.* Boston: Houghton Mifflin Co., 2005. **153**

"The Cause of the War." *The Liberator* (Boston), Sept. 6, 1861, p. 142. Available online at http://fair-se.org/the-liberator/1861/09/06/the-liberator-31-36.pdf, accessed 1/30/15. **138**

"Causes and Objects of the War." *Boston Daily Advertiser,* Nov. 18, 1861, p. 2. Available online at http://phw01.newsbank.com/cache/ean/fullsize/pl_010292015_1837_21977_907.pdf, accessed 10/29/15. **136**

Chadwick, Arthur. E-mail to Kevin L. Morgan, Jan. 12, 2016. **163**

Chapman Brothers. *Portrait and Biographical Album of St. Joseph County, Michigan. Containing Full Page Portraits and Biographical Sketches of Prominent and Representative Citizens of the County, Together with Portraits and Biographies of All the Governors of the State, and of the Presidents of the United States.* Chicago: Chapman Publishing Co., 1889. Available online at https://archive.org/details/portraitbiograph08chap, accessed 9/29/14. **148**

Charles, Robert Henry. *The Apocrypha and Pseudepigrapha of the Old Testament in English.* 2 vols. Oxford: Clarendon Press, 1913, 1976. **162**

Charlesworth, James H. *The Old Testament Pseudepigrapha: Expansions of the "Old Testament" and legends, wisdom and philosophical literature, prayers, psalms, and odes, fragments of lost Judeo-Hellenistic works.* 2 vols. New York: Doubleday, 1985. **162**

Charnwood, Baron Godfrey Rathbone Benson. *Abraham Lincoln.* Garden City, NY: Garden City Publishing Co., Inc., 1917. **152**

Chesebrough, David B. *"God Ordained This War": Sermons on the Sectional Crisis, 1830–1865.* Columbia, SC: University of South Carolina Press, 1991. **138, 156**

"Christianity and Slavery: Movement Towards Abolition." Available online at www.religioustolerance.org/chr_slav3.htm, accessed 1/4/15. **139**

Christian, Lewis Harrison. *The Fruitage of Spiritual Gifts: The Influence and Guidance of Ellen G. White in the Advent Movement.* Washington, DC: Review and Herald Publishing Assoc., 1947. Available online at http://docs.adventistarchives.org/docs/TFOSG/TFOSG1947__B.pdf, accessed 4/28/15. **181**

Chung, Peter K. "Rise of the Remnant: The Formation of the Seventh-day Adventist Church from the Era of Slavery and the Civil War." 2005. Available online at http://www.blacksdahistory.org/files/41593864.pdf, accessed 2/20/15. **140**

"The Church Is Not Post-Racial." Available online at http://www.relevantmagazine.com/reject-apathy/worldview/church-not-post-racial, accessed 4/27/15. **180**

Cincinnati Gazette. "Eternal Vigilance." *Review and Herald,* Aug. 11, 1868, pp. 124, 125. **166**

Circular (Oneida, New York). Aug. 1, 1861. **150, 184**

"Civil War." Available online at http://en.wikipedia.org/wiki/American_Civil_War, accessed 5/3/14. **165**

"Civil War Facts: Answers to Your Civil War Questions." Available online at http://www.civilwar.org/education/history/faq, accessed 2/8/15. **145**

"Civil War." *Scioto Gazette* (Chillicothe, OH), Jan. 8, 1861, p. 2. **147, 184**

Clarke, Joseph. "Is the Rebellion Quelled?" *Review and Herald,* Aug. 8, 1871, p. 63. **167, 171**

———. Letter to Uriah Smith, Feb. 24, 1878. Archives, General Conference of Seventh-day Adventists. **171**

———. "Our Country." *Review and Herald,* July 21, 1863, p. 61. **170**

———. "Our Field." *Review and Herald,* March 1, 1877, p. 72. **170**

———. "Progress of the Cause: Texas: Deckman, Dallas Co." *Review and Herald,* May 24, 1877, p. 166. **170**

———. "The Freedmen." *Review and Herald,* Sept. 14, 1876, p. 91. **171**

———. "The Judgment." *Review and Herald,* May 20, 1875, p. 166. **170**

———. "The Punishment of the South." *Review and Herald,* Jan. 23, 1866, pp. 61, 62. **170**

———. "The War! The War!!" *Review and Herald*, Sept. 23, 1862, p. 135. **170**

———. "Two Baals: Which is the Best?" *Review and Herald*, June 4, 1857, p. 37. **170**

Clarke, Joseph and Sarah. "Progress of the Cause: Texas: Deckman, Dallas Co." *Review and Herald*, March 22, 1877, p. 94. **170**

Cleveland, E. E. *Let the Church Roll On: An Autobiography*. Boise, ID: Pacific Press Publishing, 1997. **183**

Clinton Republican (Wilmington, OH), Jan. 11, 1861, p. 1. **148**

Colorado University. *General catalogue of the officers and graduates of the University of Colorado, 1877-1910*. Boulder, CO: The Boulder Publishing Company, 1911. **180**

Coulter-Smith, Graham. "Viral Creativity: Crossing the boundary between life and nonlife," Feb. 4, 2009. Available online at http://artintelligence.net/review/?p=840, accessed 1/21/15. **163**

"Compromises for the Crisis." *New York Times*, Jan. 10, 1861, p. 4. **145**

"The Conversion of Lord Palmerston in Belligerent Rights." *The Spectator*, March 15, 1862. Available online at http://archive.spectator.co.uk/article/15th-march-1862/8/the-conversion-of-lord-palmerston-on-from-the-risk, accessed 5/2/14. **154**

Cooper, William J., Jr. *Jefferson Davis, American*. New York: Alfred A. Knopf, 2000. **137**

Corliss, John Orr. "The Work in the South: Georgia." *Review and Herald*, Dec. 16, 1880, p. 397. **172**

Cornell, Merritt E. "Report of Meetings." *Review and Herald*, Feb. 11, 1862, p. 85. **146, 149**

Craven, Avery. "The 1840's and the Democratic Process." *Journal of Southern History*, vol. 16, no. 2, 1950, pp. 161–176. **138**

Crocombe, Jeff. "The Beginning of Regional Conferences in the US." Available online at http://h0bbes.wordpress.com/2006/08/07/the-beginning-of-regional-conferences-in-the-us, accessed 5/9/14. **173**

Cunningham, Horace H. *Field Medical Services at the Battles of Manassas (Bull Run)*. Athens, GA: University of Georgia Press, 1968. Available online at http://dlg.galileo.usg.edu/ugapressbks/pdfs/ugp9780820333557.pdf, accessed 1/30/15. **150**

"Current Events." *Home and Foreign Review*. London: Williams and Norgate, July 1862, vol. 1. Available online at http://books.google.com/books?id=Q35HAAAAYAAJ, accessed 9/15/15. **139, 151, 152**

Curtis, Charles F. "The Georgia Camp Meeting." *Review and Herald*, Aug. 21, 1888, p. 541. **172**

Daily Ohio Statesman (Columbus, Ohio), Nov. 2, 1860. **137**

Dattel, Eugene R. *Cotton and Race in the Making of America: The Human Costs of Economic Power*. Lanham, MD: The Rowan & Littlefield Publishing Group, 2009. **153**

Davey, Samuel. *Darwin, Carlyle, Dickens: the Fools, Jesters, and Comic Characters in Shakspeare, with Other Essays, &c.* London: J. G. Taylor, 1879. **160**

Davis, Jefferson. *Jefferson Davis, Constitutionalist: His Letters, Papers, and Speeches*. 10 vols. Edited by Rowland Dunbar. Jackson, MS: Printed for the Mississippi Dept. of Archives and History, 1923. **137**

———. *Speeches of the Honorable Jefferson Davis of Mississippi, Delivered During the Summer of 1858*. Baltimore: John Murphy and Co., 1859. Available online at https://books.google.com/books?id=o2sTAQAAMAAJ, accessed 10/22/15. **137**

———. *The Rise and Fall of the Confederate Government*. 2 vols. New York: D. Appleton and Co., 1881. Available online at https://books.google.com/books?id=qdcBAAAAMAAJ, accessed 12/15/15. **137**

Death certificate for George A. Osborne. Available online at http://cdm16317.contentdm.oclc.org/cdm/singleitem/collection/p129401coll7/id/30470, accessed 10/21/14. **149**

Degnan, James H., and Noah H. Rosenberg. "Gene tree discordance, phylogenetic inference and the multispecies coalescent." *Trends in Ecology and Evolution*, Vol. 24, pp. 332–340 (2009). **163**

De Leon, Edwin. *Secret History of Confederate Diplomacy Abroad*. Edited by William C. Davis. Lawrence: University Press of Kansas, 2005. **154**

Demyen, Ruby Clark. *The First Valle Crucis Seventh-day Adventist Church and Church School and other Mountain Stories*. Brushton, NY: Teach Services, Inc., 2003. **169**

"Destitution and Suffering at the South." *Review and Herald*, May 16, 1865, p. 189. **150, 156**

Detroit Daily Post. "Outrages in the South." *Review and Herald*, Jan. 31, 1871, p. 51. **165**

Detroit Tribune. "Report on Southern Outrages." *Review and Herald*, April 4, 1871, p. 128. **165**

Dvorak, Katherine L. *An African-American Exodus: The Segregation of Southern Churches*. Brooklyn, NY: Carlson Publishing Inc., 1991. **173**

Dittes, Albert. *A Struggle Against Great Odds: Seventh-day Adventist Origins in Post Civil War Kentucky and Tennessee*. Portland, TN: Albert Dittes, 2010. **169**

Dolgin, Elie. "Phylogeny: Rewriting evolution." *Nature*, vol. 486 (June 28, 2012), pp. 460–462. Available online at http://www.nature.com/news/phylogeny-rewriting-evolution-1.10885, accessed 7/16/14. **164**

Donald, David Herbert. *Charles Sumner and the Coming of the Civil War*. New York: Knopf, 1960. **138**

Douglas, Henry Kyd. *I Rode with Stonewall*. New York: The Great Commanders, 1995; originally published Chapel Hill, NC: University of North Carolina Press, 1940. **150**

Douglass, Herbert E. *Messenger of the Lord: The Prophetic Ministry of Ellen G. White*. Nampa, ID: Pacific Press Publishing Assoc., 1998. **155**

Downer, David. "Need of Laborers." *Review and Herald*, April 28, 1874, p. 159. **173**

Downer, David R. *The Downers of America: With Genealogical Record*. Newark, NJ: David R. Downer, 1900. **173**

Doyle, Don H. *Cause of All Nations: An International History of the American Civil War*. New York: Basic Books, 2014. **135, 137, 149**

Dudley, Charles Edward. *Thou Who Hast Brought Us: The Development of the Seventh-day Adventist Denomination Among African-Americans*. 3 vols. Brushton, NY: Teach Services, Inc., 1997. **181**

———. *The Genealogy of Ellen Gould Harmon White: The Prophetess of the Seventh-Day Adventist Church, and the Story of the Growth and Development of the Seventh-Day Adventist Denomination as It Relates to African-Americans*. Nashville, TN: Dudley Pub. Services, 1999. **64, 164**

Elkins, Nancy F. "Seventh-Day Adventists: A Study of Home Mission Work in Western North Carolina." *Appalachian Journal*, Winter 1981, p. 121. **157, 180**

Ellen G. White Estate. *The Comprehensive Index of Ellen G. White's Writings*. Mountain View, CA; Omaha, NE; and Oshawa, Ontario: Pacific Press Publishing Assoc., 1962. **144**

———. "The Genealogy of Ellen G. White: An Update." Available online at http://www.whiteestate.org/issues/genealogy.html, accessed 11/18/15. **164**

"The Emancipation Question. Is Slavery the Cause of the War?" *Newark Advocate* (Newark, OH), Dec. 20, 1861. **138, 151**

Eubanks, Rilla. "Why Should We Elevate." *The Gospel Herald*, Jan. 1900, p. 103. **175**

Evans, Emma B. "A Card." *Review and Herald*, Oct. 18, 1877, p. 127. **169**

Examiner (London), Sept. 26, 1863. Quoted by Eugene R. Dattel, *Cotton and Race in the Making of America: The Human Costs of Economic Power*. 2009, p. 188. **153**

"Exclusion of Free Blacks." Available online at http://slavenorth.com/exclusion.htm, accessed 10/22/14. **165**

"Extracts from Letters." *Review and Herald*, March 15, 1860, p. 135. **146**

"Extracts from Letters." *Review and Herald*, April 19, 1860, p. 175. **146**

Faust, Drew Gilpin. *A Sacred Circle*. Baltimore: Johns Hopkins University Press, 1977. **155**

———. *This Republic of Suffering: Death and the American Civil War*. New York: Alfred A. Knopf, 2008. **5, 145, 151, 155**

Fee, John G. "The Church, Slavery, and Caste." *Review and Herald*, Feb. 19, 1861, p. 107. **139**

Ferris, Norman B. *The Trent Affair: A Diplomatic Crisis*. Knoxville: University of Tennessee Press, 1977. **153**

Fisher, Holly. "Oakwood College Students' Quest for Social Justice Before and During the Civil Rights Era." *The Journal of African American History*, vol. 88 (Spring 2003), no. 2, pp. 110–125. **182**

"Five Most Influential SDAs—1969–1994." *Spectrum*, Dec. 1994, p. 10. **183**

Foote, William S. "Slavery." *Review and Herald*, March 1, 1860, p. 114. **143**

"Forced labour, human trafficking and slavery." Available online at http://www.ilo.org/global/topics/forced-labour/lang--en/index.htm, accessed 2/8/15. **141**

Fordham, Walter W. *Righteous Rebel: An Autobiography*. Washington DC: Review and Herald Publishing Assoc., 1991. **182**

Foreman, Amanda. "Amanda Foreman Part 3 of 4." Available online at https://www.youtube.com/watch?v=8Ezlz8uGjwA, accessed 1/22/15. **135, 150**

———. "A World on Fire: A Saga of the Civil War, at Home and Abroad." Available online at http://www.youtube.com/watch?v=-zHHPmiqa9s, accessed 3/16/13. **153**

———. *A World on Fire: Britain's Crucial Role in the American Civil War*. New York: Random House Publishing Group, 2010. **135, 153, 154**

Fortin, Denis, and Jerry Moon, eds. *The Ellen G. White Encyclopedia*. Hagerstown, MD: Review and Herald Publishing Assoc., 2013. **45, 50, 155, 157, 158, 159, 161**

"Fourth Annual Report of the N. Y. State Conference." *Review and Herald*, Oct. 31, 1865, pp. 172, 173. **165**

Franklin, John Hope. *From Slavery to Freedom: A History of Negro Americans*. New York: Random House, 1969. **177**

———. *Reconstruction: After the Civil War*. Chicago: University of Chicago Press, 1961. **166**

"Freedmen's Jubilee." *Charleston Daily Courier*, March 22, 1865. Available online at https://charlestontimemachine.files.wordpress.com/2015/02/1865_freedmens_jubilee.pdf, accessed 5/1/15. **157**

Free Press. "Union Resolutions by the State Agricultural Society." *The Western Chronicle* (Three Rivers, MI), Jan. 10, 1861, p. 2. **147**

"Free Seventh-day Adventists: A Brief Historical Sketch." Available online at http://freesda.weebly.com/our-history.html, accessed 4/1/15. **182**

Frisbie, Joseph Birchard. "Communications. From Bro. Frisbie." *Review and Herald*, Nov. 8, 1853, p. 143. **142**

"From Here and There." *The Youth's Instructor*, July 20, 1915, p. 2. **168**

"From South Carolina: Grand Procession of Colored Loyalists." *New-York Daily Tribune*, April 4, 1865, p. 6. Available online at http://chroniclingamerica.loc.gov/lccn/sn83030213/1865-04-04/ed-1/seq-6, accessed 1/27/15. **157**

Fuld, James J. *The Book of World-Famous Music: Classical, Popular, and Folk Courier Dover*. Courier Dover Publications, 2000. **149**

Futs, Will. "The Days of Noah: Understanding Ellen White's Amalgamation Statements." Available online at http://willfults.com/ellen-white-amalgamation, accessed 6/6/2014. **162**

Garden, Allen. "Religious Schism as a Prelude to the American Civil War: Methodists, Baptists, and Slavery." *Andrews University Seminary Studies*, Spring 1986, Vol. 24, No. 1, p. 17. **135**

Gates, Louisa M. "A New Year's Address to Those Engaged in Proclaiming the 'Present Truth.'" *Review and Herald*, Jan. 20, 1859, p. 70. **167**

———. "From Sister Gates." *Review and Herald*, Aug. 25, 1859, p. 111. **167**

———. "The Messages." *Review and Herald*, July 31, 1860, p. 81. **167**

Giddings, Joshua R. Letter to T. W. Higgins, Jan. 7, 1857, in *Proceedings of the State Disunion Convention Held at Worcester, Massachusetts, January 15, 1857*. Boston: 1857. Appendix, pp. 6, 7. **141**

Giem, Paul. Post. Available online at http://www.uncommondescent.com/intelligent-design/darwins-big-mistake-gradualism, accessed 7/19/14. **164**

Goddard, Samuel Aspinwall. *The American Rebellion: Letters on the American Rebellion*. London: Simpkin, Marshall & Co.; Birmingham: E. C. Osborne; Boston: Nichols and Noyes, 1870. Available online at https://books.google.com/books?id=zLcnbJV2OGsC, accessed 1/22/15. **153**

Godsmark, Otho C. "Fell With the Armor On." *Review and Herald*, Aug. 4, 1903, p. 23. **168**

———. "Progress of the Cause: Georgia." *Review and Herald*, April 10, 1888, p. 235. **172**

Goen, C. C. *Broken Churches, Broken Nation: Denominational Schisms and the Coming of the American Civil War*. Macon, GA: Mercer University Press, 1985. **135**

Golden Rule. "How to Make Infidels." *Review and Herald*, May 21, 1857, p. 19. **139**

Gospel Herald, May 1899, p. 75. **176**

"Governor Records - St. John, 1879-1883." Available online at https://www.kshs.org/p/governor-s-records-john-pierce-st-john-administration-jan-13-1879-jan-8-1883/13948, accessed April 22, 2015. **156, 177**

Graham, Ricardo B. "Black Seventh-day Adventists and Racial Reconciliation." *Perspectives: Black Seventh-Day*

Adventists Face the Twenty-first Century. Calvin B. Rock, ed. Hagerstown: Review and Herald, 1996, pp. 127–138. **183**

Graham, Roy E. *Ellen G. White, Co-Founder of the Seventh-day Adventist Church*, New York: Peter Lang Publishing, 1985. **179**

Grant, Alfred. *The American Civil War and the British Press.* Jefferson, NC, and London: McFarland & Company, Inc., Publishers, 2000. **135, 152**

Grant, Jonathan. "Heaven Bound, Earthly Good: An Historical Analysis of Race Relations in the Seventh-Day Adventist Church." A Dissertation Submitted to the Faculty of Clark Atlanta University in Partial Fulfillment of the Requirements for the Degree of Master of Arts. Department of African-American Studies. Atlanta, GA: May 2010. Available online at http://digitalcommons.auctr.edu/cgi/viewcontent.cgi?article=1716&context=dissertations, accessed 12/8/15 **139, 140, 142, 165, 169, 174, 181, 182**

Graybill, Ronald D. *E. G. White and Church Race Relations.* Washington, DC: Review and Herald Publishing Assoc., 1970. **97, 177–180**

———. *Mission to Black America: The True Story of James Edson White and the Riverboat Morning Star.* Mountain View, CA: Pacific Press Publishing Assoc., 1971. **176, 178**

———. "They're Coming to Get You, Nate." *Insight*, Aug. 10, 1971, pp. 3–9. **178**

———. "This Perplexing War: Why Adventists Avoided Military Service in the Civil War." *Insight*, Oct. 10, 1978, pp. 4–10. **159**

Ron Graybill, PhD., historian and former assistant at the Ellen G. White Estate

Greeley, Horace. *The American Conflict: A History of the Great Rebellion in the United States of America, 1860–1864: Its Causes, Incidents, and Results, Intended to Exhibit Especially Its Moral and Political Phases, with the Drift and Progress of American Opinion Respecting Human Slavery from 1776 to the Close of the War for the Union.* 2 vols. Hartford: O. D. Chase & Co.; Chicago: George & C. W. Sherwood, 1864. **145**

Greene, Alfonzo. "[Black] Regional Conferences in the Seventh-Day Adventists. (SDA) Church Compared with United Methodist [Black] Central Jurisdiction/Annual Conferences with White SDA Conferences, From 1940–2001: A Dissertation Submitted to the Faculty of the Graduate School in Candidacy for the Degree of Doctor of Philosophy Program in History." Chicago, IL: Dec. 2009. Dissertations. Paper 160. Available online at http://ecommons.luc.edu/luc_diss/160, accessed 7/8/14. **139, 165, 171, 173, 175, 180–182**

Gregory, William Henry. (Galway County) *House of Commons Debate*, July 18, 1862, vol. 168, cols. 549–569. Available online at http://hansard.millbanksystems.com/commons/1862/jul/18/resolution#column_520, accessed 5/2/14. **145, 154**

Gugliotta, Guy. "New Estimate Raises Civil War Death Toll." Available online at http://www.nytimes.com/2012/04/03/science/civil-war-toll-up-by-20-percent-in-new-estimate.html?pagewanted=all&_r=0, accessed 2/8/15. **145**

Gulliver, J. P. "The President and Congress: A Word with the Congregational Clergy." *Caledonian.* St. Johnsbury, VT, March 30, 1866, p. 1. **165**

Haloviak, Bert. "Impact of SDA Eschatological Assumptions on Certain Issues of Social Policy." Oct. 27, 1999. Available online at http://adventisthistory.wordpress.com/2008/10/26/lucy-byard, accessed 10/21/14. **182, 183**

Hamilton, Garry. "Viruses: The unsung heroes of evolution." *New Scientist*, Aug. 27, 2008, pp. 38–41. **163**

Hansen, Louis A. *From So Small a Dream.* Nashville, TN: Southern Publishing Assoc., 1968. Available online at http://www.blacksdahistory.org/files/101278383.pdf, accessed 4/16/15. **140, 165, 167, 168, 173, 175–176, 178, 180–182**

Hare, Jacob. "From Kentucky." *Review and Herald*, Jan. 30, 1872, p. 55. **168**

———. "Obituary Notices." *Review and Herald*, Feb. 27, 1872, p. 87. **168**

Harrison, C. B. Letter to Lawrence O'Bryan Branch, Dec. 2, 1860. Reprinted in W. Buck Yearns and John G. Barrett, eds., *North Carolina Civil War Documentary.* Chapel Hill: University of North Carolina Press, 1980, pp. 11–13, quoted by Stephanie McCurry, *Confederate Reckoning: Power and Politics in the Civil War South.* Cambridge: Harvard University Press, 2010, pp. 41, 43. **135**

Hart, Darryl G. and John R. Muether. *Seeking a Better Country: 300 Years of American Presbyterianism.* Phillipsburg, NJ: P & R Publishing Co., 2007. **135**

Haskell, Stephen Nelson and Uriah Smith. "S. D. Adventist General Conference." *Review and Herald*, Nov. 6, 1888, p. 698. **172**

Haskell, Stephen Nelson. "The Cause is Onward." *Review and Herald*, May 26, 1874, p. 190. **168**

Hine, Darlene Clark, William C. Hine, and Stanley Harrold. *The African-American Odyssey.* Combined Volume, 4th edition. Upper Saddle River, NJ: Pearson Prentice Hall, 2008. **165**

The History of Linn County, Iowa, Containing a History of the County, its Cities, Towns, &c., A Biographical Directory of its Citizens, War Record of its Volunteers in the late Rebellion, General and Local Statistics, Portraits of Early Settlers and Prominent Men, History of the Northwest, History of Iowa, Map of Linn County, Constitution of the United States, Miscellaneous Matter, &c. Chicago: Western Historical Co., 1878. Available online at https://books.google.com/books?id=tU80AQAAMAAJ, accessed 11/30/15. **159**

History of St. Joseph County, Michigan with Illustrations Descriptive of Its Scenery, Palatial Residences, Public Buildings, Fine Blocks, and Important Manufactories, from Original Sketches by Artists of the Highest Ability. Philadelphia: L. H. Everts & Co, 1877. Available online at http://catalog.hathitrust.org/Record/003933296, accessed 10/20/15. **146, 148, 149**

Holst, H. Von. *The Constitutional and Political History of the United States.* Chicago: Callaghan and Co., 1885, vol. 4. **145**

Holt, Michael F. *The Fate of Their Country: Politicians, Slavery Extension, and the Coming of the Civil War.* New York: Hill and Wang, 2004. **5**

"Honoring Minister Lothrop." *New York Times*, June 5, 1885. **154**

Hughes, Jennifer F. and John M. Coffin. "Human endogenous retrovirus K solo-LTR formation and insertional polymorphisms: Implications for human and viral evolution." *Proceedings of the National Academy of Sciences*, Feb. 10, 2004, vol. 101, no. 6. **164**

Hughes, John. *The Metropolitan Record*, in *The Bedford Gazette*, Nov. 8, 1861, p. 1, available online at http://chroniclingamerica.loc.gov/lccn/sn82005159/1861-11-08/ed-1/seq-1, accessed 1/22/15. **138**

Hull, Moses. "Appointments." *Review and Herald*, Jan. 14, 1862, p. 56. **149**

Humphries, Ashley Ellen. "The Migration of Westfield Quakers from Surry County, North Carolina, 1786–1828." Thesis submitted to the Graduate School at Appalachian State University. May 2013. **139**

Huxley, Thomas. *More Criticism on Darwin and Administrative Nihilism*. New York: D. Appleton and Company, 1872. **160**

Independent (New York). "The Mortara Case at Washington." *Review and Herald*, May 5, 1859, pp. 186, 187. **141**

———. "The Terrible Condition of the South." *Review and Herald*, Dec. 11, 1866, p. 9. **166**

Ingraham, William S. "Note from Bro Ingraham." *Review and Herald*, March 19, 1861, p. 144. **159**

"Interesting Extracts from Letters." *Review and Herald*, April 5, 1877, supplement, p. 4. **169**

Iowa State Census, 1885, Tama, Toledo, Toledo. Available online at https://familysearch.org/ark:/61903/1:1:H465-9W2, accessed 12/1/15. **159**

Iowa State Census, 1895, Hamilton. Available online at https://familysearch.org/ark:/61903/1:1:VT3Q-6YR, accessed 12/1/15. **159**

Iowa, State Census Collection, 1836-1925, 1856, Washington, Lime Creek, p. 18, available online at http://interactive.ancestry.com/1084/IA_67-0749/5041554, accessed 2/15/15. **167**

Isely, Jeter Allen. *Horace Greeley and the Republican Party 1853–1861: A Study of the New York Tribune*. New York: Octagon Books, Inc., 1965. **145**

"John Byington's Family." *Lest We Forget*, vol. 2, no. 1, available online at http://www.aplib.org/?page_id=299, accessed 5/13/15. **142**

"Jeff Davis Says His Loss at Bull Run was Three Thousand." *Detroit Free Press*, July 26, 1861, p. 1, available online at https://www.newspapers.com/image/118135581, accessed 2/17/16. **150**

Johnson's New Universal Cyclopædia: A Scientific and Popular Treasury of Useful Knowledge. 4 vols. Editors-in-chief Frederick A. P. Barnard and Arnold Guyot. New York: A. J. Johnson, 1877, 1881. Available online at http://catalog.hathitrust.org/Record/007705593, accessed 1/10/15. **159**

Johnson, Stephanie D. "Reading, Writing, Arithmetic . . . Our Early Beginnings." *North American Regional Voice*, Sept. 1979, p. 6. **165**

Johnson, Wilhelmina. Interview with Kevin L. Morgan, Aug. 27, 2014. **183**

Johnson, Willis Fletcher. *America's Foreign Relations*, vol. 2. New York, The Century Co., 1916. Available online at https://archive.org/stream/americasforeign02johnrich/americasforeign02johnrich_djvu.txt, accessed 1/25/15. **154**

Johns, Warren H., Tim Poirier, Ron Graybill, compilers. "EGW Private and Office Libraries." Available online at http://www.llu.edu/webapps/univ_library/speccolls/EGWPrivateLibrariesSearch.php, accessed 1/5/16. **158**

Joliet (Illinois) *Signal*, Sept. 2, 1862, p. 3. **139**

Jones, Daniel T. Letter to C. M. Kinny. March 6, 1889, GC Archives, RG 11, Box 3059, cited by Benjamin J. Baker. "A Look in the Mirror," p. 1. **174**

———. "Synopsis of the Proceedings of the General Conference Committee." *Review and Herald*, April 9, 1889, pp. 235, 236. **174**

Jones, R. Clifford. *James K. Humphrey and the Sabbath-Day Adventists*. Jackson: University Press of Mississippi, 2006. **174, 182**

Jordan, Winthrop D. *White Over Black: American Attitudes Towards the Negro 1560–1812*. Chapel Hill, NC: The University of North Carolina Press, 1968, 2002. **141**

"The Jubilee among the Freedmen. How the Slaves Celebrated Their Emancipation." *New York Times*, April 4, 1865. Available online at http://www.nytimes.com/1865/04/04/news/department-south-affairs-charleston-jubilee-among-freedmen-slaves-celebrated.html, accessed 5/3/15. **157**

Justiss, Jacob. *Angels in Ebony*. Holland, MI: Jet Printing Service Co., 1975. Available online at http://www.blacksdahistory.org/files/101257366.pdf, accessed 4/16/15. **182**

———. "A Remarkable Century of Progress." *The North American Informant*, November-December 1971, p. 1. **174**

"The Kansas-Nebraska Act." Available online at http://www.ushistory.org/us/31a.asp, accessed 10/16/14. **138**

Keeney, Harvey, and Andrew Hafer. "Appointments." *Review and Herald*, Jan. 1, 1861, p. 56. **146**

Kentucky Death Records, Fayetteville, 1903, Transit Permit 623. Available online at http://interactive.ancestry.com/1222/kyvr_7015575-1945/1203167, accessed 2/15/15. **168**

Kilgore, George Vincent. "Blind Guides." *Review and Herald*, Nov. 28, 1878, p. 170. **159**

Kilgore, Robert M. "Progress of the Cause: Texas." *Review and Herald*, April 18, 1878, p. 126. **169**

———. "Progress of the Cause: Texas" *Review and Herald*, May 17, 1877, p. 159. **170, 171**

———. "Report of the Southern Field." *General Conference Bulletin*, Oct. 21, 1889, pp. 25–27. **173**

———. "Tennessee Camp-Meeting and Nashville Institute." *Review and Herald*, Oct. 29, 1889, p. 683. **173**

———. "Texas Tent." *Review and Herald*, Sept. 6, 1877, p. 86. **173**

———. "Texas Tent: Peoria, Oct. 11." *Review and Herald*, Oct. 25, 1877, p. 135. **173**

Killen, William Francis. "Progress of the Cause: Georgia." *Review and Herald*, Aug. 30, 1881, p. 155. **171**

———. "Progress of the Cause: Georgia." *Review and Herald*, March 29, 1881, p. 202. **172**

———. "Progress of the Cause: Reynolds, GA." *Review and Herald*, Jan. 3, 1878, pp. 6, 7. **172**

———. "Progress of the Cause: Letters from the Southern Field." *Review and Herald*, Oct. 25, 1877, p. 136. **172**

Kinney, Charles M. "Progress of the Cause: Labor Among the Colored People." *Review and Herald*, Nov. 12, 1889, p. 716. **174**

———. "Progress of the Cause: Labor Among the Colored People of Topeka, Kansas." *Review and Herald*, Oct. 27, 1885, p. 668. **174**

———. "The First Official Effort for the Colored People." Cited by Delbert W. Baker, *Telling the Story*, p. 4/79 [425]. **175**

Knight, George R. *Joseph Bates: The Real Founder of Seventh-day Adventism*. Hagerstown, MD: Review and Herald Publishing Assoc., 2004. **142**

———. *Millennial Fever and the End of the World: A Study of Millerite Adventism*. Boise, Idaho: Pacific Press, 1993. **135**

Knott, Bill. "Writing Against Wrongs: Early Adventists Blistered Their Culture for Tolerating Human Slavery." *Adventist Review*, Feb. 28, 2002, p. 8–13. **142**

Koranteng-Pipim, Samuel. "Separate Black And White Conferences—Part 1: The Sin We Don't Want To Overcome." Available online at http://www.drpipim.org/church-racism-contemporaryissues-51/97-separate-black-and-white-conferences-part-1.html, accessed 1/26/15. **182**

Lane, Elbert B. "Progress of the Cause: Report of Labor: Tennessee." *Review and Herald*, May 2, 1871, p. 158. **167**

———. "The South." *Review and Herald*, Sept. 26, 1871, pp. 118, 119. **157**

Lane, Elbert B. and John Orr Corliss. "Progress of the Cause, New Market, Virginia." *Review and Herald*, March 9, 1876, p. 78. **169**

Lane, Sands H. "Progress of the Cause: The Work in Several States." *Review and Herald*, March 13, 1888, p. 172. **172**

Lawton, Graham. "Why Darwin was wrong about the tree of life." *New Scientist*, Jan. 21, 2009. Available online at http://postbiota.org/pipermail/tt/2009-February/004416.html, accessed 7/18/14. **163**

Lee, Harold L., with Benjamin Baker. *C. D. Brooks: The Man Behind the Message*. Hagerstown, MD: Review and Herald Publishing Assoc., 2013. **181–183**

Lee, Luther. *Slavery Examined in the Light of the Bible*. Syracuse, NY: Wesleyan Methodist Book Room, 1855. **144**

———. "The Bible No Refuge for Slavery." *Review and Herald*, Feb. 3, 1863, pp. 73, 74; Feb. 10, 1863, pp. 81–83; Feb. 24, 1863, pp. 97, 98; March 3, 1863, pp. 105, 106; March 10, 1863, pp. 113, 114; March 17, 1863, pp. 121–123; March 24, 1863, pp. 129, 130; April 7, 1863, pp. 146, 147; April 14, 1863, pp. 154–156; April 21, 1863, pp. 161–163; April 28, 1863, pp. 169, 170; and May 5, 1863, pp. 177, 178. **144**

Leeson, Michael A. *Commemorative Historical and Biographical Record of Wood County, Ohio*. Chicago: J. H. Beers & Co., 1897. Available online at https://books.google.com/books?id=edoyAQAAMAAJ, accessed 2/6/15. **171**

Lester, Richard I. "An Aspect of Confederate Finance During the American Civil War: the Erlanger Loan and the Plan of 1864." *Business History*, July 1, 1974, pp. 130–145. **156**

———. *Confederate Finance and Purchasing in Great Britain*. Charlottesville, VA: University Press of Virginia, 1975. **153**

Lincoln, Abraham. Aug. 22, 1862, in *The Reading Times* (Reading, PA), Aug. 25, 1862, p. 3. **138**

———. "Inaugural Address." March 4, 1861. **138**

———. Letter to Congress, July 4, 1861, in *Messages and Papers*, vol. VI, pp. 20–26. **146**

———. "Second Inaugural Address." In *Speeches and Writings*, pp. 686–687, in Faust, p. 189. **155**

———. "The Emancipation Proclamation." January 1, 1863, A Transcription. Available online at http://www.archives.gov/exhibits/featured_documents/emancipation_proclamation/transcript.html, accessed 5/2/14. **39**

Lindsay, William Schaw. *House of Commons Debate*, 18 July 1862, vol. 168, cols. 511-578. Available online at http://hansard.millbanksystems.com/commons/1862/jul/18/resolution#S3V0168P0_18620718_HOC_77, accessed 5/2/14. **152, 153**

Lindsey, David. *A. Lincoln/Jefferson Davis: The House Divided*. Cleveland: H. Allen, 1960. Available online at https://archive.org/details/alincolnjefferso00lind, accessed 1/18/15. **137**

"The Lisbon Debate." *The Cambridge City Tribune* (Cambridge City, Indiana), Jan. 13, 1870, p. 1. **159**

Litch, Josiah. "The Rise and Progress of Adventism." *Review and Herald*, May 8, 1856, p. 27. **142**

Little, Malcolm, with the assistance of Alex Haley. *The Autobiography of Malcolm X*. Brattleboro, VT: Castle Books, 1965. **181**

Logan, Rayford Whittingham. *The Betrayal of the Negro, from Rutherford B. Hayes to Woodrow Wilson*. New York: Collier Books, 1965. **177**

London, Samuel G. *Seventh-day Adventists and the Civil Rights Movement*. Jackson, MS: University Press of Mississippi, 2009. Snippet view available online at https://books.google.com/books?id=r0irGK-RSucC, accessed 4/24/15. **176, 178, 182, 183**

———. "The Sociopolitical Activism of Warren S. Banfield." available online at http://citation.allacademic.com/meta/p_mla_apa_research_citation/2/6/8/9/4/pages268947/p268947-2.php, accessed 4/12/15. **182**

Longstreet, James. *From Manassas to Appomattox*. New York: The Great Commanders, 1994; originally published Philadelphia: Lippincott, 1896. **150**

Lossing, Benson John. *The Pictorial Field Book of the Civil War in the United States of America*. 3 vols. in 1. Hartford: T. Belknap, 1874. Available online at https://books.google.com/books?id=k9wSAAAAYAAJ, accessed 1/22/15. **154**

Lovejoy, Clarence Earle. *The Lovejoy Genealogy with Biographies and History, 1470–1930: Especially recording the American descendants and the English ancestry of John Lovejoy (1622–1690) of Andover, Mass., and of Joseph Lovejoy (1684–1748) of Prince George County, Md., but also embracing all known data on other persons bearing the Lovejoy name whether or not identified with the emigrant ancestors*. New York: C. E. Lovejoy, 1930. Available online at http://babel.hathitrust.org/cgi/pt?id=wu.89061962387;view=1up;seq=11, accessed 2/8/15. **148**

Loughborough, John Norton. "All This Came." *Review and Herald*, Nov. 14, 1899, pp. 730, 731. **156**

———. "Daily Reading Course on the Spirit of Prophecy: Things Which We Have Seen and Heard." *Atlantic Union Gleaner*, Nov. 7, 1917, pp. 1, 2. **148**

———. Diary for 1883. Center for Adventist Research, Andrews University. **149**

———. "Image of the Beast." *Review and Herald*, Jan. 15, 1861, pp. 69, 70. **143**

———. "Little Time of Peace." *Review and Herald*, May 1, 1866, pp. 172, 173. **158**

———. "Meetings in Parkville, Mich." *Review and Herald*, May 29, 1860, p. 9. **146**

Harold L. Lee, director of the Bradford-Cleveland-Brooks Leadership Center on the campus of Oakwood University

———. "Remarkable Fulfillments of the Visions." *Review and Herald*, Dec. 25, 1866, p. 30. **146, 148**

———. "Report from Bro. Loughborough." *Review and Herald*, Dec. 23, 1862, p. 29. **149**

———. *Rise and Progress of the Seventh-day Adventists, with Tokens of God's Hand in the Movement and a Brief Sketch of the Advent Cause from 1831 to 1844*. Battle Creek, MI: General Conference Assoc. of the Seventh-day Adventists, 1892. Available online at http://books.google.com/books?id=fp3VAAAAMAAJ, accessed 6/13/14. **146, 147, 149, 156**

———. "Sketches of the Past—No. 121." *Pacific Union Recorder*, March 7, 1912, pp. 1, 2. Available online at http://www.adventistarchives.org/docs/PUR/PUR19120307-V11-32B.pdf, accessed 4/15/12. **146**

———. "Sketches of the Past—No. 122." *Pacific Union Recorder*, March 14, 1912, pp. 1, 2. Available online at http://www.adventistarchives.org/docs/PUR/PUR19120314-V11-33B.pdf, accessed 4/15/12. **148, 149**

———. "Special Notices: Ottawa, Illinois, Camp-Meeting." *Review and Herald*, Aug. 2, 1892, p. 493. **156**

———. *The Great Second Advent Movement: Its Rise and Progress*. Washington, DC: Review and Herald Publishing Assoc., 1905. **146, 147**

———. "The Study of the Testimonies. – No. 4." *General Conference Daily Bulletin*, Jan. 31, 1893, pp. 58–61. **146–148**

Luther, Martin. *Luther's Works*, Vol. 2: Lectures on Genesis: Chapters 6–14. Jaroslav Jan Pelikan, Hilton C. Oswald, and Helmut T. Lehmann, translators. Saint Louis: Concordia Publishing House, 1960, 1999. **157**

Magesa, Heidi. E-mail to Kevin L. Morgan, Center for Adventist Research, Andrews University, April 14, 2015. **146**

Makapela, Alven. *The Problem with Africanity in the Seventh Day Adventist Church*. New York: E. Mellen Press, 1996. **181**

Malcolm, Roy E. *The Aeolians: Directors Recall Precious Memories*. Huntsville, AL: Oakwood College, 1999. **181**

Manning, Chandra Miller. *What This Cruel War Was Over: Soldiers, Slavery, and the Civil War*. New York : Vintage Civil War Library, 2008. **152**

Marsh, Frank Lewis. *Fundamental Biology*. Lincoln, NE: Marsh, 1941. **160, 161**

Marsh, Frank Lewis, and Harold W. Clark. *The Early Writings of Harold W. Clark and Frank Lewis Marsh, a ten-volume anthology of documents, 1903–1961*. New York: Garland, 1995. **161, 164**

Marsh, Martha. Interview with Kevin L. Morgan, Sept. 9, 2014. **183**

Marshall Statesman (Marshall, Michigan), Jan. 23, 1861, p. 2. **147**

Masur, Louis. *The Civil War: A Concise History*. New York: Oxford University Press, 2011. **5**

Maynard, Douglas H. "The Forbes-Aspinwall Mission." *Mississippi Valley Historical Review*, vol. 45 (1958), p. 73. **156**

McLellan, Hugh D. and Katharine B. Lewis. *History of Gorham, Me*. Portland: Smith & Sale, Printers, 1903. **170**

McClure, Alfred C. "An Expression of Sorrow and Apology." *Adventist Review*, December 1999, North American Division edition, p. 12, available at: http://archives.adventistreview.org/9948/story1-4.htm, accessed 5/10/15). **183**

McCune, Robert K. "Progress of the Cause: From Bro. McCune." *Review and Herald*, Dec. 5, 1871, p. 198. **167**

———. "Progress of the Cause: Tennessee." *Review and Herald*, July 1, 1873, p. 22. **165, 167**

———. "Progress of the Cause: Tennessee." *Review and Herald*, May 19, 1874, p. 182. **167**

———. "Progress of the Cause: Tennessee." *Review and Herald*, Sept. 30, 1873, p. 126. **167**

———. *Review and Herald*, May 7, 1872, p. 166. **167**

McCune and others. "Progress of the Cause: From Brethren in Tennessee." *Review and Herald*, Aug. 8, 1871, p. 63. **167**

McCurry, Stephanie. *Confederate Reckoning: Power and Politics in the Civil War South*. Cambridge: Harvard University Press, 2010. **5**

McKivigan, John R. *The War against Proslavery Religion: Abolitionism and the Northern Churches, 1830–1865*. Ithaca and London: Cornell University Press, 1984. **135, 139, 170**

McPherson, James M. *For Cause and Comrades: Why Men Fought in the Civil War*. New York, Oxford University Press, 1997. **152**

———. *This Mighty Scourge: Perspectives on the Civil War*. New York: Oxford University Press, 2007. **137**

"Michigan, County Marriages, 1820-1935." St Joseph > Marriage certificates, 1832-1846, v. 1 > image 128 of 153. Available online at https://familysearch.org/pal:/MM9.3.1/TH-1-16780-39584-7?cc=1810350, accessed 1/14/16. **149**

Michigan State Gazetteer and Business Directory For 1863-4, Embracing Historical and Descriptive Sketches of All the Cities, Towns and Villages Throughout the State, Together with Classified Lists of All Professions, Trades and Pursuits, Names of All Organized Companies, State and County Officers, and full information regarding the Mercantile and Manufacturing Interests of the State. Detroit: Charles F. Clark, 1863. Available online at https://books.google.com/books?id=WS9EAQAAMAAJ, accessed 2/8/15. **148**

Miles, Norman K. "Tensions Between the Races." *The World of Ellen G. White*. Edited by Gary Land. Washington, DC: Review and Herald Publishing Assoc., 1987. **177**

Miller, Randall M., Harry S. Stout, and Charles Reagan Wilson, eds. *Religion and the American Civil War*. New York: Oxford University Press, 1998. **155**

Milman, Oliver. "Andrew Forrest signs up religious forces to fight slavery and trafficking." Available online at http://www.theguardian.com/world/2014/mar/18/andrew-forrest-signs-up-religious-forces-to-fight-slavery-and-trafficking, accessed 2/8/15. **141**

Ministerial Association of Seventh-day Adventists. *Seventh-day Adventists Believe: An Exposition of the Fundamental Beliefs of the Seventh-day Adventist Church*. 2nd edition. Nampa: ID, Pacific Press Publishing Association, 1988, 2005. **140**

Mobile *Register*. "Stimulants for the Rebels." *The Springfield* [Massachusetts] *Republican*, June 3, 1861, p. 2. Available online at http://genealogybank.com, accessed Nov. 19, 2015. **152, 184**

———. "The Slaves to Be Murdered." *The Liberator* (Boston), July 5, 1861, p. 106, col. 1. Available online at http://fair-use.org/the-liberator/1861/07/05/the-liberator-31-27.pdf, accessed 1/30/15. **152**

Morgan, Douglas. *Adventism and the American Republic: The Public Involvement of a Major Apocalyptic Movement*. Knoxville: University of Tennessee Press, 2001. **141, 142**

———. "Civil War." *The Ellen G. White Encyclopedia*, pp. 718–721. **155**

———. *Lewis C. Sheafe: Apostle to Black America*. Hagerstown, MD: Review and Herald Publishing Assoc., 2010. **175, 182**

———. "Peacemaking Heritage Series: An Abolitionist Urges Adventist Action." Feb. 29, 2008. Available online at http://spectrummagazine.org/blog/2008/02/29/peacemaking-heritage-series-abolitionist-urges-adventist-action, accessed 8/3/14. **142**

———. "The Significance of a Solid Start: Adventism and Race Relations, 1880-1920." Paper presented at the Seventh Triennial Association of Seventh-day Adventist Historians Conference, March 22, 2013, available online at http://www.sdahistorians.org/uploads/1/2/3/6/12365223/morgan_-_significance_of_a_solid_start_asdah_2013.docx, accessed 4/1/15. **181**

Douglas Morgan, PhD. History of Christianity, Washington Adventist University

Morgan, Kevin. "Scientific Research and Discovery Stimulate Controversy in Victorian Britain." HIS 5106, Dr. Michael J. Turner, Oct. 11, 2011. Available online at https://www.scribd.com/doc/255623906/Scientific-Research-and-Discovery-Stimulate-Controversy-in-Victorian-Britain, accessed 2/12/15. **160**

———. "Until We Acknowledged the Elephant in the Room: A Prophetic Reminder of the Reason for the American Civil War." Prepared in fulfillment of requirements for History 5207, Appalachian State University, Dr. Judkin Browning. May 7, 2012. Revised from instructor's comments Jan. 18, 2013. **5**

Morison, Samuel Eliot. *The Oxford History of the American People*. New York: Oxford University Press, 1965. **166**

"Mo. T. & M. Society." *Review and Herald*, Oct. 12, 1876, p. 118. **169**

Mount, Helen F. "Education of the Negro in the Military Department of the South, 1861–1865." A Thesis Submitted to the Faculty of the Department of History. The University of Arizona, 1965. Available online at http://arizona.openrepository.com/arizona/bitstream/10151/317883/1/AZU_TD_BOX40_E9791_1965_297.pdf, accessed 1/22/15. **151**

"Mount Vernon Academy Center of Race Issue." *The Lancaster Eagle-Gazette* [Lancaster, Ohio], July 31, 1962, p. 8. **183**

Müller, Fritz. *Facts and Arguments for Darwin*. London, Murray, 1869. **160**

Murphy, Jim. *The Boys' War: Confederate and Union Soldiers Talk about the Civil War*. Boston, MA: Houghton Mifflin Harcourt, 1993. **150**

Mushegian, Arcady R., et al. "Large-Scale Taxonomic Profiling of Eukaryotic Model Organisms: A Comparison of Orthologous Proteins Encoded by the Human, Fly, Nematode, and Yeast Genomes." *Genome Research*, Vol. 8 (1998), pp. 590–598. **163**

Nam, Julius. "Adventists in American Courts—The Sunday Law Cases." *Spectrum Forum*, January 11, 2013, available online at http://spectrummagazine.org/article/julius-nam/2013/01/11/adventists-american-courts%E2%80%94-sunday-law-cases, accessed 2/10/15. **179**

Nashville City Directory. The Ninth Annual Issue. Nashville, Tennessee: Wheeler, Marshall & Bruce, March 1873. Available online at http://interactive.ancestry.com/2469/13036347/1125698778, accessed 2/10/15. **167**

National Association for the Advancement of Colored People. *Thirty Years of Lynching in the United States, 1889–1913*. New York: Negro Universities Press, 1969. Available online at http://msa.maryland.gov/megafile/msa/speccol/sc5300/sc5339/000070/000000/000056/restricted/html/naacp-0001.html, accessed 1/18/15. **99**

Negro, His Ethnological Status; or, Is the Negro a Beast? Austin, TX: Harpoon Pub. Co., 1867?, 1908? (this edition can be no earlier than 1880). **157**

Nevins, Allan. *The Emergence of Lincoln: Prologue to Civil War, 1859-1861*. **135**

———. *War for the Union: War Becomes Revolution, 1862–1863*. New York: Charles Scribner's Sons, 1959, vol. 2. Available online at https://archive.org/stream/warfortheunionvo010196mbp/warfortheunionvo010196mbp_djvu.txt, accessed 8/5/14. **145**

"The New American Minister to Russia." *Nevada State Journal*, June 6, 1885, p. 1. **154**

New Bedford [Massachusetts] Republican Standard. "The War." *Review and Herald*, June 10, 1862, pp. 11, 12. **156**

Newbern (New Bern, NC) *Daily Progress*, Aug. 29, 1862, p. 2. **138, 139**

New Lexicon Webster's Dictionary of the English Language. New York: Lexicon Publications, Inc., 1988. **170**

"News and Miscellany: Home News: The Catholics Among the Freemen." *Review and Herald*, Dec. 18, 1866, p. 20. **175**

"News and Miscellany." *Review and Herald*, Jan. 15, 1867, p. 68. **165**

"News and Miscellany." *Review and Herald*, April 16, 1867, p. 224. **165**

"News and Miscellany: The Tennessee Election." *Review and Herald*, July 9, 1867, p. 61. **165**

"News of the Week." *The Spectator*, Jan. 31, 1863. Available online at http://archive.spectator.co.uk/article/31st-january-1863/1/news-of-the-week, accessed 5/2/14. **156**

New York Age, Feb. 28, 1907, section 1, p. 20. **177**
New York Age, May 16, 1907, section 3, p. 8. **177**
New York Age, May 23, 1907, section 3, p. 10. **178**
New-York Daily Tribune, Oct. 17, 1851. **145**
New York Herald, July 24, 1861, col. D. **150**

———. "Wendell Phillips Spouting Foul Treason." *The Liberator* (Boston), Aug. 15, 1862, p. 129. Available online at http://fair-use.org/the-liberator/1862/08/15/the-liberator-32-33.pdf, accessed 1/23/15. **152**

New York Marriage Index. Available online at http://search.ancestry.com/cgi-bin/sse.dll?db=NYCmarriageindexes&h=3163739, accessed 2/24/15. **182**

New-York Tribune, Jan. 12, 1861, p. 4. Available online at http://chroniclingamerica.loc.gov/lccn/sn83030213/1861-01-12/ed-1/seq-4 , accessed 12/23/15. **147**

New-York Tribune. "The [American] Tract Society," *Review and Herald*, Oct. 15, 1856, p. 185. **144**

Nichol, Francis D. *Ellen G. White and Her Critics: An Answer to the Major Charges that Critics Have Brought Against Mrs. Ellen G. White*. Washington, DC: Review and Herald Publishing Assoc., 1951. **155, 161**

Nix, James R., compiler; Fylvia Fowler Klin, editor. *The Spirit of Sacrifice & Commitment: Experiences of Seventh-day*

Adventist Pioneers. Nampa, ID: Pacific Press Publishing Association, 2000. **178**

Norman, R. Steven, III. "Edson White's Southern Work Remembered." *Southern Tidings*, Oct. 1995, pp. 2, 3. **174**

———. "Southern Union Trail of Adventists." *Southern Tidings*, Jan. 2010, pp. 12–19. **169**

———. "The Early History of South Central Conference, 1863–1945," p. 12. Available online at www.blacksdahistory.org/files/40633669.ppsx, accessed 4/14/15. **167**

Numbers, Ronald L., and Jonathan M. Butler, ed. *The Disappointed: Millerism and Millenarianism in the Nineteenth Century* (Knoxville: The University of Tennessee Press, 1993). **140**

Numbers, Ronald L., Arthur I. Brown, William Bell Riley William Vance Trollinger, George McCready Price, Harold Willard Clark, and Frank Lewis Marsh. *Creationism in Twentieth-century America. 8: The Early Writings of Harold W. Clark and Frank Lewis Marsh, a ten-volume anthology of documents, 1903–1961.* New York: Garland, 1995. **161**

Oakes, James. *Freedom National: The Destruction of Slavery in the United States, 1861–1865.* New York and London: W. W. Norton & Co., 2013. **136–138, 145, 147**

"Obituaries: Olvin." *Review and Herald*, March 31, 1904, p. 23. **178**

"Obituary Notices: Byard." *Atlantic Union Gleaner*, Dec. 17, 1943, p. 6. **182**

"Obituary Notices: Horr." *Review and Herald*, Oct. 29, 1895, p. 703. **166**

"Obituary Notices: Keeney." *Review and Herald*, Oct. 21, 1884, p. 671. **149**

O'Malley, Maureen A. and Eugene V. Koonin. "How stands the Tree of Life a century and a half after *The Origin*?" Available online at http://www.ncbi.nlm.nih.gov/pmc/articles/PMC3159114, accessed 7/16/14. **163**

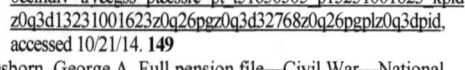

James Oakes, PhD.
Professor of History and the Humanities Professor at The Graduate Center, City University of New York

Osborne, Squire. "Greenup Co., Ky." *Review and Herald*, March 4, 1873, p. 94. **168**

———. "Kentucky and Tennessee." *Review and Herald*, Aug. 8, 1878, p. 51. **169**

———. "Progress of the Cause: Greenup Co., Kentucky." *Review and Herald*, April 23, 1872, p. 151. **168**

———. "Progress of the Cause: Green Co., Ky." *Review and Herald*, Jan. 1, 1875, p. 6. **168**

———. "Progress of the Cause: Kentucky." *Review and Herald*, April 1, 1875, p. 110. **168**

———. "Progress of the Cause: Kentucky." *Review and Herald*, Feb. 10, 1876, pp. 46, 47. **168**

———. "Progress of the Cause: Kentucky." *Review and Herald*, Sept. 30, 1875, p. 102. **168**

Osborn, Frank A. "U.S. Civil War Soldier Records and Profiles, 1861-1865." Available online at http://search.ancestry.com/cgi-bin/sse.dll?db=civilwar_histdatasys&h=3640943&ti=0&indiv=try&gss=pt&ssrc=pt_t51630505_p13231001623_kpidz0q3d13231001623z0q26pgz0q3d32768z0q26pgplz0q3dpid, accessed 10/21/14. **149**

Osborn, George A. Full pension file—Civil War—National Archives. **148**

———. "U.S. Civil War Soldier Records and Profiles, 1861-1865." Available online at http://search.ancestry.com/cgi-bin/sse.dll?db=civilwar_histdatasys&h=1842903&ti=0&indiv=try&gss=pt&ssrc=pt_t51630505_p13231002316_kpidz0q3d13231002316z0q26pgz0q3d32768z0q26pgplz0q3dpid, accessed 10/21/14. **149**

Osborn, Rebecca B., Find A Grave Memorial #70539378. Available online at http://www.findagrave.com/cgi-bin/fg.cgi?page=pv&GRid=70539378&Pipi=43144097, accessed 1/10/15. **149**

Osborn, Ronald. "True Blood: Race, Science, and Early Adventist Amalgamation Theory Revisited." *Spectrum*, vol. 38, no. 4. Fall 2010. Available online at http://www.scribd.com/doc/56488321/True-Blood-Race-Science-and-Early-Adventist-Amalgamation-Theory-Revisited, p. 4, accessed 6/23/14. **158, 162**

"Our Russian Minister." *Salt Lake Evening Democrat*, June 5, 1885, p. 2. **154**

Owsley, Frank Lawrence. *I'll Take My Stand: The South and the Agrarian Tradition*. New York: Harper and Row, 1962. **136**

Pace, John K. II, Clement Gilbert, Marlena S. Clark, and Cedric Feschotte. "Repeated horizontal transfer of a DNA transposon in mammals and other tetrapods." *Proceedings of the National Academy of Sciences*, vol. 105, no. 44, Nov. 4, 2008, p. 17023. Available online at http://www.pnas.org/content/105/44/17023.full, accessed 12/15/15. **163**

Papers of Jefferson Davis. 11 vols. Baton Rough: Louisiana State University Press, 1971–. **151**

"Papists among the Freedmen." *Signs of the Times*, April 8, 1875, p. 176. **175**

Paulson, David. Letter to Ellen White, April 19, 1906. **162**

Payne, Buckner H. ("Ariel"). "The Negro: What Is His Ethnological Status? Is he the progeny of Ham? Is he a descendent of Adam and Eve? Has he a soul? Or is he a beast in God's nomenclature? What is his status as fixed by God in creation? What is his relation to the white race?" Second edition. Cincinnati, OH: published for the proprietor, 1867. **157**

"Peaceful Disunion." *New-York Tribune*, Jan. 11, 1861, p. 6. **145**

Perkins, Howard Cecil, ed. *Northern Editorials on Secession*. 2 vols. Gloucester, MA: Peter Smith, 1964. **137**

Philadelphia Inquirer, Jan. 29, 1861, p. 2. **152**

Phillips, Wendell. *Disunion: Two Discourses at Music Hall, on January 20th, and February 17th, 1861.* Boston: Robert F. Wallcut, 1861. Available online at https://books.google.com/books?id=AnV2AAAAMAAJ, accessed 12/2/15. **135**

"Pigs and Humans Share 112 DNA Mutations, Say Scientists" Available online at http://tech.firstpost.com/news-analysis/pigs-and-humans-share-112-dna-mutations-say-scientists-212100.html, accessed 9/14/14. **164**

Pitman, Sean D., M.D. "Pseudogenes and Other Forms of 'Junk' DNA." Available online at http://www.detectingdesign.com/pseudogenes.html, accessed 9/23/14. **164**

"Please Notice." *Review and Herald*, Nov. 30, 1876, p. 176. **169**

Poirier, Timothy L. E-mail to Kevin L. Morgan, April 13, 2015. **179**

Pollard, Leslie N. "The Cross-Culture Challenging a Church as it Begins a New Millennium." *Adventist Review*, Feb. 2000, pp. 20–24. Available online at http://adventistreview.org/200-05/story2.htm, accessed 1/4/15. **141**

"Popular Sovereignty." *Merriam-Webster Dictionary*. Available online at http://www.merriam-webster.com/dictionary/popular%20sovereignty, accessed 10/16/14. **136**

Porter, Stephen T. "The Mighty Walk." *Liberty*, May/June 2013. Available online at http://www.libertymagazine.org/article/the-mighty-walk, accessed 1/8/15. **182**

Premium Tract. "Is Slavery Sanctioned by the Bible?" *Review and Herald*, Oct. 1, 1861, pp. 138–140. **144**

Prescott, Frank Williams. *Tariff Legislation 1859–1862: Its Relation to Protection and Political Activities*. Master's thesis, University of Wisconsin: 1921. Available online at http://babel.hathitrust.org/cgi/pt?id=wu.89089883987, accessed 8/3/14. **146**

Proceedings of the State Disunion Convention Held at Worcester, Massachusetts, January 15, 1857. Boston: printed for the committee, 1857. Available online at https://ia700303.us.archive.org/20/items/proceedingsofsta00mass/proceedingsofsta00mass_bw.pdf, accessed 8/3/14. **141**

"Prosperity of the Freedmen." *Review and Herald*, Nov. 28, 1871, p. 192. **166**

"Publications." *Review and Herald*, Aug. 23, 1864, p. 104. **144**

"Publishing House Notes." *The Southern Union Worker*, Oct. 14, 1915, p. 329. **168**

Putnam, Carol. "AMALGAMATION: The Racist Doctrine Seventh-Day Adventists Don't Want You to Know," available online at http://new.exchristian.net/2010/09/amalgamation-racist-doctrine-seventh.html, accessed 4/12/15. **157**

Quynn, William R., editor. *The Diary of Jacob Engelbrecht, 1818-1878*. 3 vols. Frederick, MD: Historical Society of Frederick County, 1976. **145**

Raimo, John W. *A Guide to Manuscripts Relating to America in Great Britain and Ireland*. Rev. ed. London: Mansell Publishing, 1979. **153**

Raleigh Daily Telegram, May 13, 1871, p. 3. Available online at https://www.newspapers.com/image/58183416, accessed 1/24/16. **170**

Raymond, Henry J. "Crushing Rebellion. The Greatest Battle Ever Fought on the Continent... The Rebels Routed and Driven Behind the Manassas Lines." *New York Times*, July 22, 1861, p. 1. **150, 184**

"The Rebel Loss Nearly Four Thousand." *Detroit Free Press*, July 26, 1861, p. 1. **150**

Read, David C. *Dinosaurs: An Adventist View*. Keene, TX: Clarion Call Books, LLC, 2009. **161**

"Rebel Account of the First Skirmish at Bull's Run." *The New York Herald*, July 23, 1861, p. 1. **150**

"Receipts. For Review and Herald." *Review and Herald*, Oct. 1, 1857, p. 176. **166**

"Receipts. For Review and Herald." *Review and Herald*, Feb. 6, 1866, p. 80. **166**

"Receipts. For Review and Herald." *Review and Herald*, July 14, 1868, p. 64. **167**

"The Reign of Terror in the South." *Review and Herald*, Aug. 25, 1868, p. 158. **166**

Religious Telescope. "The Wicked Go Unpunished." *Review and Herald*, Oct. 23, 1866, p. 163. **166**

Remley, Mary A. "Progress of the Cause: Tennessee." *Review and Herald*, July 15, 1875, p. 22. **167**

"Results from the 1860 Census." Available online at http://www.civil-war.net/pages/1860_census.html, accessed 10/20/14. **137**

"The *revised* Dred Scott Case Collection: History of Dred Scott." Available online at http://digital.wustl.edu/dredscott/history.html, accessed 2/17/15. **170**

Reynolds, Louis Bernard. *We Have Tomorrow: The Story of American Seventh-day Adventists with an African Heritage*. Hagerstown, MD: Review and Herald Publishing Assoc., 1984. **139, 172, 174, 181, 182**

Richards, Samuel P. *Sam Richards's Civil War Diary: A Chronicle of the Atlanta Home Front*. Edited by Wendy Hamand Venet. Athens, GA: The University of Georgia Press, 2009. **151**

Richmond Climax (Richmond, KY), July 29, 1903, p. 4. **168**

Robertson, John. *Michigan in the War*. Lansing, MI: State Printer, 1882. **149**

Robinson, Dores E. "Amalgamation Versus Evolution." DF 316. Available online at http://drc.whiteestate.org/read.php?id=13624, accessed 6/11/14. **161**

———. Letter to George McCready Price, dated April 29, 1931, DF 31D8, egw_4563.pdf. Available online at http://drc.whiteestate.org/read.php?id=135960, accessed 1/20/15. **161**

Rock, Calvin, ed. *Institutional Loyalty Versus Racial Freedom: The Dilemma of Black Seventh-day Adventists*. Nashville, TN: Vanderbilt University, 1984. **174**

———. *Perspectives: Black Seventh-day Adventists Face the Twenty-first Century*. Hagerstown, MD: Review and Herald Publishing Assoc., 1996. **182**

Rowe, David L. *God's Strange Work: William Miller and the End of the Word*. Grand Rapids, MI: Wm. B. Eerdmans Publishing Co., 2008. **140**

Rozwenc, Edwin C., ed. *The Causes of the American Civil War*. Lexington, MA: D. C. Heath and Co., 1961. **135–138, 149**

Rupert, Greenberry George. "Progress of the Cause: Georgia." *Review and Herald*, Sept. 7, 1886, p. 571. **173**

Rust, Alfred B., Elbridge G., and Joseph Clarke. "Progress of the Cause: Texas." *Review and Herald*, April 5, 1877, p. 111. **170**

Saul, Norman E. and Richard D. McKinzie. *Russian-American Dialogue on Cultural Relations, 1776-1914*. Columbia: University of Missouri Press, 1997. Available online at http://books.google.com/books?id=irnw4ksE-RQC, accessed 5/5/15. **154**

Schellhous, Lorancie. "A Request." *Review and Herald*, Feb. 25, 1862, p. 104. **149**

———. "From Bro. Schellhous." *Review and Herald*, July 22, 1858, p. 79; Jan. 13, 1859, p. 63; Dec. 8, 1859, p. 23; Dec. 11, 1860, p. 31; July 16, 1861, p. 55; Jan. 17, 1865, p. 63; July 3, 1866, p. 39; March 3, 1868, p. 187; Aug. 25, 1868, p. 156. **149**

———. *Life of Lorancie Schellhous: Written by him in March, 1873*. Available online at http://trees.ancestry.com/tree/61048794/downloadmedia/d0896455-f9d2-4e1a-a1d0-3265b4578343?mediatype=Story, accessed 5/7/14. **149**

Schell, William G. *Is the Negro a Beast?* Moundsville, WV: Gospel Trumpet Pub. Co., 1901. A response to Charles Carroll. **158**

"The Scheme to Exterminate the Colored Race." *Southern Christian Intelligencer*, Aug. 5, 1965. Quoted in *Review and Herald*, Sept. 5, 1865, p. 107. **165**

Scherer, Lester B. *Slavery and the Churches in Early America, 1619–1819*. Grand Rapids, MI: William B. Eerdmans, 1975. **139**

Schwarz, R. W. *Light Bearers to the Remnant*. Mountain View, CA: Pacific Press Publishing Assoc., 1979. **168, 170, 180, 182**

"Scuds in the Political Heavens." *Review and Herald*, April 24, 1866, p. 164. **158**

"S.D.A. Accomplishments in Interracial Relations–1934." Available online at http://documents.adventistarchives.org/Resources/RegionalConf/RCO-01.pdf, accessed 1/12/15. **174**

Seaman, Edwin R. "The Days of Noah and the Sons of Man." *Review and Herald*, June 13, 1854, pp. 157, 158. **141**

"Secession Movement." *Kalamazoo Gazette*, Jan. 11, 1861, p. 3. **147, 151, 184**

Seilhamer, George Overcash. *Leslie's History of the Republican Party, vol. 1. Narrative and Critical History*. 1856–1898. New York: L. A. Williams Publishing and Engraving Co., 1903. Available online at http://booksnow1.scholarsportal.info/ebooks/oca1/31/leslieshistoryof01seiluoft/leslieshistoryof01seiluoft.pdf, accessed 10/25/15. **165**

Selcer, Richard F. *Civil War America, 1850 to 1875*. New York: Facts on File, Inc., 2006. **139**

"Senate History. 1851-1877. July 21, 1861: Senators Witness the First Battle of Bull Run." Available online at http://www.senate.gov/artandhistory/history/minute/Witness_Bull_Run.htm, accessed 12/27/15. **150**

Sentinel (Milwaukee, WI), June 10, 1885, p. 4. 19th Century U.S. Newspapers. Accessed 1/28/15. **154**

Sepúlveda, Ciro. "Booker T. Washington, Ellen G. White, and Adventists Manual Training Schools," presented at the Seventh Triennial Association of Seventh-day Adventist Historians Conference, March 22, 2013, at Union College in Lincoln, Nebraska, available online at http://www.sdahistorians.org/uploads/1/2/3/6/12365223/washington_and_white.docx, accessed 3/30/15. **176**

———. *Ellen White on the Color Line: The Idea of Race in a Christian Community*. Leominster, MA: Biblos Press, 1997. Available online at http://www.oakwood.edu/historyportal/Faculty/Color%20Line.pdf, accessed 5/14/14. **6, 140, 174, 175, 177, 181**

Sepúlveda, Ciro, with Lea Hardy. *The Ladies of Oakwood: The Power of the So-called Powerless*. Huntsville, AL: Oakwood College Press, 2003. Available online at https://ia601706.us.archive.org/3/items/ladiesofoakwoodp2003sepu/ladiesofoakwoodp2003sepu.pdf, accessed 2/23/15. **122**

Ciro Sepúlveda, PhD., retired professor, Oakwood University

"Seventh-day Adventists." *The Yazoo Sentinel*, June 7, 1900, quoted in "The Southern Field Closing to the Message." *The Gospel Herald*, Oct. 1900, p. 86. **180**

Seward, William Henry. "The Degeneracy of the United States." *Review and Herald*, March 15, 1860, p. 132. **138**

Sheffield City Libraries, Department of Local History. *Wharncliffe Muniments: Estate & personal letters & papers*. Sheffield, 1955. **156**

SHELL BARK. "Our Washington Correspondence." *The Western Chronicle* [Three Rivers, MI], Dec. 20, 1860, p. 2. **148, 184**

Shigley, Gordon. "Amalgamation of Man and Beast: What Did Ellen White Mean?" *Spectrum*, June 1982, pp. 10–19. **158**

Singleton, Harold Douglas. "A Short History of the Work of Seventh-day Adventists among the Negroes of North America before 1909, submitted for Social Science Seminary and World Politics." 1932. **173**

"The Slave Experience: Education, Arts, & Culture. Original Documents." Available online at http://www.pbs.org/wnet/slavery/experience/education/docs1.html, accessed 2/8/15. **142**

Smith, Ben. "Georgia Geneticist Challenges Evolution, Links Humans to Pigs." July 29, 2013. Available online at http://saportareport.com/blog/2013/07/mccarthy_human_pig_chimp_evolution, accessed 9/14/14. **164**

Smith, Michael Thomas. *The Enemy Within: Fears of Corruption in the Civil War North. A Nation Divided: Studies in the Civil War Era*. Charlottesville: University of Virginia Press, 2011. **5**

Smith, Uriah. "Explanation Wanted," *Review and Herald*, June 27, 1895, p. 30. **152**

———. "In the Question Chair." *Review and Herald*, Nov. 5, 1901, p. 721. **160**

———. "Is Slavery Dead?" *Review and Herald*, June 20, 1865, p. 20. **165**

———. "Objections to the Visions." *Review and Herald*, June 12, 1866, p. 16. **159, 161**

———. "Politics." *Review and Herald*, Sept. 11, 1856, p. 152. **142**

———. "Report of the Third Annual Session of the General Conference of S. D. Adventists." *Review and Herald*, May 23, 1865, pp. 196, 197. **165**

———. *Review and Herald*, Sept. 2, 1858, p. 124. **136**

———. *Review and Herald*, Feb. 27, 1866, p. 104. **165**

———. *Review and Herald*, March 27, 1866, p. 137. **165**

———. "The Conference." *Review and Herald*, April 13, 1876, p. 116. **168**

———. "The Degeneracy of the United States." *Review and Herald*, June 17, 1862, p. 22. **138**

———. "The Dragon Voice." *Review and Herald*, Feb. 5, 1857, p. 106. **141**

———. "The National Sin." *Review and Herald*, Aug. 20, 1861, p. 94. **143**

———. *The Visions of Mrs. E. G. White: A Manifestation of Spiritual Gifts According to the Scriptures*. Battle Creek, MI: Seventh-day Adventist Publishing Assoc., 1868. **51, 159–161**

———. "The War, and Its Cause." *Review and Herald*, Nov. 12, 1861, pp. 188, 189. **144**

———. "The Warning Voice of Time and Prophecy." *Review and Herald*, June 23, 1853, pp. 17–19. **141**

———. "Traitors in Power." *Review and Herald*, Feb. 4, 1862, pp. 77, 78. **151**

Smith, Uriah, George W. Amadon, and J. M. Aldrich. "Remarks." *Review and Herald*, Jan. 23, 1866, p. 63. **159**

Snook, Benjamin Franklin. "From Bro. Snook." *Review and Herald*, July 25, 1865, pp. 62, 63. **159**

———. "Report from Bro. Snook." *Review and Herald*, April 23, 1861, pp. 180, 181. **170**

———. "Testimony No. 9." *Review and Herald*, March 3, 1863, p. 109. **160**

———. "The War and Our Duty." *Review and Herald*, Oct. 14, 1862, p. 159. **160**

Snook, Benjamin Franklin and William Henry Brinkerhoff. "The Visions of E. G. White, Not of God." Cedar Rapids, IA: Cedar Valley Times Book and Job Printers, 1866. Available online at http://www.ellenwhiteexposed.com/snook/visionsc.htm, accessed 8/4/14. **51, 147, 152, 157, 159**

Snyder, John. "Notice." *Review and Herald*, July 12, 1877, p. 24. **169**

"Sola scriptura." Available online at https://en.wikipedia.org/wiki/Sola_scriptura. Accessed 1/4/16. **162**

Southwestern Adventist College. Alumni Association. *Lest We Forget, The Heritage of Southwestern Adventist College, Where Students Learn to Live*. Keene, TX: College Press, 1985. **141**

Spalding, Arthur Whitefield. *Captains of the Host, First Volume of a History of Seventh-day Adventists Covering the Years 1845–1900*. Washington, D. C: Review and Herald Publishing Assoc., 1949. Available online at http://documents.adventistarchives.org/Books/CH1949.pdf. **140, 165, 167–169, 172–174**

———. *Footprints of the Pioneers*. Washington, DC: Review and Herald Pub. Assn., 1947. **169**

———. "Lights and Shades in the Black Belt: An Evil Heritage." *The Youth's Instructor*, April 6, 1915, pp. 3, 4, available online at http://documents.adventistarchives.org/Periodicals/YI/YI19151416-V63-14.pdf, accessed 10/18/15. **168**

———. "Lights and Shades in the Black Belt: An Evil Heritage (Concluded)." *The Youth's Instructor*, April 13, 1915, pp. 3–5, available online at http://documents.adventistarchives.org/Periodicals/YI/YI19151423-V63-15.pdf, accessed 10/18/15. **168**

———. "Lights and Shades in the Black Belt: A Rising Storm." *The Youth's Instructor*, May 11, 1915, pp. 3, 4, available online at http://documents.adventistarchives.org/Periodicals/YI/YI19151511-V63-19.pdf, accessed 10/18/15. **168**

———. "Lights and Shades in the Black Belt: A Rising Storm (Concluded)." *The Youth's Instructor*, May 25, 1915, pp. 3–5, available online at http://documents.adventistarchives.org/Periodicals/YI/YI19151525-V63-21.pdf, accessed 10/18/15. **168**

———. "Lights and Shades in the Black Belt: Emancipation." *The Youth's Instructor*, June 8, 1915, pp. 3–5, available online at http://documents.adventistarchives.org/Periodicals/YI/YI19151608-V63-23.pdf, accessed 10/18/15. **168**

———. "Lights and Shades in the Black Belt: Emancipation (Concluded)." *The Youth's Instructor*, June 15, 1915, pp. 3, 4, available online at http://documents.adventistarchives.org/Periodicals/YI/YI19151615-V63-24.pdf, accessed 10/18/15. **168**

———. "Lights and Shades in the Black Belt: The Gospel Among the Slaves." *The Youth's Instructor*, April 20, 1915, pp. 3–5, available online at http://documents.adventistarchives.org/Periodicals/YI/YI19151430-V63-16.pdf, accessed 10/18/15. **168**

———. "Lights and Shades in the Black Belt: The Gospel Among the Slaves (Continued)." *The Youth's Instructor*, April 27, 1915, pp. 3–5, available online at http://documents.adventistarchives.org/Periodicals/YI/YI19151437-V63-17.pdf, accessed 10/18/15. **168**

———. "Lights and Shades in the Black Belt: The Gospel Among the Slaves (Concluded)." *The Youth's Instructor*, May 4, 1915, pp. 3–5, available online at http://documents.adventistarchives.org/Periodicals/YI/YI19151504-V63-18.pdf, accessed 10/18/15. **168**

———. "Lights and Shades in the Black Belt: Containing the Story of the Southern Missionary Society, the Oakwood School, and the Hillcrest School." Unpublished book manuscript. Office Document File: 376.0. Washington, DC: E. G. White Publications, 1914. Available online at http://www.blacksdahistory.org/files/46593763.pdf, accessed 4/16/15, and at: http://docs.adventistarchives.org/docs/LS/LS1914__C.pdf, accessed 6/13/14. **117, 168, 169, 171–176, 178–181**

———. *Origin and History of Seventh-day Adventists*. 4 vols. Washington, DC: Review and Herald Publishing Assoc., 1962. **167–170, 172–174**

———. *The Men of the Mountains: The Story of the Southern Mountaineer and His Kin of the Piedmont; with an Account of Some of the Agencies of Progress among Them*. Nashville, TN; Atlanta, GA: Southern Publishing Assoc., 1915. **168**

"Special Oakwood Edition." *Adventist Heritage*, March 1996. Available online at http://www.blacksdahistory.org/files/42131641.pdf, accessed 1/9/15. **181**

Spetner, Lee M. "Reviewing *The Evolution Revolution*, the NCSE Offers Uninformed Criticism that Misses the Point." Available online at http://www.evolutionnews.org/2016/01/reviewing_the_e102281.html, accessed 1/13/16. **163**

"Springville Items." *The Portsmouth Times* (Portsmouth, Ohio), March 18, 1876, p. 3. **173**

Spurgeon, Charles Haddon. "The World on Fire." *Review and Herald*, Aug. 21, 1879, pp. 65–67. Original sermon available online at http://ccel3.calvin.edu/ccel/spurgeon/sermons19.xxxvii.html, accessed 1/6/15. **157**

"Squire Osborne." Find A Grave Memorial #90198607. Available online at http://www.findagrave.com/cgi-bin/fg.cgi?page=gr&GRid=90198607&ref=acom, accessed 2/12/15. **168**

"Squire Osborn in the U.S. and International Marriage Records, 1570-1900." Available online at http://search.ancestry.com/cgi-bin/sse.dll?indiv=1&db=WorldMarr_ga&gss=angs-d&pcat=34&h=911069&ml_rpos=1, accessed 2/15/15. **167**

Stafford, Tim. "The Abolitionists." ChristianHistory.net. Available online at http://www.christianitytoday.com/ch/1992/issue33/3321.html, accessed 4/23/12. **139**

Starr, Louis Morris. *Bohemian Brigade: Civil War Newsmen in Action*. New York: Knopf, 1954. **150**

State of Michigan Proceedings of the Public Domain Commission, vol. 6, Lansing, MI: Wynkoop Hallenbeck Crawford, Co. State Printers, 1915. https://books.google.com/books?id=4cDPAAAAMAAJ, accessed 11/8/15. **148**

"State of the Cause in Michigan." *Review and Herald*, June 2, 1863, pp. 5–7. **146**

Stearns, Charles. *The Way to Abolish Slavery*. Boston: the author, 1849. Available online at http://babel.hathitrust.org/cgi/pt?id=loc.ark%3A%2F14060%2Ft4jm2c54j;page=root;view=plaintext;size=100;seq=13;num=9, accessed 4/25/12. **139**

Stephens, Alexander. "Cornerstone Address." In Wakelyn, *Southern Pamphlets*, pp. 405, 406. **137**

Stickney, William B. "Links in the chain of Violence—the Maltreatment of Women, and the Murder of Whites and Blacks." *Review and Herald*, Aug. 28, 1866, pp. 102, 103. **165**

"St. John Amuses His Audience." *The InterOcean* (Chicago, IL), June 30, 1891, p. 1. Available online at http://www.newspapers.com/image/33757175, accessed 4/22/15. **156**

St. John, Hiram Allen, and John Boardman Craw. "Testimonial." *Review and Herald*, Dec. 14, 1876, p. 192. **170**

Story, Joseph. *Commentaries on the conflict of laws, foreign and domestic: in regard to contracts, rights, and remedies, and especially in regard to marriages, divorces, wills, successions, and judgments.* Boston: Little, Brown; London: A. Maxwell and Son, 1846. **138**

Stowe, Harriet Beecher. "The Church and the Slave Trade." *Review and Herald*, Nov. 20, 1860, pp. 2, 3. **139**

Stowell, Daniel. " 'We Have Sinned and God Has Smitten Us!' John H. Caldwell and the Religious Meaning of Confederate Defeat." *Georgia Historical Quarterly*, vol. 78, Spring 1994, pp. 1–38, in Wyatt-Brown, *Religion and the American Civil War*, p. 32. **155**

Strayer, Brian E. "Remembering the Radical Politics of the Pioneers: John Byington." January 25, 2015. Available online at https://adventistpeace.wordpress.com/2015/01/25/john-byingtons-radical-abolitionism-by-brian-strayer, accessed 2/8/15. **141, 142**

———. "John Byington: First General Conference President, Circuit-Riding Preacher, and Radical Reformer," book manuscript currently at Pacific Press Publishing Assn. (forthcoming). **139, 141, 144**

———. *Where the Pine Trees Softly Whisper: the History of Union Springs Academy.* Union Springs, NY: Alumni Association, Union Springs Academy, 1992. **181**

Stringer, Carrie L. "Death of Elder W. H. Green." *Field Tidings*, Jan. 2, 1929, p. 5. **181**

Sumners, J. W. "The 'Grandfather Clause,'" *Lawyer and Banker and Southern Bench and Bar Review*, vol. 7, no. 1 (February 1914), Charles Ellewyn George, editor, pp. 39–50. Available online at https://books.google.com/books?id=knizAAAAIAAJ, accessed 2/3/15. **177**

Sunday Record (Battle Creek, MI), Jan. 31, 1904, section 2. **177**

Sun (New York). "Not Cured Yet." *Review and Herald*, Aug. 8, 1865, p. 79. **165**

Taft, William Howard. *Presidential addresses and state papers, from March 4, 1909 to March 4, 1910.* New York: Doubleday, Page & Co., 1910. **177**

Taylor, Charles O. "Progress of the Cause: Georgia." *Review and Herald*, April 10, 1879, p. 118. **169**

———. "Progress of the Cause: Georgia." *Review and Herald*, Jan. 4, 1877, p. 7. **168**

———. "Progress of the Cause: Georgia." *Review and Herald*, Oct. 18, 1877, p. 126. **169**

———. "Progress of the Cause: Reynolds, GA." *Review and Herald*, April 18, 1878, p. 127. **169, 171, 171**

———. "Progress of the Cause: Reynolds, GA." *Review and Herald*, March 14, 1878, p. 86. **172**

———. "Progress of the Cause: Reynolds, GA." *Review and Herald*, Jan. 3, 1878, pp. 6, 7. **172**

———. "Quitman, GA." *Review and Herald*, Sept. 20, 1877, p. 101. **168**

"Taylor C. O. Rev. Adventist." *Shole's Georgia State Gazetteer, 1879-80*, p. 648. Available online at http://interactive.ancestry.com/2469/41199_1220706242_4012-00673/1411226991, accessed 2/15/15. **169**

Taylor, Peter Alfred. *House of Commons Debate*, 18 July 1862, vol. 168, cols. 511–578. Available online at http://hansard.millbanksystems.com/commons/1862/jul/18/resolution#S3V0168P0_18620718_HOC_77, accessed 5/2/14. **154**

Taylor, Rob. "Kangaroo genes close to humans." Nov. 18, 2008. Available online at http://www.reuters.com/article/2008/11/18/us-australia-kangaroos-idUSTRE4AH1P020081118, accessed 4/5/15. **164**

"Tennessee Conference Proceedings." *Review and Herald*, Nov. 12, 1889, pp. 716, 717. **168**

"Testimony for the Church No. 9, is now ready." *Review and Herald*, Jan. 27, 1863, p. 72. **145, 155**

Times (London), Jan. 16, 1863. In Bennett, p. 138. **153**

Times-Picayune (New Orleans, LA), June 15, 1861, p. 2, col. 2. Available online at http://www.newspapers.com/image/28345920, accessed 8/3/14. **145**

———, Sept. 25, 1877, p. 2. **171**

Toloken, Steve. "Creationist Joins Forces With Scientists: Fossil Discoveries Help 2 Theories." *Daily Press*, Nov. 27, 1994. Available online at http://articles.dailypress.com/1994-11-27/news/9411270004_1_fossils-ancient-whales-scientists, accessed 6/23/14. **162**

Trowbridge, Carol. *Andrew Taylor Still: 1828–1917.* Kirksville, MO: The Thomas Jefferson University Press, 1991. Available online http://www.fulcrumosteopatia.com/app/download/5706889210/Trowbridge+Andrew+Taylor+Still.pdf, accessed 12/16/15. **148**

Tubb, Benjamin R. "Civil War Music: The Battle Hymn of the Republic." Available online at http://www.civilwar.org/education/history/on-the-homefront/culture/music/the-battle-hymn-of-the-republic/the-battle-hymn-of-the.html, accessed 12/16/15. **149**

Turner, George H. *Record of Service of Michigan Volunteers in the Civil War, 1861–1865.* Vol. 17. Kalamazoo, MI: Ihling Bros. & Everard, 1905. Available online at http://interactive.ancestry.com/18555/dvm_PrimSrc000301-01494-1/2922, accessed 8/4/14. **149**

United States Congress, *Congressional Record: Proceedings and Debates of the 85th Congress, Vol. 103, Part 10.* U. S. Government Printing Office, 1957. **177**

United States War Department. *The War of the Rebellion: A Compilation of the Official Records of the Union and Confederate Armies*, Series 4. 70 vols. Washington, DC: Government Printing Office, 1902. Available online at http://books.google.com/books?id=Ydo4AQAAMAAJ, accessed 9/2/14. **137**

Urban, John W. *My Experiences Mid Shot and Shell and in Rebel Den, a Graphic Recital of Personal Experiences Throughout the Entire Civil War.* Lancaster, PA: for the author, 1882; Philadelphia: J. H. Moore, 1892. **150**

Van Slyke, Hanna Maria. "Among the Freedmen." *Review and Herald*, Feb. 22, 1877, p. 59. **169**

———. "Coming." *Review and Herald*, Aug. 12, 1875, p. 49. **169**

———. "Coming." *The Golden Sickle*, Jan. 15, 1887, p. 9. **169**

Vecsey, George. "7th Day Adventists Elect Black Chief." *New York Times*, Jan. 12, 1979, p. A20. ProQuest Historical Newspapers. **183**

Victor, Orville James. editor. *Incidents and Anecdotes of the War: Together with Life Sketches of Eminent Leaders, Narratives of the Most Memorable Battles for the Union.* New York: James D. Torrey, 1862. **150**

———. *The History, Civil, Political and Military, of the Southern Rebellion, From Its Incipient Stages to Its Close. Comprehending, also, All Important State Papers, Ordinances of Secession, Proclamations, Proceedings of Congress, Official Reports of Commanders, Etc. Etc.*, vol. 2. New York: James D. Torrey, 1861. **150**

Waggoner, Joseph H. "Modern Spiritualism." *The Signs of the Times*, Sept. 4, 1879, p. 267. **181**

———. "Questions." *Review and Herald*, May 6, 1862, p. 182. **156**

———. "National Degeneracy." *Review and Herald*, Aug. 12, 1858, pp. 100, 101. **143**

———. "Trip to Indiana." *Review and Herald*, Feb. 11, 1862, p. 85. **149**

Wakelyn, Jon L. *Southern Pamphlets on Secession, November 1860–April 1861*. Chapel Hill: University of North Carolina Press, 1996. **137**

Walker, E. S. "Response of the Battle Creek Church." *Review and Herald*, July 25, 1865, p. 63. **159**

Walsh, Eric. "Who Stopped the Movement?" recorded Feb. 28, 2009. Available online at https://www.audioverse.org/english/sermons/recordings/1463/who-stopped-the-movement.html, accessed 1/3/15. **181**

Ward, Andrew. *The Slaves' War: The Civil War in the Words of Former Slaves*. Boston: Houghton Mifflin Harcourt, 2009. **150, 173**

Warren, Mervyn A. *King Came Preaching: The Pulpit Power of Dr. Martin Luther King Jr.* Downers Grove, IL: InterVarsity Press, 2001. **182**

———. *Oakwood! A Vision Splendid Continues*. Huntsville, AL: Oakwood College, 1996, 2010. Available online at www.blacksdahistory.org/files/101258125.pdf, accessed 4/16/15. **181**

———. "Oakwood? Oh, Yes . . ." *Southern Tidings*, February 2016, pp. 8–10. **182**

Mervyn A. Warren, PhD., Provost and senior Vice President Oakwood University

"The War." *Harper's Weekly*, May 4, 1861, p. 274, cols. 1, 2. Available online at http://www.sonofthesouth.net/leefoundation/civil-war/1861/may/news-civil-war.htm, accessed 4/23/12. **20, 145, 151**

Washington, Marjorie Hyer. "Seventh-Day Adventists Elect a Black President." *The Washington Post*, Jan. 13, 1979, p. A8. ProQuest Historical Newspapers. **183**

Waterloo Courier (Waterloo, IA), July 22, 1869, p. 4. **159**

———. July 28, 1870, p. 1. **159**

Waters, Andrew. *Prayin' to Be Set Free: Personal Accounts of Slavery in Mississippi*. Winston-Salem, NC: John F. Blair, 2002. **172**

Webster, Noah. *An American Dictionary of the English Language*. (New York: S. Converse, 1828). Available online at www.christiantech.com, accessed 2/2/15. **46, 140, 150**

Weekly Democratic Statesman (Austin, TX), Aug. 22, 1878, p. 2. Available online at http://www.newspapers.com/image/49688632, accessed 1/27/15. **171**

Weekly Democratic Statesman (Austin, TX), Nov. 25, 1880, p. 1. Available online at http://www.newspapers.com/image/50533406, accessed 1/27/15. **171**

Western Chronicle (Three Rivers, MI), Dec. 13, 1860, p. 2. **153**

"What Congress Might and Should Do to Save the Union." *New-York Tribune*, Jan. 11, 1861, p. 4. **149**

Wheeler, Gerald. *James White: Innovator and Overcomer*. Hagerstown, MD: Review and Herald Publishing Assoc., 2003. **156**

Wheeler, Joe. *Abraham Lincoln: A Man of Faith and Courage*. New York: Howard Books, 2008. **136**

Wheeler, Richard. *A Rising Thunder: From Lincoln's Election to the Battle of Bull Run: An Eyewitness History*. New York, NY: HarperCollins, 1994. **150, 151**

White, Arthur Lacey. "Ellen G. White: A Brief Biography." Available online at http://www.whiteestate.org/about/egwbio.asp, accessed 2/16/15. **140**

———. *Ellen G. White, Volume 2: The Progressive Years, 1863–1876*. Hagerstown, MD: Review and Herald Publishing Assoc., 1985. **145**

———. *Ellen G. White, Volume 4: The Australian Years, 1891–1900*. Hagerstown, MD: Review and Herald Publishing Assoc., 1985. **176**

———. *Ellen G. White, Volume 5: The Early Elmshaven Years, 1900–1905*. Hagerstown, MD: Review and Herald Publishing Assoc., 1981. **176**

———. Letter to "Dear Friend," Chicago, Illinois, Nov. 8, 1861. Q&A File Number 43-C-49, available online at http://ellenwhite.org/content/file/why-southern-work-not-published-today-43-c-40#document, accessed 12/4/15. **176**

———. Letter to Dr. Donald R. Gibbs, Cortland, New York, July 20, 1971 (egw_3831.pdf). Available online at http://drc.whiteestate.org/read.php?id=114564, accessed 1/20/15. **161**

———. Letter to Hedwig Jemison, Nov. 2, 1964, available online at http://www.andrews.edu/library/car/cardigital/digitized/wdf/b17092693-004.pdf, accessed 5/5/15. **146**

White, Ellen G. *The Ellen G. White Letters & Manuscripts with Annotations*. Hagerstown, MD: Review and Herald Publishing Assoc., 2014. **141**

———. *The Great Controversy Between Christ and Satan*. Mountain View, CA: Pacific Press Publishing Assoc., 1888, 1907. **15, 140, 163**

———. *Notebook Leaflets from the Elmshaven Library*. St. Helena, CA, 1945). **146**

———. *The Oakwood Manual Training School* [SpTB12]. 1908. **181**

———. *Patriarchs and Prophets [The Story of Patriarchs and Prophets: As Illustrated in the Lives of Holy Men of Old]*. Washington, DC: Review and Herald Publishing Assn., 1890, 1958. **45, 57, 60, 158, 162, 163**

———. *A Sketch of the Christian Experience and Views of Ellen G. White*. Saratoga Springs, NY: James White, 1851. **141, 158**

———. *The Southern Work*. Washington, DC: Review and Herald Publishing Assoc., 1966. **174–180, 182**

———. *The Spirit of Prophecy*, vol. 1. Battle Creek, MI: Steam Press of the SDA Publishing Assn., 1870. **45, 57, 58, 61, 157, 161, 162**

———. *The Spirit of Prophecy*, vol. 4. Battle Creek, MI: Steam Press of the SDA Publishing Assn., 1884. **163, 178**

———. *Spiritual Gifts*, vol. 1. Battle Creek, MI: James White Publisher, 1858. **58, 141, 158**

———. *Spiritual Gifts*, vol. 2. Battle Creek, MI: James White Publisher, 1860. **145**

———. *Spiritual Gifts, Important Facts of Faith, in Connection with the History of Holy Men of Old*, vol. 3. Battle Creek, MI: James White Publisher, 1864. **55, 57, 58, 60, 157, 160, 162**

———. *Spiritual Gifts, Important Facts of Faith: Laws of Health and Testimonies Nos. 1–10*, vols. 4a and 4b. Battle Creek, MI: James White Publisher, 1864. **58, 144–147, 156, 158, 162**

———. *Testimonies for the Church*, vol. 1, comprised of Testimony 1 (1855); 2 (1856) 3, 4 (1857); 5 (1859); 6 (1861); 7, 8 (1862); 9 (1863); 10 (1864); 11, 12, 13 (1867); 14 (1868). Mountain View, CA: Pacific Press Publishing Assn., 1881, 1902, 1948. **135, 140, 141, 144, 147, 150–159, 164, 174**

———. *Testimonies for the Church*, vol. 2, comprised of Testimony 15, 16 (1868); 17 (1869); 18, 19 (1870); 20 (1871). Mountain View, CA: Pacific Press Publishing Assn., 1881, 1902, 1948. **162**

———. *Testimonies for the Church*, vol. 5, comprised of Testimony 31 (1882); 32 (1885); 33 (1889). Mountain View, CA: Pacific Press Publishing Assn., 1902, 1948. **162**

———. *Testimonies for the Church*, vol. 7. Mountain View, CA: Pacific Press Publishing Assn., 1902. **175, 176**

———. *Testimonies for the Church*, vol. 8. Mountain View, CA: Pacific Press Publishing Assn., 1904. **178**

———. *Testimonies for the Church*, vol. 9. Mountain View, CA: Pacific Press Publishing Assn., 1909. **177, 179–181, 183**

———. "To the Little Remnant Scattered Abroad." Portland, ME, April 6, 1846. Available online at http://library.ellenwhite.org/content/file/little-remnant-scattered-abroad-df-68#document, accessed 5/7/15. **135**

EGW articles, by order of publication

———. "To the Young." *Review and Herald*, July 25, 1854, p. 197. **144**

———. "Duty of Parents to Their Children." *Review and Herald*, Sept. 19, 1854, pp. 45, 46. **162**

———. "To the Church." *Review and Herald*, June 12, 1855, pp. 246. **144**

———. "Communication from Sister White." *Review and Herald*, Jan. 10, 1856, p. 118. **144**

———. "Brethren and Sisters." *Review and Herald*, Feb. 21, 1856, pp. 167. **144**

———. "He Went Away Sorrowful, for He Had Great Possessions." *Review and Herald*, Nov. 26, 1857, pp. 18, 19. **144**

———. "The Future." *Review and Herald*, December 31, 1857, p. 59. **144**

———. "A Warning." *Review and Herald*, April 15, 1858, p. 174. **144**

———. "The Sinner's Trials." *Review and Herald*, April 28, 1859, pp 181, 182. **144**

———. "Testimony for the Church, No. 5." *Review and Herald*, June 16, 1859, p. 32. **141**

———. "Power of Example." *Review and Herald*, June 25, 1861, pp. 37–39. **144**

———. "Communication from Sister White: Slavery and the War." *Review and Herald*, Aug. 27, 1861, pp. 100–102. **19, 144, 168**

———. "An Extract from a Letter Written to a Distant Female Friend." *Review and Herald*, Sept. 16, 1862, p. 126. **140**

———. "Seth and Enoch." *The Signs of the Times*, Feb. 20, 1879, p. 58. **162**

———. "Joseph in Egypt." *The Signs of the Times*, Jan. 8, 1880, p. 1. **162**

———. "A Living Church." *Review and Herald*, June 3, 1880, pp. 353, 354. **162**

———. "Among the Churches: Freshwater." *The Signs of the Times*, Feb. 16, 1882, pp. 80, 81. **162**

———. "The Primal Object of Education." *Review and Herald*, July 11, 1882, pp. 433, 434. **174**

———. "Importance of Education." *Review and Herald*, Aug. 19, 1884, pp. 529, 530. **174**

———. "Marrying and Giving in Marriage." *Review and Herald*, Sept. 25, 1888, pp. 609, 610. **162**

———. "No Caste in Christ." *Review and Herald*, Dec. 22, 1891, pp. 785, 786. **174, 179**

———. "The Good Shepherd's Estimate of a Lost Sheep." *The Signs of the Times*, Nov. 20, 1893, pp. 35, 36. **158**

———. "Work Among the Colored People." *Review and Herald*, April 2, 1895, pp. 209, 210, in *The Southern Work*, pp. 19, 22. **175**

———. "An Appeal for the Southern Field." *Review and Herald*, Nov. 26, 1895, pp. 753, 754, in *The Southern Work*, pp. 26, 27. **176**

———. "An Appeal for the South.—2." *Review and Herald*, Dec. 3, 1895, pp. 769, 770, in *The Southern Work*, pp. 32, 33. **176**

———. "An Appeal for the South.—3." *Review and Herald*, Dec. 10, 1895, pp. 785, 786, in *The Southern Work*, pp. 38. **176**

———. "An Example in History." *Review and Herald*, Dec. 17, 1895, pp. 801, 802, in *The Southern Work*, pp. 42, 43. **176**

———. "Am I My Brother's Keeper?" *Review and Herald*, Jan. 21, 1896, pp. 33, 34. **162**

———. "Lift Up Your Eyes and Look on the Field." *Review and Herald*, Jan. 28, 1896, pp. 49, 50, in *The Southern Work*, p. 60. **141, 176**

———. "Volunteers Wanted for the Southern Field." *Review and Herald*, Feb. 4, 1896, p. 65. **176**

———. "Whole-hearted Service." *The Signs of the Times*, Feb. 1, 1899, pp. 82, 83. **164**

———. "Trust in God." *The Gospel Herald*, March 1901, p. 22. **180**

———. "The Collection for the Colored Work." *Review and Herald*, Sept. 28, 1905, pp. 7, 8. **180**

———. "Lessons From the Life of Solomon—No. 20: 'Be Ye Separate.' " *Review and Herald*, Feb. 1, 1906, pp. 8, 9. **162**

———. "The Enmity." *The Signs of the Times*, Feb. 17, 1909, pp. 99, 100. **163**

EGW letters, by order of writing

———. Letter 1 (April 7), 1847 to Joseph Bates, in *The Ellen G. White Letters & Manuscripts with Annotations*, vol. 1, pp. 112–117. **141**

———. Letter 2 (Feb. 23), 1861, to "Dear friend William." **146**

———. Letter 16 (Aug. 3), 1861, to Church at Roosevelt, NY, in *Manuscript Releases*, vol. 5, p. 60. **140**

———. Letter 24, 1862, to Alexander Ross, in *Testimonies for the Church*, vol. 1, pp. 359–360. **140, 155**

———. Letter 9 (March 22), 1868, to Joseph Clarke. **170**

———. Letter 24 (Sept.), 1870, to J. E. and Emma White, in *Manuscript Releases*, vol. 20, p. 331. **155**

———. Letter 36 (July), 1880, to the brethren at Woodland [California]. **174, 181**

———. Letter 18 (Oct. 18), 1890, to J. H. Kellogg. **175**

———. Letter 73 (Nov. 25), 1890, to Uriah Smith, in *The Ellen G. White 1888 Materials*, p. 732. **160**

———. Letter 5 (July 24), 1895, to "Brethren in Responsible Positions in America." **176**

———. Letter 73 (Nov. 20), 1895, p. 2, to A. O. Tait, in *The Southern Work*, p. 72. **178**

———. Letter 80a (Aug. 16), 1895, to J. E. and Emma White. **141**

———. Letter 90 (June 5), 1899, to A. F. Ballenger, in *The Southern Work*, pp. 84–86. **178, 180**

———. Letter 165 (Oct. 22), 1899, to F. E. Belden, in *Manuscript Releases*, vol. 4, pp. 13–15. **177, 178**

———. Letter 84 (July 16), 1901, to "Brethren in Denver." In *Manuscript Releases*, vol. 4, p. 18. **180**

———. Letter 113 (Aug. 13), 1901. **179**

———. Letter 206 (Dec. 13), 1902, to W. C. White, in Graybill, *E. G. White and Church Race Relations*, p. 93. **179**

———. Letter 105 (June 1), 1903, to G. I. Butler. **147**

———. Letter 141 (July 12), 1903, to W. C. White. **147**

———. Letter 87 [Feb. 15], 1904, to W. C. White. **147**

———. Letter 99 (Feb. 23), 1904, to J. E. and Emma White, in *Manuscript Releases*, vol. 4, pp. 23, 90. **178**

———. Letter 313 (Nov. 2), 1904, to "Brethren and Sisters." **181**

———. Letter 206 (June 14), 1906, to David Paulson, in "Correct Views Concerning the Testimonies: A Reply to an Inquirer." *Review and Herald*, Aug. 30, 1906, pp. 8, 9. **162**

———. Letter 317 (Sept. 24), 1907, to Nashville Church, in *Manuscript Releases*, vol. 4, pp. 30, 31. **178**

———. Letter 304 (Oct. 19), 1908, to Churches in Washington, D.C., in *Manuscript Releases*, vol. 4, p. 32. **180**

———. Letter 36, 1912, to "Friend." **179**

EGW manuscripts, by order of writing

———. Ms. 4, 1883. **155**

———. Ms. 6 (prepared for a tract March 20), 1891. "Our Duty to the Colored People" (written Nov. 4, 1889), published in *The Southern Work*, pp. 9–17. **135, 174, 175**

———. Ms. 22 (Oct. 20), 1889. "Diary, October 1889."**173**

———. Ms. 24 (Jan. 1), 1891. "The Work in the Southern Field." **178**

———. Ms. 22a (Nov. 20), 1895. "Interview re Work Among the Colored People." Available online at http://drc.whiteestate.org/read.php?id=18228. **178**

———. Ms. 7 (Feb. 3), 1896. **175, 179**

———. Ms. 65 (April 25, copied), 1899. **164**

———. Ms. 118 (Aug. 21, copied), 1899, in Graybill, *E. G. White and Church Race Relations*, pp. 75, 76. **179**

———. Ms. 45 (May 14), 1904. **182**

———. Ms. 60 (June 21), 1904. Talk at Oakwood. **179, 181**

———. Ms. 114 (Sept. 17), 1904, in *A Place Called Oakwood*, pp. 125, 126. **180**

———. Ms. 94 (Sept. 1), 1905, from Loma Linda, in *Testimonies for the Church*, vol. 9, p. 195. **181**

———. Ms. 196 (April 29), 1907. **179**

———. Ms. 123, 1908, in SpTB12, pp. 4–16. **181**

———. Ms. 15 (April 26), 1909. "Words of Encouragement to Self-Supporting Workers." **179**

White Estate Trustees. "Comments on the Ellen G. White Statements Relative to the Revival of Slavery." Available online at http://drc.whiteestate.org/files/6785.pdf, accessed 1/25/15. **178**

White, James Springer. "Brief Report." *Review and Herald*, Jan. 15, 1861, p. 72. **146**

———. "New and Important Work." *Review and Herald*, Aug. 25, 1868, p. 160. **161**

———. "Sunday Battles." *Review and Herald*, Feb. 9, 1864, p. 84. **151**

———. "Testimony for the Church, No. 7 is ready." *Review and Herald*, Feb. 18, 1862, p. 96. **144**

———. "The American Board and Slave Trade." *Review and Herald*, Dec. 11, 1860, p. 32. **139**

———. "The Nation." *Review and Herald*, Aug. 12, 1862, p. 84. **144**

———. "The Nebraska Bill." *Review and Herald*, March 7, 1854, p. 56. **141**

———. "The South." *Review and Herald*, Dec. 9, 1880, p. 376. **169**

———. "The War Question." *Review and Herald*, Oct. 14, 1862, pp. 159, 160. **159, 160**

———. "The Watch Tower." *Review and Herald*, Feb. 28, 1878, p. 65. **176**

———. "The Work in the South." *Review and Herald*, May 31, 1877, p. 172. **173**

———. "Correct Views Concerning the Testimonies: A Reply to an Inquirer." *Review and Herald*, Aug. 30, 1906, pp. 8, 9. **162**

White, James and Uriah Smith. "Special Session of the General Conference." *Review and Herald*, April 6, 1876, p. 108. **168**

White, James Edson. "At Hickory, N.C." *The Gospel Herald*, June 1900, p. 46. **180**

———. "Beginning Work. Steamer Morning Star." *The Gospel Herald*, June 1900, p. 37. **176**

———. "Explanations of Financial Report. Field Expense and Aid." *The Gospel Herald*, June 1900, p. 52. **180**

———. "False Accusation." *The Gospel Herald*, Oct. 1900, pp. 89, 90. **178**

———. Letter to Ellen G. White, May 18, 1893. Available online at http://ellenwhite.org/content/correspondence/white-je/002860pdf, accessed 12/29/15. **175**

———. Letter to Ellen G. White, Aug. 10, 1893. Available online at http://ellenwhite.org/content/correspondence/white-je/002872pdf accessed 12/29/15. **176**

———. Letter to Ellen G. White, Oct. 31, 1893. **176**

———. Letter to Ellen G. White, May 14, 1899; May 25, 1899; Aug. 19, 1899; Aug. 24, 1899; Nov. 20, 1899. **178**

———. Letter to M. A. Cornwell, Oct. 10, 1899. **178**

———. Letter to N. W. Allee, Feb. 16, 1900. **178**

———. Letter to W. C. White, March 7, 1909. **180**

———. "Morning Star Group of Southern Missionary Workers." *The Gospel Herald*, March 1899, pp. 68, 69. **176**

———. "Relief for the Suffering." *The Gospel Herald*, March 1899, pp. 61, 62. **178**

———. "Sick and in Prison." *The Gospel Herald*, January 1901, p. 2. **178**

———. "The Southern Field Closing to the Message." *The Gospel Herald*, Oct. 1900, p. 86. **180**

———. "The Southern Work: Mob Violence." Battle Creek, Michigan: June 9, 1899. Excerpted in James R. Nix, *The Spirit of Sacrifice & Commitment: Experiences of Seventh-day Adventist Pioneers*, p. 177. **178**

White, Ronald C. *A. Lincoln: A Biography*. New York: Random House, 2009. **149**

White, Walter F. "The Eruption of Tulsa." *The Nation*, vol. 112, no. 292 (June 29, 1921), pp. 909, 910. Available online at https://books.google.com/books?pg=PA910&dq, accessed 2/3/15. **179**

White, William Clarence. Letter to J. N. Loughborough, Nov. 20, 1899. WCW Letterbook 14, p. 337. **147**

———. Letter to L. E. Froom, Dec. 13, 1934. **140**

———. Letter to L. E. Froom, Jan. 8, 1928, in *Selected Messages*, book 3, pp. 459, 460. **140**

———. Letter to Pastor W. G. Kneeland, Jan. 18, 1924, DF 316. **161**

———. "Some Early Statements—Why Not Reprinted?" DF 316, Ellen G. White Estate branch office/archives, Loma Linda University, California. **158, 162**

White, William C., Dores E. Robinson, and Arthur White. "The Spirit of Prophecy and Military Service." Washington, DC: Ellen G. White Publications, June 15, 1956. **144**

Whittington, G. P. "Thomas O. Moore, Governor of Louisiana, 1860–1864." *The Louisiana Historical Quarterly*, vol. 13 (Jan. 1930), no. 1, pp. 5–31. **151**

Wiley, Bell Irvin. *The Life of Billy Yank*. Indianapolis, Bobbs-Merrill, 1952. **32, 152**

Willey, T. Joe. "A Beast in the Garden: Amalgamation of Man and Beast Challenges the Unity of Mankind." Available online at http://www.docin.com/p-412350824.html, accessed 6/8/14. **161**

———. "Amalgamation of Man and Beast: Solving the Riddle." A presentation by Dr. T. Joe Willey at the San Diego Adventist Forum, Oct. 13, 2007. **157, 158**

"William F Killen in the U.S. Civil War Soldier Records and Profiles, 1861-1865." Film number M226, roll 34. **172**

"Will of John Killen 11 Feb 1869 Houston County, GA." Available online at http://files.usgwarchives.net/ga/houston/wills/k4500002.txt, accessed 2/10/15. **172**

Woese, Carl. "The Universal Ancestor." *Proceedings of the National Academy of Sciences USA*, vol. 95, no. 12, pp. 6854-6859 [June 1998]. Available online at http://www.pnas.org/content/95/12/6854.full.pdf, accessed 2/5/15). **163**

Wood, Todd Charles. "Species Variability and Creationism." *Origins*, 2008, Number 62, pp. 6–25. Accessed online at http://www.grisda.org/origins/62006.pdf, accessed 12/15/15. **161, 164**

Woodward, C. Van. *The Strange Career of Jim Crow*. New York: Oxford University Press, 1966. **100, 177**

Woldman, Albert A. *Lincoln and the Russians*. Cleveland, World Pub. Co., 1952. **154**

Wright, Jared, and Alisa Williams. "Dwight Nelson's MLK-Weekend Sermon Spurs Petition to Eradicate Ethnic Conferences." Available online at http://spectrummagazine.org/article/2015/01/22/dwight-nelsons-mlk-weekend-sermon-spurs-petition-eradicate-ethnic-conferences, accessed 1/27/15. **183**

Wyatt-Brown, Bertram. "American Abolitionism and Religion." Available online at http://nationalhumanitiescenter.org/tserve/nineteen/nkeyinfo/amabrel.htm, accessed 4/25/12. **139**

———. *Religion and the American Civil War*. New York: Oxford University Press, 1998. **155**

Yazoo City *Herald*, June 1, 1900. Quoted in *The Gospel Herald*, Oct. 1900, p. 88, 89, in Graybill, pp. 70, 71. **179**

Yazoo Sentinel, June 7, 1900. Quoted in "The Southern Field Closing to the Message." *The Gospel Herald*, Oct. 1900, p. 86. **180**

Yearns, W. Buck and John G. Barrett, eds., *North Carolina Civil War Documentary*. Chapel Hill: University of North Carolina Press, 1980. **137**

"Yes, We Have a Christian Sabbath." *Examiner and Chronicle* (New York), Oct. 4, 1877. **171**

Young, Robert A. *The Negro: A Reply to Ariel*. Nashville, TN: J. W. M'Ferrin & Co., 1867. **158**

Zimmer, Carl. "Festooning The Tree Of Life." Available online at http://blogs.discovermagazine.com/loom/2008/07/17/festooning-the-tree-of-life/#.Vlo2INKrR0t, accessed 11/28/15. **207**

Scriptural and Pseudepigraphal Index

Genesis 1:24, 25 **164** 1:27 **55** 3:15 **163** 4:26 **56** 6 **56** 157 6:1 **56** 6:2 **56**, **59** 6:4 **48**, **59** 6:11 **54**, **55**, 6:12 **55** 6:13 **54**, **55** 6:20 **164** 7 **157** 7:1, 2 **61** 7:14 **164** 8 **157** 8:19 **164** 9–14 **157** 9:2, 3 **59**
Exodus 22:19 **54** 32:7 **162**
Leviticus 18:23 **54**, **159**, **160** 18:24 **159**, **160** 20:12 **54**, **160**
Deuteronomy 32:26-30 **38**
Joshua 10:13 **163**
2 Samuel 1:18 **163** 12:7 **151**
1 Kings 11:1–8; 16:31–33 **48**
2 Chronicles 18:4–17 **151**
Nehemiah 13:23–27 **57**
Job 19:26 **140**
Psalms 56:8 **158** 75:8 **17**
Ecclesiastes 7:29 **63**
Isaiah 58:5–7 **34**, 58:13 **171**
Jeremiah 25:15, 26, 31 **17**
Hosea 4:12 **151**
Amos 9:10 **151**
Obadiah 1:16 **158**
Micah 2:8, 9; 3:5 **151**

Matthew 7:14 **135** 12:29 **143** 13:27, 28 **63** 22:30 **56** 24:38, 39 **57** 25:38, 39 **17** 28:19, 20 **180**
Mark 3:27 **143** 12:25 **56**
Luke 11:17 **136** 21:25, 26 **17**
John 1 **56** 1:12 **56** 3:16 **171** 3:23 **171** 14:1–3 **140**
Acts 8:38 **171** 13:27, 42, 44; 16:13; 17:2 **140** 17:26 **51**, **52**, **56**, **160**
Romans 3:31; 5:1, 2; 7:22; 8:4, 7 **140** 13:13 **171**
1 Corinthians 7:19 **140** 15:33 **57** 15:39 **162** 15:53, 54 **140**
2 Corinthians 5:8 **150** 6:14 **56**
Galatians 5:23 **171**
Ephesians 2:8–10 **140**
1 Thessalonians 4:14 **140** 4:15 **155** 4:17 **155**, **171**
2 Thessalonians 2:8 **171**
1 Timothy 1:8–11 **140**
Hebrews 8:1, 2 **140** 8:10; 10:16 **140** 13:3 **17**
1 John 3:2 **114**
Revelation 3:11 **155** 6:15 **144**, **158** 13 **142** 13:11 **143** 18:12 **143**, **144** 18:13 **143**, **144**, **152** 20:5 **171** 22:7 **155** 22:12 **140**, **155** 22:20 **155**

Book of Jubilees **55** 5:2, 3; 7:23, 24 **162**
Jasher 4:16–19 **62**

The *Scriptural and Pseudepigraphal Index* uses the order of Scripture. Pseudipigraphal works are at the end.

Photo Documentation Index

Page

1 ... Young men in suits pointing heavenward. Purchased from http://www.shutterstock.com.

3 ... "Abraham Lincoln, February 9, 1864." http://www.homeworkshop.com/wp-content/uploads/2009/11/Abraham-Lincoln-seated-Feb-9-1864.jpg, accessed 4/15/15.

5 ... "Ellen G. White, 1864." © Ellen G. White Estate, Inc.

7 ... The elephant in the room.

8 ... "Alexander Stephens, Vice President of the Confederacy" [c. 1866]. Available online at www.history.com, accessed 4/15/15.

8 ... "Jefferson Davis, President of the Confederacy." Available online at http://www.historyinanhour.com/2012/06/26/american-civil-war-timeline, accessed 4/15/15.

9 ... "Lincoln defending his 'House Divided' speech during the Lincoln-Douglas debate." Available online at http://www.bobcrespo.com/wp-content/uploads/2014/06/house-divided.jpg, accessed 4/15/15.

10 ... "Map of Southern Secession, 1860–1861." Available online at https://mmsperryas.files.wordpress.com/2012/06/secession-order-map.jpg, accessed 5/7/15.

11 ... "Albert Barnes, Presbyterian clergyman." Presbyterian Historical Society. Painted by J. Neagle, engraved by J. Sartain, Sansom St. Phila. Published September 1837 by J.S. Earle of Philadelphia. Available online at https://commons.wikimedia.org/wiki/File:Albert_Barnes.jpg, accessed 12/13/15.

11 ... "Harriet Beecher Stowe." 1852. Gurney & Sons. Bowdoin College Museum of Art. Available online at https://upload.wikimedia.org/wikipedia/commons/7/70/Harriet_Beecher_Stowe_c1852.jpg, accessed 12/15/15.

12 ... "Evangelist Charles G. Finney." Available online at https://commons.wikimedia.org/wiki/File:Charles_g_finney.jpg, accessed 12/13/15.

12 ... "William Miller." Available online at http://commons.wikimedia.org/wiki/Category:William_Miller_(preacher)#/media/File:William_Miller.jpg, accessed 4/1/15.

13 ... "Abolitionist William Lloyd Garrison." Library of Congress. Britannica Online for Kids. Available online at http://kids.britannica.com/comptons/art-143618/William-Lloyd-Garrison, accessed 12/13/15.

13 ... "Adventist preachers Charles Fitch and Joshua V. Himes." Available online at: http://es.slideshare.net/rolandomireles/lnea-de-tiempo-adventista and http://pastorrussell.blogspot.com/2009/11/joshua-vaughan-himes-18051895.html and http://library.ellenwhite.org/content/file/joshua-v-himes-engraved-j-sartain-phila-boston?numFound=12286&collection=true&curr=389&sqid=2012538526&f%5B0%5D=bundle%3Afiles#image, accessed 4/15/15.

14 ... "Ellen G. White, 1859." H. C. White, photographer, Monroe, WI, 1859. © Ellen G. White Estate, Inc.

16 ... "J. N. Andrews." © Ellen G. White Estate, Inc.

16 ... "Joshua R. Giddings." Tintype, c. 1855. Yale Collection of American Literature, Beinecke Rare Book and Manuscript Library. Available online at https://commons.wikimedia.org/wiki/File:Bust_length_portrait_of_Joshua_R._Giddings._Melaineotype,_ninth_plate.jpg, accessed 12/15/15.

16 ... "Joseph Bates." © Ellen G. White Estate, Inc.

17 ... "Uriah Smith." © Ellen G. White Estate, Inc.

19 ... "Communication from Sister White": The first portion of Ellen White's counsel about the Civil War, published in the *Review and Herald* following the Battle of Bull Run. *Review and Herald*, Aug. 27, 1861, p. 100. Available online at http://documents.adventistarchives.org/Periodicals/RH/RH18610827-V18-13.pdf, accessed 1/18/15.

20 ... "Horace Greeley, editor." Available online at http://americanadsm.com/americana-election-night-rock-out-with-your-vote-out, accessed 4/14/15.

20 ... "Cassius Marcellus Clay." Matthew Brady, photographer. Library of Congress. Available online at http://commons.wikimedia.org/wiki/File:Cassius_Marcellus_Clay_abolitionist_-_Brady-Handy.jpg, accessed 4/1/15.

20 ... "Abraham Lincoln, February 9, 1861." By Christopher S. German, last portrait sitting in Springfield, Illinois, before leaving for Washington, D.C., to assume the presidency. Library of Congress. Available online at http://commons.wikimedia.org/wiki/File:Lincoln_O-43_by_German,_1861.jpg, accessed 4/1/15.

21 ... "Ellen G. White" (1864). © Ellen G. White Estate, Inc.

21 ... A bayonet charge. "The War for the Union, 1862 – A Bayonet Charge." Winslow Homer, artist. (Rama/Wikimedia Commons). "Visualizing the Civil War." Available online at http://www.studio360.org/story/122951-mathew-brady-and-winslow-homer, accessed 1/26/15.

21 ... Cannon firing. Available online at http://www.wrcbtv.com/story/17342129/park-service-seeks-volunteers-to-fire-artillery, accessed 1/26/15.

21 ... "Parkville officiants James and Ellen White, Joseph H. Waggoner, Uriah Smith, and J. N. Loughborough." J. W. Becheller collection of Adventist pioneers. Center for Adventist Research, Andrews University.

22 ... "A Harvest of Death, Gettysburg, July 4, 1863." Timothy H. O'Sullivan, photographer. Printed by Alexander Gardner. Huntington Library. Available online at http://huntington.org/WebAssets/Templates/content.aspx?id=17630, accessed 12/16/15. The photo was taken days after the conflict and was artificially staged. It being a Union victory, the Northern dead were already buried.

22 ... "Living conditions at Andersonville prison." National Park Service reenactment. "Civil War Series: The Prison Camp at Andersonville." Available online at http://www.nps.gov/parkhistory/online_books/civil_war_series/5/sec4.htm, accessed 4/14/15.

22 ... "J. N. Loughborough and John Byington." J. W. Becheller collection of Adventist pioneers. Center for Adventist Research, Andrews University.

23 ... "Nathan Osborn" with his signature. *History of St. Joseph County, Michigan* (1887), p. 230.

23 ... "Confederate pictorial envelope, Charleston, S.C., ca. 1861." Huntington Library, Art Collections, and Botanical Gardens. Available online at http://huntington.org/WebAssets/Templates/content.aspx?id=17630, accessed 12/16/15

24 ... "Julia Ward Howe." Getty Images. Available online at http://www.huffingtonpost.com/matthew-albracht/peace-mothers-day_b_3226405.html, accessed 12/18/15.

24 ... " 'Battle Hymn of the Republic' first published in *The Atlantic Monthly*, February 1862." Available online at http://www.loc.gov/resource/amss.cw100430.0, accessed 10/22/15.

25 ... "The Roosevelt Seventh-day Adventist Church." Available online at http://rooseveltsdachurch.org, accessed 4/14/15.

25 ... "Lieutenant Henry Kyd Douglas, CSA." Available online at http://farm8.staticflickr.com/7019/6738715913_6de3442c83_z.jpg, accessed 4/14/15.

25 ... "Col. William Willis Blackford." Available online at http://www.encyclopediavirginia.org/Blackford_W_W_18 31-1905, accessed 4/14/15.

26 ... "Henry J. Raymond." Library of Congress. Available online at http://hd.housedivided.dickinson.edu/files/images/HD_raymondHJ.jpg, accessed 4/14/15.

27 ... "First Battle of Bull Run, by Kurz and Allison." Available online at http://upload.wikimedia.org/wikipedia/commons/4/48/First_Battle_of_Bull_Run_Kurz_%26_Allison.jpg, accessed 4/15/15; with angel by Joe Maniscalco.

28 ... "General Edmund Kirby Smith, CSA." Library of Congress.

28 ... "General Irvin McDowell." Matthew Brady, photographer. Library of Congress.

29 ... "John Wesley Urban, Infantry, USA." Available online at http://image2.findagrave.com/photos/2011/307/38617496_132040851067.jpg, accessed 4/14/15.

29 ... "Horace Bushnell, Congregational clergyman." Available online at http://www.congregationallibrary.org/get-connected/beacon-street-diary?page=31, accessed 4/14/15.

32 ... "John C. Calhoun, South Carolina Senator." Matthew Brady, photographer, March 1849, beinecke.library.yale.edu, available online at http://upload.wikimedia.org/wikipedia/commons/b/b9/John_C_Calhoun_by_Mathew_Brady%2C_March_1849.jpg, accessed 4/14/15.

33 ... "Wendell Phillips, abolitionist crusader and orator." Matthew Brady, photographer. Available online at http://www.old-picture.com/mathew-brady-studio/Phillips-Wendell.htm, accessed 4/14/15.

34 ... "A slave family near Savanna, Georgia. Insuring a steady supply of cotton for their factories helped English businessmen and politicians overlook Southern slavery." Available online at http://www.history.com/topics/black-history/slavery/pictures/slave-life/slave-family-in-cotton-field-near-savannah, accessed 4/14/15.

36 ... "James Mason and John Slidell, Confederate diplomats." Available online at http://civilwardailygazette.com/2011/12/26/they-will-be-cheerfully-liberated-mason-slidell-to-be-freed, accessed 8/29/14.

37 ... "Methodist Bishop George Foster Pierce." From the William Wynn Mood photo album, United Methodist Archives, Wofford College, Spartanburg, South Carolina. Available online at https://www.flickr.com/photos/wofford_archives/3118989684, accessed 3/17/15.

39 ... "Lincoln's preliminary reading of the Emancipation Proclamation before his cabinet in July 1862. Francis Bicknell Carpenter, artist." From left to right, the men in the portrait are: Secretary of War Edward Stanton (seated), Secretary of the Treasury Salmon P. Chase, President Lincoln, Secretary of the Navy Gideon Welles, Secretary of the Interior Caleb B. Smith, Postmaster General Montgomery Blair, Attorney General Edward Bates, Secretary of State William Seward (seated in front of the table). Library of Congress. Available online at http://www.whitehousehistory.org/whha_classroom/classroom_documents-1863.html, accessed 4/14/15.

40 ... "Ellen G. White's VISIONS in relation to CIVIL WAR events." Kevin L. Morgan.

42 ... "Major General John Porter Hatch assumed military command of Charleston from February to August 1865, following the city's surrender." Library of Congress.

43 ... "Brigadier General Rufus Saxton, organizer of the first regiment of liberated slaves, the First South Carolina Colored Volunteers." Saxton served for four months in 1865 as the first assistant commissioner of the Freedmen's Bureau assigned to Georgia, South Carolina, and Florida. Library of Congress. Available online at http://coolcivilwarnames.wordpress.com, accessed 4/15/15.

43 ... "Freed slaves watching parade." *Harper's Weekly*, Dec. 2, 1865.

44 ... "A hand-scrawled message on a hearse declared: 'Slavery is Dead.' " Picture represents what was described, it does not depict the actual parade. Available online at http://www.grandcarriages.com/funeral/Funeral.html, accessed 4/14/15.

47 ... "Louis Agassiz, biologist and geologist." "Louis Agassiz." wikipedia. Available online at http://en.wikipedia.org/wiki/Louis_Agassiz, accessed 1/21/15.

47 ... "Elbert B. Lane." Center for Adventist Research, Andrews University.

47 ... "Charles Haddon Spurgeon." From "The Spurgeon Lectures." Available online at http://www.mbts.edu/spurgeon/, accessed 1/21/15.

48 ... "Martin Luther." "Martin Luther." Available online at http://www.xn--ktphane-n2ab.net/manset/517-martin-luther.html, accessed 4/15/15.

48 ... "T. Joe Willey, PhD." Available online at http://sandiegoadventistforum.org/node/473, accessed 4/14/15.

51 ... "Benjamin F. Snook and William H. Brinkerhoff." J. W. Becheller collection of Adventist pioneers. Center for Adventist Research, Andrews University.

51 ... "Uriah Smith." © Ellen G. White Estate, Inc.

52 ... "People groups mentioned by Uriah Smith in his rebuttal: the Bushmen, . . ." Available online at http://upload.wikimedia.org/wikipedia/commons/5/5c/Bosquimanos-Grassland_Bushmen_Lodge,_Botswana_09.jpg, accessed 4/19/15.

52 ... "the Hottentots, . . ." "Nama Family Group - Circa 1900." ("Hottentot" is the colonial name for the Nama people.) Available online at http://www.ezakwantu.com/Gallery%20Herero%20and%20Namaqua%20Genocide.htm, accessed 4/14/15.

52 ... "and the Digger Indians." "California Native American Indians in 1863." Available online at http://usslave.blogspot.com/2014/11/california-native-american-indians-in.html, accessed 4/14/15.

53 ... "Frank Lewis Marsh." GC Archives.

53 ... "W. C. White." Center for Adventist Research, Andrews University.

53 ... "W. G Kneeland" (Warren George Kneeland). "Emergency Passport Applications, Argentina thru Venezuela, 1906-1925 1915-1925 Volume 004: Great Britain and Possessions," p. 297/462. Issue date: 9 June 1924. Available at: http://interactive.ancestry.com/1174/32296_1220705228_0035-00330/2202306, accessed 4/19/15.

61 ... "Amateur paleontologist Robert Correia in 1993." From "Dinosaurs What and Why?" recorded April 24, 1993.

Photo Documentation Index

62 ... "Chromosomes within the nucleus of a cell" Available online at http://www.wisegeek.com/what-are-chromosomes.htm, accessed 12/24/15. "Bacterial horizontal gene transfer." Available online at http://wps.prenhall.com/wps/media/objects/1143/1171012/9_1.html, accessed 12/24/15.

63 ... "Darwin's 1837 simplistic sketch of his conception of the relation between life forms." "Evolution: Charles Darwin was wrong about the tree of life." *theguardian*, Jan. 21, 2009. Available online at http://www.theguardian.com/science/2009/jan/21/charles-darwin-evolution-species-tree-life, accessed 1/21/15.

63 ... "A representation of the actual relations of organisms after DNA comparisons." Illustration available online at http://photos1.blogger.com/blogger/4566/894/1600/hgt-bacteria-bl.1.jpg, accessed 11/28/15. For an explanation of the representation, see Carl Zimmer, "Festooning The Tree Of Life," available online at http://blogs.discovermagazine.com/loom/2008/07/17/festooning-the-tree-of-life/#.Vlo2INKrR0t, accessed 11/28/15).

67 ... "Ku Klux Klan robe." Available online at http://americanhistory.si.edu/brown/history/1-segregated/detail/kkk-robe.html, accessed 4/15/15.

69 ... "A slave cabin." Once a slave hut, it housed male students at the Oakwood Training School in 1896. From *Adventist Heritage*, March 1996, Issue 17.1, pp. 6, 54

69 ... "Elbert B. Lane, first Seventh-day Adventist minister in the South." Available online at https://h0bbes.wordpress.com/2006/08/07/the-beginning-of-regional-conferences-in-the-us, accessed 4/15/15.

70 ... "Elbert B. Lane preaching in a train station." Fred Collins, illustrator, in Spalding, *Origin and History*, p. 170, modified by Kevin L. Morgan to conform to photo of E. B. Lane. Available online at http://blacksdahistory.org/files/40749920.pdf, accessed 4/15/15.

71 ... "The Jonathan Allison family, charter members of the Edgefield Junction Church in Tennessee. Two Allison sons became ministers—Thomas H. Allison, known for his musicianship and preaching in the South and Midwest, and Jonathan W. Allison, Sr., who worked in the South and West. Allison's son, Jonathan W. Allison, Jr., pastored in the Midwest and at the University Boulevard church in Los Angeles." Available online at http://blacksdahistory.org/files/40749920.pdf, accessed 4/15/15.

72 ... "Powder Mills, Kentucky, Seventh-day Adventist Church, built 1878." Courtesy Albert Dittes.

73 ... "Charles O. Taylor" (c. 1859). J. W. Becheller collection of Adventist pioneers. Center for Adventist Research, Andrews University.

76 ... "D. M. Canright." © Ellen G. White Estate, Inc.

76 ... "Joseph Clarke." J. W. Becheller collection of Adventist pioneers. Center for Adventist Research, Andrews University.

77 ... "Dred Scott." Wood engraving in *Century Magazine*, 1887. Library of Congress.

80 ... "William Francis Killen and his wife Martha." Contributed by Dawn Marcus Sparacio on ancestry.com.

80 ... "Otho C. Godsmark." © Ellen G. White Estate, Inc.: L. T. Nicola Album Collection.

81 ... Tent Meeting. *Review and Herald*, June 9, 1859, p. 24.

81 ... "Sands H. Lane." Center for Adventist Research, Andrews University: L. T. Nicola Album Collection.

82 ... "Seventh-day Adventist historian A. W. Spalding." Center for Adventist Research, Andrews University.

83 ... "Robert M. Kilgore." Center for Adventist Research, Andrews University.

84 ... "Elder Charles M. Kinney." Available online at http://www.blacksdahistory.org/great-black-sda-evangelists.html, accessed 4/15/15.

86 ... "Elder Alonzo Barry." Available online at www.blacksdahistory.org/great-black-sda-evangelists.html, accessed 4/15/15.

88 ... "The Birmingham First Seventh-day Adventist Church provides a contemporary example of racial cooperation." *Southern Tidings*, February 2012.

90 ... " 'Le bon-Samaritain' [The Good Samaritan]. Aimé Morot, 1880." Available online at https://www.tumblr.com/search/aime%20morot, accessed 4/15/15.

92 ... "A young black cotton sharecropper standing in before a cotton field in Pulaski County, Arkansas." Available online at http://www.globalresearch.ca/debt-slavery-in-america-the-forgotten-history-of-sharecropping/5356693, accessed 4/15/15.

94 ... "James Edson White." Review and Herald Publishing Assoc., © Ellen G. White Estate, Inc.

94 ... "Will Palmer." © Ellen G. White Estate, Inc.: L. T. Nicola Album Collection.

94 ... "The 'Morning Star,' as Edson enlarged it in 1896." © Ellen G. White Estate, Inc.

95 ... "Locations of schools begun through the 'Morning Star.' " *The Gospel Herald*, Oct 1899, p. 88. Caption in original reads: "This map shows the present field of operation of the Southern Missionary Society, as mentioned in articles in this paper. In addition will be seen Star Landing, a piece of woodland bought as a fuel station for the 'Morning Star,' and Cottonwood Landing, the home of Albert Jones, who first took the truth to Calmar."

95 ... "A selection of Edson White's books." Honor Him Publishers.

96 ... "*Morning Star* Southern Missionary Workers." *The Gospel Herald*, March 1899, p. 68.

97 ... "Clarence C. Crisler, literary assistant to Ellen G. White." Available online at http://www.theseventhunders.com/gallery/displayimage.php?album=1&pos=34, accessed 4/15/15.

97 ... "W. E. B. Du Bois" (1911). Addison N. Scurlock, photographer, displayed in National Portrait Gallery, Washington, DC. Available online at http://commons.wikimedia.org/wiki/File:Motto_web_dubois_original.jpg, accessed 4/15/15.

97 ... "Booker T. Washington" (1911). Available online at http://www.lisarivero.com/2013/02/23/booker-t-washington-and-w-e-b-du-bois, accessed 4/15/15.

98 ... "The Fifteenth Amendment."

99 ... "William Howard Taft, 27th U. S. President" (1909). Library of Congress.

99 ... "Lynchings from 1909–1918." National Association for the Advancement of Colored People. *Thirty Years of Lynching in the United States, 1889–1913*, p. viii.

100 ... "A sign of segregation at a Greyhound Bus station in Rome, Georgia." Available online at http://www.pbs.org/wgbh/americanexperience/freedomriders/issues/jim-crow-laws, accessed 4/15/15.

101 ... "Chapel and parsonage, Calmar, Mississippi." "History of the South Central Conference," by R. Steven Norman, III. Available online at http://www.scribd.com/doc/180349855/South-Central-Conference-Early-History-pps, accessed 4/15/15.

102 ... "Albion Fox Ballenger." Available online at https://newenglandpastor.files.wordpress.com/2012/11/

ballenger.jpg and http://www.smyrna.org/op/2014/November_2014/op_14_11.htm, accessed 4/15/15.

103... "Old Plantation Mansion, Huntsville." *Adventist Heritage*, March 1996, Issue 17.1, p. 6.

106... "W. C. White" (1907). "Ellen G. White in Family Group, Elmshaven, California 1907." © Ellen G. White Estate, Inc.

106... "Ellen G. White" (1907). "Ellen G. White in Family Group, Elmshaven, California 1907." © Ellen G. White Estate, Inc.

106... "D. E. Robinson." © Ellen G. White Estate, Inc.

106... "P. T. Magan." © Ellen G. White Estate, Inc.

107... "African Americans taken captive during Tulsa Race Riot, June 1921." Library of Congress.

112... "Fred Rogers and family, R. T. Nash and family, and Franklin G. Warnick at the Day School in Lintonia." *Gospel Herald*, June 1900, p. 42.

113... "Ellen White at a special meeting of educators at the Oakwood Industrial School, June 21, 1904. Edson is first at the left in the front row, and Willy is third from the left. F. R. Rogers is in the third row, far left." © Ellen G. White Estate, Inc.

Front row, beginning at the left: (1) Elder James Edson White, (2) Mrs. Ellen G. White, (3) Elder W. C. White, (4) Elder Smith Sharp, (5) Prof. J. E. Tenney, and (6) Elder N. W. Allee.

Second row: (1) Elder W. F. McNeely, (2) Elder S. B. Horton, (3) Elder R. M. Kilgore, (4) A. F. Harrison, and (5) John Macmillan.

Third row: (1) Prof. F. R. Rogers, (2) Elder H. G. Thurston, (3) Elder J. O. Johnston, (4) A. Fort, (5) Brother Dart, and (6) Prof. E. B. Melendy.

Fourth row: (1) T. O'Rell and (2) S. M. Jacobs. Available online at https://photo.egwwritings.org/index.php?album=People&image=28.jpg, accessed 4/15/15.

115... "Martin Luther King, Jr., delivering his 'I have a dream' speech." "Ga Rep. Paul Broun statement on MLK's 'I Have a Dream' speech." Available online at http://www.examiner.com/article/ga-rep-paul-broun-statement-on-mlk-s-i-have-a-dream-speech, accessed 4/27/15.

116... "Timeline of Ellen G. White's Counsels in the Context of National Events."

117... "Opening of Southern Missionary Society Schools"

118... "The Vicksburg Mission School started by Edson White 1895 (see also *Gospel Herald*, May 1898, p. 5)." *The Gospel Herald*, May 1898, p. 4; June 1900, p. 38.

118... "Agricultural program at the Hillcrest School Farm, Nashville, Tennessee." © Ellen G. White Estate, Inc.

118... "Anna Knight, the first Black missionary to India, attended the Hillcrest School Farm." © Ellen G. White Estate, Inc.

118... "Shireman's 'Colored' School, Hildebran, North Carolina, c. 1903. Courtesy Barry Mahorney.

119... "Students at the Lintonia Mission School: (left to right) Robert Walker, Flanigan Wicks, Nettie Williams, Little Walker, Parlee Jones." *Gospel Herald*, June 1900, p. 50.

119... "(left to right) Lelar Knighton, Rosa Jones, Olive Knighton at the Wilsonia Mission School." *Gospel Herald*, June 1900, p. 50.

119... "Larger group of students at the Mission School in Lintonia." *Southern Tidings*, October 1995, p. 3; *Southern Tidings*, February 2001, p. 10.

120... "Oakwood Principal Solon M. Jacobs with students and workers, displaying the school's new riding plow, 1897." General Conference Archives

121... "Oakwood School faculty and students, 1910." © Ellen G. White Estate, Inc.

121... "Anna Knight with the star from the *Morning Star*. c. 1960." © Ellen G. White Estate, Inc. Available online at http://library.ellenwhite.org/content/file/miss-anna-knight-and-star-anna-knight-pioneer-black-teacher-and-medica#image, accessed 4/15/15.

122... "Barry Black." "U.S. Senate Chaplain Barry Black to preach at Oakwood University Seventh-day Adventist Church." Available online at http://www.al.com/living/index.ssf/2014/12/barry_black_at_oakwood.html, accessed 4/15/15.

122... "Dr. Eva B. Dykes." Available online at https://rosessupposes.wordpress.com/2010/01/22/eva-b-dykes, accessed 4/15/15.

122... "Chessie Harris." Available online at http://www.blacksdahistory.org/chessie-harris.html, accessed 4/15/15.

122... "Inez Booth." "Inez Booth made a lifetime out of reaching those in jail." Available online at http://blog.al.com/breaking/2010/08/inez_booth_made_a_lifetime_out.html, accessed 4/15/15.

122... "Calvin Edwin Mosely, Jr." Center for Adventist Research, Andrews University. Louis B. Reynolds Collection, Andrews University.

122... "Frank Loris Peterson." "The historical roots of the SDA African-American community and PUC are intertwined from the start." Available online at http://www.blacksdahistory.org/files/45788769.ppt, accessed 4/16/15.

122... "Wintley Phipps." Available online at http://www.itickets.com/artists/10623/Wintley%20Phipps_concert, accessed 4/15/15.

123... "Malcolm X." Available online at http://newsone.com/2885219/ps-201-flushing-queens-malcolm-x, accessed 4/15/15.

123... *"The Fruitage of Spiritual Gifts."* Available online at http://www.cellarstories.com/cgi-bin/cellarstories/150462.html, accessed 4/15/15.

125... "Lewis C. Sheafe." Available online at www.blacksdahistory.org/Lewis_Sheafe.html, accessed 4/15/15.

125... "John W. Manns." "John Wesley Manns in the U.S. Passport Applications, 1795-1925." Available online at http://search.ancestry.com/cgi-bin/sse.dll?db=USpassports&h=1009780&indiv=try&o_vc=Record:OtherRecord&rhSource=6061, accessed 4/2/15.

125... "James K. Humphrey." Center for Adventist Research, Andrews University.

126... "James L. Moran." Available online at images.adventistarchives.org/view/ARAI/ARAI1938-P44-01.jpg.html, accessed 11/17/15.

126... "Lucille Lewis Byard." Taken from *The North American Regional Voice*, August 1987, p. 4. Available online at http://documents.adventistarchives.org/Periodicals/RV/RV19870801-V09-06.pdf, accessed 10/21/2015.

127... "Evangelist E. E. Cleveland." Available online at http://blacksdahistory.org/black-sda-preacher-hall-of-fame.html, accessed 4/15/15.

128... "Irene Morgan *The African American*, June 15, 1946.

128... "W. S. Banfield, one-time state NAACP president." "Black Seventh-day Adventists in Civil Rights." Available online at http://www.blacksdahistory.org/black-sdas-in-civil-rights.html, accessed 4/15/15.

129... "Oakwood students with school sign at the 1965 march." Available online at http://www.blacksdahistory.org/Timelines.html, accessed 4/15/15.

129... "Program autographed for Mervyn Warren by Martin Luther King, Jr., and Ralph Abernathy, March 19, 1962." Courtesy Dr. Mervyn A. Warren. *Southern Tidings*, February 2016, p. 8.
130... "Nelson, Hale, and Holloway at the Layman's Leadership Conference." Available online at http://www.blacksdahistory.org/files/45460276.pdf, accessed 4/16/15.
130..."Neal C. Wilson [1975]." "Henry Wright with Neal Wilson, then president of North American Division and later General Conference president." Available online at http://www.columbiaunionvisitor.com/photo-gallery-pastor-wrights-ministry-over-the-years/neil-wilson, accessed 4/16/15.
130..."C. D. Brooks [1966]." Available online at http://www.columbiaunionvisitor.com/wp-content/uploads/2014/02/C.D.-in-1966.jpg, accessed 4/16/15.
131..."Charles Bradford." "Town Hall American of the Year, Dr. Charles E. Bradford, Vice President of the General Conference of Seventh-day Adventists, Washington, D.C." Center for Adventist Research, Andrews University.
131..."Robert Pierson." Available online at http://www.blacksdahistory.org/a-preacher-was-born.html, accessed 11/10/14.
131..."Dr. Ron Smith." Available online at http://www.floridaconference.com/wp-content/uploads/2013/07/Ron-Smith.jpg, accessed 4/16/15.
132..."Dwight Nelson, pastor Pioneer Memorial Church." Available online at http://www.adventfm.org, accessed 4/16/15.
132..."Ricardo B. Graham, president Pacific Union Conference." Available online at http://paucadmin.adventistfaith.org/president, accessed 4/17/15.
132..."Baptismal candidates at Fort Myers Shores Church: (left to right) Nigel Loney, Roger Johnson, Pedro Nuñez, Jean Paul, Nancy Bartolet, Sarah Noack, and Claudette Loney" *Southern Tidings*, May 2014.
133..."Wilhelmina Johnson teaching at Vacation Bible School." Taken at the Aiken Seventh-day Adventist Church, June 1996. Honor Him Publisher.
133..."Martha Marsh." Taken at the funeral of her sister, Mary Brown, August 31, 2008. Honor Him Publishers.
134... "Ellen White's early vision of the pathway to heaven." Source unknown.
184..." Photographs and newspaper clippings about slavery and the beginning of the American Civil War."
184...Five generations of slaves in South Carolina, c. 1862 (Library of Congress), taken at Smith's Plantation, Beaufort, South Carolina.
184... "Neutrality," by John Tenniel, at *Punch*, 1863, with original dialogue, "Mrs. North: "How about the Alabama, you wicked old man?" Mrs. South: "Where's my rams? Take back your precious consuls — there!!!" Available online at http://imgarcade.com/1/cotton-diplomacy, accessed 12/18/15.
184...Uncle Tom's Cabin. Available online at http://utc.iath.virginia.edu/interpret/exhibits/winship/winship.html, accessed 12/18/15.
184...Abraham Lincoln's last studio portrait, Feb. 5, 1865 (Library of Congress) with his signature. Available at http://handwritinguniversity.com/newsletters/kathi3.html, accessed 12/18/15 .
184... "Civil War." *Scioto Gazette* (Chillicothe, OH), Jan. 8, 1861, p. 2. **(See chapter 2, endnote 25.)**
184... "The National Crisis." *New York Times*, Dec. 29, 1860. Available online at http://www.rarenewspapers.com, accessed 12/20/15.

184... "The Crittendon compromise seems to be gaining friends..." from "The Secession Movement." *Kalamazoo Gazette*, Jan. 11, 1861, p. 3. **(See chapter 4, endnote 5.)**
184... "But we will weather the storm..." from "Our Washington Correspondence." *Western Chronicle*, Dec. 20, 1860, p. 2, by SHELL BARK. **(See chapter 2, endnote 29.)**
184... "To Arms! To Arms! Your Country Calls." Civil War recruitment poster. Available online at http://civilianmilitaryintelligencegroup.com/3997/civil-war-union-recruitment-posters, accessed 12/22/15.
184... African American Army Teamsters, Cobb Hill, Virginia (Library of Congress).
184... "National Affairs: The Defeat." *The Circular* (Oneida, New York), Aug. 1, 1861. Available online at http://www.rarenewspapers.com, accessed 12/20/15. **(See chapter 3, endnote 7.)**
184... "The Stampede from Bull Run.—from a sketch by our special artist." (N. Y. Public Library Picture Collection).
184... "Crushing Rebellion," *New York Times*, July 22, 1861, p.1. Henry J. Raymond reporter. **(See chapter 3, endnote 7.)**
184... "Servile insurrection is a part of their program..." from Mobile *Register*. "Stimulants for the Rebels." *Springfield Daily Republican*, June 3, 1861, p. 2. Available online at http://genealogybank.com, accessed Nov. 19, 2015. **(See chapter 4, endnote 24.)**
184... Ellen G. White, 1858. Center for Adventist Research, Andrews University.
186..."Benjamin Baker, PhD., assistant archivist and historian, General Conference of Seventh-day Adventists." Available online at http://www.columbiaunionvisitor.com/wp-content/uploads/2014/02/Benjamin-Baker.jpg, accessed 4/16/15.
186... "Delbert Baker, PhD., vice president, General Conference of Seventh-day Adventists." Available online at http://imgick.al.com/home/bama-media/width620/img/breaking/photo/delbert-bakerjpg-ed265c7dc79e99e4.jpg, accessed 4/16/15.
191..."Ronald Graybill, PhD., historian and former assistant at the Ellen G. White Estate." Available online at https://www.adventisthealth.org/white-memorial/pages/about-us/foundation/about-the-foundation/centennial/video-stories.aspx, accessed 4/15/15.
193..."Harold L. Lee, director of the Bradford-Cleveland-Brooks Leadership Center on the campus of Oakwood University." Available online at http://www.adventistbookcenter.com/c-d-the-man-behind-the-message.html, accessed 4/26/15.
195..."Douglas Morgan, PhD. History of Christianity, Washington Adventist University." Available online at https://www.wau.edu/images/Latest_News/Meet_our_faculty_bios/Douglas-Morgan.jpg, accessed 4/16/15.
196..."James Oakes, PhD. Professor of History and the Humanities Professor at The Graduate Center, City University of New York." Available online at http://www.law.yale.edu/news/16744.htm, accessed 4/17/15.
198..."Ciro Sepúlveda, PhD., retired professor, Oakwood University." Available online at http://warinheavenwaronearth.com/wp-content/uploads/2012/06/Sepulveda_Ciro_smallerfile_noborder-250x350.jpg, accessed 4/16/15.
201..."Mervyn A. Warren, PhD., Provost and senior Vice President Oakwood University." Courtesy Oakwood University. Available online at http://blog.al.com/breaking/2010/07/mervyn_warren_named_interim_pr.html, accessed 4/16/15.

General Index

A

abolition, -ism, -ist(s) 5, 10–13, 16, 18, 20, 25, 30, 32–34, 38, 41, 47, 67, 98, 104, 116, 135–139, 141–143, 145, 149, 152, 153, 170
Adams, Aaron H. (member Parkville, MI, church) 146
Adams, John Quincy 138
Adventism 89, 120, 121, 130
Adventist(s) (sometimes meaning "Seventh-day Adventist(s)") 3, 5, 6, 12–16, 23, 38, 50, 89, 90, 111, 112, 120, 123, 125, 126, 128, 140, 143, 144, 146, 148, 149, 156, 159, 160, 162, 171, 173, 181, 183
  Sabbatarian, or seventh-day Sabbath keeping 14–16, 21, 141, 143, 146
Advent Review and Sabbath Herald (also *Review and Herald*) 11, 15, 17–19, 41, 47, 51, 65–70, 74, 76, 86, 89, 93, 109, 136, 138, 139, 165, 166, 169, 170
Aeolians 122
Agassiz, Louis *47*
Agee, Anna (African American Adventist Vicksburg teacher) 96
"Age of Washington" 97
Alabama 11, 73, 74, 79, 82, 98, 117, 120, 126–129, 134, 147, 156, 169, 173, 175–177
Aldrich, J. H. (from Parkville SDA) 146
Aldrich, J. M. 159
Allee, N. W. 104, 105
Allegheny Conference of Seventh-day Adventists 127
Allegheny East Conference of Seventh-day Adventists 132, 183
Allison, Jonathan W., Jr. *71*
Allison, Jonathan W., Sr. *71*
Allison, Thomas H. *71*
Altadena Seventh-day Adventist Church 181
"amalgamation of man and beast" 45, 51, 54, 57–59, 159, 160, 161, 164
amendment 151
  Fifteenth 98, 99, 152, 166
  Fourteenth 100, 165
  Thirteenth 49, 65, 78, 116, 144, 165
America 8, 11, 15, 18, 36, 38, 97, 115, 116, 135, 138, 139, 141, 143, 144, 152, 155, 156, 168, 181, 182
  in prophecy, sometimes with dragon-like voice 15, 142, 143
American Anti-Slavery Society 11, 13, 170
American Bible Society 12, 139
American Board of Commissioners for Foreign Missions in Boston for the Episcopal Church 12

American Colonization Society 13
American Missionary 17, 18, 66, 68
The American Sentinel 170
American slavery 16, 136
American Tract Society 12, 139
Anaconda Plan, General Scott's 145
Anderson, Dirk 61
Anderson, E. Marcella 2
Anderson, Eric 144, 146, 151, 155, 158
Anderson, Herb L. (pastor) 133
Andersonville prison 22
Andrews, John Nevins 16
angel(s) 3, 36, 50, 56, 58, 59, 110, 155, 167
  at Manassas (Bull Run) 27, 28, 116
antediluvian(s) 48, 54, 55, 57, 63
anti-slavery 11, 13–15, 18, 20, 34, 36, 41, 144, 145, 153, 156, 170
Anti-Slavery Society 170
  American 11, 13, 170
  Chittenden County, Vermont 142
  Fairhaven, Massachusetts 16
  St. Lawrence County, New York 141
Appalachian State University 3, 5
Arkansas 23, *92*, 107, 116, 151, 156
armies/army 21, 23, 25–30, 32, 33, 36, 38, 65, 79, 83, 140, 145, 146, 150, 151, 156, 165
arms 30, 31, 78, 137, 147, 151, 166
Army of the Potomac 151
Arthur, Neal 129
Asia 85
Astrap, William J. (convert in Mississippi) 176
Australia 85, 87, 89, 109, 121
Aydelott, Benjamin Parham 46

B

Bahamas Mission 53
Baker, Benjamin 3, 87, 88, 120, 124, 131, 182, *186*
Baker, Delbert 107, *186*
Bala, Kansas 146
Ballenger, Albion Fox 93, *102*
Baltimore, Maryland 35, 175
Banfield, Warren S. 122, *128*
Baptism, baptismal 70, 73, 74, 80, *132*, 134, 167, 171
Baptists 7, 117, 169, 172
Barnes, Albert *11*, 139
Barrett, Edwin S. 26, 27
Barry, Alonzo 86
base crime 45, 54, 57–60, 162, 164
Baskerville, E. L. 122
Bates, Joseph *16*, 141
Baton Rouge, Louisiana 31, 151
battle(s) 9, 21, 22, 25–30, 33, 40, 41, 78, 107,
136, 144, 145, 147, 150, 156, 166
  of Antietam 40
  of Ball's Bluff 40
  of Chancellorsville 37, 40
  of Chattanooga, Tennessee 40
  of Chickamauga, Georgia 40
  of Fredericksburg 40
  of Gettysburg 22, 38, 40, 155
  of Manassas (Bull Run), First 19, 25–27, 40, 41, 116, 144, 147, 150
    panic in 26–29
  of Manassas (Bull Run), Second 40
  of Palmito Ranch, Texas 156
  of Petersburg 40
  of Shiloh 40, 166
  of South Mountain 22, 40, 148
  of Spotsylvania 40
  of Stones River 40
  of Vicksburg 40
  of the Wilderness 40
  of Wilson's Creek 40
  Seven Days' 35, 40
Battle Creek, Michigan 19, 31, 40, 41, 65, 72, 80, 83, 87, 94, 149, 159, 173
Battle Creek Sanitarium 121
Battle Creek *Sunday Record* 98
Battle Hymn of the Republic 23, *24*
Battle, Maurice 122
Battles, Will 129
beast(s) 13, 16, 45–51, 53–55, 57–59, 62, 93, 142, 157–162, 164
  brute 16, 49, 93, 157
  flesh of 162
Beatty, John 32
Beecher, Henry Ward 30, 156
Bee, Barnard Elliott (General) 26
Belden, Frank E. 104
belief(s) 8–10, 16, 17, 53, 54, 78, 85, 125, 140, 171, 172, 181
Bell, Goodloe Harper 165
Berea College 116, 145
Bertrand, Emile (teacher Freedmen's school) 66
Birmingham First Seventh-day Adventist Church 88
Black, Barry *122*
black codes (of 1865, 1866) 69, 166
black disenfranchisement 181
Blackford, William Willis (Lieutenant Colonel, CSA) 25, 150
black voters 65, 86, 98
  registered 177
black worker(s) 114, 120, 180, 182
Blanchard, Jonathan (Congregationalist abolitionist) 170
blood, mixed 56

The *General Index* does not duplicate page references for titles in the *Bibliographical Index*. Italicized bold page numbers are for picture captions.

General Index

Bloomington, Illinois **9**
Blow, Peter (master of Dred Scott) **170**
bondage **16, 17, 42, 68, 69, 143, 156, 178**
Bonner, John S. **157**
Booth, Inez *122*
Boston **11, 12, 20, 32, 154**
Boston *Daily Advertiser* **32**
Bourdeau, Daniel T. **75, 169**
Bovee, Oran (member Parkville SDA Church) **146**
Bowles, Charles **12**
Bradford, Charles E. **122,** *131*
Bradwell, J. P. (minister) **66**
Brady, Michigan, Seventh-day Adventist Church **149**
Branson, Roy **181**
Branson, William Henry **128**
Brinkerhoff, William (also misspelled "Brinkerhoof") **45,** *51,* **147, 152, 157, 159–161**
brinkmanship **32, 151**
Bristow, Mary Beckley **33**
Britain(s), Great **135, 138, 152, 153**
Britton, Dr. Mary A. **175**
Brooks, Charles D. **122,** *130,* **131, 183**
Brooks County, Georgia **80, 171**
Brooks, Steven **133**
brotherhood **86, 89, 110, 115, 123, 131, 134, 175**
Browning, Judkin J. **3, 5, 135**
Brown, Calline (former slave) **172**
Brown, John (song) **23, 32, 42, 149, 165**
Brownlow, Senator William G. **78**
Brownson, Dr. Orestes A. **30, 138**
brutes **13, 15, 30, 49, 50, 141**
Bryant, Franklin Henry **96,** **119, 176, 180**
Buchanan, James **136, 138, 151**
Buckner, T. B. (African-American Seventh-day Adventist minister) **174**
Bull, Malcolm (Oxford lecturer) **124**
Bull Run **19,** *25–27,* **29, 39, 40, 144, 150**
Burgess, Monroe **129**
Burner, David **68**
Burnham, Lieut. P. F. **66**
Burr Oak, Michigan, Seventh-day Adventist Church **149**
Bushmen *52*
Bushnell, Horace **29**
Butler, George I. **83, 181**
Byard, Lucille Lewis and James *126,* **183**
Byington-Amadon, Martha D. **146**
Byington, Anson **17, 142, 143**
Byington, Catharine (wife of John) **142**
Byington, John **3, 17,** *22,* **140–142, 144, 146, 149**

C

Cain, Cainites **48, 55, 56, 59–61**
calcified pragmatism **123**
Caldwell County, Missouri **75, 169**
Caldwell, Dr. J. E. **94**
Calhoun, John C. **7,** *32,* **136, 151, 152**

Callagher, F. H. **144**
Calmar, Mississippi **95,** *96, 101,* **109, 178**
Campbell, Charles S. **153**
Campbell, Duncan Andrew **34**
Campbell, John **158**
Campbell, Michael W. **158**
Canales, Fernando **129**
Canright, Dudley M. **73, 75,** *76,* **79, 155, 156, 169**
Caribbean islands **85**
Carnegie, Andrew **98**
Carroll County, Tennessee **166**
Carroll, J. H. (Seventh-day Adventist pastor) **125**
Carter, Robert **122**
Catholics **91, 138, 169, 176**
Caucasian **46, 64, 100, 101, 110, 158, 163**
causes of secession and the Civil War **7–9, 11, 18, 32, 33, 39, 41, 135, 136–138, 159**
Central States Conference **127**
Chadwick, Arthur V., PhD (research professor in the Biology and Geology Department at Southwestern Adventist University) **3, 61, 163**
Chambers, Ruth **126**
Charity Mission School, Montgomery, Alabama **117**
Charleston **32, 41–43, 151**
Cheatham, William L. **127**
Cheever, George B. **30**
Chicago **106, 107, 127, 158**
Chicago riots in 1919 **107**
children of Seth **59, 60**
Chiles, J. Alexander (attorney) **175**
Christ **5, 6, 12–14, 16, 29, 50, 64, 70, 74, 85, 87–92, 95, 97, 103, 104, 109–114, 116, 117, 123–125, 139, 143, 144, 155, 168, 169, 171, 174, 175, 180**
Christadelphians **14**
Christian Anti-Slavery Conventions and the Church Anti-Slavery Society **170**
Christian, Lewis Harrison **123, 124**
Christian nation **18, 110**
Christian(s) **6, 7, 13, 14, 18, 29, 34, 52, 54, 70, 82, 89, 90, 92, 100, 101, 108, 110, 111, 114, 116, 120, 124, 128, 129, 173**
and slavery **11, 12, 50, 79**
Church of God (Adventist) **160**
church organization **14, 70, 76, 124, 132, 146**
civil rights **98, 128, 129, 131, 175**
Civil Rights Acts 1870, 1871, 1875 **116**
Civil Rights Case of 1883 **100**
civil war **12, 23, 34, 147, 148, 154**
Civil War, the American **3, 5, 6, 12, 14, 16, 18, 19, 23, 25, 31, 38, 39, 41, 45, 53, 65, 68, 105, 116, 117, 135, 136, 140, 144, 145, 149, 156, 158, 172, 173, 177, 182**
Clarke, Joseph **16, 75–79, 83, 167, 170, 171**
Clarke, Sarah **76, 170**
Clarke, Yolanda **180**
Clark, Harold W. **53, 162, 164**

Clarksdale Mission School, Clarksdale, Mississippi **117**
classes in society **35, 38, 51, 52, 60, 66, 67, 73, 81, 82, 84, 89, 91, 103, 113, 128, 152, 160, 166, 173, 174, 178**
"class of very large animals" **61**
Clay, Cassius Marcellus *20,* **145, 152**
Cleveland, E. E. **122,** *127,* **129**
Cobb, Paul **129**
Cole, V. O. **95**
Collie, Alexander **39**
Colon, Michigan, Seventh-day Adventist Church **149**
"color line" (segregation) **83, 87, 89, 100, 104, 108, 112, 113, 116, 131, 174**
Colored Farmers Alliance **86**
Colored Orphans' Home **104**
Columbus Mission School, Columbus, Mississippi **117**
commandment(s) **55, 59, 60, 70, 149, 156, 160, 162, 171**
Confederacy **7, 9, 11, 23, 30, 32–36, 134, 136, 137, 147, 152–156, 172**
Confederate(s) **8, 23, 25, 26, 28–31, 35–37, 39, 40, 65, 100, 135, 145, 150–154, 177**
Confederate States of America (CSA) **23,** *25, 28,* **30, 100, 135, 153, 154, 177**
"confusion" in Ellen White's statements
at Manassas (Bull Run) **26–29**
before the flood from amalgamation **45, 52, 54, 55, 57, 64, 164**
between human and animal races **52**
from interracial marriages **110, 116**
general, at the return of Jesus **154**
general, when England declares war **36, 37, 135**
in Scripture **54, 160**
of the slave master at the return of Jesus **141, 158**
utmost, before war **155**
with marriage between believers and unbelievers **60**
congregation **22, 146**
black **85, 86, 124, 125, 167**
mixed **73, 74, 86, 88, 125, 133, 169**
Congregational, Congregationalist(s) **29, 30, 67, 142, 170**
Congress **7, 16, 20, 65, 67, 78, 100, 137, 138, 141, 143, 144, 146–149, 151, 165**
Constitution (United States), -al, -alism, -ally, unconstitutional **8, 9, 11, 23, 76, 78, 98–100, 108, 116, 128, 136–138, 142, 143, 147–149, 151, 152, 165, 170, 177**
Corliss, John Orr **65, 75, 84**
Cornell, Merritt E. **83, 146, 149**
Correia, Robert ("Dinosaur Bob") *61,* **162**
corrupt, -ed, -ing, -ion **45, 46, 49, 51, 54, 55, 57, 59, 60, 62–64, 77, 93**
cotton **7, 32, 35, 93, 97, 115, 135, 137, 153, 154**

Cotton States and International Exposition **97, 115**
Cottrell, Roswell Fenner **75, 165**
Cox, Jeter Mark (pastor) **126**
Cranmer, Gilbert **159**
crime **28, 43, 45, 48–51, 54, 57, 58–60, 77, 136, 150, 162, 164, 165**
Crimean War **154**
Crisler, Clarence C. *97*, **98, 177**
Crisler, Dr. J. A. **101**
Crittenden Compromise **147**
Crittenden, John J. (Kentucky Congressman) **147**
Curry, Gloria (member of the Aiken Seventh-day Adventist Church) **133**

D

Dahlgren, Admiral John A. **42**
Dallas County **79**
Dancer, J. W. *96*
Darwin, Charles **62,** *63*, **160, 164**
Darwinism **53**
"daughters of men" **47, 48, 56, 59–62**
Davis, Jefferson *8*, **9, 23, 30, 31, 33, 42, 67, 134, 137, 151, 153, 154**
Day Neighborhood Mission School, Ellisville, Mississippi **117**
Democrat, -ic **9, 86, 137, 143, 147, 148, 177**
denomination(s), -al, -ally **6, 7, 12, 14, 18, 46, 65, 74, 84, 93, 101, 111, 121, 125, 126, 128, 131, 139, 146, 168, 170–173, 176, 179, 180**
Dicks, Ann (member of the Aiken Seventh-day Adventist Church) **133**
Dickson, Louis **125**
Digger Indians **52, 161**
dinosaur(s) **61, 162**
disenfranchisement (taking away voting rights) **98, 115, 181**
Dixon, Mineola **122**
DNA **62–64, 163, 164**
Douglas, Henry Kyd *25*
Douglass, Frederick **139**
Douglas, Stephen A. **9, 136–138**
Downer, David **83**, **173**
dream, -s, -ed **14, 21, 114, 115, 125, 141**
Du Bois, William E. B. *97*, **98**
Dwinell, Israel E. **39**
Dykes, Eva B. **121,** *122*

E

East St. Louis, Illinois, massacre at **107**
Edgefield Junction **65, 69, 71, 72, 86, 167, 174**
education, -al **6, 14, 38, 65, 68, 75, 80, 82, 89, 91, 92, 98, 106, 108, 115–117, 120, 122, 176, 176, 179, 180, 181**
Elaine, Arkansas **107**
"elephant in the room" (slavery) **5, 7, 8, 11, 135**
Elkins, Nancy F. **157**
Ellen G. White Estate **64, 159, 179**

Ellisville Mission School, Ellisville, Mississippi **117**
Elzey, Colonel Arnold **28**
emancipation **32, 35, 38, 39, 46, 78, 87, 117, 134–136, 138, 145, 147, 152, 153, 155, 156**
Emancipation Proclamation **14, 34, 37,** *39*, **40, 116, 144, 152, 153**
Emancipation Society **37**
Emerson, Dr. John (master of Dred Scott) **170**
empire **35, 47, 136, 154**
Engelbrecht, Jacob **145**
England **3, 5, 7, 33–39, 41, 64, 135, 139, 149, 152–154, 156**
Ensign, Martha V. **146**
enslaved **5, 18, 117, 141, 142**
Episcopalians **117**
equality, black/racial/social **6, 8, 83, 85, 86, 98, 108–112, 116, 123, 124, 127, 137, 158, 177**
Eruption of Tulsa **107**
Erving, Williemae **122**
Eubanks, Rilla (student at Lintonia school) **175**
Europe, -an **30, 35, 36, 85, 124, 126, 135, 153, 154**
evolution, -ary **53, 62, 141, 163, 164**
amalgamation versus **161**
expel slavery from the union **137**
extinction, ultimate of slavery **8–10**

F

faithful vs. unfaithful line **56, 57, 61, 64**
fast, national, to end slavery **34, 39–41, 156, 159**
Fee, John G. **139, 145**
Finney, Charles **11,** *12*
Fire-Eaters **8**
Fire Zouaves **26**
Fitch, Charles *13*
flesh **55, 62, 162**
Flood **45–51, 54, 55, 57–59, 61–64, 158, 160–162, 164, 173**
Florence, P. M. **133**
Florida **11, 73, 78, 80, 86, 116, 127, 128, 147, 151, 156, 168**
Flowerfield, Michigan, Seventh-day Adventist Church **148, 149**
Foote, William S. **143**
Forbes, John (US agent) **38, 156**
Fordham, Henry J., III **183**
Fordham, Walter **182**
Foreman, Amanda **37, 135, 153**
former slave(s) **6, 29, 44, 67, 69, 75, 115, 117, 139, 156, 172**
Fort Barrancas **151**
Fort Jackson **151**
Fort McRae **151**
Fort Moultrie **151**
Fort Pike **31**
Fort Pulaski **151**

Fort St. Phillips **151**
Fort Sumter **21, 40**
Fourth Estate (the press) **135**
Fox, William F. (historian and statistician) **145**
Fox, Ruben (former slave) **172**
Foy, William Ellis *12*
France **135, 153, 154**
Franklin, John Hope **97**
freedman, -men **65–70, 74–76, 78–80, 82, 84–87, 89, 91, 93, 117, 120, 165, 166, 168, 171, 175, 176**
Freedmen's Bureau **65–67, 165**
freedom(s) **5, 15, 29, 33, 34, 38, 42, 43, 47, 67, 78, 91, 93, 115, 141, 143, 157, 170**
free labor **9, 137**
Fremont, John Charles (General) **156**
French, Rev. Mansfield (an American Methodist Episcopal clergyman and anti-slavery activist, army chaplain, and a personal friend of Abraham Lincoln) **44**
French, William H. (abolitionist) **142**
Fresno, California **146**
Frisbie, Joseph Birchard **142**
The Fruitage of Spiritual Gifts **123**
Fugitive Slave Act (Law) **7, 15, 16, 29, 77, 116, 141, 143, 147, 148, 151**
fundamental Seventh-day Adventist beliefs **140**
Futs, Will **162**

G

Garrison, William Lloyd *13*, **30, 139, 145**
Gates, Louisa M. **69, 166, 167**
General Conference Bulletin **86, 174**
General Conference (of Seventh-day Adventists) **17, 40, 65, 73, 80, 82, 83, 85, 87, 88, 108, 120–123, 125–128, 130, 131, 140, 142, 149, 156, 173, 174, 181, 182**
gene(s), genetic(s), genomes **3, 45, 46, 47, 62, 63, 163, 164**
Georgia **11, 20,** *34*, **38, 40, 68, 73, 80, 82, 97–99, 106, 115, 125, 134, 151, 156, 166, 169, 171, 172, 176**
Giddings, Joshua R. (influential Republican) *16*, **30, 141**
Gladstone, William Ewart (British Prime Minister) **153**
Glover, Charles Smith "vision lover" **146**
Godsmark, Otho C. **75,** *80*, **82, 169, 172, 173**
Godsmark, Richard **172**
Good Samaritan **89,** *90*, **92**
Gospel Herald **101, 176**
The Gospel Sickle **170**
government(s) **7–11, 16–18, 21, 23, 35, 36, 52, 65, 66, 76–79, 100, 117, 135–139, 142–144, 147, 148, 151–154, 156, 160, 174**
Graham, Ricardo B. *132*
grandfather clause **98, 165, 177**
Grant, Alfred (author) **135**
Grant, Ulysses **39, 40, 65, 79**

Graybill, Ronald D. **97, 108, 109, 112, 115, 160, 177–179,** *191*
Graysville, Tennessee **120**
The Great Controversy **15**
Greeley, Horace **11,** *20***, 139**
Greene, Alfonso, Jr. **86, 112**
Greene, Alfonso, Sr. **129**
Greenup County **72, 73, 167**
Greenville Mission School, Greenville, Mississippi **117**
Green, William H. (Negro Dept. secretary, 1918–1928) **181**
Grimké, Angelina and Sarah **139**
Gulliver, John Putnam **67, 165**
Gurney, Heman S. **142**

H

Hacker, J. David (demographic historian) **145**
Hafer, Andrew (from Parkville SDA Church) **146**
Halladay, Fred W. *96*
Halladay, Isa C. Wekell *96*
Hall v. deCuir **100**
Haloviak, Bert **126**
Hammond, Edmund **35**
Hare, Jacob **72**
Hare, Milton **129**
Hare, R. A. (administrator Washington Sanitarium) **127**
Harpers Ferry raid **165**
Harper's Weekly **20, 30,** *43*
Harris, Chessie *122*
Hatch, John Porter (General) *42***, 43**
Hayes, Rutherford B. **100, 116, 177**
The Health Reformer **170**
Hendryx, Truman **13**
Hillcrest School Farm *118***, 119, 180**
Hilliard cousins (abolitionists) **141**
Himes, Joshua V. *13*
Holland, Harvey **129**
horizontal gene transfer (HGT) **3,** *62***, 163, 164**
Horr, Samuel and Betsey **166**
Hottentots *52***, 161**
"House Divided" speech of Lincoln **8,** *9*
Howe, Julia Ward **23,** 149
Howell, Clark, editor of the *Atlanta Constitution* **98**
Hughes, John (archbishop of New York) **138**
Hughes, Louis (former slave) **29**
Hull, Moses (Seventh-day Adventist minister) **149**
Humphrey, James Kemuel **125, 126**
Huntsville, Alabama *103***, 120, 122, 126, 177**
Huntsville School Farm **120**
Huxley, Thomas, "Darwin's bulldog" **160**
hybrid animals, hybridization (e.g. platypus) **58, 158, 161, 163, 164**

I

ignorance **28, 49, 50, 79, 84, 91, 93, 158, 160**

image of Christ, God, divine **16, 45, 50, 54, 55, 57, 59–60, 90, 91, 162, 164**
Indiana **70, 149**
Indian Territory **100**
Ingraham, William S. **51,** *159*
integration **85, 90, 124, 127, 131, 132, 182**
intermarriage **45–47, 55, 57, 60, 61, 110, 116, 157**
intervention
  God's **5, 13, 29, 41, 116**
  England's **37, 154**
Iowa **33, 51, 72, 83,** *96***, 116, 159, 160, 167, 168**

J

Jackson, Andrew **47, 148, 151**
Jackson Mission School, Jackson, Mississippi **117**
Jackson, "Stonewall" **25, 37, 40, 150**
Jacobs, Solon M. (Principal Oakwood) *120*
Jay, Hamilton, Esq. **78**
Jefferson, Thomas **138**
Jensen, Anna *96*
Jesus **6, 13, 14, 50, 56, 57, 63, 70, 85, 87, 88, 90, 91, 109, 110, 114, 132, 134, 140, 158, 174**
Jim Crow **69, 120**
Joe's Walk, Mississippi **95**
"John Brown's Body" ("John Brown's Song") **23,** *42***, 149**
Johnson, Andrew **67**
Johnson County, Texas **171**
Johnson, Prince (former slave) **172**
Johnson, Stephanie D. **65**
Johnson, Wilhelmina (member of the Aiken Seventh-day Adventist Church) *133*
Jones, Parlee (student Lintonia) *119*
Jones, Rosa (student Wilsonia) *119*
Jones, Susan (former slave) **172**
Jordan, G. M. and F. **76**
Jordan, Winthrop D. (author *White Over Black*) **141**
Joslyn, Roger D. (President of the American Society of Genealogists) **64,** *164*
jubilee of freedom **41,** *42***, 78, 158**
Juniata Mission School, Alabama School **117**

K

Kalamazoo Gazette **31,** *147*
Kansas **16, 17, 39, 77, 84, 138, 146, 156, 174**
Kansas-Nebraska Act (Nebraska bill) **7, 9, 10, 16, 116, 136, 138**
Keeney (also misspelled "Kinney" and "Kinne"), Harvey (Parkville, Michigan elder) **23, 146, 148, 149**
Keeney, Sarah **146**
Kelley, Abby **139**
Kellogg, Dr. John Harvey **104**
Kellogg, John P. **156**

Kentucky **32, 33, 72, 73, 75, 83, 85, 86, 100, 116, 127, 145, 147, 167–170, 173**
Kilgore, George Vincent **159**
Kilgore, John Lindsay **79,** *83***, 140**
Kilgore, Robert M. **79,** *83***, 84, 88, 140, 169, 171, 173**
Killen, Charles S., Eva, Herbert, Mattie, Robert, Susie, William Lane (children of William F. and Martha A. P.) **172**
Killen, Edmund **80, 172**
Killen, John (father of William Francis) **172**
Killen, Leah **172**
Killen, Martha Ann Permelia *80***, 172**
Killen, Mattie, Madison, Eddie, Leah, Rachel, and Annie (children of Edmund and Leah Killen) **172**
Killen, William Francis *80***, 82, 84, 171, 172, 173**
Killen, Will L. **172**
Killingsworth, J. A. **171**
"kinds," biblical **64, 164**
King, Martin Luther, Jr. **114,** *115***,** *129***, 133**
King, N. B. *96*
King, S. H. **79**
Kinney, Charles M. *84***–86,** *120***, 173, 174**
Kinney, John **46**
Kirby's Digest **101**
Knauft, Daniel **2**
Kneeland, Warren G. *53*
Knight, Anna *118***, 119,** *121***,** *122***, 180**
Knighton, Lelar and Olive (students at Wilsonia) *119*
Ku Klux Klan **67, 78, 79, 165**

L

Lake, Jud **3**
Lake Region Conference **127**
Landrith, Dr. Ira A. **108**
Lane, Elbert B. **47,** *69***–71, 75, 86, 167, 172**
Lane, Sands Harvey **75, 80,** *81***, 172**
Lanphear, A. **165**
Laymen's Leadership Conference (LLC) **130**
leadership, black **125, 127, 128**
leadership, white **114**
Leavitt, Joshua (Congregationalist abolitionist) **170**
Lee, Harold L. **120, 131, 182,** *193*
Lee, Luther (Methodist minister) **144**
Lee, Robert E. **40, 65, 67, 156**
Legette, Frank E., III **132**
Lester, Charles Edwards **153**
Lester, Richard I. **35**
Lewis, Jannith **122**
Lewis, John L. **12**
life forms **64**
Lime Creek, Iowa **167**
Lincoln, Abraham *3***, 6, 8–11,** *20***, 23, 30, 31, 35, 37–39, 41, 135–139, 144, 145, 151–153, 155, 156**
  Inaugural Address **11, 37**

Lindsay, William Schaw 31, 34, 35
Linnaeus, Carl 161
Lintonia, Mississippi 95, *96*, 101, 105, 112, *119*, 175, 176
literature societies 74
Littlejohn, Etta 131
Livermore, Thomas Leonard (historian and statistician) 145
Lockhart, Keith 124
Lockport, Michigan 146
Logan, Rayford 97
London *Daily News* 135
London, England 35–37, 39
London *Examiner* 153
London, Samuel, Jr. 130
London *Spectator* 36
London *Times* 20, 36, 38, 153, 156
"long, dark night," the 97, 115
Longstreet, James (General) 28
The Lost Cause 166
"lost sons in the war" 23, 148
Lothrop, George V. N. (Ambassador to Russia) 154
Loughborough, John N. 3, *21–23*, 84, 125, 143, 146–149, 156, 158
Louisiana 11, 31, 40, 44, 73, 98, 116, 136, 151, 156, 165, 177
Louisiana Purchase 136
Louisville, Kentucky 85, 86, 167, 174
Louisville, New Orleans and Texas Railroad v. Mississippi 100
Lovejoy, Dr. Anson 148
Lowe, Harry 86
Lower judicatories 12, 139
Luther, Martin *48*
lynching(s) 83, *99*, 100, 107, 108, 115, 133
Lyons, Lord Richard (British Ambassador) 35

M

Madison, James 138
Magan, Percy T. *106*
Mahorney, Barry 3, *118*
Mahoney, John P. 78
Malcolm X *123*
Manassas (see Battle of) 19, 25, 27, 29, 40, 41, 116, 144, 150
Manns, John Wesley *125*
Marsh, Frank Lewis 53, 161, 162, 164
Marsh, Martha *133*
Martin, Myles (reporter) 130
Maryland, Marylander 22, 23, 32, 35, 40, 75, 116, 140, 142, 175
Mason, James (ambassador, CSA) 31, *36*, 135
Maynard Rifle 31
McAdoo, Ben 129
McClellan, George B. (General) 35
McClure, Alfred C. 183
McCune, Robert Kirkwood 69–72, 167
McDowell, Irvin (General) *28*, 150

McElhany, J. Lamar 126, 182
McGoodwin, Maceo 129
McKivigan, John R. 5, 12, 135
McPherson, James M. 5, 33
Medlin, Green (freedman minister) 75
Melancon, Artie 122
Menander 57
Mennonites 139
Merivale, Herman 46
Methodist(s) 7, 37, 117, 135, 139, 141, 142, 144, 146, 148
Micaiah 30, 151
Michigan 19, 21, 22, 31, 40, 94, 144, 146–148, 154, 159, 171, 174
microRNA 62, 164
Miller, William (minister) *12*, 13, 135
Millet, Garland J. (Oakwood president) 129
Milne, Admiral (British Navy) 154
mission school 96, 117, *119*
Mississippi 11, 20, 31, 40, 73, 83, 89, 95, *96*, 100, *101*, 103–105, 109, 112, 113, 115–117, 119, 127, 131, 137, 147, 156, 177, 178
Missouri 40, 75, 79, 84, 88, 100, 136, 140, 169
Missouri Compromise 116, 136, 138, 147, 170
Mobile Mission School, Mobile, Alabama 117
Mongoloid race 64, 163
Monroe, Don 129
Monroe, James 138
Monterey, Michigan, Seventh-day Adventist Church 146, 149
Moore, T. O. (Louisiana governor) 31
Moore, Isaiah 96
Moore, J. R. 96
Moran, James L. (college president) *126*
Morgan, Douglas 16, 141, 155, 181, *195*
Morgan, Irene *128*
Morgan, Isham 134
Morgan, Jefferson Davis 134
Morgan, Joseph 134
The Morning Star 94–96, 101, 102, 117, 178
Morton, Samuel George 46
Mosely, Calvin Edwin *122*
Mott, Lucretia (Quaker) 139
Mulatto(es) (also misspelled "molatoes") 13, 64, 142, 158
murder, -ing 13, 16, 34, 66, 68, 78, 99, 107, 166, 178
Murphy, Thomas (convert in Mississippi) 176

N

"nadir" of American race relations 97
Nash, R. T. *96*, *112*
Nashville 67, 69, 75, 86, 105, 106, 108, *118*–120, 167, 168, 169, 176, 181
Natchez Mission School, Natchez, Mississippi 117

Nathan (the prophet) 30, 151
National Association for the Advancement of Colored People (NAACP) 98, *128*, 129, 175
National Association for the Advancement of Worldwide Work Among Colored Seventh-day Adventists 182
naturalists 52, 53, 161
Near East 85
needle, threading the 97, 132
Negro race 6, 16, 45, 51, 53, 64, 108, 110, 114, 117, 153, 158, 161, 168, 180
Negro suffrage 78
Nelson, Dwight (pastor) *132*
Nelson, Russ *129*
Nelson, W. E. (General Conference treasurer) 127
neutrality, England's 34, 152, *184*
Newellton Mission School, Newellton, Louisiana 117
Newton, Michigan, Seventh-day Adventist Church 149
New-York Daily Tribune 7, 20, 41–43, 145, 147, 149, 156
New York Herald 23
New York Times 20, 26, 35, 150, 152, 153
Noah 55–57, 59–61, 158
Norman, R. Steven, III 3, 169
North American Division of Seventh-day Adventists 128, 131, 132, 183
North American Negro Department 123, 181
North American Regional Voice 65
North Carolina 2, 5, 23, 32, 65, 68, 74, 75, 82, 98, 99, 116, 119, 133, 142, 156, 165, 166, 169, 172
Northeastern Conference 127
Northern States 7, 9, 37, 66
Nyquist, Paul (president Moody Bible School) 180

O

Oakes, James 136, *196*
Oakwood 112, *120*–122, 126, *129*, 131, 133, 177, 179, 181, 183
Oberlin College 11
Ohio 16, 32, 33, 65, 69, 129, 141, 149, 160, 167, 170, 171
Oklahoma 98, 100, 107, 116
Olvin, Nathan W. 101, 102, 178
Osborne, M. M. (White Adventist Vicksburg teacher) 96
Osborne, Squire 72, 73, 82, 83, 167–169, 173
Osborn, Frank and George 22, 23, 148, 149
Osborn, James 168
Osborn (also misspelled Osborne), Nathan (judge) 22, *23*, 148
Osborn, Rebecca (Foster) 23, 148, 149
Osborn, Ronald 50, 60, 61
Osterman, Eurydice 122
Owen, G. K. (minister) 75

General Index

Owen, Robert Dale **46**
Owsley, Frank Lawrence (historian) **7, 136**

P

Pacific Islands **85**
Page, Sarah **107**
Palmer, Will *94, 96*, **176**
Palo Alto, Mississippi **95**
Paludan, Phillip Shaw **37**
Parker, Alonzo (preacher-martyr) **116**
Parks, Rosa **128**
Park Street Church (Boston) **11**
Parkville, Michigan **19, 21–23, 40, 146–149**
Parliament **5, 34–36, 154**
Parliamentary (House of Commons) debates **5, 34, 35, 37, 154**
Patagonians **52**
Paul **51, 52, 57**
Paulson, David **162**
Payne, Buckner H. "Ariel" **49, 50, 158**
people of color **6, 18**
Perry, Houston County, Georgia **74, 173**
perversion **54, 55**
Peterson, Frank Loris **121**, *122*
Pettus, Edmund W. **151**
Phelps, Amos A. (Congregationalist abolitionist) **170**
Philadelphia *Inquirer* **32**
Phillips, Wendell *33*, **65**
Phipps, Wintley *122*
picket(s) (also misspelled "piquets") **13, 37, 140**
Pierce, George Foster *37*
Pierson, Robert *131*
Pinckney, Charles Cotesworth **138**
Pioneer Memorial Church **132**
Plessy v. Ferguson **100, 116**
Poland, Joseph P. **142**
Pollard, Edward **29**
Pope Pius, IX **154**
popular sovereignty **7, 9, 136, 138**
Porter, Andrew (Union colonel) **28**
Powder Mills, Kentucky, Seventh-day Adventist Church **72, 73, 169**
prejudice(s) **6, 45, 46, 48, 52, 66, 75, 81–83, 86–90, 92, 93, 95, 97, 101–105, 108, 109, 110, 112–114, 116, 120, 122, 130–132, 156, 174, 183**
Presbyterian(s) **7, 11, 12, 108, 117, 139, 146, 170**
Price, George McCready **161, 164**
projections of the length of the Civil War **20, 21**
prophecy **12, 14, 15, 17, 72, 77, 142, 143, 155, 163**
prophetic gift, word **143, 144, 145, 149**
prophet(s) (false) **30, 142, 151, 156**
pro-slavery **49, 143, 155**
pseudepigrapha **55, 163**
Pulaski County, Arkansas **92**
Pulaski, Iowa *96*
Pulaski, Tennessee **67**

punish, -ment **27–29, 37, 38, 41, 49, 68, 77, 82, 116, 141, 142, 165**

Q

Quakers (Society of Friends) **117, 139**
quasi-polygynist **157**

R

Race(s), long-lived **45, 54, 55**
    relations **97, 104, 108, 109, 130, 131, 133, 134, 181**
    "three great" **62, 163**
racial
    equality **6, 123**
racism **127, 130, 131, 181, 183**
Randall, James G. (historian) **136**
Raymond, Henry J. *26*
rebellion **18–20, 31–33, 36, 37, 40, 77–79, 138, 140, 144, 147, 150, 159, 160, 166, 174**
Reconstruction **66, 68, 78, 82, 111, 140, 177**
regional conferences **124, 126, 127, 132, 133, 183**
religion **12, 14, 92, 114, 122, 139, 175, 176**
Religious Telescope **67**
Reno, Nevada **84**
Republican(s) **8–11, 65, 78, 79, 136, 137, 141, 145, 148, 171, 174, 177**
Review and Herald cafeteria **181**
Reynolds, Georgia **73, 169, 172**
Reynolds, Louis B. **139, 181**
Richardson, Stephen (Ministerial Director of the Allegheny East Conference) **183**
rights, black (civil, human, and Constitutional) **5, 8–10, 12, 15, 41, 43, 65–67, 76, 86, 97, 98, 100, 101, 116, 124, 128, 129, 131, 137–139, 141, 157, 165, 175, 177**
rights, Southern (Constitutional) **8, 10, 42, 43, 66, 135, 137, 138**
RNA **163**
Robinson, Dores Eugene **53**, *106*, **161**
Rochester, New York **16, 140**
Rogers, Chester *96*
Rogers, Fred R. *96*, **101, 104, 105, 111,** *112*, **181**
Rogers, Minnie *96*
Roman Catholic Church (Rome) **154, 175, 176**
Roosevelt Seventh-day Adventist Church **19**, *25*, **40, 140**
Ross, Alexander (Adventist sympathetic to secession and slavery) **140**
Rowe, Elder **126**
Rowland, Dick **107**
Rupert, G. G. (Seventh-day Adventist minister) **173**
Russell, Lord Earl **35, 136**
Russell, William Howard (British journalist) **26, 150**
Russia(n) **85, 145, 154**

Rust, Alfred B. and Elbridge G. **76, 171**

S

Sabbath **14, 70–75, 79, 80, 83, 84, 86, 111–113, 125, 129, 140, 146, 147, 149, 156, 159, 167, 168, 171–173, 179**
Sabbath-keeper(s), observers **65, 71, 72, 77, 80, 83, 84, 140, 144, 148, 149, 171**
Sabbath School **85, 114, 172**
safety **78, 128, 140**
San Diego Chapter of the Association of Adventist Forums **48, 157**
San Francisco Chronicle **85**
sanitarium **121, 126, 127**
Satan **15, 50, 59, 60, 88, 93, 143, 163, 178, 179**
Saviour **15–17, 50, 56, 88, 109–111, 155, 171, 175**
Saxton, Rufus (Brigadier General) **42–44**
Scales, William C. **122**
Scandinavia, -ian **85, 114**
Schellhous [also misspelled Shelhouse], Leonard E. **22, 23, 148, 149**
Schellhous, Lorancie **149**
Schlesinger, Arthur M., Jr. (historian) **136**
school(s), -room, -house **3, 6, 42, 43, 65, 66, 68, 70, 72, 75, 76, 79, 80, 82, 91, 93, 95, 96, 104, 105, 108, 114–117, 119, 120–122, 125, 127–130, 133, 142, 146, 165, 167, 168, 171, 172, 175, 176, 180, 181**
    for blacks **66, 68, 75, 76, 79, 91, 93, 95**, *96*, **104, 105, 115, 117, 119–122, 127, 133, 142, 165, 168, 175, 176, 180, 181**
Schramm, Frank H. *96*
Scott, Burrell and Bonnie, and the Mount Vernon Academy admission denial **183**
Scott, Dred (also misspelled "Dread") **8, 77, 116, 136, 170**
Scott, Maggie *96*
Scriptures **14, 58, 60, 74, 91, 93, 94, 108, 162, 168**
Seaman, Edwin R. **16**
Sebastian, W. H. *96*
secession(s), -ist(s) **7, 8, 11, 19–21, 23, 31, 32, 35, 37, 38, 41, 137, 140, 144, 147, 151, 152**
Sedler, Mary (from Parkville SDA) **146**
segregation **6, 67, 69, 82, 84, 86, 87, 98,** *100*, **101, 104, 112, 115, 116, 122–124, 126–128, 132, 181**
Sepúlveda, Ciro **6, 89, 95, 122,** *198*
Seth, descendents of **48, 55, 56, 59, 60, 61**
Seventh-day Adventist(s) (also S. D. Adventists) **5, 6, 12, 14–19,** *25*, **34, 39–41, 44, 51, 64, 65,** *69*, **72, 73, 75–77, 79, 80,** *82–88*, **91–93, 95, 101, 102, 104–106, 108, 109, 111, 112, 115–117, 119–134, 139, 140, 141, 143, 144, 146, 147, 149, 150, 155–**

157, 159, 160, 165–167, 168, 170, 172, 174, 176, 179, 180, 181
   first church building in the South 169
   organization of 6, 14, 22, 65, 70, 73, 76, 83, 86, 124, 127, 132, 146, 149, 159, 167, 169, 170, 172, 174, 182
   segregation within 113, 123
Seventh-day Adventists Believe 14
Seward, William Henry 135, 136, 138, 153
Seymour, Horatio, ex-governor New York 11, 166
Sheafe, Lewis C. *125*, 182
Sherman, William Tecumseh (General) 40
Shireman, Daniel T. *118*, 119, 180
Shull's Mill, North Carolina 75
The Signs of the Times 170
Sister White 51, 53, 146, 148, 149, 159
skin, color of 85, 93, 114, 115, 180
Slaughter, Anna 96
Slaughter House Cases 100
slaveholder(s), -ing 8, 12, 13, 66, 67, 139, 144, 170
slave law(s) 16, 29, 77, 141, 143, 151
slave-master(s) 15, 30, 49, 50, 158
slave owners 115, 138
slave power 33, 137, 144
slave property 137, 147
slavery 3, 5–18, 20, 23, 25, 28–41, 44, 47, 49, 50, 65, 67, 68, 74, 76–78, 82, 84, 86, 92, 93, 98, 102, 104–106, 116, 120, 134–141, 142, 143, 144, 147, 149–153, 156, 158, 159, 165, 170, 174, 178, 179, 181, 183
   abolish, -ed, -ing, abolition of, (also destroy, done away, end, exterminate) 11, 13, 18, 20, 25, 31–34, 38, 41, 67, 78, 104, 116, 120, 138, 141, 143, 147, 152, 153, 156, 165
   nationalizing 9
   sin of 28, 38, 78, 150
slaves' names of Joseph Morgan (author's third great grandfather), Wilcox County, Alabama 134
slaves, pious (bondmen) 50, 141, 158
slave states 7, 10, 18, 20, 23, 42, 116, 142, 144, 147
slave trade 12, 147
Slidell, John (ambassador, CSA) 31, *36*, 135, 153
Smith, Edmund Kirby (General) *28*, 150
Smith, Gerrit (abolitionist) 30
Smith, Hoke 99
Smith, Ron *131*
Smith, Sheridan Sidney 160
Smith, Uriah 15–18, *21*, 30, 45, *51*–53, 67, 79, 136, 141–143, 150, 151, 155, 157, 159–161, 166
Snook, Benjamin Franklin 45, *51*, 147, 152, 157, 159–161
social equality 6, 98, 108, 109, 111, 112, 116, 127

Sojourner Truth (Isabella Van Wagener) 139, 142
Solomon 48, 56, 57, 60, 140, 149
"sons of God" 47, 48, 55, 56, 59–61, 114
Soule, Orlando 75, 169
South America 85
South Atlantic Conference 127, 133
South Carolina 7, 11, 21 23, 32, 40, 41, 43, 73, 116, 133, 137–139, 142, 151, 152, 156
South Central Conference 127, 133
Southern (or Confederate)
   aristocracy 9, 33
   Confederacy 32, 33
   explanation for secession 7
   masters 34
   nationalism 65, 135
   people 10, 37, 81, 98, 137, 170
   prejudices 101, 104
   preparedness 30, 31, 116
   prison 140
   rebellion 20, 31, 37
   slaveholders 8
   slavery 7, 135, 152
   states 7, 9, 11, 14, 20, 23, 30, 32, 64, 70, 75, 83, 100, 103, 105, 114, 116, 136–138, 153, 158, 174, 179
   whites 120, 165
Southerners 29, 30, 37, 47, 80, 144, 151, 152, 170
   white 69, 70
Southern field 73, 83, 84, 97, 103, 105, 108, 110, 112, 178
Southern Independence Association 35, 153
Southern Missionary Society 95, 168, 180
Southern Missionary workers 96
Southern Tidings 3
Southern Union Conference 128, 131
"Southern work" 117
South Side Church of Salem, Massachusetts 39
Southwestern Adventist University 3, 157
Southwest Region Conference 127
Spalding (also spelled Spaulding), Arthur Whitefield 82, 84, 102, 112, 117, 168, 171, 172, 176, 179–181
Spalding, Bishop Martin J. 175
species 45, 51, 52, 59, 61–63, 159–161, 163, 164, 174
   confused 45, 58, 59, 61, 62
Spence, James (British businessman) 35
Spectator of London 37, 156
spiritual gifts 14, 22, 148
Sprague, Rosetta Douglass 139
Springville, Kentucky 173
Spurgeon, Charles Haddon 47, 48
Stafford, Randolph P. 129
Standish, Timothy G. 158
Stanton, Elizabeth Cady 139
Stearns, Charles 11
Steele, Mrs. A. S. 104

Stephens, Alexander H. 7, *8*, 10, 20
Stephenson, Dan G. *96*, 101
Steps to Christ 14
Still, William 12
St. John, Gov. John P. 39, 156, 174
St. Joseph County, Michigan 146, 148
St. Lawrence County 141, 142
St. Louis, Missouri 84, 85, 88, 170
Stone, A. L. (pastor in Boston) 11
Storrs, George 142
Stowe, Harriet Beecher *11*
Strachan, M. C. (African American teacher) 96
suffrage 65, 66, 78, 97, 165, 170, 176
Sumner, Charles 30, 138
Sunday Law(s) 143, 179
Sunday-Sabbath 178, 180
Sunday, work(ing) on 105, 111
Syvanen, Michael (biologist) 163

T

Taft, William Howard (President) 99
Tait, A. O. 106, 179
Tappan, Lewis (Congregationalist abolitionist) 170
tariff 7, 136, 151
Taylor, Charles O. *73*, 75, 80, 169, 171, 172
Taylor, Peter Alfred 37
teacher(s) 11, 42, 66, 68, 79, 91, 93, 95, 96, 105, 122, 126, 127, 130, 133, 165, 166, 180
Tennessee 23, 32, 40, 65–67, 69, *71*, 72, 73, 75, 78, 86, 94, 108, 116, *118*, 120, 127, 130, 166, 167, 169, 170, 173
tent (for meetings) 72, 73, 76, 80–83, 133, 146, 173, 178
"Testimonies for the Church" 156
"Testimony for the Church, No. 4" 145
"Testimony for the Church, No. 7" 19, 31, 38, 41, 67, 144, 147
"Testimony for the Church, No. 9" 19, 38, 40, 140, 144, 145, 155, 156, 158, 159, 170
Texas 11, 68, 75, 76, 79, 83, 100, 120, 151, 156, 163, 173, 174
third angel's message 73, 85, 165
three angels' messages 149, 172
Tillman, Benjamin 98, 106
Times of London 20, 36, 39, 156
tract society 84
   American 12, 139
   International 94
   Missouri Missionary and 169
   New England 169
treason 38, 77
tree of life 45, 58
tree of life, evolutionary 62, *63*, 163, 164
Trent Affair 31, 36, 40
troop(s) 23, 26–28, 31, 35, 40, 42, 66, 100, 138, 150, 151, 156, 177
Troy, John A. 148
Trump, S. W. *96*

General Index

Tulsa, Oklahoma *107*, **108**
Tulsa Race Riot *107*

U

Underground Railroad **79**, **142**
Union City, Michigan, Seventh-day Adventist Church **149**
Union, the **6–8**, **11**, **18–20**, **22**, **23**, **25**, **28**, **29**, **31–33**, **35**, **38**, **39**, **41**, **46–48**, **52**, **56**, **59**, **61**, **62**, **78**, **79**, **83**, **135–138**, **141**, **145**, **148–151**, **153–155**, **159**, **166**
   forces **19**, **25–29**, **41**
   soldiers **23**, **28**, **33**, **150**
United States v. Cruikshank **100**
United States v. Reese **100**
Urban, John Wesley (infantryman) *29*
Utopia Park **125**

V

Valle Crucis, North Carolina **75**, **169**
Van Slyke, Hanna Maria **75**, **169**
Vicksburgh, Michigan, Seventh-day Adventist Church **149**
Vicksburg Mission School **117**, *118*
Vicksburg, Mississippi **40**, **89**, **91**, **95**, *96*, **101**, **102**, **113**, **116**, **117**, **131**, **176**
Victoria, Queen **34**, **152**
Victor, Orville James (historian) **28**
violence **54**, **55**, **58**, **59**, **62**, **66–68**, **77**, **79**, **98–100**, **102**, **104**, **105**, **107**, **111**, **136**, **138**, **150**, **151**, **161**, **166**, **181**
Virginia **20**, **23**, **27**, **28**, **32**, **40**, **44**, **75**, **98**, **116**, **126**, **128**, **138**, **140**, **142**, **151**, **156**, **177**
Virginia Revised Code of 1819 **142**
viruses **63**, **163**, **164**
vision(s), Ellen G. White's **5**, **6**, **14**, **15**, **19**, **21–23**, **25**, **27**, **31**, **34**, **40**, **45**, **51–54**, **116**, **140**, **144–149**, **159**
vote(s), -ed, -ers, -ing (see also suffrage) **7**, **11**, **17**, **65**, **66**, **73**, **76**, **78**, **86**, **98**, **127**, **128**, **136**, **138**, **139**, **152**, **159**, **165**, **166**, **171**, **176**, **177**, **182**, **183**

W

Waggoner, Joseph H. *21*, **38**, **143**, **146**, **149**
Walker, Little and Robert (students at Lintonia Mission School) *119*
Walsh, Eric **123**, **181**
Warnick, Franklin G. **96**, *112*
Warren, Mervyn A. *201*
Washington, Booker T. **97**, **98**, **115**, **177**
Washington County, Iowa **159**, **167**
Washington, DC **23**, **26**, **28**, **29**, **31**, **104**, **112**, **116**, **123**, **125**, **129**, **137**, **139**, **147**, **148**, **152**
Washington, George **138**
Washington Sanitarium **126**, **127**
Washington's solution **98**
Weld, Theodore (abolitionist) **12**
Wellcome, Isaac C. **37**

West, Jesse (pastor) **133**
West Virginia **74**
Wheeler, Gerald **156**
Whig **10**
White, Arthur L. **14**, **161**, **176**
White, Ellen (G.) **5**, **6**, *14*, **15**, **18**, **19**, *21*, **22**, **23**, **25**, **27–41**, **44–64**, **67**, **83–97**, **100–117**, **120–126**, **130**, **133**, **140**, **141**, **142**, **144–149**, **154–164**, **170**, **174–177**, **179**, **180–182**
   death of **14**, **123**, **177**, **179**
   predictions of
      "A large number of States are going to join that State" **21**
      "As the defenders of truth refuse to honor the Sunday-Sabbath, some of them will be thrust into prison, some will be exiled, some will be treated as slaves" **178**
      "God [will] not give the Northern army wholly into the hands of a rebellious people, to be utterly destroyed by their enemies" **38**
      "If England thinks it will pay, she will not hesitate a moment to improve her opportunities to exercise her power and humble our nation" **36**, **37**
      "If the object of this war had been to exterminate slavery, then, if desired, England would have helped the North" **34**
      "Slavery ... alone ... lies at the foundation of the war" **25**, **32**, **116**
      "There will be a most terrible war" **21**
      "There are those in this house who will lose sons in that war" **21**, **146**
      "When England does declare war, all nations will have an interest of their own to serve, and there will be general war, general confusion" **36**, **37**, **135**
   statements about
      black human rights
         before the Civil War **15**, **49**, **50**, **116**, **141**, **158**
         during the Civil War **15**, **25**, **28–30**, **32–35**, **38**, **49**, **50**, **67**, **116**, **140**, **157**, **159**
         following the Civil War **15**, **56**, **85–93**, **97**, **100**, **102–106**, **108–111**, **116**, **174**, **175**, **178**, **179**
         in the 20th Century **105–117**, **120**, **121**, **125**, **177**, **179**, **180**
      "races of men" **45**, **46**, **51**, **53**, **59**, **61**, **62**, **158**, **160**, **163**
      "general war" **36**, **37**, **135**
      the "almost endless varieties of species of animals" **45**, **51**, **59**, **62**, **160**, **161**
   the "booming of the cannon" **21**, **23**, **147**
   the revival of slavery **105**, **106**, **116**

White, Emma McDearmond **96**, **154**
white enfranchisement and black disenfranchisement **181**
white fear(s) **99**, **115**
white guilt **134**
White, James Edson **89**, **93–96**, **101**, **102**, **104**, **105**, **109**, *113*, **116**, **117**, **119**, **120**, **131**, **154**, **165**, **175–178**, **181**
White, James Springer *21*, **53**, **83**, **141**, **143**, **144**, **146**, **156**, **159–161**
white leaders, -ship **114**, **116**, **125**, **127**, **181**
White, Maria (former slave) **172**
white privilege **128**, **133**, **180**
white race **47**, **48**, **87**, **110**, **158**
white supremacy **8**, **67**, **108**
white trash **82**, **173**
White, Walter F. **107**, **108**
White, William C. (W. C. or Willy) **15**, *53*, **61**, *106*, *113*, **147**, **179**
Wicks, Flanigan (student at Lintonia Mission School) **119**
Wild Flower, Fresno County, California **146**
Wiley, Bell **33**
Willey, T. Joe *48*, **49**
Williams, Nettie (student at Lintonia Mission School) **119**
Williams v. Mississippi **100**
Wilson, Henry (Senator) **30**
Wilson, Neal C. *130*, **131**
Wilson, North Carolina **133**
Wilson, Woodrow **123**
Wilsonia, Mississippi **95**, **117**, *119*
Wisconsin **14**, **69**, **72**, **83**, **160**, **166**, **167**, **170**, **173**
Woldman, Albert A. **154**
Woodfork, R. L. **122**
Woodruff, Colonel Stewart L. **42**
Woodward, C. Van **100**
Woodward, Henry M. **148**
Wool, John E. (General) **148**
worship **48**, **50**, **60**, **73**, **80**, **88**, **89**, **91**, **92**, **105**, **109**, **112**, **113**, **115**, **116**, **132**, **142**, **146**, **169**, **173**
Wright, Michigan, Seventh-day Adventist Church **146**

Y

Yahweh **61**, **62**
Yancey, William Lowndes (Confederate commissioner to Britain and France) **135**
Yazoo City Herald **111**
Yazoo City Mission School, Yazoo City, Mississippi **117**
Yazoo City, Mississippi **95**, *96*, **101**, **102**, **104**, **109**, **119**
Yazoo River **95**, **176**
yoke, break(ing) every **33**, **34**, **36**
yoke with unbelievers **56**
The Youth's Instructor **168**, **170**, **179**, **180**

We invite you to view the complete
selection of titles we publish at:

www.TEACHServices.com

Scan with your mobile
device to go directly
to our website.

Please write or email us your praises, reactions, or
thoughts about this or any other book we publish at:

info@TEACHServices.com

TEACH Services, Inc., titles may be purchased in bulk for
educational, business, fund-raising, or sales promotional use.
For information, please e-mail:

BulkSales@TEACHServices.com

Finally, if you are interested in seeing
your own book in print, please contact us at

publishing@TEACHServices.com

We would be happy to review your manuscript for free.

www.ingramcontent.com/pod-product-compliance
Lightning Source LLC
Chambersburg PA
CBHW080540170426
43195CB00016B/2622